Reshaping Retirement Security

Reshaping Retirement Security

Lessons from the Global Financial Crisis

EDITED BY

Raimond Maurer,
Olivia S. Mitchell,
and Mark J. Warshawsky

OXFORD
UNIVERSITY PRESS

OXFORD
UNIVERSITY PRESS

Great Clarendon Street, Oxford, OX2 6DP,
United Kingdom

Oxford University Press is a department of the University of Oxford.
It furthers the University's objective of excellence in research, scholarship,
and education by publishing worldwide. Oxford is a registered trade mark of
Oxford University Press in the UK and in certain other countries

First Edition published 2012

Impression: 1

British Library Cataloguing in Publication Data
Data available

Library of Congress Cataloging in Publication Data
Data available

ISBN 978–0–19–966069–8

Printed in Great Britain by
MPG Books Group, Bodmin and King's Lynn

Preface

Over the past few years, the worldwide financial crisis has brought deep changes in capital and labor markets, old-age retirement systems, and household retirement and consumption patterns. Around the world, plan sponsors, fiduciaries, policymakers, and households have gained a new awareness of retirement risk. This volume, the newest in our Pension Research Council/Boettner Center Series, draws out lessons learned regarding how retirement planning and long-term financial security have changed in the wake of the turmoil. This book is a welcome addition to all concerned with the future of financial security in retirement around the globe.

In the process of preparing this book, several key people and institutions played essential roles. Superb editorial comments were provided by my co-editors Raimond Maurer and Mark J. Warshawsky. On behalf of the Council, I thank both of them, as well as the many contributors to the volume, the reviewers who helped bring this work to fruition, and the Council's Advisory Board on whom we rely for guidance. This manuscript was expertly prepared and thoroughly edited by Andrew Gallagher with assistance from Irene Shaffer and Heather Shrigley. We are particularly grateful for the intellectual and financial sustenance provided by our Senior Partners and the Institutional Members of the Pension Research Council, listed elsewhere in this volume. The Wharton School graciously provided access to conference facilities and more through its Impact Conference funding. Additional financial support was received from the Pension Research Council, the Boettner Center for Pensions and Retirement Research, and the Ralph H. Blanchard Memorial Endowment at the Wharton School of the University of Pennsylvania.

I also express continued appreciation for the fine collaboration with Oxford University Press, which hosts the Pension Research Council Series on retirement security. On behalf of the Pension Research Council and the Boettner Center for Pensions and Retirement Security of the Wharton School of the University of Pennsylvania, we are pleased to continue in our tradition of research and dissemination on pensions and retirement security around the world.

Olivia S. Mitchell
Executive Director, Pension Research Council
Director, Boettner Center for Pensions and Retirement Research
The Wharton School, University of Pennsylvania

Contents

List of Figures

List of Tables

List of Abbreviations

AAA	American Academy of Actuaries
ACLI	American Council of Life Insurers
ACMBPRA	Access to Care for Medicare Beneficiaries and Pension Relief Act
AEI	American Enterprise Institute
AIME	average indexed monthly earnings
AMEX	American Stock Exchange
AR1	autoregressive model
BC	business cycle
BEA	Bureau of Economic Analysis
BLS	Bureau of Labor Statistics
BVI	German Investment and Asset Management Association
CAFR	Comprehensive Annual Financial Report
CAMS	Consumption and Activities Mail Survey
CB	cash balance
CCBR	Composite Corporate Bond Rate
CD	certificate of deposit
CEIOPS	Committee of European Insurance and Occupational Pensions Supervisors
CEX	Consumer Expenditure Survey
CPI	Consumer Price Index
CPS	Current Population Survey
CRR	Center for Retirement Research
CRS	Congressional Research Service
CRSP	Center for Research in Security Prices
CWHS	Continuous Work History Sample
DB	defined benefit
DC	defined contribution
DFG	German Science Foundation
DOL	US Department of Labor
DYNASIM3	Urban Institute's dynamic microsimulation model

EBRI	Employee Benefit Research Institute
EIN	Employer Identification Number
EIOPA	European Insurance and Occupational Pensions Authority
EOY	End-of-Year
EPS	earnings per share
ERA	early retirement age
ERISA	Employee Retirement Income Security Act
EU	European Union
FIP	Funding Improvement Plan
FPL	federal poverty level
FRA	full retirement age
FRB	Board of Governors of the Federal Reserve System
GDP	gross domestic product
GNP	Gross National Product
HCE	highly compensated employee
HRS	Health and Retirement Study
ICI	Investment Company Institute
IRA	individual retirement account
IRC	Internal Revenue Code
IRS	Internal Revenue Service
LRA	late retirement age
MPPAA	Multiemployer Pension Plan Amendments Act
MRRC	Michigan Retirement Research Center
NAR	National Association of Realtors
NASDAQ	National Association of Securities Dealers Automated Quotations
NBER	National Bureau of Economic Research
Netspar	Network for Studies on Pensions, Aging and Retirement
NIA	National Institute on Aging
NRA	normal retirement age
NYSE	New York Stock Exchange
OASDI	Old Age, Survivors, and Disability Insurance
OECD	Organisation for Economic Co-operation and Development
OTC	over-the-counter

PBGC	Pension Benefit Guaranty Corporation
PBO	pension benefit obligation
PEBES	Personal Earnings and Benefit Estimate Statement
PEP	pension equity plan
Pew	Pew Center on the States
PIA	primary insurance amount
PIMS	Pension Insurance Modeling System
PPA	Pension Protection Act
PRA	Pension Relief Act
PSCA	Profit Sharing/401k Council of America
PSID	Panel Study of Income Dynamics
QC	quarter of coverage
RCS	Retirement Confidence Survey
RRC	Retirement Research Consortium
S&P	Standard & Poor's
SCF	Survey of Consumer Finances
SEC	Securities Exchange Commission
SER	Summary Earnings Record
SIPP	Survey of Income and Program Participation
SSA	Social Security Administration
SSAB	Social Security Advisory Board
SSI	supplemental security income
SZW	Netherlands Ministry of Social Affairs and Employment
TDF	target-date fund
WHO	World Health Organization
WRERA	Worker, Retiree, and Employer Recovery Act

Notes on Contributors

Andrew G. Biggs is a Resident Scholar at the American Enterprise Institute (AEI), where his work focuses on Social Security, pensions, and related retirement and budgetary issues. Prior to joining AEI, he served as a staff member to President Bush's 2001 Commission to Strengthen Social Security, on the staff of the White House National Economic Council in 2005, and as deputy commissioner for policy and principal deputy commissioner of the Social Security Administration. He holds a Bachelor's degree from the Queen's University of Belfast, Master's degrees from Cambridge University and the University of London, and a Ph.D. from the London School of Economics.

Lans Bovenberg is a Professor of Economics at Tilburg University. In 2003, he won the Spinoza prize—the second Dutch social scientist ever to win this prize. With the prize money, he founded the research network Netspar (Network for Studies on Pensions, Aging and Retirement) in which various pension funds, insurance companies, public agencies, and universities participate. He has published extensively in the leading international journals on a wide variety of topics: public economics, tax policy, environmental economics, institutional economics, pensions and aging, international macroeconomics, and labor economics.

Barbara A. Butrica is a Senior Research Associate at the Urban Institute, where she studies issues related to the economic security of the boomer generation, pensions, Social Security, and the engagement of older adults. She previously served as an analyst at Mercer Human Resource Consulting, where she worked with employers to identify the best human capital practices for their own organizations. Before that she was an economist at the Social Security Administration, where she developed a detailed knowledge of Social Security regulations. In 1998, she received her Ph.D. in Economics from Syracuse University.

Jingjing Chai is a doctoral student in the Department of Finance at Goethe-University, Frankfurt, where she teaches courses on Financial Mathematics, as well as Law and Finance. She received her business degree in Finance and Quantitative Methods from Goethe-University, Frankfurt, in 2007.

Robert L. Clark is Professor of Economics and Professor of Management, Innovation, and Entrepreneurship, North Carolina State University. He has conducted research examining retirement decisions, the choice between defined benefit (DB) and defined contribution (DC) plans, the impact of pension conversions to DC and cash balance plans, the role of information and communications on 401(k) contributions, government regulation of pensions, and Social Security. He has recently completed books examining the development of state and local retirement plans in the twentieth century and retiree health plans for public sector employees. Professor Clark earned a BA from Millsaps College and an MA and Ph.D. from Duke University.

Julia Coronado is Chief Economist, North America for BNP Paribas' global market economics team. Prior to joining BNP Paribas, Julia was a Senior US Economist at Barclays Capital in New York, where she helped formulate the forecast for the US Economy and Fed policy. She has deep expertise in aging issues and worked as Director of Retirement Research at Watson Wyatt Worldwide. She currently serves on the Advisory Board of the Pension Research Council at the Wharton School and received the Ph.D. in Economics from the University of Texas.

Karen Dynan is Vice President, Co-director of the Economic Studies program, and the Robert S. Kerr Senior Fellow at the Brookings Institution, where she focuses on macroeconomic and household finance issues. Prior to joining Brookings, she had worked with the Federal Reserve Board as a Senior Advisor. She has also served as a Senior Economist at the White House Council of Economic Advisers and as a Visiting Assistant Professor at Johns Hopkins University. She received her Ph.D. in Economics from Harvard University and her AB from Brown University.

Jason J. Fichtner is Senior Research Fellow at the Mercatus Center at George Mason University, a university-based research, education, and outreach organization that works with scholars, policy experts, and government officials to bridge academic learning and real-world practice. Previously, he served in several positions at the Social Security Administration, including the Deputy Commissioner of Social Security (Acting), Chief Economist and Associate Commissioner for Retirement Policy. He has also served as a Senior Economist with the Joint Economic Committee of the United States Congress. His primary research interests are Social Security, federal tax policy, budget issues, and policy proposals to increase saving and investment. He received the BA from the University of Michigan; the MPP from Georgetown University; and the Ph.D. in Public Administration and Policy from Virginia Tech.

Alan Glickstein is a senior retirement consultant in the Dallas office of Towers Watson. He specializes in the strategic design and financing of total compensation packages, with a particular concentration in the retirement benefit area. His areas of focus include cash balance plans, retirement research, and the financial and risk management aspects of benefit plans. He also leads Towers Watson's national consulting team with respect to accounting for stock-based compensation. He is an Enrolled Actuary with the Internal Revenue Service and an Associate of the Society of Actuaries. He holds a BA in Mathematics from Queens College.

Eli Greenblum is a member of the Office of the Chief Actuary for The Segal Company and serves on their national actuarial policy committee. In addition to his consulting activities, the performance of actuarial valuations on behalf of plan sponsors, and PPA'06 certification/remedial plan efforts, he also works to navigate retirement plan issues with labor and management representatives engaged in the collective bargaining process. Mr Greenblum has over twenty-five years of actuarial consulting experience, having served as the consulting actuary for select multiemployer and public sector clients. He is a member of the American Academy of Actuaries (AAA) Pension Practice Council and Pension Committee, as well as chair of the AAA Multiemployer Plans Subcommittee. He earned a BA in Mathematics from the State University of New York at Albany.

Tomeka Hill is a Senior Research Associate for Towers Watson, where her interests include retirement and savings behavior of employees. Her research has focused on the impact of changes in retirement plan design, phased retirement, and general labor force trends in the United States. She received her BS degree in Mathematics from Duke University, her MS degree in Statistics from American University, and her Ph.D. in Economics from Cornell University.

Michael Hurd is a Senior Principal Researcher at RAND and the Director of the RAND Center for the Study of Aging. His published research covers a wide range of topics in the economics of aging, including the structure of private pensions and Social Security and their effects on retirement decisions, the economic status of the elderly, the determinants of consumption and saving, the use of health care services, the relationship between socioeconomic status and mortality, and the effects of the Great Recession. He is on the editorial board of the *Journal of Population Ageing* and a member of the Board of Directors of the Western Economic Association International. He received a Master's degree in Statistics and a Ph.D. in Economics from the University of California, Berkeley.

Richard W. Johnson is a Senior Fellow at the Urban Institute, where he directs the Program on Retirement Policy and is an expert on older Americans' employment and retirement decisions. Recent studies include analyses of older adults' employment during the 2007–10 economic downturn, occupational change at older ages, changes over time in job demands, and work impediments at older ages. He has also written extensively about retirement preparedness, including studies of the financial and health risks people face as they approach retirement, economic hardship in the years before Social Security's early eligibility age, and gender differences in pension wealth. He received his Ph.D. in economics from the University of Pennsylvania.

Raimond Maurer holds the endowed Chair of Investment, Portfolio Management, and Pension Finance in the Finance Department at the Goethe-University, Frankfurt. His research focuses on asset management, life-time portfolio choice, and pension finance. He serves in professional capacities for the Society of Actuaries, the Association of Certified International Investment Analysts, and the Advisory Board of the Wharton School's Pension Research Council. He received his habilitation, his Ph.D., and his Diploma in Business from Mannheim University.

Judith F. Mazo is a Senior Vice President for The Segal Company's Washington, DC office. She is responsible for directing research and providing guidance on public policy, legislative and regulatory issues, and other matters of interest to Segal clients. Prior to joining Segal, she was engaged in private law practice in Washington, DC, specializing in Employee Retirement Income Security Act (ERISA) and serving as special counsel to the US Pension Benefit Guaranty Corporation (PBGC) and as a consultant to the Pension Task Force of the Committee on Education and Labor of the US House of Representatives. Ms Mazo has also served on the US Department of Labor's ERISA Advisory Council and chaired its Working Groups on Cash Balance Plans and on Disclosures Regarding Health Care Quality. She received her J.D. with honors from Yale Law School and her BA from Wellesley College.

Olivia S. Mitchell is the International Foundation of Employee Benefit Plans Professor of Insurance and Risk Management at the Wharton School, University of Pennsylvania. Her main areas of interest are private and public insurance, risk management, public finance, labor markets, compensation, and pensions with both a US and an international focus. She received the BA in Economics from Harvard University and the MS and Ph.D. in Economics from the University of Wisconsin-Madison.

Theo Nijman is the Van Lanschot professor in Investment Theory at Tilburg University. His recent work covers topics such as pension fund management, the optimal individual pension contract, measurement and management of inflation, interest and longevity risk, and performance attribution and measurement. He is Scientific Director of the Network for Studies on Pensions Aging and is the Academic Coordinator of Inquire Europe, which brings together investment professionals interested in understanding and developing quantitative solutions to investment problems. He received the Ph.D. in Econometrics from Free University.

John W. R. Phillips is a Labor Economist at the National Institute on Aging (NIA) Division of Behavioral and Social Research. He serves as Health Scientist Administrator for Retirement Research, as well as Project Scientist for the Health and Retirement Study. His prior supervisory posts include Director of the Social Security Administration (SSA) Office of Policy Research and several years as the Chief of the Population and Social Process Branch at the NIA Division of Behavioral and Social Research. Earlier in his career, he served as an economist and federal project officer at SSA, conducting research on retirement and administering the SSA Retirement Research Consortium cooperative agreements. He received his Ph.D. in Economics from Syracuse University in 1997.

Ralph Rogalla is an Assistant Professor of Finance at Goethe-University, Frankfurt. His current areas of research are pension fund management and households' optimal life-cycle decision-making. He received his Diploma in Economics from Technical University Berlin and his Ph.D. in Finance from Goethe University, Frankfurt.

Susann Rohwedder is a Senior Economist at RAND, Associate Director of the RAND Center for the Study of Aging, and an affiliate member of the faculty of the Pardee RAND Graduate School. Her research focuses on the economics of aging in the areas of household consumption and saving behavior, retirement, and expectation formation. She has written on the impact of public pensions on household saving, on the adequacy of retirement resources of US households near retirement, on the effect of retirement on cognitive ability, on spending and saving patterns among the older population, on consumption- and income-based poverty measures at older ages, and on individuals' expectations about future Social Security benefits and longevity. She obtained her Ph.D. in Economics from University College London and holds Master's degrees from the University of Warwick and the Sorbonne in Paris.

Barbara A. Smith is a Senior Economist in the Office of Retirement Policy at the Social Security Administration, where her research interests focus on the intersection of Social Security and financial education. Prior to joining the Social Security Administration, she was a Senior Supervisory Policy Analyst in the Consumer and Community Affairs Division of the Board of Governors of the Federal Reserve System. Before working at the Federal Reserve Board, she established and directed the Financial Education Project at the Organisation for Economic Co-operation and Development in Paris, France. Under her supervision, the Project produced the first major international study of financial education programs. She has also worked as a Senior Economist at the US Government Accountability Office in Washington, DC, where she was responsible for leading projects on Social Security and pension issues. Ms Smith has taught economics at Old Dominion University in Norfolk, Virginia, and worked as a research associate at Mathematica Policy Research and as a junior economist at the Council of Economic Advisers. She received her Ph.D. from the University of Michigan.

Karen E. Smith is a Senior Research Associate at the Urban Institute. Her main area of expertise is the design and implementation of microsimulation models in a social policy environment. Over the past twenty-five years, she has developed microsimulation models for Social Security, pensions, taxation, wealth and savings, labor-supply, charitable giving, health expenditure, student aid, and welfare reform. Her recent work includes estimating the income and asset accumulation patterns of the adult population, analyzing the retirement decision, evaluating the effect of disability on earnings and mortality, and using statistical matching to impute earnings, taxes, and spouse characteristics. She received her BA in Computer Science and Economics from the University of Michigan.

Ning Tang is an Assistant Professor in the Department of Finance in the College of Business Administration at San Diego State University. Her research mainly focuses on household portfolio choice, investment behavior, pension and benefit plan design, and insurance and risk management. She received her Ph.D. from the Wharton School of the University of Pennsylvania.

Stephen P. Utkus is the Director of the Vanguard Center for Retirement Research, where he conducts and sponsors research on retirement savings and retirement benefits. He is a member of the Advisory Board of Wharton's Pension Research Council, and he is currently Visiting Scholar at the Wharton School of the University of Pennsylvania. He received the BS in Computer Science from the Massachusetts Institute of Technology and the MBA in Finance from the Wharton School of the University of Pennsylvania.

Mark J. Warshawsky is Director of Retirement Research at Towers Watson, a global human capital consulting firm. He conducts and oversees research on employer-sponsored retirement programs and policies, Social Security, financial planning, and health care financing. He is a co-author of the *Fundamentals of Private Pensions, Ninth Edition*, 2009, published by Oxford University Press, and of *Retirement Income: Risks and Strategies*, forthcoming, published by MIT Press. Previously, he held senior-level economic research positions at the Internal Revenue Service, the Federal Reserve Board in Washington, DC, and TIAA-CREF, where he established the Paul A. Samuelson Prize. He received a Ph.D. in Economics from Harvard University and a BA with Highest Distinction from Northwestern University.

David Wray is the President of the Profit Sharing/401k Council of America (PSCA), a national, non-profit association of 1,200 companies that sponsor profit sharing and 401(k) plans for over 5 million employees. Previously, he was the 2004 Chair of the Department of Labor's ERISA Advisory Council, which advises the Secretary of Labor on benefits issues, and was a member of the Certified Financial Planner Board of Standards Advisory Board. He has produced numerous articles and publications, including *Take Control with Your 401(k)*. He received a BA from Creighton University and an MA from the University of Colorado.

Chapter 1

Retirement Security and the Financial and Economic Crisis: An Overview

Raimond Maurer, Olivia S. Mitchell, and Mark J. Warshawsky

The global financial and economic crisis has brought about numerous changes in the outlook for retirement security. This volume summarizes the lessons learned by practitioners, academics, and policy analysts, who explore how retirement planning and long-term financial security have changed following the crisis. The global financial meltdown has had important repercussions for capital market returns, labor market earnings, household retirement and consumption patterns, old-age Social Security systems, and pension plan resilience. Both defined benefit (DB) and defined contribution (DC) plans have been shaken by the recent economic shocks. Stakeholders have gained a new appreciation of the need to identify, mitigate, and finance risk faced by beneficiaries, plan sponsors, and other players in the retirement finance field, including government. In the future, improved understanding of risk is essential—and as the financial and economic collapse now confirms, risk will always play a part in retirement planning.

How the crisis affected different groups

The financial and economic crisis of 2008–9 wiped out about a quarter of US household net worth, an outcome that will have long-term impacts on retirement saving and economic behavior. As Julia Coronado and Karen Dynan (2012) note, one group heavily hit was the Baby Boomers, who, on the verge of retirement, had to alter their consumption and retirement plans as a result of these unpleasant developments. Their behavior will have substantial macroeconomic repercussions, inasmuch as this group holds a dominant share of assets. Despite the fact that persons aged 55–64 represent only 17 percent of the total US population (US Census Bureau, 2011), they command one-third of stock market assets and one-quarter of the nation's housing stock. So when household net worth as a percent of disposable income fell back to where it was in the early 1990s, 'this group was particularly vulnerable to the declines in stock and housing prices', explains Dynan. 'They felt the brunt of it.'

Accordingly, it is hardly surprising that this age group also cut spending aggressively. Following the 2000 recession, the cohort aged 55–64 had the highest increase in spending, up by almost 7 percent in 2000–2. But from 2000 to 2009, this group also had the sharpest drop in spending; that is, 8 percent. Further, after-tax income for persons aged 55–64 rose 7 percent after the 2000 downturn, but it fell 4 percent, more recently. These declines were even more pronounced for the age 65+ group, which experienced a 14 percent increase in after-tax income following the prior recession, but a 4 percent drop in 2007–9. What people are consuming has also changed: younger persons cut spending on credit-related items, particularly vehicles, whereas the 55–64-year-olds made drastic cuts across the board. Most notably, they cut food expenditures almost 7 percent compared to the prior economic cycle, whereas all other age groups (except those aged 25–34) increased food spending, even during the crisis. Expenditures for apparel for persons aged 55–64 also declined 21 percent, the most for any age group during the crisis. Continuing to work has also been a form of adjustment for those who lost significant savings during the crisis and could not afford to wait for an economic rebound to recoup those losses before retirement.

Meanwhile, saving rates rose from 1 to 2 percent in the years leading up to the crisis, to 6 percent in 2010—similar to saving rates prior to the stock market run-up of the 1990s. Moreover, households along the age continuum are also borrowing less: cash-in mortgage refinancing is now outpacing cash-out transactions, whereas heading into the crisis in 2007, cash-out deals made up nearly 90 percent of refinancing transactions. Households are also taking a more conservative approach to financial investments.

These patterns are broadly echoed in a simulation analysis by Butrica et al. (2012), who point out that almost 9 million jobs were lost between December 2007 and February 2010, sending US unemployment to its highest level since World War II. Of those who lost jobs, 43 percent were out of work for more than six months, making it difficult for them to get new jobs as skills depreciated and job networks grew cold. Men, youth, and African Americans were more likely than others to become unemployed, and three-quarters of those unemployed in 2010 believe that joblessness will have a major impact on their lives. Of those out of work more than seven months, 70 percent dipped into savings, 56 percent borrowed from family or friends, and 24 percent skipped mortgage or rent payments. Meanwhile, wages stagnated, wealth declined for three-fifths of Americans, and overall poverty increased 17 percent.

To estimate the potential long-term impacts of the recession on retirement compared to what would have been expected before the downturn, the researchers undertook a microsimulation effort. Their projections indicate that incomes at age 70 will shrink by 4 percent, for persons aged 55–64 by about 1 percent, and for the younger workers (aged 25–34 in 2008) by about 5 percent. Social Security benefits depend on labor market earnings, and these benefits too are projected to decline by about 5 percent for persons aged 25–34. Overall, wealthier people will suffer greater losses to their expected retirement income in absolute terms, because they have more to lose. Johnson also notes that 'this recession could be worse than previous ones, and the long-term impact could be worse', due to longer-term scarring effects of unemployment on older workers.

Michael Hurd and Susann Rohwedder (2012) are concerned that older people with less time to make up for lost saving will need to alter spending and consumption. Comparing the less volatile 2001–7 period with the 2007–9 period, they show that postcrisis, spending dropped dramatically for older people. Spending falls anyway with age, but the effect was eight times larger for persons aged 51–64; for persons aged 65+, the spending decline was about half again as large, postcrisis. Their data are underscored by responses to an Internet survey where 85 percent of respondents who cut spending said they are worried about the economic future.

'Even people not affected directly by the stock market or housing are worried about the economy', Hurd reports. One reason is that people are very pessimistic about housing values: only one-third of the respondents expect their home to be worth more in a year. Stock market expectations are also dismal: precrisis, more than half the respondents said markets would improve the following year but a year later, in 2009, the figure dropped to just 20 percent. While this is not rational based on twenty-year historical returns, Hurd believes that people have momentum expectations influenced strongly by what has happened recently. Even those with income and assets sufficient to insulate them are still concerned about how their children will fare. Mean anticipated bequests dropped from $535,000 in 2008 to $436,000 in 2009. Even though the National Bureau of Economic Research has determined that the 2009–10 recession is over, Hurd adds, 'It is certainly not over from the viewpoint of our respondents.'

Social Security comprises a major source of income for retirees, a topic examined by Fichtner et al. (2012). In particular, they investigate how peoples' benefit-claiming patterns are changing, using birth cohort data to isolate trends. The age of first-time Social Security claims had been declining since 1997, and the percentage of beneficiaries claiming at the earliest opportunity hit a trough in 2007, with 34 percent of men eligible for Social Security payments signing up to collect their benefits. But the trend turned around at the peak of the crisis in 2008, when the percentage rose to 35 percent; a year later it was up again, to 36 percent. The researchers also find a correlation between state unemployment rates and the number of beneficiaries opting to take benefits early.

Defined contribution plans during the downturn

The economic downturn severely affected DC plan participants. Going into the crisis, David Wray (2012) observes that DC plans were enjoying momentum: the 2006 Pension Protection Act (PPA) made permanent several favorable changes that first went into effect in 2001, and this bill cleared the way for auto-enrollment in DC plans. In his view, DC plans were quite resilient over the period 2006–10: no DC plans were terminated except at companies that went out of business. Moreover, three-quarters of all plans maintained employer contribution levels; only 15 percent suspended contributions, while 4 percent reduced and 5 percent boosted payments in 2009. The following year, these figures shifted to 78, 9, 4, and 9 percent, respectively. The number of plans offering immediate eligibility to new hires and automatic enrollment also rose steadily throughout the crisis and many plans added investment allocation support. The share of plans offering target-date funds (TDFs) rose from 43 to 79 percent over 2006–10, representing extremely rapid change in the normally slow-to-evolve pension world.

Wray also points out that DC participants stayed the course; in 2006, plans experienced a 2.5 percent resignation rate, rising to 3.1 percent in 2008, dropping back to 2 percent in 2010. Participants with loans against their 401(k) holdings declined slightly during the crisis, from 24 percent in 2006 to 23 percent in 2009. DC plan assets also responded to the crisis: in 2006, DC assets stood at $3.6 trillion, fell to $2.7 trillion in 2008, and recovered back to $3.9 trillion, a record high. 'Clearly there was no massive flight from the system by participants', Wray observes. Yet the volatility experienced during this period appears to have had an impact on asset allocation. DC participants had 73 percent of their investments in equities and 27 percent in fixed income investment in 2006, which shifted to 68 and 32 percent, respectively, in 2010. Rather than finding that DC retirement saving vehicles failed, he argues that the DC plan passed its stress test.

To gain more insight into DC participant behavior during the crisis, Ning Tang et al. (2012) examine how trading patterns changed in 401(k) plans. Drawing on Vanguard data, the authors point out that only 2.5 percent of plan participants traded between January 2006 and March 2009. Nevertheless, trading did rise 23 percent in the second half of the period, beginning in September 2008 at the height of the crisis. They also find a strong shift away from equities: flows to stock declined almost

4 percent, down 1 percent from the precrisis phase, and 11 percent after the shock hit. On examining characteristics of people who traded, they conclude that the average plan trader was a 46-year-old male who had accumulated $115,000 in assets during ten years in the plan. During the crisis, however, more women with lower total wealth and trading experience began to trade.

The researchers also focus on trader motivation and discover that market volatility boosted investor awareness of the risk associated with equities. Prior to the crisis, many traders were apparently momentum-driven, but during the downturn they engaged in some contrarian behavior—'they were trying to buy on the dips', explains Tang. 'This is a surprise.' It also appears that when plan participants receive their quarterly statements, this also shaped trading patterns. Nevertheless, they conclude that inertia dominated trading behavior in 401(k) plans, overall.

The long-term impacts of the financial and economic crisis on DC plan participants cannot yet be evaluated, so one group of analysts has modeled what these outcomes might be. Using a dynamic programming model, Jingjing Chai et al. (2012) explore how people of different ages will respond to the shocks they have experienced in consumption, employment, and retirement over their remaining lifetimes. The researchers focus on both short- and long-term 'scarring' effects on the young and the middle-aged; that is, those aged 20 and 55 when the shock occurred. The model inputs data on labor and capital markets, work and retirement, and housing to gauge the impact on consumption, leisure, asset allocation, retirement decisions, and annuitization. The authors predict that most workers will remain employed longer: for those currently in their 20s and in their 50s, the average retirement age is predicted to rise by more than a year.

Compared to what would have been expected in 'normal' periods, they also project both short- and long-term changes in asset allocation. For those currently aged 20, equity investments will fall by nearly 20 percent initially and return to normal levels by age 30. Thereafter, when this cohort is aged 40–80, its equity weighting is predicted to rise by 5–10 percent and to 10 percent by age 80. For those currently aged 55, the equity fraction is predicted to fall by nearly 10 percent right away, and then rise by age 60 and beyond. As for consumption, the model predicts a larger consumption loss for young people in the earlier years. Yet, explains Maurer, there is a substantial, persistent consumption loss for both age groups. 'The young will compensate for the consumption drop by enjoying more leisure, but the older group will consume less and have to work more.'

How defined benefit plans managed during the crisis

Many concerned with retirement security have been interested in how DB retirement programs fared during the crisis. The downturn had a dramatic impact on corporate, single-employer DB pensions, according to Mark J. Warshawsky's analysis (2012) of funding levels, contributions, and proposed reforms. Using Fortune 1000 data, he shows that aggregate funding rose to 106 percent in 2007, fell to 77 percent in 2008, and then edged slightly up to 83 percent in 2010. The improvement was due to a rise in asset values, but it was tempered by declines in the discount rate and the effect of that change on pension liabilities. And though funding levels are up, Warshawsky notes that there's still a long way to go. He also compares asset allocation patterns in DB and DC plans through the crisis. Starting in the mid-1990s, both plan types began to increase equity holdings; by 2006, each had about 70 percent of assets in equities. In 2007, the paths diverged, with equities rising to more than 70 percent of DC assets, while the fraction in stock dropped steadily for DB plans to under 50 percent by 2009. Equities rose again as a percentage of DC plan assets in 2009, along with share prices, illustrating that the decline for DB plans was a conscious choice by plan sponsors to de-risk their plans.

'We are still grappling with the issue of who should bear pension plan risk', Warshawsky indicates. He suggests that DB plan contributions will need to be boosted in the future and notes that reform proposals include new types of plans that split the difference between the employer and employee, regarding where risks are borne. This is already happening, in light of the dramatic shift in plan type offered. In 1998, new hires were offered a DB plan at seventy-two of the Fortune 100 companies (sixty-six traditional DBs and six hybrids). Today, only fourteen offer a traditional DB plan (and seventeen offer a hybrid plan). Meanwhile, the number of companies offering only a DC retirement program to new hires has increased from twenty-eight to sixty-nine.

Multiemployer plans are the subject of an analysis by Judith F. Mazo and Eli Greenblum (2012), which examines how union plans used the PPA of 2006 to stabilize their finances. The authors identify three categories they call the red, yellow, and green zones: plans with sound finances all deemed 'safe' and in the green zone; plans at least 80 percent funded and facing a deficit in seven years are classified as 'endangered' and in the yellow zone; and plans in 'critical' danger of being deficient, or insolvent, in four to five years fall into the red zone. Trustees of yellow- and red-zone plans had to establish rehabilitation plans. Of the more than 400 plans examined, 9 percent were in the red zone in 2008, rising to 29 percent in 2010; 80 percent were in the green zone in 2008, falling to just over half 53 in 2010; and 11 percent of the firms were in the yellow zone in 2008, with

18 percent now in this category. Nonetheless, of the plans in the red zone, the majority were progressing to recovery. Of those still facing insolvency, most were in dying industries or overwhelmed by large numbers of retirees. In order to move forward, many plans reduced benefits and asked employees to pay a greater share of contributions.

Hybrid plans blend characteristics of both DB and DC pensions, and they have become more popular following passage of the PPA, according to Robert Clark et al. (2012). The first US hybrid pension plan was created in 1985 by Bank of America, and this plan type enjoyed a surge during the 1990s. Companies sought to convert to hybrid plans due to changes in accounting rules, employee preferences for more mobile pensions, compensation packages de-emphasizing retirement, and some DB plan overfunding. Yet the trend was halted by lawsuits in the late 1990s arguing that these plans violated federal pension laws and statutes regarding age discrimination. In 2006, with passage of the PPA, hybrid plans received safe harbor from age discrimination claims. The researchers contend that the funded status of DB plans of firms was not an important predictor of the conversion to hybrid plans. Instead, companies with a smaller market capitalization but large pension obligations and assets relative to capitalization were more likely to convert to a hybrid.

The financial crisis has also affected pensions in other countries. For instance, in the Netherlands, it forced a profound reexamination of risk and guarantees in the country's occupational retirement plans. Bovenberg and Nijman (2012) explain that the Netherlands has a first-tier government pension to protect against poverty, on top of which occupational pension funds provide a second tier of retirement income linked to earnings. Dutch occupational pensions are of the DB variety, and they historically enjoyed high levels of funding with assets amounting to 130 percent of liabilities in 2000. During the crisis, however, pension funding ratios fell due, in part, to a drop in asset prices and also to a fall in nominal interest rates. As a result, occupational retirement pension funds reduced nominal benefits that many beneficiaries had thought were 'guaranteed'. In fact, as the authors point out, it has become clear that the participant is the ultimate risk-bearer.

The financial crisis has triggered reforms to preserve the Dutch DB-style plans. Many of their pensions have asset buffers that enable risk-sharing across generations and smooth out fluctuations in financial markets. Nonetheless, these mechanisms also have problems in that they lack transparency and do not make clear who bears the burden of funding shortfalls. Inasmuch as reforms implemented in 2010 restricted raising premiums as a way to absorb risk, the authors note that 'participants will have to share in shocks to the system one way or another'.

Public sector pensions have also faltered in the wake of the crisis, as pointed out by Andrew Biggs (2012). His analysis asks whether public pension funds have altered their portfolios to adjust the risk assumed after losing nearly $1 trillion in asset value during the crisis. The debate is driven by the fact that public employee pensions were already underfunded going into the crisis and assets are roughly 25 percent below levels in 2007. Moreover, expected asset return levels are set by state legislatures, and if a legislature sets the discount rate at 8 percent (typical in the public sector), plan administrators are driven to find a portfolio that can deliver that return—at the same time that projected asset returns have declined.

To determine how public plans reacted to the downturn, Biggs studies thirty major plans representing about half of all the public pension assets under management. To determine whether plans have 'doubled down' on risk in order to catch up on returns, reduced risk to preserve funding, or held steady, he looks at asset allocations pre- and postcrisis. In 2007, the plan portfolios were heavy on equities, with a median target of 57 percent; US bonds were 26 percent of assets; and alternative investments were about 8 percent. In 2010, equities had declined to 52 percent, bonds were stable, and alternative investments rose significantly to 15 percent. In all, fourteen of the plans under study boosted increased risk, five reduced risk, and eleven held steady. Mean returns rose from 6.35 percent in 2007 to 6.51 percent in 2010. Biggs concludes that higher risk may do little to help with public plan shortfalls.

Conclusion

There is little doubt but that the financial and economic crisis—and its continuing fallout—profoundly shook the foundations of retirement security in America and around the world. When pressed to recommend reforms postcrisis, many would recommend enhancing financial advice for plan participants, emphasizing flexibility, and the positive effect of working another one or two years to make up for investment losses in the downturn. Adding to this is the great and continuing need for financial education, essential as the retirement system moves increasingly toward personal account pensions.

But perhaps most important of all is the need for greater understanding of risk throughout the retirement security system, along with new approaches to reengineering retirement pensions. This includes revisiting asset allocation patterns and embedding rebalancing efforts to better ensure retirement security. This volume outlines some successes and some failures, along with the lessons learned.

References

Biggs, A. G. (2012). "How Have Public Sector Pensions Responded to the Financial Crisis?", in R. Maurer, O. S. Mitchell, and M. J. Warshawsky, eds., *Reshaping Retirement Security: Lessons from the Global Financial Crisis.* Oxford, UK: Oxford University Press.

Bovenberg, L., and T. Nijman (2012). "Collective Pensions and the Global Financial Crisis: The Case of the Netherlands", in R. Maurer, O. S. Mitchell, and M. J. Warshawsky, eds., *Reshaping Retirement Security: Lessons from the Global Financial Crisis.* Oxford, UK: Oxford University Press.

Butrica, B. A., R. W. Johnson, and K. E. Smith (2012). "The Potential Impact of the Great Recession on Future Retirement Incomes", in R. Maurer, O. S. Mitchell, and M. J. Warshawsky, eds., *Reshaping Retirement Security: Lessons from the Global Financial Crisis.* Oxford, UK: Oxford University Press.

Chai, J., R. Maurer, O. S. Mitchell, and R. Rogalla (2012). "Lifecycle Impacts of the Financial Crisis on Optimal Consumption-Portfolio Choices and Labor Supply", in R. Maurer, O. S. Mitchell, and M. J. Warshawsky, eds., *Reshaping Retirement Security: Lessons from the Global Financial Crisis.* Oxford, UK: Oxford University Press.

Clark, R. L., A. Glickstein, and T. Hill (2012). "Adopting Hybrid Pension Plans: Effects of Economic Crisis and Regulatory Reform", in R. Maurer, O. S. Mitchell, and M. J. Warshawsky, eds., *Reshaping Retirement Security: Lessons from the Global Financial Crisis.* Oxford, UK: Oxford University Press.

Coronado, J. and K. Dynan (2012). "Changing Retirement Behavior in the Wake of the Financial Crisis", in R. Maurer, O. S. Mitchell, and M. J. Warshawsky, eds., *Reshaping Retirement Security: Lessons from the Global Financial Crisis.* Oxford, UK: Oxford University Press.

Fichtner, J. J., J. W. R. Phillips, and B. A. Smith (2012). "Retirement Behavior and the Global Financial Crisis", in R. Maurer, O. S. Mitchell, and M. J. Warshawsky, eds., *Reshaping Retirement Security: Lessons from the Global Financial Crisis.* Oxford, UK: Oxford University Press.

Hurd, M., and S. Rohwedder (2012). "Effects of the Economic Crisis on the Older Population: How Expectations, Consumption, Bequests and Retirement by the Older Population Responded to Market Shocks", in R. Maurer, O. S. Mitchell, and M. J. Warshawsky, eds., *Reshaping Retirement Security: Lessons from the Global Financial Crisis.* Oxford, UK: Oxford University Press.

Mazo, J. F. and E. Greenblum (2012). "Multiemployer Pension Plans in the Financial Crisis", in R. Maurer, O. S. Mitchell, and M. J. Warshawsky, eds., *Reshaping Retirement Security: Lessons from the Global Financial Crisis.* Oxford, UK: Oxford University Press.

Tang, N., O. S. Mitchell, and S. P. Utkus (2012). "Trading in 401(k) Plans during the Financial Crisis", in R. Maurer, O. S. Mitchell, and M. J. Warshawsky, eds., *Reshaping Retirement Security: Lessons from the Global Financial Crisis.* Oxford, UK: Oxford University Press.

US Census Bureau (2011). *Age and Sex Composition 2010.* 2010 Census Briefs. Washington, DC: US Census Bureau. http://www.census.gov/prod/cen2010/briefs/c2010br-03.pdf

Warshawsky, M. J. (2012). "Corporate Defined Benefit Pension Plans and the Financial Crisis: Impact and Sponsor and Government Reactions", in R. Maurer, O. S. Mitchell, and M. J. Warshawsky, eds., *Reshaping Retirement Security: Lessons from the Global Financial Crisis.* Oxford, UK: Oxford University Press.

Wray, D. (2012). "A Stress Test for the Private Employer Defined Contribution System", in R. Maurer, O. S. Mitchell, and M. J. Warshawsky, eds., *Reshaping Retirement Security: Lessons from the Global Financial Crisis.* Oxford, UK: Oxford University Press.

Part I

Rethinking Retirement in the New Economic Era

Chapter 2

Changing Retirement Behavior In the Wake of the Financial Crisis

Julia Coronado and Karen Dynan

The financial crisis and the ensuing Great Recession left huge scars on household balance sheets. Stock prices remain below their peak of the fall of 2007. Home prices fell more than one-quarter from their 2006 peak and continue to fall. Households have shed some of their debt (in large part through defaults), but the decline has not been nearly as large as the decline in the value of their assets, leaving the ratio of debt to assets well above its precrisis range. Looking across age groups, households approaching retirement have seen the largest decline in wealth. These households were in their peak life cycle wealth accumulation years when the crisis hit, and they were holding much of this wealth in equities or homes. With fewer years of earnings ahead than their younger counterparts, they have fewer options to make up for this loss in wealth and must make a number of significant economic decisions as a result.

This chapter examines how households approaching retirement have adjusted to these balance sheet developments. To date, much of the evidence on this question has come from surveys that ask households how they are adjusting or plan to adjust (cf. Sass et al., 2010; Hurd and Rohwedder, 2011). Such evidence is useful but remains limited, in that intentions do not always correspond to actions. This chapter complements the survey evidence with a careful look at the available data on what households approaching retirement are actually doing—how households are adjusting their consumption, labor supply, and asset allocation.

We begin with a review of macroeconomic and financial developments over the past few years and then explore exactly how these developments have affected the financial conditions of households in different age groups. Next, we turn to the different margins on which households may be adjusting. We look at patterns of consumption and labor supply across age groups, using past recessions as a benchmark; we also examine financial decisions, including willingness to borrow and asset allocation.

Whereas the survey evidence is mixed on whether households are adjusting to their wealth losses by trimming their spending, households do seem to have adjusted on this margin. In particular, households on the cusp of retirement have seen a sharp and broad-based decline in their spending, in contrast to a fairly muted reduction for households in the age categories on either side of this group. Patterns of labor force participation by age are consistent with survey data, indicating a strong inclination toward deferring retirement to make up for the losses. Finally, the financial crisis appears to have left an imprint on financial behavior, with a significant reduction in willingness to take on debt and considerable wealth having been moved out of higher-risk equity funds and into lower-risk bond funds.

Boom and bust in the early 2000s

To set the stage for our analysis, it is useful to briefly review the events of the past decade and their implications for household finances. Following a brief and mild recession in 2001, the United States saw considerable run-ups in stock prices and home prices paired with solid economic growth and low rates of unemployment. Aggregate household net worth relative to disposable income rose sharply to a high of 6.4 in mid-2007, noticeably above the peak reached during the stock market bubble of the late 1990s (Figure 2.1).

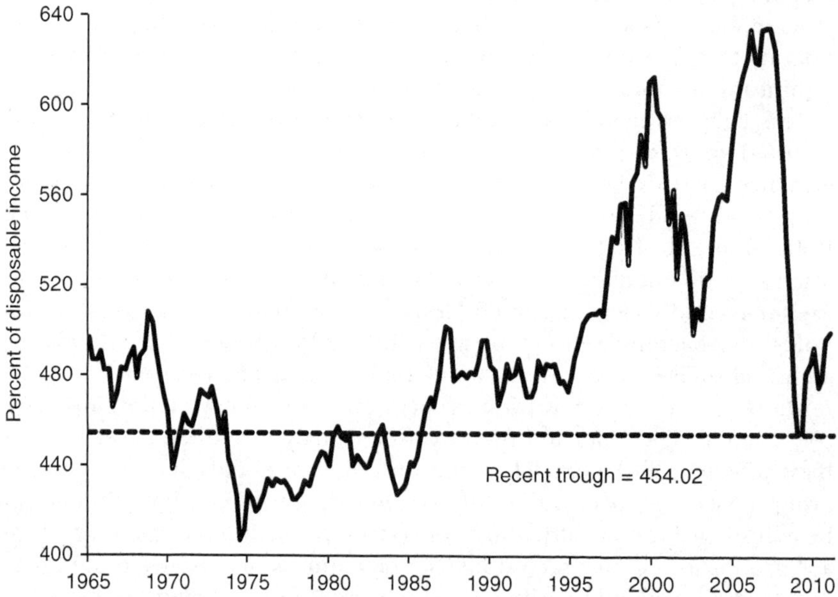

Figure 2.1 Household net worth as a percent of disposable income: 1965–2011
Source: Board of Governors of the Federal Reserve System (2011*a*).

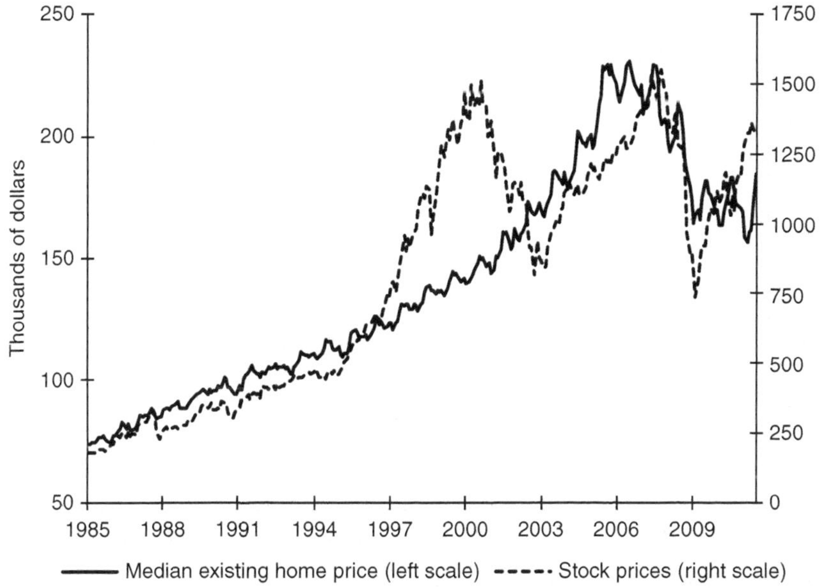

Figure 2.2 US stock and home prices: 1985–2010

Source: National Association of Realtors (2011); Standard and Poor's (2011*a*).

Ultimately, the good times proved transitory, however. Home prices began to decline in 2006, and stock prices turned down in late 2007 (Figure 2.2).

Housing played a special role in the recent economic cycle. In retrospect, home values clearly rose above levels that could be justified by economic fundamentals. Housing has historically been the most widely held asset among US households, and it became even more broadly based as homeownership rates rose from the 63–66 percent range observed between 1965 and 1998 to around 69 percent between 2004 and 2007 (Figure 2.3). The expansion in home ownership was fueled, in part, by a slackening of mortgage underwriting standards, including a sharp rise in the prevalence of the so-called 'affordable' mortgages. However, many of these mortgages proved to be unsustainable in the absence of continued home price appreciation. As home prices began to fall, losses mounted at financial institutions and many collapsed or threatened to do so. In turn, credit conditions began to tighten, leading to yet more defaults and credit losses, until the United States found itself in the most severe financial crisis and economic downturn since the Great Depression.

Stock ownership has also expanded in recent decades. The Survey of Consumer Finances (SCF) conducted by the Federal Reserve Board shows an increase in stock ownership (both directly and indirectly held) from

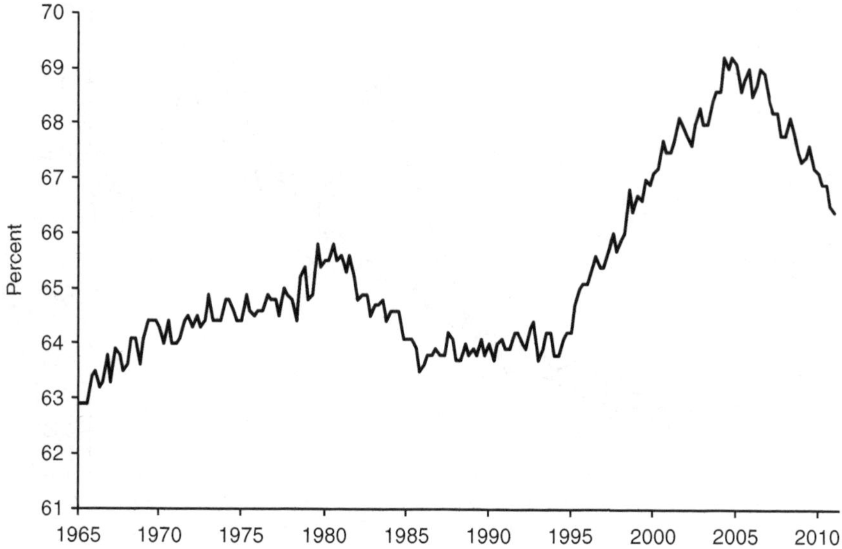

Figure 2.3 US homeownership rate: 1965–2011
Source: US Census Bureau (2011).

37 percent of households in 1992 to 51 percent in 2007 (Aizcorbe et al., 2003; Bucks et al., 2009). Homeowners tended to have greater exposure to stock than renters, with 63 percent holding equity in 2007 (about two-and-a-half times the corresponding share of renters). Amid the boom in equity and home values, consumers took on unprecedented amounts of debt. The ratio of household debt to disposable income (Figure 2.4) rose steadily in the 1980s and 1990s as the liberalization of financial markets and improvements in technology for assessing risk increased access to credit and lowered the cost of borrowing. The trend sharply accelerated in 2002, with household debt surging above 100 percent of disposable income and reaching a peak of 130 percent in the third quarter of 2007. Rising debt levels left household vulnerable to shocks that left them with elevated debt obligations relative to their available resources (Dynan, 2009).

By early 2009, aggregate stock market wealth was 50 percent below its peak in October 2007, while the value of aggregate household real estate holdings were down one-quarter from their peak two years prior. The ratio of household wealth to disposable income bottomed out at 4.5 in early 2009, its lowest level since the mid-1980s. The combination of elevated debt burdens and depleted balance sheets left households under enormous strain. The ratio of debt to asset values, which had shown fairly subdued growth between 2002 and 2007 because of rising asset values, exploded upward with the collapse in asset values.

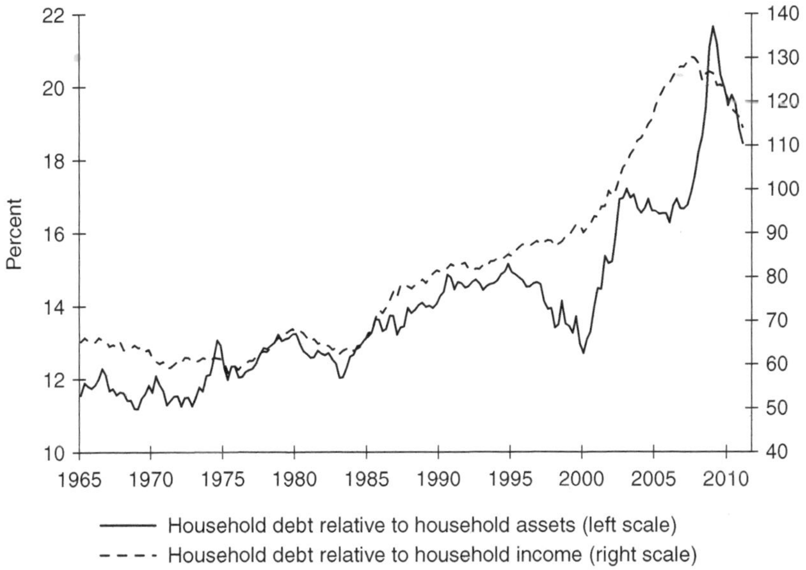

Figure 2.4 Measures of US household stress resulting from debt: 1965–2011
Source: Board of Governors of the Federal Reserve System (2011*a*).

The recession also had a profound effect on employment conditions. Nearly 9 million jobs were lost to the downturn. When employment conditions reached their trough in late 2009, the unemployment rate was over 10 percent and the 'underemployment rate' (which includes part-time workers that would like to be fully employed and workers not actively seeking a job because they are discouraged) was 17.2 percent. Since that time, the economy has remained weak and improved only modestly in terms of broader conditions and household financial conditions. More than one in twelve workers is still without a job. Long-term unemployment trends have been particularly troubling, with the fraction of workers unemployed for twenty-seven weeks or more, at 4 percent, still well above the range seen for decades prior to this recession. The ratio of household wealth to income has recovered a bit, but it remains no higher than it was in the early 1990s.

Impact of the Great Recession on the finances of different age groups

We use the SCF to explore the effect of the rise and fall of asset prices on the financial position of households in different age groups: it contains comprehensive and high-quality information about the balance sheets of

TABLE 2.1 Household median net worth in 2007 by age of head ($ 2010)

Age of head (years)	Median net worth ($)
<35	12,268
35–44	90,844
45–54	192,564
55–64	265,063
65–74	250,815
75+	223,366

Source: Authors' calculations from the 2007 Survey of Consumer Finances (FRB, 2011*b*).

US households, as well as data on household income, demographics, and attitudes. Conducted by the Federal Reserve Board on a triennial basis since 1983, the last full wave that is publicly available contains information collected during the second half of 2007; nevertheless, the Federal Reserve has recently released data on median net worth for selected demographic groups from a follow-up survey of the 2007 respondents conducted in the latter half of 2009.[1] In principle, we could use the SCF micro data to group households by the age ranges most pertinent to this analysis, but we are limited to 'standard' SCF age groupings because the key 2009 data are presented that way based on the age of household head: younger than age 35, 35–44, 45–54, 55–64, 65–74, and 75+. Households approaching retirement—the main target of our analysis—are likely to be concentrated in the 55–64 age group.

Life cycle economic theory predicts that household wealth will peak at retirement and, indeed, in the SCF, households with heads aged 55–64 tend to have higher wealth than their counterparts in other age groups. The first column of Table 2.1 shows that median net worth rose with the age of the head for households in their working years, peaking at $265,000 in the 2007 SCF (measured in 2010 dollars) for households aged 55–64. Median net worth fell off for older age groups, though the decline is not as pronounced as the increase during the working years.

Households approaching retirement also tend to have more exposure to equity price fluctuations. As can be seen in the first panel of Table 2.2, the share of households owning stock (both directly and indirectly through mutual funds, defined contribution retirement plans, and the like) in the 55–64 age group was a shade lower than that for the 45–54 age group in 2007 (59 versus 61 percent). Yet conditional on owning stocks, median stock holdings and the share of assets represented by stocks were considerably higher for the 55–64 age group than for any other age group. The

TABLE 2.2 Household assets by age of head: ownership, holdings, and portfolio shares (in 2007; $ 2010)

Age of head (years)	Equity			Residential real estate			Other financial assets		
	Share owning	Median for owners		Share owning	Median for owners		Share owning	Median for owners	
		Amount ($)	Share of assets		Amount ($)	Share of assets		Amount ($)	Share of assets
<35	0.39	7,559	0.06	0.42	183,344	0.79	0.89	5,238	0.10
35–44	0.54	26,925	0.09	0.69	225,251	0.71	0.93	14,772	0.08
45–54	0.61	47,146	0.11	0.79	256,682	0.67	0.93	29,649	0.11
55–64	0.59	82,033	0.15	0.83	246,205	0.58	0.97	40,860	0.13
65–74	0.52	61,289	0.10	0.86	209,536	0.62	0.96	44,107	0.14
75+	0.40	42,955	0.12	0.79	157,152	0.66	0.97	30,068	0.21

Source: Authors' calculations from the 2007 Survey of Consumer Finances (FRB, 2011*b*).

TABLE 2.3 Household debt by age of head: ownership, holdings, and ratio to income (in 2007; $ 2010)

Age of head (years)	Share with debt	Median conditional on having debt	
		Amount ($)	Ratio to income
<35	0.84	37,863	0.91
35–44	0.86	111,054	1.44
45–54	0.87	100,504	1.20
55–64	0.82	63,112	0.98
65–74	0.66	42,043	0.84
75+	0.31	13,620	0.44

Source: Authors' calculations from the 2007 Survey of Consumer Finances (FRB, 2011*b*).

second panel of Table 2.2 shows that households with heads between ages 55 and 64 also had relatively sizable holdings of residential real estate. The ownership rate was 83 percent for this group—a bit lower than that for the next age group, but higher than that of other age groups. The median amount of real estate owned (conditional on owning) was $235,000, also at the top end of the range for the various age groups.

Although older working households appear to have more risk in terms of assets than households in other age groups in 2007, the liabilities side of their balance sheet was not as risky. As can be seen in Table 2.3, at 82 percent, the share of households in the 55–64 age group with debt (including mortgage obligations as well as any consumer loans) in 2007

TABLE 2.4 Distribution of selected assets and debt by age of head: 2007

Age of head (years)	Equities	Residential real estate	Other financial assets	Debt	*Memo: population share*
<35	0.02	0.09	0.03	0.19	0.22
35–44	0.10	0.17	0.10	0.26	0.20
45–54	0.24	0.25	0.25	0.28	0.21
55–64	0.31	0.23	0.29	0.19	0.17
65–74	0.21	0.15	0.19	0.08	0.11
75+	0.12	0.10	0.14	0.02	0.11

Source: Authors' calculations from the 2007 Survey of Consumer Finances (FRB, 2011*b*).

was a bit lower than the shares for households in the 35–44 and 45–54 age groups. Moreover, conditional on having debt, the median amount of debt and the ratio of debt to income, at about $60,000 and one, were considerably lower for the 55–64 age group than for the next two younger groups.

Table 2.4 pulls this information together, showing the share of aggregate assets of different types and debt owned by households in different age groups in 2007. Households with heads between 55 and 64 years old owned 31 percent of equities, 23 percent of residential real estate, and 29 percent of other financial assets, despite accounting for just 17 percent of the population (final column). Their share of debt was roughly on par with their population share, considerably higher than for older households, but a good bit lower than for households with heads between ages 35 and 54.

Figure 2.5 shows trends in inflation-adjusted median net worth of different age groups over time. As can be seen, median net worth in 2009 was lower than its precrisis value for all age groups, with large declines in the 45–54, 55–64, and 65–74 age groups. At $222,000, median net worth for those aged 55–64 in the 2009 SCF was down $60,000 from the peak seen for that age group in the 2004 SCF and was roughly the same as in 2001 SCF. All told, the patterns suggest a considerable hit to the resources of households approaching retirement relative to what they likely expected prior to the financial crisis.

While the collapse in asset values had an outsized impact on people nearing retirement, it does not appear that this age group was disproportionately hurt by the rapid deterioration in labor market conditions. As shown in Table 2.5, all age groups experienced a much larger increase in unemployment relative to prior cycles. However, in percentage terms, workers aged 55 and older saw a smaller increase in their unemployment rate than those in other age groups, except for those under the age of 24, just as in prior recessions. Workers aged 55 and over generally have an unemployment rate below the national average owing to their greater

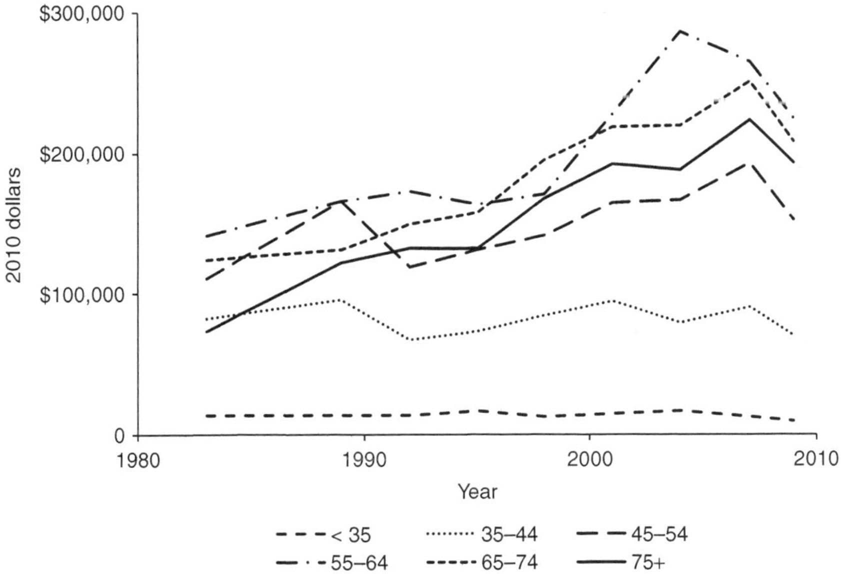

Figure 2.5 Median household net worth ($ 2010) by household head age over time
Source: Authors' calculations from the Survey of Consumer Finances (FRB, 2011*b*).

experience and more senior positions, and they currently enjoy the lowest unemployment rate of any age group. That said, workers nearing retirement certainly experienced far more joblessness and job insecurity than was typical in the past, and while we cannot break down the long-term unemployed by age, this group has no doubt been part of this trend at a time in their life where their remaining work horizon is much shorter than for younger cohorts. Thus, while they were hit proportionately, the longer-run damage to their living standard may well be more severe.[2]

Three margins of adjustment to the crisis

Because of their considerable holdings of financial and real estate assets, older workers were hurt hardest by the dual decline in equity values and home prices at a time in their lives when many were likely planning an exit from the labor force before long. Economic theory tells us that there are a number of changes in behavior that such a sizable shock to wealth and income security might elicit. First, older workers might choose to save more, reducing current consumption in order to reduce the damage to their planned spending in retirement. Second, this group might choose to stay in the labor force longer than planned. An additional year of work has a powerful impact on retirement resources, although such a response will only be available to those for whom work is available. Finally, given that the losses experienced in the values of stock portfolios and home values were quite likely well beyond anything most households had thought was likely or possible, households might reevaluate their risk tolerance or how to express their risk preferences through changes in their portfolio allocation. Each of these responses has implications for household retirement security, as well as for the macroeconomy. We examine each of these three margins of behavior by looking at both evidence on what households say they are doing (or planning to do) and micro and macro data that shed light on what they are doing in practice.

Changes in saving behavior

Reducing spending and raising saving is one way in which households are able to rebuild or conserve their life cycle saving. One would expect such effects to be most pronounced for households nearing retirement and in retirement given the considerable size of their losses (and, for the retired group, the greater difficulty of reentering the labor force so as to increase labor income). Note, though, that households who mainly suffered losses via lower home values might not have to trim nonhousing spending if they were planning to live in their homes for the foreseeable future because the present discounted value of expected housing consumption fell commensurately. One would not expect a large wealth effect on the spending of younger households, since they suffered much smaller losses and they have many years to restore their retirement saving. However, younger (and older) households might reduce spending because of a loss in income regardless of their rate of saving. They also might increase saving for precautionary reasons if they have raised their assessment of the underlying riskiness of the economic environment they face. Finally, the tight supply of credit over the past few years might also have damped consumption, although one would expect this to be a bigger issue for less creditworthy younger households and for this effect to fade as credit conditions ease.

Survey evidence on households' inclination to change their saving behavior in the wake of the crisis is mixed. For example, the Center for Retirement Research at Boston College surveyed roughly 1,300 workers between the ages of 45 and 59 in mid-2009 about how they were responding to the financial downturn and found fairly modest reported effects on saving (Sass et al., 2010). Two-thirds of surveyed households reported no change in how much they save for retirement through 401(k) accounts, individual retirement accounts (IRAs), and other accounts. On the other hand, about 60 percent of respondents to the 2009 SCF between the ages of 50 and 61 reported they would spend less if their wealth decreased; many of these households also indicated a material increase in their desired precautionary saving (Duke, 2011).

The aggregate evidence suggests that households have significantly ramped up their saving; the personal saving rate, which bottomed out between 1 and 2 percent in the years just prior to the financial crisis, jumped to close to 6 percent during the crisis, and it has remained elevated even as the recovery has progressed. The current level is similar to that seen prior to the stock market run-up of the 1990s. It may be that, when asked by a survey, households think about saving as an active decision to invest money in a retirement account rather than including paying down debt, spending less, and keeping larger cash balances on hand. Indeed, while household debt has been shrinking in large part due to defaults and charge-offs, a recent analysis by the New York Fed showed that households actively paid down consumer debt in 2009; and, while net borrowing turned positive in 2010, it has remained well below prior norms (Brown et al., 2011).

To explore more concretely how the events of the past several years may have changed the spending and saving behavior of households (particularly those nearing retirement), we look at patterns of spending using data from the *Consumer Expenditure Survey* (CEX) conducted by the Bureau of Labor Statistics (BLS). The BLS collects detailed data on expenditures from roughly 7,000 households per quarter, with each household providing this information for up to four successive quarters before being rotated out of the sample. Limited information about the income, demographic characteristics, assets, and liabilities of the respondents is also gathered.

Annual averages of CEX variables by demographic group are published on the US Department of Labor Bureau of Labor Statistics website.[3] Our analysis focuses on a measure of consumption spending that roughly matches the Personal Consumption Expenditures concept in the National Income and Product Accounts excluding direct spending on housing (rent and owners' imputed rent). We exclude rent and owners' imputed rent because changes in these categories have a strong relationship to house price movements, and so may represent households' investment decisions, in addition to their consumption decisions. However, the results would not be materially different if we were to focus on total consumption. To construct our consumption measure, we start with total CEX expenditures and then subtract mortgage payments, property tax and insurance expenditures, home maintenance expenditures, rent payments, and pension and life insurance expenditures.

As a check on the data, Figure 2.6 shows trends in the levels of after-tax income, nonhousing consumption, and home values. Past studies have shown that CEX aggregates do not track national accounts data very tightly over time, for a variety of purported reasons, including conceptual differences in the measures, limited coverage of high-income households, and trends in the degree of underreporting.[4] Still, one would expect the patterns to make some sense in the context of macroeconomic developments, and they do. Average consumption and income both declined after the onset of the recession in late 2007, with consumption declining more than income, consistent with a rise in the saving rate. The average value of owned homes peaked in 2006 and fell thereafter, returning by 2009 to its lowest value since 2004.

By age group (not shown), average household income and consumption are highest for households with heads between ages 45 and 54 and lowest for households with heads aged 65+. Households with heads aged 45–64 have the highest average home value, with households with heads younger than 35 having the lowest. This pattern likely reflects in part the younger households having a lower homeownership rate (recall that these are not conditional averages)—the percent of these households owning a home over the past decade averaged 48 percent, compared with 75–80 percent

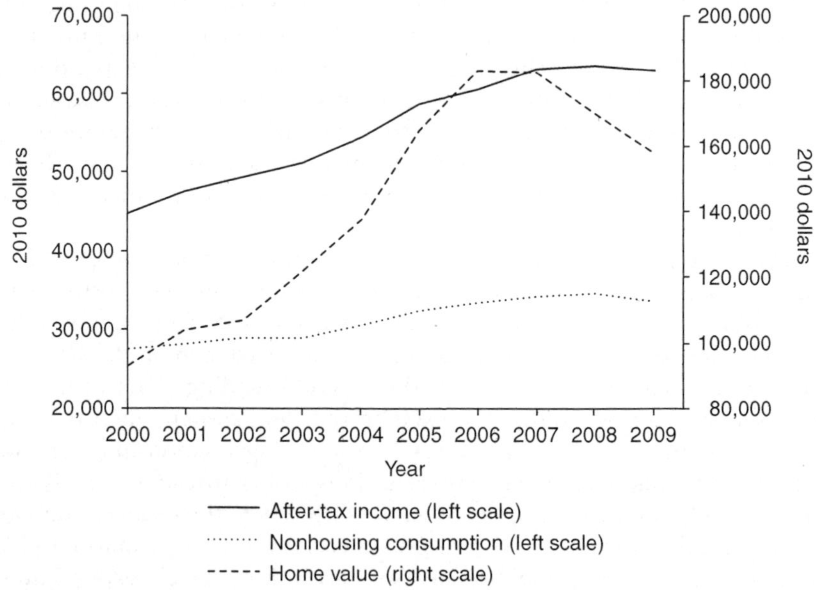

Figure 2.6 US average household income, consumption, and home value over time
Source: Authors' calculations from the Consumer Expenditure Survey (BLS, 2011*a*).

for the middle-aged groups. Households in the oldest group also had a homeownership rate of around 80 percent, though a slightly lower average home value. The percent decline in house prices from their peak level was largest for households in the 25–34 age group (26 percent), with these households experiencing the largest drop in homeownership (4 percentage points). For other age groups, the decline in average home value was in the neighborhood of 15 percent.

The heart of our analysis of the CEX data focuses on changes in spending between the business cycle peak and two years later. Thus, for the latest recession, we consider changes between 2007 and 2009. We compare results across several dimensions. We look across age groups, with a focus on households with heads between 55 and 64, as that group is the most likely to be on the cusp of retirement.[5] We also look across business cycles, comparing changes from the current episode with those experienced during the recession in the early 2000s. For this earlier cycle, we calculate changes between 2000 and 2002, as high-frequency data put the start of the recession in early 2001, implying that the peak based on annual averages was 2000. In order to abstract from the influence of differential price trends over the two periods, we divide all variables by the deflator for Personal Consumption Expenditures from the National Income Accounts. Finally, we compare results across selected categories of spending, since relative movements in the more discretionary or credit-sensitive categories may also be telling about how the financial crisis and recession affected households' behavior.

Table 2.5 shows our results. Looking at changes for the 2007–9 period (Column 3), households with heads in the 55–64 age group show a much larger drop in nonhousing consumption than their counterparts in the next youngest category. The larger drop likely in part reflects the larger drop in after-tax income they experienced (bottom panel of table), but the difference in the income change is much smaller than that in the consumption change.[6] Younger households (those with heads aged 25–44) also experienced fairly large drops in nonhousing consumption between 2007 and 2009. These households experienced smaller income declines than that in the group aged 55–64, and they also experienced smaller declines in wealth (in dollar terms). However, as discussed later, younger households tend to be more reliant on credit and thus may have been more constrained by the tightness in credit conditions. The decline in nonhousing consumption for those aged 55–64 stands out when the 2007–9 changes are compared to those observed in the previous business cycle (Column 4). All age groups showed noticeably weaker consumption in the recent episode, but the biggest difference by far was for those approaching retirement.

Spending patterns for the oldest age group (households with heads 65 and above) are somewhat puzzling. One might have expected spending to weaken most noticeably in this group given the greater difficultly it

TABLE 2.5 Changes in real spending and income by age of head: 2002–9

	Age of head (years)	% change		Difference in changes
		2000–2	2007–9	
Nonhousing consumption	25–34	−1.6	−7.9	−6.3
	35–44	1.7	−7.7	−9.4
	45–54	0.1	−2.2	−2.3
	55–64	6.6	−8.3	−14.8
	65+	1.4	−1.7	−3.1
Food expenditures	25–34	0.7	−0.7	−1.4
	35–44	0.3	1.4	1.1
	45–54	−4.2	0.2	4.4
	55–64	4.1	−2.4	−6.6
	65+	3.7	4.9	1.2
Apparel expenditures	25–34	−6.5	−14.2	−7.7
	35–44	−12.4	−2.9	9.5
	45–54	−17.2	−16.9	0.3
	55–64	2.4	−18.6	−20.9
	65+	1.7	−0.8	−2.5
Vehicle expenditures	25–34	−0.2	−30.7	−30.5
	35–44	11.3	−36.2	−47.5
	45–54	5.3	−3.1	−8.4
	55–64	3.7	−20.6	−24.3
	65+	−7.6	−9.0	−1.4
After-tax income	25–34	4.5	−.5	−5.1
	35–44	5.4	−2.8	−8.2
	45–54	6.8	−2.9	−9.7
	55–64	7.0	−4.0	−11.0
	65+	14.1	−4.4	−18.5

Note: Relative to the business cycle peak.

Source: Authors' calculations from various Consumer Expenditure Surveys (BLS, 2011*a*).

presumably had adjusting its labor supply. However, the response of this group for the 2007–9 period was among the most muted, both in absolute terms and relative to the last recession. One possibility is that these households viewed their future retirement income streams as safe, relative to those of households exposed to risk from job loss. This oldest cohort has relatively high levels of defined benefit pension coverage, and though these plans have become severely underfunded as a result of the crisis, those receiving benefits have been unaffected. In addition, those older households still owning their homes may have been planning to stay in these homes so that the drop in home values translated into lower implicit future rent. That said, given the SCF evidence that this group saw a very large decline in its net worth, the issue warrants more investigation.

Comparing responses across categories of spending, food consumption showed much smaller declines for all age groups than broader consumption (and, in some cases, it increased). This pattern is consistent with food being more of a necessity than other types of goods and services. By contrast, spending in the more discretionary categories, such as apparel and, in particular, motor vehicles, fell much more noticeably. For households with heads aged 55–64, apparel spending fell close to 20 percent between 2007 and 2009, in sharp contrast to the modest rise seen between 2000 and 2002. Spending by this group on vehicles fell similarly. Of note, households in the two youngest age groups saw an even larger decline in spending on vehicles between 2007 and 2009, though not in spending on apparel. This pattern could reflect the sharply reduced availability of auto loans, given that younger households tend to hold fewer liquid assets and thus presumably are more reliant on credit to finance large purchases.[7]

To recap, both data limitations and the complicated nature of the underlying economic environment preclude us from drawing very precise conclusions. Roughly speaking, though, the patterns suggest that tight credit conditions limited the spending of households with heads younger than age 45. Equally striking are the patterns for older households, presumably less likely to be constrained by credit availability. The spending of households with heads between ages 45–54 and 65+ showed a fairly slight weakening after the recession began. However, the group bracketed by these two age categories—where households approaching retirement are concentrated—declined in a sharp and broad-based way. This pattern is consistent with the view that these households, at least in part, are attempting to make up for their financial losses (and perhaps lower expected future returns) by cutting consumption and raising saving.

Changes in labor supply

A particularly powerful way for those nearing retirement to make up for financial losses is to defer retirement, as a year of additional earnings can make a considerably larger difference than raising one's saving rate by a few percentage points even for several years. The likely labor supply effect would probably be smaller for younger households, given their smaller financial losses and for retired households, who presumably find it harder and less desirable to reenter the labor force.

There is some evidence that many households have extended their planned retirement ages. Roughly, 40 percent of respondents reported delaying their retirement dates, with most intending to work longer by four or more years (Sass et al., 2010). Two-thirds of preretirement SCF respondents reported that they expected to delay retirement by a year or more relative to their expectations in 2007 (Duke, 2011). Likewise, the Employee Benefit Research Institute (2011) shows between 20 and 25 percent of workers reporting delaying their retirement each year after 2009, up from a range of 10–15 percent before the crisis. The vast majority cited changes in employment prospects or finances as reasons for the delay. Similarly, the percentage of respondents saying they expect to retire at age 70 or later shot up from 16 percent in 2006 to 25 percent in 2011. Clearly, for older workers who are still employed, delaying retirement is a strong margin of preference to shore up resources.

The labor force participation response also shows up in the macroeconomic data when we look at changes in men's labor force participation by age group across this and prior business cycles.[8] The behavior of men aged 55+ stands in stark contrast to other age groups (Table 2.6). Labor force participation generally declines a bit during recessions, with the youngest and oldest households seeing the largest changes. During the Great Recession, all of the younger age groups saw pronounced declines in participation and the aggregate labor force participation rate dropped

TABLE 2.6 Employment conditions and choices by age, through the recession

Age group (years)	June 2011	Peak-to-trough change in current cycle		Average for past recessions	
		First difference	% change	First difference	% change
Unemployment rate					
All	9.2	5.7	130	3.5	90
16–24	17.3	9.2	93	5.6	67
25–34	9.6	6.4	145	3.8	112
35–44	7.8	5.8	176	3.0	114
45–54	7.3	4.7	152	2.5	100
55+	7.0	3.8	119	2.2	86
Labor force					
All	70.5	−1.4	−1.9	−0.2	−0.3
16–24	55.9	−3.9	−6.4	−1.0	−1.4
25–34	89.1	−1.9	−2.1	−0.1	−0.1
35–44	91.6	−0.7	−0.8	−0.1	−0.1
45–54	86.4	−0.5	−0.6	0.1	0.1
55+	46.6	1.0	2.2	−0.6	−1.0

Note: Change from May 2007 (recent low for overall unemployment rate) to October 2009 (recent high for overall unemployment rate).

Source: Authors' calculations from the US Department of Labor (BLS, 2011*b*).

1.4 percentage points. However, workers aged 55+ actually increased their rate of participation by 1 percentage point over the period (and have seen further increases, on net, since then). This continues a long-term trend that probably reflects declining pension coverage and increasing life expectancies among other factors, but its resilience during a recession, when all other age groups are leaving the labor force, is a striking indication that an important way to recoup lost resources is through continued work. The exception is for older workers who lost their jobs through the downturn and have had a hard time finding work; this group will have to rely on increased saving or simply accept reduced consumption in retirement.

Changes in portfolio allocation

A final margin on which one might expect to see some adjustment is the way in which households allocate their portfolios. Although it is possible that some households might move into higher-return riskier investments to make up for their losses, a more plausible story is that they have shifted to a more cautious position, having lived through a painful illustration of the downsides of taking on risk.

The Bricker et al. (2011) analysis of the 2007 and 2009 waves of the SCF concluded that balance sheet changes over this period primarily reflected changes in asset values, rather than changes in the composition of household portfolios. However, the attitudinal question in the survey pointed to a material decline in households' willingness to take risk. Among households with heads aged 50–61, the share of households unwilling to take any financial risk increased by 5–10 percentage points (Duke, 2011). Another survey found that 30 percent of respondents reported changing the allocation of their retirement accounts, with most in this category shifting away from stocks (Sass et al., 2010).

There is also evidence in aggregate data for what is either a change in risk preferences or a recalibration of how to express risk tolerance, in light of the magnitude of recent shocks. The reduction in active consumer borrowing noted earlier may in part reflect a reduced taste for debt. This would be consistent with the fact that the repayment rate on credit cards is at the high end of its historical range (Figure 2.7). Some of this is probably related to supply—those consumers who still have access to credit are more creditworthy and inclined to pay down debt. Supply factors also probably are one influence on another trend: that toward 'cash-in' mortgage refinancings. The share of 'cash-out' mortgage refinancings (those that involved an increase of more than 5 percent of the balance) reached 88 percent at the peak of the housing boom, but has

Figure 2.7 US credit card repayment behavior: 1993–2011

Note: Three-month average as a percent of total balance. *Source*: Standard and Poor's (2011*b*).

since plunged to less than 30 percent. Meanwhile, the share of recent refinancing transactions involving the pay down of principal ('cash-in' refinancing) has been quite elevated by historical standards (Figure 2.8). Declining home values and home equity, and tightening credit standards, probably mean that to access current low rates homeowners are required by lenders to pay down principal in many cases. But the fact that they are willing to do so, even in light of declining home values, is impressive. Perhaps the traditional retirement behavior of paying off the mortgage evidenced by the very low debt holdings of households aged 65+ is reasserting itself.

In addition to a reduced taste for leverage, households also appear to be channeling their financial assets into less risky investments. As shown in Figure 2.9, mutual fund flows into fixed income bond funds were massive following the crisis, outstripping the magnitude of stock market inflows seen in the late 1990s. Meanwhile, equity mutual funds have seen net outflows in recent years that only recently turned positive. Thus, while the stock market has staged an impressive rally in the past two years, fewer investors have benefited from it. Figure 2.10 shows that stock market trading volumes are well down from their peaks and are nearing volumes that predate the last two stock booms. As more data become available, we will be able to tell with greater precision whether it is the older generation driving this trend. Yet, because they hold most of the stock wealth, they

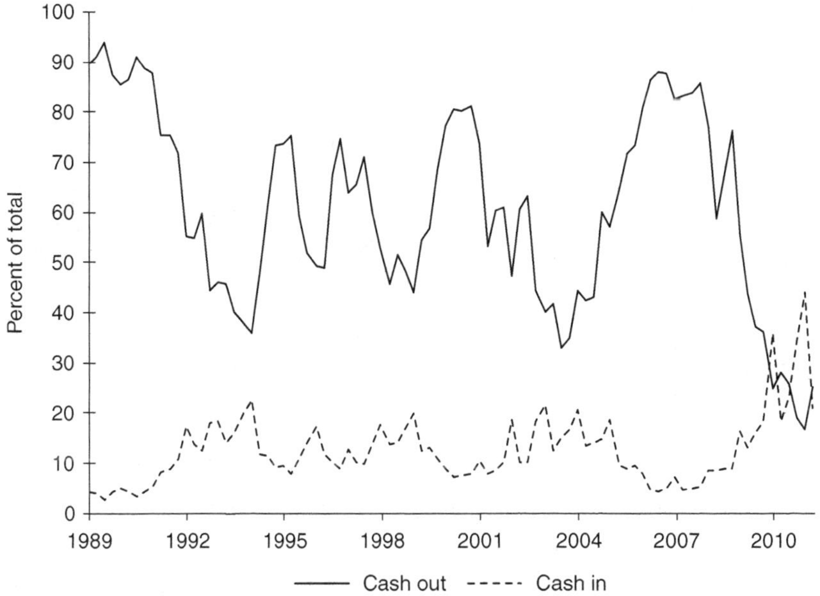

Figure 2.8 US mortgage refinancing transactions: 1989–2011

Source: Freddie Mac (2011).

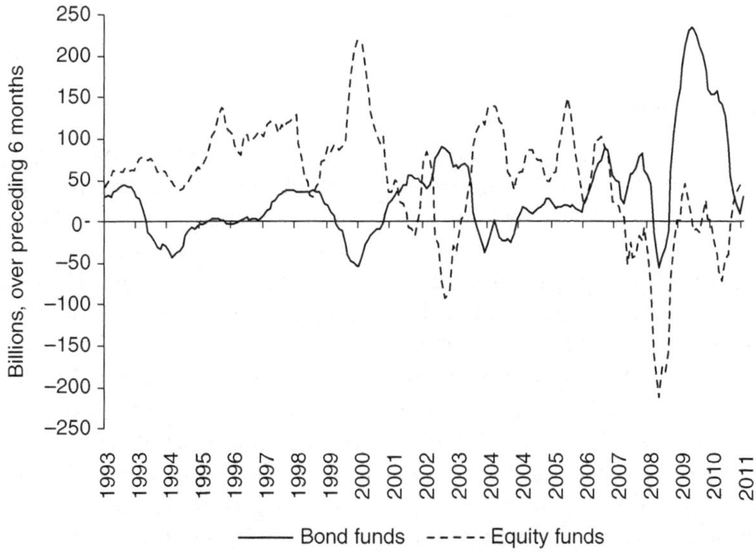

Figure 2.9 Net cash flows into US mutual funds: 1993–2011

Source: Investment Company Institute (2011).

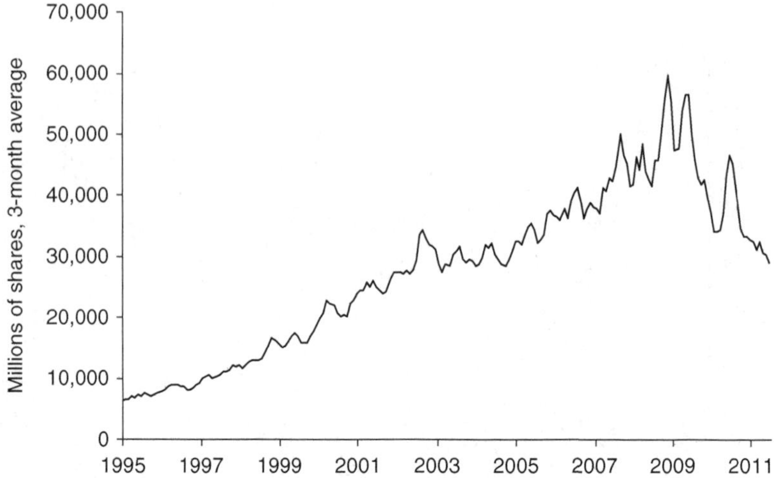

Figure 2.10 New York Stock Exchange trading volumes: 1995–2011
Source: New York Stock Exchange (2011).

have reason to be more cautious given their reduced horizon for making up losses. Surveys suggest a reduced interest in equity investments, so the likelihood is that older workers' portfolios have shifted.

Conclusion

Evidence on consumption and labor force participation over the past several years suggests that households nearing retirement are making up for financial losses by increasing saving and deferring retirement. They also appear to have reduced financial risk exposure by taking on less leverage and moving their portfolios in a more conservative direction. These findings complement survey data indicating that households were inclined to make such changes to their behavior.

In addition to responding to financial losses experienced during the Great Recession, households are also forming expectations around how they believe large unfunded liabilities in public and private pensions and health care programs are likely to be resolved. The losses suffered in recent years probably understate the overall loss of retirement resources. A key question is whether the behavioral changes discussed in this chapter will be sufficient to allow older households approaching retirement to avoid making a material cut in their retirement standards of living. This question should be a priority for future research as individual- and household-level data become available for this period and the years that follow.

Acknowledgments

We thank John Soroushian for excellent research assistance, and David Richardson and participants at the Pension Research Council Spring Symposium for helpful comments. The views expressed are our own and not those of BNP Paribas, the Brookings Institution, or their affiliates.

Endnotes

1. For more description of the follow-up survey, see Bricker et al. (2011).
2. For further discussion of possible long-run implications, see Tang et al. (2012).
3. See http://www.bls.gov/cex/csxstnd.htm
4. See, for example, Attanasio (1998).
5. A sharper test would involve isolating patterns for the nonretired households in this group, but we do not have these data. We can say, though, that households approaching retirement look to be concentrated in this group, as the average number of earners per household is a little lower than that for the next youngest group, and much higher than that for the next oldest group.
6. These income changes should be taken with a grain of salt, given that the core mission of the survey is really to collect expenditure information and many researchers over the years have expressed doubts about their degree of accuracy. Similar reasoning is behind our decision not to conduct the analysis in terms of saving rates.
7. The greater presumed credit dependence of this group is consistent with findings by Gourinchas and Parker (2002) and others that consumption tracks income much more closely for households with heads below the age of 40.
8. We concentrate on men, as women's labor force participation has exhibited a structural increase in recent decades that make cyclical patterns more difficult to detect.

References

Aizcorbe, A., A. Kennickell, and K. Moore (2003). "Recent Changes in US Family Finances: Evidence from the 1998 and 2001 Survey of Consumer Finances", *Federal Reserve Bulletin*, 89 (January): 1–32.

Attanasio, A. P. (1998). "Cohort Analysis of Saving Behavior by US Households", *Journal of Human Resources*, 33(3): 575–609.

Board of Governors of the Federal Reserve System (FRB) (2011*a*). *Flow of Funds Accounts of the United States.* Washington, DC: FRB. http://www.federalreserve.gov/releases/z1/current/

—— (2011*b*). *Survey of Consumer Finances (1983, 1989, 1992, 1995, 1998, 2001, 2004, 2007 Waves, and 2009 Panel).* Washington, DC: FRB. http://www.federalreserve.gov/pubs/oss/oss2/scfindex.html

Bricker, J., B. Bucks, A. Kennickell, T. Mach, and K. Moore (2011). "Surveying the Aftermath of the Storm: Changes in Family Finances from 2007 to 2009", Federal Reserve Board Finance and Economics Discussion Series Paper No. 2011-17 (March).

Brown, M., A. Haughwout, D. Lee, and W. van der Klaauw (2011). "Have Consumers Been Deleveraging?", *Liberty Street Economics Blog,* Federal Reserve Bank of New York. http://libertystreeteconomics.newyorkfed.org/2011/03/have-consumers-become-more-frugal.html

Bucks, B., A. Kennickell, T. Mach, and K. Moore (2009). "Changes in US Family Finances from 2004 to 2007: Evidence from the Survey of Consumer Finances", *Federal Reserve Bulletin,* 95 (February): A1–A55.

Bureau of Labor Statistics (BLS) (2011*a*). *Consumer Expenditure Survey Current Expenditure Tables by Age of Reference Person.* Washington, DC: BLS.

—— (2011*b*). *Labor Force Statistics from the Current Population Survey.* Washington, DC: BLS.

Duke, E. A. (2011). "Changed Circumstances: The Impact of the Financial Crisis on the Economic Condition of Workers Near Retirement and of Business Owners." Remarks to the Virginia Association of Economists (March 24).

Dynan, K. E. (2009). "Changing Household Financial Opportunities and Economic Security", *Journal of Economic Perspectives,* 23(Fall): 49–68.

Employee Benefit Research Institute (2011). "The 2011 Retirement Confidence Survey: Confidence Drops to Record Lows, Reflecting 'the New Normal' ", EBRI Issue Brief 355, March 2011.

Freddie Mac (2011). *Refinance Activities Reports.* Washington, DC: Freddie Mac.

Gourinchas, P. and J. A. Parker (2002). "Consumption Over the Life Cycle", *Econometrica,* 70(January): 47–89.

Hurd, M. and S. Rohwedder (2011). "The Effects of the Economic Crisis on the Older Population: How Expectations, Consumption, Bequests and Retirement by the Older Population Responded to Market Shocks", in R. Maurer, O. S. Mitchell, and M. J. Warshawsky, eds., *Reshaping Retirement Security: Lessons from the Global Financial Crisis.* Oxford, UK: Oxford University Press.

Investment Company Institute (ICI) (2011). *Fund and Market Statistics.* Washington, DC: ICI.

National Association of Realtors (NAR) (2011). *Existing Home-Sales Information.* Chicago, IL: NAR.

New York Stock Exchange (NYSE) (2011). *NYSE Euronext Data Library.* New York, NY: NYSE.

Sass, S. A., C. Monk, and K. Haverstick (2010). "Workers' Response to the Market Crash: Save More, Work More?" Center for Retirement Research at Boston College Brief #10-3 (February).

Standard & Poor's (S&P) (2011*a*). *S&P 500.* New York, NY: S&P.
—— (2011*b*). *U.S. Credit Card Quality Index.* New York, NY: S&P.
Tang, N., O. S. Mitchell, and S. P. Utkus (2012) "Trading in 401(k) Plans during the Financial Crisis," in R. Maurer, O. S. Mitchell, and M. J. Warshawsky, eds., *Reshaping Retirement Security: Lessons from the Global Financial Crisis.* Oxford, UK: Oxford University Press.
US Census Bureau (2011). *Housing Vacancies and Homeownership.* Washington, DC: US Census Bureau.

Chapter 3

Potential Impacts of the Great Recession on Future Retirement Incomes

Barbara A. Butrica, Richard W. Johnson, and Karen E. Smith

The Great Recession, as many analysts dubbed the 2007–9 economic downturn, lived up to its name. Economic activity plummeted, millions of workers lost their jobs, and unemployment soared (Elsby et al., 2010). Many Americans were out of work for more than twelve months (Pew Economic Policy Group, 2010), and wages stagnated for those able to keep their jobs (Mishel and Shierholz, 2010). As incomes fell, families struggled to make ends meet and poverty rates surged (DeNavas-Walt et al., 2010; Godofsky et al., 2010; Hurd and Rohwedder, 2010). Declining tax revenues and expanding public expenditures swelled the federal deficit and squeezed state and local governments (Congressional Budget Office, 2010; McNichol et al., 2011). Although the National Bureau of Economic Research declared the recession is over in 2009, many analysts predict that unemployment will stay above its pre-recession level for years (Eberts, 2011).

One result of the Great Recession is its impact on future retirees. Earlier research showed that the 2008 stock market crash could erode retirement security for high-income workers, most likely to hold equities (Butrica et al., 2009, 2010). But high unemployment could reduce future retirement incomes for a broader segment of the population, since in addition to reducing earnings, job loss will lower Social Security and pension credits, and leave workers with less income to set aside for retirement. This chapter uses the Urban Institute's dynamic microsimulation model (DYNASIM3) to examine the likely impacts of the Great Recession on future retirement incomes. The analysis projects average incomes to age 70 for adults who were aged 25–64 in 2008, and compares them to what retirees would have received if the recession had not occurred.

Our results show that the Great Recession will modestly reduce future retirement incomes. This drop results almost entirely from the anemic wage growth that occurred during the recession, which our model assumes will permanently reduce future wages. Employment declines will have little effect on future aggregate retirement incomes because most workers remained employed during the recession, and the losses that occurred are generally inconsequential when averaged over decades-long careers. Retirement incomes will fall most sharply for high-socioeconomic-status groups, who have the most to lose, but relative income losses will not vary much across groups. Those workers who were youngest when the recession began will be hit hard, since they are most likely to lose their jobs, and the impact of lower wages will accumulate over their entire careers. But retirement incomes will also fall substantially for those now in their late 50s, because the drop in the economy-wide average wage will lower the index factor in the Social Security benefit formula, permanently reducing their annual benefits.

Methodology

To assess the impact of the Great Recession on future retirement security, we project incomes at age 70 for adults aged 25–64 in 2008 and compare them to what older adults would have received had the recession not occurred. We focus on income at age 70 because the vast majority of adults have retired by then. The impact of high unemployment on future retirement incomes will likely depend on one's stage of the life course when the recession hit. To capture these differences, the analysis compares outcomes by ten-year cohorts, ranging from those aged 25–34 in 2008 (who turn 70 between 2044 and 2053) to those aged 55–64 in 2008 (who turn 70 between 2014 and 2023).

Projections come from the Urban Institute's Dynamic Simulation of Income Model, known as DYNASIM3. This model starts with a self-weighting sample of 103,072 individuals from the 1990 to 1993 panels of the United States Census Bureau's Survey of Income and Program Participation (SIPP) and ages this starting sample in yearly increments to 2085, using parameters estimated from longitudinal data sources. DYNASIM3 then projects demographic and economic changes annually from 1993 to 2085. The model integrates many important trends and group-level differences in life-course processes, including birth, death, schooling, leaving home, first marriage, remarriage, divorce, disability, work, retirement, and earnings. It projects the major sources of income and wealth annually from age 15 until death, including employment, earnings, Social Security benefits, benefits from employer-sponsored defined benefit (DB) pensions, supplemental security income (SSI), retirement accounts (defined contribution or DC plans, individual retirement accounts (IRAs), and Keoghs), and other assets (saving, checking, money market, certificates of deposit (CDs), stocks, bonds, equity in businesses, vehicles, and nonhome real estate, less unsecured debt).

We examine the impact of the Great Recession on lifetime employment and several income measures, including own lifetime earnings, per capita household lifetime earnings, and per capita household income at age 70. Individuals are considered employed in a given year if they have any earnings, even if they worked relatively few hours because they were unemployed for part of the year. (The Social Security Trustees follow the same convention when setting their employment targets.) As a result, employment rates calculated in DYNASIM3 do not match those from Bureau of Labor Statistics (BLS), which are annual averages of monthly employment.[1] Own lifetime earnings are reported in 2010 dollars and averaged from ages 22 to 62. Per capita household earnings, which we term 'shared lifetime earnings', are computed as half of the husband's and wife's earnings in years when an individual is married and own earnings in years when single. As with own lifetime earnings, shared lifetime earnings are indexed to 2010 dollars and averaged from ages 22 to 62. Both measures include years with zero earnings. Per capita household income includes all income received by the individual and spouse, divided by 2 if married. It excludes income of other household members. Because income and asset distributions are highly skewed, we drop individuals in the top 1 percent of the income distribution to lessen the impact of these outliers on reported means. All financial amounts are reported in constant 2010 dollars (adjusted by the projected change in the consumer price index).

Our baseline simulation uses the Social Security Trustees' 2010 assumptions (Social Security Board of Trustees, 2010), which account for the actual and projected effects of high unemployment and lower wages from the Great Recession. Our alternative scenario, designed to simulate outcomes if the recession had not occurred, is based largely on the Trustees' 2008 assumptions (Social Security Board of Trustees, 2008). One complication is that some differences between the 2008 and 2010 Trustees' assumptions were unrelated to the recession. For example, the Trustees changed their assumptions about mortality and immigration after 2008. They also increased their long-range real wage growth assumptions from 1.1 to 1.2 percent per year, because the Affordable Care Act, signed by President Obama in March 2010, is expected to reduce employers' health care spending and boost earnings. To isolate the changes in the Trustees' assumptions between 2008 and 2010 related to the recession, we use adjusted 2008 targets in the no-recession simulation. That simulation uses the employment and disability onset rates from 2008 and assumes that real wages grow at the 2008 assumed rate through 2010, after which they grow at the higher rates assumed by the Trustees in 2010. Both the baseline and no-recession simulations, then, capture the expected impact of health reform on projected wage growth. The no-recession scenario also uses the 2008 price growth series through 2010 and aligns price growth with the 2010 assumptions for later years.[2] As a result, the no-recession simulation includes permanently higher average earnings and price targets than the baseline simulation in all years after 2007. All other parameters in the no-recession simulation rely on the 2010 Trustees' assumptions.

Findings

Figure 3.1 shows actual and projected employment rates for persons aged 16–64 under the baseline scenario, where the impact of the Great Recession is evident. Employment rates fall from 82 to 75 percent for men and from 77 to 71 percent for women between 2007 and 2010. After 2010, employment rates are projected to gradually recover, stabilizing at about 80 percent for men and 74 percent for women in 2016.

Figure 3.2 shows projected labor earnings paths for the two scenarios, in 2010 dollars. Real earnings fall between 2007 and 2009 in the baseline scenario, but then grow at about 2 percent per year in the no-recession scenario. By the time earnings growth rates converge again in the two scenarios in 2010, average real earnings in the no-recession scenario exceed those in the baseline scenario by 6 percent, a differential that

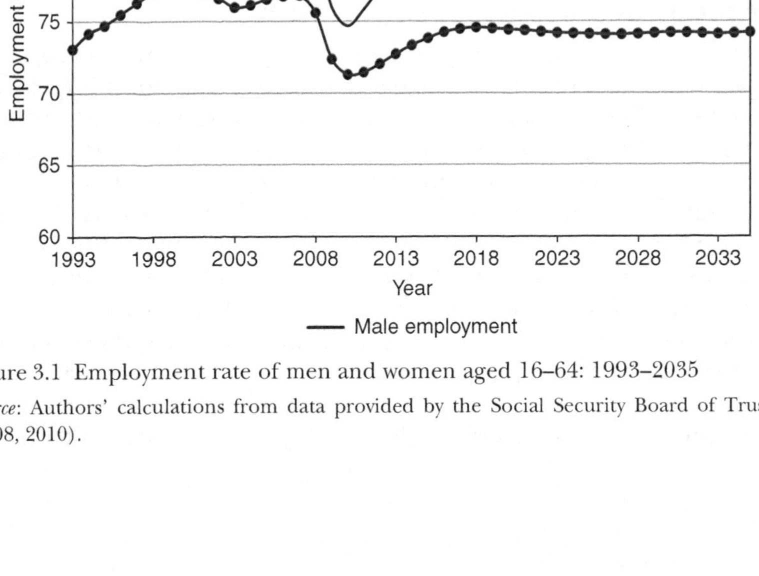

Figure 3.1 Employment rate of men and women aged 16–64: 1993–2035

Source: Authors' calculations from data provided by the Social Security Board of Trustees (2008, 2010).

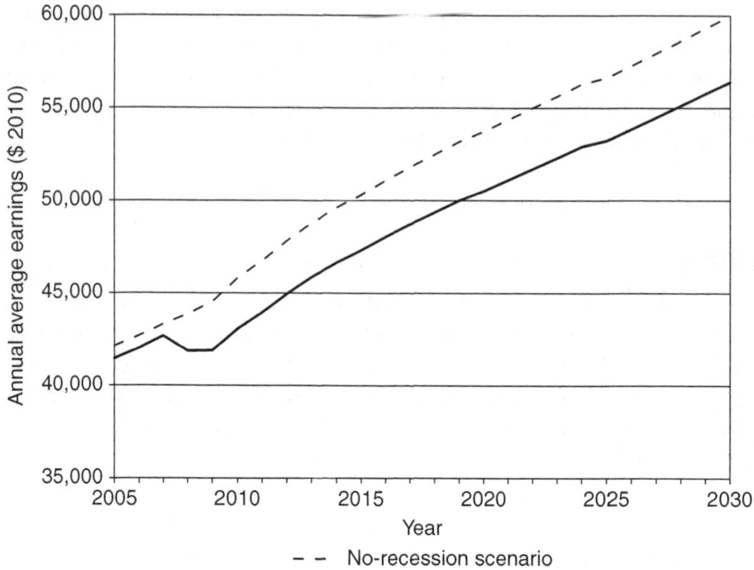

Figure 3.2 Average earnings of workers by simulation in $ 2010: 2005–30

Source: Authors' calculations from data provided by the Social Security Board of Trustees (2008, 2010).

persists throughout the projection period. The absolute value of the real wage differential in the two scenarios grows from about $2,700 in 2010 to $3,200 in 2020 to $3,600 in 2030. The projected price targets do not differ much between the two scenarios.

The recession's impact on employment

Table 3.1 shows simulated employment rates in 2010 when actual unemployment peaked under the baseline scenario, and the absolute and percentage change relative to the no-recession scenario. In 2010, we estimate that 71.1 percent of 25–64-year-olds were working (had earnings), 3.4 percentage points (4.6 percent) below the share that would have been employed had the recession not occurred. The hardest hits were the 35–44-year-olds, whose employment rate declined by 3.9 percentage points (5 percent). In contrast, the 55–64-year-olds were least affected. Because older workers were less likely to lose their jobs than younger workers during the Great Recession (as in previous recessions) (Johnson and Mommaerts, 2011; Johnson and Park, 2011), their employment rate declined by only 2.5 percentage points (4 percent). Men, blacks, Hispanics, those who did not complete high school, and those with intermittent

TABLE 3.1 Employment rates in 2010, adults aged 25–64

	Employment rate (%)					Absolute change due to recession					Percent change due to recession				
Age in 2008		25–34	35–44	45–54	55–64		25–34	35–44	45–54	55–64		25–34	35–44	45–54	55–64
Year age 70	All	2044–53	2034–43	2024–33	2014–23	All	2044–53	2034–43	2024–33	2014–23	All	2044–53	2034–43	2024–33	2014–23
All	71.1	74.1	73.8	74.7	59.8	−3.4***	−3.7***	−3.9***	−3.3***	−2.5***	−4.6	−4.8	−5.0	−4.2	−4.0
Gender															
Female	67.8	70.7	71.2	72.6	54.5	−2.5***	−2.9***	−3.0***	−1.9***	−2.1**	−3.6	−3.9	−4.0	−2.6	−3.7
Male	74.8	77.8	76.4	77.0	65.9	−4.4***	−4.4***	−4.9***	−4.9***	−3.0***	−5.6	−5.4	−6.0	−6.0	−4.4
Race/ethnicity															
Non-Hispanic white	75.3	79.8	78.1	78.8	63.6	−3.3***	−3.8***	−3.9***	−3.1***	−2.4***	−4.2	−4.5	−4.8	−3.8	−3.6
Non-Hispanic black	67.2	78.0	73.9	68.5	38.3	−4.0***	−2.9**	−4.4***	−4.7***	−4.1*	−5.6	−3.6	−5.6	−6.4	−9.7
Hispanic	58.2	60.3	59.0	58.1	51.5	−3.9***	−4.3***	−4.4***	−4.2**	−1.6	−6.3	−6.7	−6.9	−6.7	−3.0
Asian/native American	62.6	59.8	64.3	67.6	59.0	−2.4**	−2.5	−2.2	−2.3	−2.8	−3.7	−4.0	−3.3	−3.3	−4.5
Education															
Did not complete high school	38.9	42.6	40.4	38.7	33.3	−4.2***	−5.2***	−4.7***	−4.8***	−1.5	−9.7	−10.9	−10.4	−11.0	−4.3
High school graduate/some college	71.1	75.4	74.1	75.5	57.3	−3.7***	−3.9***	−4.3***	−3.7***	−2.8***	−4.9	−4.9	−5.5	−4.7	−4.7
College graduate	83.1	82.4	84.9	87.7	75.8	−2.5***	−2.9***	−2.8***	−1.8**	−2.4**	−2.9	−3.4	−3.2	−2.0	−3.1
Years worked from age 15 through 2010															
≤10	35.0	44.9	29.2	22.6	18.9	−3.0***	−3.9***	−2.5**	−2.3	−0.8	−7.9	−8.0	−7.9	−9.2	−4.1
11–29	77.2	89.1	81.5	63.4	36.8	−3.7***	−3.2***	−4.0***	−4.5***	−2.4*	−4.6	−3.5	−4.7	−6.6	−6.1
30+	81.6	0.0	96.5	90.3	71.1	−2.6***	0.0	−2.4***	−2.6***	−2.7***	−3.1	–	−2.4	−2.8	−3.7

(Continued)

TABLE 3.1 Continued

	Employment rate (%)					Absolute change due to recession					Percent change due to recession				
Age in 2008		25–34	35–44	45–54	55–64		25–34	35–44	45–54	55–64		25–34	35–44	45–54	55–64
Year age 70	All	2044–53	2034–43	2024–33	2014–23	All	2044–53	2034–43	2024–33	2014–23	All	2044–53	2034–43	2024–33	2014–23
Own lifetime earnings quintile															
Bottom	29.9	28.7	31.2	33.2	25.5	−2.7***	−2.9**	−3.1**	−3.2**	−1.4	−8.3	−9.2	−9.0	−8.8	−5.2
Second	69.3	75.7	72.2	74.3	51.9	−4.5***	−5.4***	−5.6***	−3.5***	−2.9**	−6.1	−6.7	−7.2	−4.5	−5.3
Third	79.7	84.3	83.1	83.1	65.8	−3.7***	−3.8***	−4.3***	−4.0***	−2.0	−4.4	−4.3	−4.9	−4.6	−2.9
Fourth	86.1	89.5	89.9	89.4	73.3	−3.2***	−3.0***	−3.0***	−3.2***	−3.5***	−3.6	−3.2	−3.2	−3.5	−4.6
Top	90.6	92.5	92.6	93.4	82.4	−3.0***	−3.1***	−3.4***	−2.7***	−2.8***	−3.2	−3.2	−3.5	−2.8	−3.3

Notes: *** Significant at 1% level; ** at 5% level; * at 10% level. Sample excludes individuals with incomes in the top 1 percent of the income distribution. Years worked is the number of years with positive earnings from age 15 through 2010. Own lifetime earnings is the average of wage-indexed earnings from age 15 until 2010. Quintiles are calculated within age groups.

Source: Authors' computations from DYNASIM3 projections.

employment histories and lower wages were generally hit harder by the recession than others. In the youngest age group, employment rates fell by 10.9 percent for those lacking high school diplomas, but only 3.4 percent for college graduates.

Projecting outcomes to age 70 shows the effects of the recession compounded over a lifetime. Although employment rates fell by 3.4 percentage points in 2010—at the peak of the downturn in the labor market—most workers retained their jobs or received at least some earnings in the year they became unemployed. As a result, the average number of years worked between ages 22 and 62 is projected to decline by less than 1 percent for all cohorts (Table 3.2). Among the youngest age group, 66 percent are projected to work 30 or more years over their lifetimes. This share is only 0.5 percentage points below what it would have been had the recession not occurred. The recession will have very little impact on lifetime work years for those closest to retirement when the downturn began.

Projected incomes for future retirees

Although the Great Recession will not shorten worklives, it is projected to reduce average own lifetime earnings by 3.4 percent, because the economic downturn interrupted the growth in hourly wages (Table 3.3). The impact will be greater for workers who were relatively young in 2008 and will spend much of their careers in the new, lower-wage labor market, and smaller for older workers, who will spend few years in the less-inviting labor market. For example, the recession will reduce average own lifetime earnings 4.8 percent for those aged 25–34 in 2008, but only 0.7 percent for those aged 55–64. Results are similar for husbands' and wives' shared lifetime earnings.

Our projections also indicate that the recession will reduce Social Security benefits in two ways. Because benefits are based on the average highest thirty-five years of earnings, the decline in annual earnings after 2008 will directly reduce future benefits. Benefits will receive an additional hit because they are indexed to the economy-wide average earnings in the year the beneficiary turns age 60. Strong growth in average wages before age 60 raises future Social Security benefits, even for those whose own wages did not increase much, because the indexing means that all earnings received before age 60 count more in the benefit formula than they would if average wages grew more slowly. Our baseline scenario assumes that the recession will permanently reduce earnings after 2008, in turn reducing the index factor in the Social Security benefit formula for everyone who turns 60 after 2008. As a result, future Social Security benefits will generally decline more sharply than lifetime earnings, especially for those approaching age 60 in 2008. Average own Social Security benefits will drop

TABLE 3.2 Projected work histories of future retirees at age 70

	Baseline work history					Absolute change due to recession					Percent change due to recession				
Age in 2008		25–34	35–44	45–54	55–64		25–34	35–44	45–54	55–64		25–34	35–44	45–54	55–64
Year age 70	All	2044–53	2034–43	2024–33	2014–23	All	2044–53	2034–43	2024–33	2014–23	All	2044–53	2034–43	2024–33	2014–23
Average age worked	31.1	31.1	31.2	31.2	30.8	−0.1	−0.1	−0.2	−0.2	−0.1	−0.3	−0.3	−0.6	−0.6	−0.3
Distribution of years worked (%)															
≤10	8	7	8	8	9	0.1	0.1	0.0	0.2	0.1	1.2	1.4	0.0	2.5	1.1
11–29	24	27	23	22	22	0.3	0.4	0.6	0.4	0.0	1.3	1.5	2.7	1.8	0.0
30+	68	66	69	69	68	−0.5*	−0.5	−0.6	−0.5	−0.1	−0.7	−0.7	−0.9	−0.7	−0.1

Notes: Sample excludes individuals with incomes in the top 1 percent of the income distribution. Years worked is the number of years with positive earnings between ages 22 and 62.

Source: Authors' computations from DYNASIM3 projections.

TABLE 3.3 Projected income of future retirees at age 70

	Average income (thousands of $ 2010)					Absolute change due to recession (thousands of $ 2010)					Percent change due to recession				
Age in 2008		25–34	35–44	45–54	55–64		25–34	35–44	45–54	55–64		25–34	35–44	45–54	55–64
Year age 70	All	2044–53	2034–43	2024–33	2014–23	All	2044–53	2034–43	2024–33	2014–23	All	2044–53	2034–43	2024–33	2014–23
Own lifetime earnings	36.6	42.2	39.5	32.9	30.5	−1.3***	−2.1***	−1.8***	−0.7**	−0.2	−3.4	−4.8	−4.3	−2.2	−0.7
Shared lifetime earnings	36.0	41.7	38.7	32.6	30.2	−1.3***	−2.1***	−1.7***	−0.7***	−0.2	−3.4	−4.8	−4.2	−2.2	−0.7
Own Social Security benefits	17.1	19.5	18.0	16.2	14.5	−0.7***	−1.0***	−0.8***	−0.6***	−0.2***	−4.1	−4.6	−4.5	−3.8	−1.4
Per capita household Social Security benefits	16.1	18.3	16.7	15.2	13.6	−0.6***	−0.7***	−0.7***	−0.6***	−0.2***	−3.8	−3.9	−4.2	−4.0	−1.5

Notes: *** Significant at 1% level; ** at 5% level; * at 10% level. Sample excludes individuals with incomes in the top 1 percent of the income distribution. Own lifetime earnings is the average of wage-indexed earnings between ages 22 and 62. Shared lifetime earnings is the average of wage-indexed shared earnings between ages 22 and 62, where shared earnings are half the total earnings of the couple in the years when married and individual earnings in years when not married.

Source: Authors' computations from DYNASIM3 projections.

1.4 percent for those aged 55–64 in 2008, and 3.8 percent for those aged 45–54, or about twice the decline in lifetime earnings.[9] For those aged 25–34, who will spend almost their entire careers in the postrecession labor market, the percentage decline in Social Security benefits roughly equals the percentage decline in lifetime earnings.

The recession will also affect other sources of retirement income outside of Social Security. Lower earnings will reduce wealth in employer retirement plans and limit workers' ability to save outside of them. Unemployed workers may be forced to dip into their retirement savings at relatively young ages to meet current consumption needs. Moreover, the recession will curtail postretirement earnings.

Table 3.4 reports projected average per capita household income at age 70. We suggest that the recession will reduce annual household income by 4.1 percent (or $2,100 per person in 2010 dollars) for those closest to retirement when the recession hit, and by 4.9 percent (or $3,200 per person) for those farthest from retirement. For those aged 55–64 in 2008, average retirement incomes will drop more steeply than average Social Security benefits, primarily because their age-70 earnings will fall 9 percent and their income from assets outside of pension and retirement plans will fall 4.7 percent. Earnings at age 70 will drop so much for this age group because many lost their jobs late in life and will never become reemployed. We project that the recession will reduce age-70 employment rates by 2.3 percentage points for those aged 55–64 in 2008, but by only 0.2 percentage points for later cohorts (not shown). Wealth outside of pension plans falls for those near retirement when the recession hit, because the recession forced many to dip into their savings to meet current consumption needs, and they have little time to recoup their lost savings. For the youngest adults in 2008, the recession depresses overall retirement income by about the same percentage as Social Security benefits.

The recession's impact on income sources is projected to vary across the income distribution. Retirees in the bottom income quintile receive most of their household income (around 71 percent) from Social Security benefits. As a result, the projected drop in Social Security benefits for these retirees' accounts for nearly the entire decline in their age-70 income. By contrast, retirees in the top income quintile receive relatively little of their household income (around 16 percent) from Social Security benefits, so the projected benefit decline explains only part of their total income losses. Although they will receive more Social Security benefits than lower income retirees (despite the program's progressivity) and the recession will reduce their benefits more, this cut will account for only about 16 percent of the total income decline (averaged across all cohorts). Instead, the projected decline in household income for the highest income retirees is driven mostly by drops in income from nonpension assets and

TABLE 3.4 Average per capita household income of future retirees at age 70 by income source and income quintile

	Average per capita household income (thousands of $ 2010)					Absolute change due to recession (thousands of $ 2010)					Percent change due to recession				
Age in 2008		25–34	35–44	45–54	55–64		25–34	35–44	45–54	55–64		25–34	35–44	45–54	55–64
Year age 70	All	2044–53	2034–43	2024–33	2014–23	All	2044–53	2034–43	2024–33	2014–23	All	2044–53	2034–43	2024–33	2014–23
All															
Total income	54.5	61.1	57.8	49.3	49.0	−2.4***	−3.2***	−2.4***	−2.1***	−2.1***	−4.3	−4.9	−4.0	−4.1	−4.1
Earnings	11.5	13.3	12.8	10.0	9.6	−0.6***	−0.6**	−0.2	−0.6**	−1.0***	−5.2	−4.5	−1.6	−5.9	−9.0
DB pension benefits	4.2	3.9	3.7	3.9	5.8	−0.2**	−0.3*	−0.2	−0.2	0.0	−4.8	−7.5	−5.4	−5.1	0.0
DC assets	6.1	6.8	6.8	5.8	5.0	−0.2***	−0.5***	−0.3**	−0.1	−0.1	−3.3	−7.2	−4.5	−1.8	−2.1
Social Security benefits	16.1	18.3	16.7	15.2	13.6	−0.6***	−0.7***	−0.7***	−0.6***	−0.2***	−3.8	−3.9	−4.2	−4.0	−1.5
SSI benefits	0.1	0.1	0.1	0.1	0.2	0.0**	0.0	0.0	0.0	0.0	0.0	0.0	0.0	0.0	0.0
Nonpension assets	16.5	18.8	17.7	14.2	14.9	−0.7***	−0.8*	−0.8**	−0.6*	−0.7*	−4.3	−4.3	−4.5	−4.3	−4.7
Bottom quintile															
Total income	10.4	11.5	10.4	10.0	9.5	−0.4***	−0.4***	−0.4***	−0.3***	−0.1	−3.9	−3.5	−3.9	−3.1	−1.1
Earnings	0.6	0.7	0.6	0.5	0.6	0.0	0.0	0.0	0.0	0.0	0.0	0.0	0.0	0.0	0.0
DB pension benefits	0.3	0.3	0.3	0.3	0.3	0.0	0.0*	0.1	0.0	0.0	0.0	0.0	50.0	0.0	0.0
DC assets	0.3	0.4	0.4	0.3	0.3	0.0	0.0**	0.1	0.0	0.0	0.0	0.0	33.3	0.0	0.0
Social Security benefits	7.4	8.3	7.3	7.2	6.5	−0.3***	−0.3**	−0.3**	−0.3***	−0.1	−4.1	−3.7	−4.2	−4.2	−1.6
SSI benefits	0.6	0.5	0.6	0.6	0.8	0.0**	0.1	0.0	0.0	0.1	0.0	25.0	0.0	0.0	14.3
Nonpension assets	1.1	1.3	1.2	1.1	0.8	−0.1***	0.0	−0.1**	−0.1**	0.0	−9.1	0.0	−8.3	−9.1	0.0

(*Continued*)

TABLE 3.4 Continued

	Average per capita household income (thousands of $ 2010)					Absolute change due to recession (thousands of $ 2010)					Percent change due to recession				
Age in 2008		25–34	35–44	45–54	55–64		25–34	35–44	45–54	55–64		25–34	35–44	45–54	55–64
Year age 70	All	2044–53	2034–43	2024–33	2014–23	All	2044–53	2034–43	2024–33	2014–23	All	2044–53	2034–43	2024–33	2014–23
Middle quintile															
Total income	36.8	39.8	38.1	34.7	33.9	−1.8***	−2.2***	−2.1***	−1.5***	−1.3***	−4.7	−5.3	−5.2	−4.1	−3.6
Earnings	6.3	7.1	6.9	5.7	5.6	−0.4***	−0.4*	−0.3	−0.4*	−0.6***	−6.3	−5.6	−4.4	−6.9	−10.2
DB pension benefits	2.7	2.2	2.2	2.5	4.0	−0.1***	−0.1	−0.2	−0.2*	−0.2	−3.7	−4.5	−8.7	−7.7	−5.0
DC assets	4.3	4.3	4.5	4.2	4.0	−0.2***	−0.3*	−0.4***	−0.1	−0.1	−4.7	−6.8	−8.5	−2.4	−2.6
Social Security benefits	17.3	19.4	18.2	16.5	14.8	−0.5***	−1.0***	−0.6***	−0.5***	−0.1	−3.0	−4.7	−3.4	−3.1	−0.7
SSI benefits	0.0	0.0	0.0	0.0	0.0	0.0	0.0	0.0	0.0	0.0	0.0	0.0	0.0	0.0	0.0
Nonpension assets	6.0	6.7	6.3	5.6	5.5	−0.4***	−0.5**	−0.6***	−0.2	−0.2*	−6.6	−7.4	−9.1	−3.6	−3.7
Top quintile															
Total income	141.9	162.2	152.9	124.2	125.7	−6.2***	−7.9***	−5.3***	−5.5***	−6.1***	−4.2	−4.7	−3.3	−4.2	−4.6
Earnings	33.6	39.8	37.5	28.7	27.0	−1.3***	−1.6	0.3	−1.6*	−2.7***	−3.6	−3.8	0.9	−5.2	−9.2
DB pension benefits	11.6	11.1	10.5	10.6	15.2	−0.7**	−1.2	−1.0	−0.3	0.0	−6.0	−9.5	−8.3	−2.9	0.0
DC assets	16.4	19.0	18.5	14.9	12.5	−0.5*	−1.0	−0.4	−0.3	−0.3	−3.1	−4.8	−2.2	−2.1	−2.5
Social Security benefits	22.0	25.5	23.0	20.6	18.1	−1.0***	−1.0***	−1.2***	−1.0***	−0.5***	−4.1	−3.6	−4.8	−4.4	−2.8
SSI benefits	0.0	0.0	0.0	0.0	0.0	0.0	0.0	0.0	0.0	0.0	0.0	0.0	0.0	0.0	0.0
Nonpension assets	58.4	66.9	63.4	49.4	52.9	−2.6***	−3.0	−3.0*	−2.2*	−2.5	−4.3	−4.2	−4.5	−4.3	−4.6

Notes: *** Significant at 1% level; ** at 5% level; * at 10% level. Sample excludes individuals with incomes in the top 1 percent of the income distribution. Quintiles are calculated within age groups. The sum of the components of income does not always equal total income because of rounding. DB = defined benefits, DC = defined contributions, and SSI = supplemental security income.

Source: Authors' computations from DYNASIM3 projections.

TABLE 3.5 Projected number and share of adults at age 70 with low incomes

	Baseline simulation					Absolute change due to recession					Percent change due to recession				
Age in 2008		25–34	35–44	45–54	55–64		25–34	35–44	45–54	55–64		25–34	35–44	45–54	55–64
Year age 70	All	2044–53	2034–43	2024–33	2014–23	All	2044–53	2034–43	2024–33	2014–23	All	2044–53	2034–43	2024–33	2014–23
Percent with income below 100% FPL	4.9	3.9	5.0	5.4	5.5	0.2	0.1	0.3	0.3	0.2	4.3	2.6	6.4	5.9	3.8
Percent with income below 125% FPL	7.3	5.7	7.1	7.9	8.6	0.5***	0.5*	0.5*	0.5*	0.5	7.4	9.6	7.6	6.8	6.2
Number with income below 100% of FPL (thousands)	6,971	1,444	1,863	2,039	1,663	284.5	37.0	111.8	113.3	60.5	4.3	2.6	6.4	5.9	3.8
Number of income below 125% FPL (thousands)	10,385	2,111	2,645	2,982	2,600	711.3***	185.2*	186.3*	188.8*	151.1	7.4	9.6	7.6	6.8	6.2

Notes: *** Significant at 1% level; ** at 5% level; * at 10% level. Sample excludes individuals with incomes in the top 1 percent of the income distribution. FPL = federal poverty level.

Source: Authors' computations from DYNASIM3 projections.

earnings at age 70. For the youngest age group, 38 percent of their projected total loss is in nonpension asset income and 20 percent is in earnings. For the oldest age group, 41 percent of their projected total loss is in nonpension asset income and 44 percent is in earnings.

The recession-induced decline in household income is also projected to increase the number of Americans living in or near poverty at age 70. Table 3.5 reports the number and percentage of adults surviving to age 70 with incomes below 100 and 125 percent of the federal poverty level (FPL). We focus on those below the higher threshold because many with incomes that slightly exceed the FPL struggle financially (Zedlewski and Butrica, 2008). Moreover, the official poverty measure does not fully capture households' health care spending needs, a particularly pressing concern for many older Americans. The National Academy of Sciences developed a revised poverty threshold that better accounts for out-of-pocket spending (Citro and Michael, 1995). The 2009 poverty rate for adults aged 65 and older under this revised measure was about equal to the share with incomes below 125 percent of the official poverty threshold, suggesting that 125 percent of the FPL is an appropriate indicator for financial hardship at older ages (DeNavas-Walt et al., 2010; Short, 2010).

Across the four cohorts, the share of adults projected to have incomes below 125 percent of the FPL at age 70 will increase 7.4 percent because of the recession. The impact will grow over time, increasing 6.2 percent for those closest to retirement in 2008 and 9.6 percent for the youngest group. Among those aged 25–64 in 2008, the recession will leave an additional 711,000 adults with incomes below 125 percent of the FPL.[4]

Variation in projected outcomes by individual characteristics

Table 3.6 shows how the recession's impact on average per capita household income at age 70 is projected to vary across the population. Although employment rates fell most dramatically during the recession among those with the least education and earnings, these groups are unlikely to experience the sharpest declines in future retirement incomes. In absolute terms, incomes at age 70 will fall most for those with the highest incomes, who have most to lose. In relative terms, however, high-socioeconomic-status groups will not lose much more income than less privileged groups, because the large absolute losses for affluent groups represent only a small share of their total income. Within the youngest age group, the recession will reduce age-70 incomes for the highest income retirees by 4.7 percent, compared with 3.5 percent for the lowest income retirees.

TABLE 3.6 Average projected per capita household income of future retirees at age 70, by personal characteristics

Age in 2008	Average per capita household income (thousands of $ 2010)					Absolute change due to recession (thousands of $ 2010)					Percent change due to recession				
		25–34	35–44	45–54	55–64		25–34	35–44	45–54	55–64		25–34	35–44	45–54	55–64
Year age 70	All	2044–53	2034–43	2024–33	2014–23	All	2044–53	2034–43	2024–33	2014–23	All	2044–53	2034–43	2024–33	2014–23
All	54.5	61.1	57.8	49.3	49.0	−2.4***	−3.2***	−2.4***	−2.1***	−2.1***	−4.3	−4.9	−4.0	−4.1	−4.1
Gender															
Female	51.8	58.4	54.6	47.4	46.1	−2.5***	−3.2***	−2.5***	−1.9**	−2.3***	−4.7	−5.1	−4.4	−3.9	−4.8
Male	57.5	63.9	61.1	51.4	52.5	−2.4***	−3.1***	−2.2**	−2.3***	−1.9**	−4.1	−4.6	−3.5	−4.3	−3.5
Race/ethnicity															
Non-Hispanic white	62.4	72.0	67.3	56.1	55.7	−2.6***	−3.6***	−2.4***	−2.2***	−2.2***	−4.1	−4.7	−3.5	−3.8	−3.8
Non-Hispanic black	34.8	41.4	37.4	30.0	26.7	−1.6**	−1.6	−1.8	−1.6	−1.3	−4.4	−3.7	−4.6	−5.0	−4.5
Hispanic	34.9	43.5	34.1	28.2	25.7	−2.3***	−2.4*	−2.7**	−1.5	−1.6	−6.3	−5.3	−7.4	−5.0	−5.8
Asian/native American	46.8	52.2	50.6	42.5	36.7	−2.9**	−3.8*	−2.4	−1.7	−2.9	−5.7	−6.8	−4.6	−3.8	−7.2
Education															
Did not complete high school	22.9	27.7	24.1	20.5	18.7	−1.0*	−1.2	−1.2	−1.0	−0.5	−4.0	−4.0	−4.6	−4.4	−2.7
High school graduate/some college	44.9	51.7	46.9	41.0	40.4	−2.0***	−2.5***	−1.9**	−1.7***	−1.9***	−4.3	−4.7	−3.9	−4.0	−4.5
College graduate	82.6	85.1	86.2	78.4	78.5	−3.6***	−4.5***	−3.3**	−3.3**	−3.3**	−4.2	−5.1	−3.7	−4.0	−4.0

(Continued)

TABLE 3.6 Continued

	Average per capita household income (thousands of $ 2010)					Absolute change due to recession (thousands of $ 2010)					Percent change due to recession				
Age in 2008		25–34	35–44	45–54	55–64		25–34	35–44	45–54	55–64		25–34	35–44	45–54	55–64
Year age 70	All	2044–53	2034–43	2024–33	2014–23	All	2044–53	2034–43	2024–33	2014–23	All	2044–53	2034–43	2024–33	2014–23
Years worked															
≤10	19.0	20.7	18.9	18.5	18.1	−1.0*	−1.2	−1.5	−0.5	−0.7	−4.8	−5.3	−7.3	−2.8	−3.9
11–29	35.4	41.2	35.3	31.1	32.5	−1.6***	−1.7	−1.4	−1.7**	−1.3	−4.3	−3.9	−3.7	−5.2	−3.8
30+	65.5	73.4	70.1	58.9	58.6	−2.6***	−3.6***	−2.4***	−2.1***	−2.5***	−3.9	−4.7	−3.3	−3.5	−4.1
Social Security benefit status															
Retired, spouse, or survivor	59.8	66.6	63.6	54.4	53.7	−2.6***	−3.5***	−2.6***	−2.0***	−2.2***	−4.2	−5.0	−4.0	−3.6	−4.0
Disabled beneficiary	39.0	45.3	42.5	33.9	32.7	−1.6**	−1.7	−1.4	−1.9*	−0.6	−3.9	−3.6	−3.1	−5.3	−1.9
SSI	7.1	6.9	6.7	7.2	7.5	0.0	0.1	−0.1	0.1	0.0	0.0	1.6	−1.6	1.5	0.0
Not beneficiary	24.6	20.0	20.6	25.6	33.0	−0.7	−1.1	0.2	−0.6	−1.7	−2.9	−5.0	1.0	−2.4	−4.9
Own lifetime earnings quintile															
Bottom	24.4	27.9	23.8	23.8	22.0	−1.3***	−1.2	−1.6*	−1.5*	−0.7	−4.9	−4.0	−6.3	−5.9	−3.3
Second	34.4	39.4	34.4	31.0	32.6	−1.8***	−2.4**	−1.7*	−1.4*	−1.7*	−5.0	−5.8	−4.7	−4.2	−4.9
Third	45.7	51.7	48.1	41.5	41.2	−2.1***	−2.3*	−2.0*	−1.7**	−2.0**	−4.4	−4.3	−4.0	−3.9	−4.6
Fourth	63.6	68.3	70.4	56.9	57.7	−3.0***	−4.4***	−2.2	−2.6**	−2.3*	−4.4	−6.1	−3.1	−4.4	−3.9
Top	104.5	118.2	112.2	93.6	91.6	−4.2***	−5.2**	−4.5**	−3.4**	−3.9**	−3.9	−4.2	−3.9	−3.5	−4.1
Shared lifetime earnings quintile															
Bottom	16.9	19.8	16.6	15.3	15.8	−0.6**	−0.2	−0.8*	−0.6	−0.5	−3.6	−1.1	−4.8	−4.0	−3.2
Second	31.3	35.3	31.4	28.5	29.8	−1.8***	−2.5***	−2.0***	−1.3**	−1.3	−5.4	−6.7	−6.0	−4.3	−4.1
Third	45.7	49.2	48.0	42.4	42.9	−1.6***	−1.6	−1.5	−1.5*	−1.9*	−3.3	−3.1	−3.0	−3.4	−4.2
Fourth	64.3	68.9	69.3	60.1	57.8	−3.7***	−6.0***	−3.1**	−2.6**	−3.0**	−5.4	−8.0	−4.2	−4.2	−4.9
Top	114.5	132.4	123.7	100.5	98.8	−4.5***	−5.2**	−4.5**	−4.4***	−4.1**	−3.8	−3.8	−3.5	−4.2	−4.0

Household income quintile															
Bottom	10.4	11.5	10.4	10.0	9.5	−0.4***	−0.4***	−0.4***	−0.3***	−0.1	−3.9	−3.5	−3.9	−3.1	−1.1
Second	22.5	24.7	23.1	21.3	20.5	−1.1***	−1.5***	−1.3***	−0.8***	−0.6***	−4.5	−5.6	−5.2	−3.8	−3.0
Third	36.8	39.8	38.1	34.7	33.9	−1.8***	−2.2***	−2.1***	−1.5***	−1.3***	−4.7	−5.3	−5.2	−4.1	−3.6
Fourth	61.2	67.2	64.3	56.6	55.5	−2.9***	−3.6***	−3.1***	−2.3***	−2.6***	−4.5	−5.1	−4.5	−3.9	−4.5
Top	141.9	162.2	152.9	124.2	125.7	−6.2***	−7.9***	−5.3***	−5.5***	−6.1***	−4.2	−4.7	−3.3	−4.2	−4.6

Notes: *** Significant at 1% level; ** at 5% level; * at 10% level. Sample excludes individuals with incomes in the top 1 percent of the income distribution. Own lifetime earnings is the average of wage-indexed earnings between ages 22 and 62. Shared lifetime earnings is the average of wage-indexed shared earnings between ages 22 and 62, where shared earnings are half the total earnings of the couple in the years when married and individual earnings in years when not married. Quintiles are calculated within age groups.

Source: Authors' computations from DYNASIM3 projections.

TABLE 3.7 Projected survival rates at age 70 by sex, education, and employment status between 2008 and 2013

Age in 2008	Female			Male		
	Employed each year (%)	Not employed at least one year (%)	Absolute difference	Employed each year (%)	Not employed at least one year (%)	Absolute difference
25–34 years						
All	86.7	83.2	−3.5***	82.0	77.5	−4.5***
Did not complete high school	77.2	81.2	4.0	70.2	72.0	1.8
High school graduate/some college	83.6	81.7	−1.9	80.1	75.8	−4.3***
College graduate	90.2	87.7	−2.5**	86.6	86.1	−0.5
35–44 years						
All	86.1	82.8	−3.3***	83.2	75.8	−7.4***
Did not complete high school	77.9	80.2	2.3	70.2	69.8	−0.4
High school graduate/some college	83.6	82.3	−1.3	81.3	75.6	−5.7***
College graduate	89.8	86.4	−3.4***	86.6	82.0	−4.6***

45–54 years						
All	88.2	81.9	−6.3***	85.5	73.6	−11.9***
Did not complete high school	78.4	80.4	2.0	79.1	69.1	−10.0***
High school graduate/ some college	86.6	81.6	−5.0***	83.4	73.5	−9.9***
College graduate	91.5	85.4	−6.1***	89.1	78.9	−10.2***
55–64 years						
All	93.8	87.1	−6.7***	91.0	80.3	−10.7***
Did not complete high school	89.6	85.8	−3.8	83.6	77.4	−6.2*
High school graduate/ some college	93.1	87.1	−6.0***	90.0	79.3	−10.7***
College graduate	95.3	88.4	−6.9***	93.2	83.8	−9.4***

Notes: *** Significant at 1% level; ** at 5% level; * at 10% level. Table includes all individuals aged 25–64 living in the United States in 2008. The ‘employed each year’ category includes individuals with positive earnings in all years between 2008 and 2013. The other category includes all individuals with no earnings in at least one year between 2008 and 2013. The survival rate is the share of the 2008 population that survives to age 70.

Source: Authors’ computations from DYNASIM3 projections.

Although, the recession will cut future incomes for high-socioeconomic-status groups, they will remain much better off than others.

Differential survival mutes the observed variation in retirement incomes at age 70. Table 3.7 shows survival rates by employment status. Among men aged 45–54 in 2008, 85.5 percent of those who worked every year between 2008 and 2013 will survive to age 70, compared with only 73.6 percent of those with at least one year of zero earnings during that period—about a 12 percentage point difference. These results suggest that the impact of the recession would be even worse had these individuals survived to age 70. Additionally, we would likely observe more significant effects for the recession if we compared retirement outcomes at younger ages.

Conclusion

Our projections indicate that the Great Recession, by many measures the most severe economic downturn since the Great Depression, will modestly reduce future retirement incomes for today's workers. Workers unemployed for many months accumulate fewer Social Security and employer-sponsored pension credits, and are less able to contribute to retirement accounts or save in other ways. Most workers, however, remained employed during the recession, and the reduction in work years for those who lost their jobs was generally inconsequential when averaged over decades-long careers. More important for future retirement incomes is the wage stagnation that the recession triggered, since people can never make up lost wages. Lower wage growth affects nearly all workers, not just the relatively few who lost their jobs. Our results show that average age-70 incomes for those aged 25–64 when the recession began will fall 4.3 percent from the levels that would have prevailed had the recession not occurred, almost entirely because of the long-term reduction in wages.

Unemployment rates rose sharply during the recession for workers with limited education, yet the recession will not disproportionately reduce their retirement incomes. Because lower-socioeconomic-status groups are less likely to have pensions or to accumulate significant retirement savings even in good times, they had less to lose. The most disadvantaged are also less likely to survive into old age. Low-income and less-educated workers have certainly suffered during the recession, with unemployment leaving many impoverished. And even modest retirement income losses could significantly reduce their economic well-being in later life, because their resources are so limited even in the absence of the recession. Nonetheless, retirement incomes will fall most sharply for well-educated, high-income workers, the same groups that have borne the brunt of the stock market crash associated with the financial crisis (Butrica et al., 2009, 2010).

Projecting incomes over the next forty years involves much uncertainty, and future developments could lead to outcomes very different from our forecasts. Retirement projections are more certain for those who were in their late 50s when the recession began. The recession will undoubtedly reduce their Social Security income because the index factor in the benefit formula is lower today than it would have been had the recession not occurred. Moreover, those older workers who lost their jobs in the recession have limited employment prospects and little chance of extending their working lives. Unlike workers who were young when the recession hit, and have years to adjust before retiring, there is little older workers who can do to offset their recession-induced losses.

Appendix

This appendix provides additional information about how the DYNASIM3 model projects employment, earnings, pensions, retirement accounts, other assets, and income.

Employment and earnings. DYNASIM3 projects the likelihood that an individual works each year as a function of age, sex, race and ethnicity, education, health and disability status, geographic region, marital status, student status, number of young children, spouse characteristics (employment, age, disability, and education), immigrant status, Social Security benefit status, cohort, and the state-specific unemployment rate. The likelihood also includes an estimated individual-specific error term that captures nonvarying individual preferences that are independent of observed characteristics. The model classifies an individual as employed if his or her expected probability of working exceeds a given random number. The selection criteria are adjusted so that our employment projections for men and women within particular age groups hit the Social Security Trustees' targets.[5]

DYNASIM3 uses a similar set of explanatory variables to assign hourly wages and annual hours of employment to those projected to work. Annual earnings are the product of the hourly wage and annual hours worked. DYNASIM3 adjusts the underlying predicted annual wage for real wage growth based on the Trustees' economic assumptions. It also aligns the annual earnings of workers to hit the Trustees' annual earnings targets.

Pensions. DYNASIM3 projects pensions from employer-sponsored DB plans, cash balance (CB) plans, and retirement accounts. Information about pension coverage on current and past jobs, pension contribution rates, and account balances come from SIPP self-reported information. Projected DB pension information reflects plan structures through

December 2008, including DB pension plan freezes and conversions to CB plans. Various data sources and models described below are used to project job changes, pension coverage, pension participation, and pension contributions into the future.

DYNASIM3 projects DB pensions using the Pension Benefit Guaranty Corporation's (PBGC) Pension Insurance Modeling System (PIMS) DB plan formulas, which are randomly assigned to DB participants based on broad industry, union status, and firm size categories, and are an indicator of whether the firm offers dual (DB and DC) coverage. The model uses actual benefit formulas to calculate benefits for federal government workers and military personnel, and uses tables of replacement rates from BLS to calculate replacement rates for state and local government workers. The model also varies the probability of selecting a joint and survivor annuity by gender, education, family health status, wealth, and expected pension income. It also varies DB cost-of-living adjustments by employment sector (i.e. private, federal, state, and local). The model projects conversions of pension plan type (from DB to CB or DB to DC) using actual plan change information for plans included in the PIMS data.

Most DB plan formulas assign DB pension income as a function of plan earnings and job tenure. Most private pensions require five years of employment before workers are vested in the DB plan. Any shortening of job tenure directly reduces expected DB pension income.

Retirement accounts. DYNASIM3 starts with the self-reported SIPP retirement account balance. Because of documented deficiencies in the SIPP asset data (Czajka et al., 2003; Smith et al., 2005), asset balances in retirement accounts (as well as financial assets outside of retirement accounts) in the starting SIPP sample are adjusted to align with asset distributions from the 2007 Survey of Consumer Finances (SCF). Individuals are also assigned an individual-specific risk tolerance based on SCF data. An individual's share of retirement account assets invested in equities varies by age and risk tolerance, with high-risk and younger individuals investing more in equities than low-risk and older individuals.

The model uses historical price changes and returns for stocks, long-term corporate bonds, and long-term government bonds through 2008 to grow portfolios. Investment experience varies for each individual because the model sets rates of return stochastically, using historical means and standard deviations. We account for the 2008 stock market crash, which reduced equity values by 37 percent, by assuming that the market recovers to half of its projected precrash value by 2017 (Butrica et al., 2010). Specifically, the model assumes a 10.7 percent average real rate of return on stocks from 2009 to 2017 before resuming its historic average real return of 6.5 percent. DYNASIM3 assumes mean real rates of return of 3.5 percent for corporate bonds, 3 percent for government bonds, and standard deviations of 17.28 percent for stocks and 2.14 percent for bonds.[6] The 6.5 percent real return on stocks reflects a capital appreciation of about 3.5 percent and a dividend yield of around 3 percent, in line with the long-term performance of the S&P 500. The model subtracts 1 percentage point from annual stock and bond returns to reflect administrative costs.

The model allows some workers to cash out retirement account balances with job changes or job losses. Younger workers, workers with lower account balances, and workers who lose their jobs are more likely to cash out retirement account balances than are older workers, those with higher balances, and those who stay on their jobs or move seamlessly from one job to another. High unemployment contributes to lower lifetime DC pension savings through lost contributions (and returns on lost contributions) when out of work and to hardship withdrawals.

Financial assets. The model uses random-effects models to project financial assets. DYNASIM3 starts with SIPP self-reported financial assets (saving, checking, money market, and certificate of deposit balances, stocks, bonds, equity in businesses, vehicles, and nonhome real estate, less unsecured debt). We adjust the SIPP starting values to align with the household asset distribution from the 2007 SCF. Unlike retirement accounts that are directly invested in stock and bond portfolios, financial assets accumulate and decumulate as a function of family characteristics and earnings and projected wage differentials. The main economic explanatory variable is individual lifetime earnings relative to the cohort average. Individuals with above-average lifetime earnings accumulate assets faster than those with below-average lifetime earnings. A spell of unemployment will lower a worker's average compared with one who remains employed continuously. The longer the unemployment spell, the greater is the differential in lifetime earnings relative to the cohort average and the greater is the impact on projected assets. Assets accumulate at the family level, so husbands and wives equally share family assets. We assume that couples split assets at divorce and survivors inherit the assets of deceased spouses.

The model projects nonpension financial assets over three separate age ranges: up to age 50, from age 51 to retirement, and from retirement to death. Equations projecting assets to age 50 were estimated on the Panel Study of Income Dynamics (PSID) (Toder et al., 2002). Equations projecting assets from age 51 to retirement were estimated on the first seven waves of the Health and Retirement Study (HRS) (Smith et al., 2007). Equations projecting assets from retirement to death were estimated on a synthetic panel of SIPP data (Toder et al., 1999). The latter two data sets included historic earnings from the Social Security Administration's Summary Earnings Record (SER) data.

Other income sources. DYNASIM3 projects income from various other sources to generate a measure of total household income. Social Security income is computed based on the benefit formula, projected lifetime earnings, and an equation projecting benefit take-up. SSI is also computed using benefit formulas that vary by state. The model projects SSI eligibility based on age, disability, family income, and assets. It then projects participation based on family characteristics and benefit size.

The model computes income from retirement accounts and financial assets each year as the real (price indexed), actuarially fair, annuity income a family would receive if it annuitized 80 percent of its total wealth. We use the calculated annuity value to assign only that year's income from retirement accounts and financial assets. The annuity factor is recalculated each year to reflect changes in wealth as individuals age, based on the projections of wealth accumulation and spend-down and changes in life expectancy and marital status as individuals survive to older ages. For married couples, the model assumes a 50 percent survivor annuity.

We measure income from financial wealth and retirement accounts as potential annuities to ensure comparability with DB pension and Social Security benefits, which are also annuities. Without this adjustment, the model would overstate the loss in retirement well-being from the shift from DB pension income to DC assets. A dollar in DB pension wealth produces more income by standard measures than a dollar in DC wealth because measured DB income counts both a return on accumulated assets and some return of principal, while measured income from financial wealth and DC retirement accounts includes only the return on accumulated assets. The income measure we use therefore differs conceptually from asset income as measured by the United States Census Bureau (as well as many analysts), which includes only the return on assets (interest, dividends, and rental income) and excludes the potential consumption of capital that could be realized if people spent down their wealth.

The model also projects income of nonspouse family members. We use this income primarily for determining poverty status, as these family members' incomes and characteristics are included in the standard poverty measure. We include spousal income in our measure of family income but exclude incomes of other family members in this report.

Acknowledgments

The research reported herein was pursuant to a grant from the Social Security Administration (SSA), funded as part of the Retirement Research Consortium (RRC). The findings and conclusions expressed are solely those of the author and do not represent the views of SSA, any agency of the Federal Government, the RRC, the Urban Institute, its board, or its funders.

Endnotes

1. Another difference is that the DYNASIM3 model includes institutionalized adults, overseas military personnel, and residents of US territories, whereas the Bureau of Labor Statistics uses the civilian noninstitutionalized US resident population.
2. The underlying price and wage targets affect various other projections, including the Social Security wage base (the taxable maximum), the indexing of wages for the calculation of Social Security benefits (AIME and PIA), SSI benefit parameters, stock and bond rates of return, and interest rates. Changes in economic conditions also affect retirement and Social Security benefit claiming, as well as marriage, divorce, fertility, and schooling outcomes.
3. Some people in the oldest age group turned 60 before 2008. The recession will not affect their Social Security benefits much.
4. Poverty rates projected in the DYNASIM3 model are lower than the official poverty rates calculated by the Census Bureau because DYNASIM3 includes the annuitized value of 80 percent of household assets in the income measure. The Census income measure includes only the return on capital (dividend, interest, and rental income). See the Appendix for more details.
5. The random error term follows an autoregressive (AR1) process so that random shocks include both a current and lagged effect.
6. The assumed rates of return are those recommended by the Social Security Administration's Office of the Chief Actuary for the President's Commission to Strengthen Social Security (President's Commission to Strengthen Social Security, 2001). The standard deviations are derived from real returns over the 55-year period between 1952 and 2007 for large company stocks and Treasury bills reported in Ibbotson Associates (2008). Inflation assumptions follow the 2010 intermediate assumptions used by the Social Security Trustees (Social Security Board of Trustees, 2010).

References

Butrica, B., K. Smith, and E. Toder (2009). *Retirement Security and the Stock Market Crash: What Are the Possible Outcomes?* Washington, DC: The Urban Institute.

——, —— and —— (2010). "What the 2008 Stock Market Crash Means for Retirement Security", *Journal of Aging & Social Policy*, 22(4): 339–59.

Citro, C. and R. T. Michael (1995). *Measuring Poverty: A New Approach.* Washington, DC: National Academy Press.

Congressional Budget Office (2010). *The Budget and Economic Outlook: Fiscal Years 2011 to 2021.* Washington, DC: Congressional Budget Office.

Czajka, J., J. Jacobson, and S. Cody (2003). *Survey Estimates of Wealth: Comparative Analysis and Review of the Survey of Income and Program Participation.* Washington, DC: Social Security Administration.

DeNavas-Walt, C., B. D. Proctor, and J. C. Smith (2010). *Income, Poverty, and Health Insurance Coverage in the United States: 2009.* Current Population Reports P60-238. Washington, DC: United States Census Bureau.

Eberts, R. W. (2011). "When Will US Employment Recover from the Great Recession?", *International Labor Brief,* 9(2): 4–12.

Elsby, M. W., B. Hobijn, and A. Sahin (2010). "The Labor Market in the Great Recession," NBER Working Paper 15979. Cambridge, MA: National Bureau of Economic Research.

Godofsky, J., C. Van Horn, and C. Zukin (2010). *American Workers Assess an Economic Disaster.* New Brunswick, NJ: John J. Heldrich Center for Workforce Development, Rutgers University.

Hurd, M. and S. Rohwedder (2010). "Effects of the Financial Crisis and Great Recession on American Households", NBER Working Paper 16407. Cambridge, MA: National Bureau of Economic Research.

Ibbotson Associates (2008). *Stocks, Bonds, Bills, and Inflation (SBBI) 2008 Yearbook: Market Results for 1926–2007.* Chicago, IL: Ibbotson Associates.

Johnson, R. W. and C. Mommaerts (2011). "Age Differences in Job Loss, Job Search, and Reemployment", Program on Retirement Policy Discussion Paper No. 22-01. Washington, DC: The Urban Institute. http://www.urban.org/url.cfm?ID 412284.

—— and J. S. Park (2011). "Can Unemployed Older Workers Find Work?" Older Americans' Economic Security No. 25. Washington, DC: The Urban Institute.

McNichol, E., P. Oliff, and N. Johnson (2011). *States Continue to Feel Recession's Impact.* Washington, DC: Center on Budget and Policy Priorities.

Mishel, L. and H. Shierholz (2010). *Recession Hits Workers' Paychecks.* EPI Briefing Paper No. 277. Washington, DC: Economic Policy Institute.

Pew Economic Policy Group (2010). *A Year or More: The High Cost of Long-Term Unemployment.* Philadelphia, PA: Pew Charitable Trusts.

President's Commission to Strengthen Social Security (2001). *Strengthening Social Security and Creating Personal Wealth for all Americans: Report of the President's Commission.* Washington, DC: President's Commission to Strengthen Social Security.

Short, K. S. (2010). "Who Is Poor? A New Look with the Supplemental Poverty Measure", SEHSD Working Paper 2010-15. Washington, DC: US Census Bureau.

Smith, K. E., M. Favreault, and D. Cashin (2005). *Modeling Income in the Near Term 4.* Washington, DC: The Urban Institute.

——, ——, C. Ratcliffe, B. A. Butrica, E. Toder, and J. M. Bakija (2007). *Modeling Income in the Near Term 5.* Washington, DC: The Urban Institute.

Social Security Board of Trustees (2008). *The 2008 Annual Report of the Board of Trustees of the Federal Old-Age and Survivors Insurance and Disability Insurance Trust Funds.* Washington, DC: Board of Trustees.

—— (2010). *The 2010 Annual Report of the Board of Trustees of the Federal Old-Age and Survivors Insurance and Disability Insurance Trust Funds.* Washington, DC: Social Security Board of Trustees.

Toder, E., C. E. Uccello, J. O'Hare, M. Favreault, C. Ratcliffe, K. E. Smith, G. T. Burtless, and B. Bosworth (1999). *Modeling Income in the Near Term—Projections of Retirement Income through 2020 for the 1931–1960 Birth Cohorts.* Washington, DC: The Urban Institute.

——, L. Thompson, M. Favreault, R. Johnson, K. Perese, C. Ratcliffe, K. E. Smith, C. Uccello, T. Waidmann, J. Berk, R. Woldemariam, G. Burtless, C. Sahm, and D. Wolf (2002). *Modeling Income in the Near Term: Revised Projections of Retirement Income through 2020 for the 1931–1960 Birth Cohorts.* Washington, DC: The Urban Institute.

Zedlewski, S. R. and B. A. Butrica (2008). "More Older Americans are Poor than the Official Poverty Measure Suggests." Older Americans' Economic Security No. 15. Washington, DC: Urban Institute.

Chapter 4

Effects of the Economic Crisis on the Older Population: How Expectations, Consumption, Bequests, and Retirement Responded to Market Shocks

Michael Hurd and Susann Rohwedder

The financial crisis that unfolded rapidly in the latter part of 2008 developed into a recession that stands out from other recessions of the post-World War II era in several important ways. The stock market began to decline in October 2007. At first moderate, the pace of the decline increased rapidly, coinciding with the troubles in the financial sector that began in September 2008. By March 2009, the S&P 500 had lost more than 50 percent from its peak 2007 level (Coronado and Dynan, 2012). The swings in the economic environment have been unequalled since the Great Depression, and the crisis has also affected several markets simultaneously (housing, stock, and labor market), consequently providing a number of channels through which individuals and their households might be affected. The economic crisis and the subsequent increase in the unemployment rate operated through several channels, affecting people of different ages in differing ways.

The at-retirement population has been vulnerable to negative shocks in the equity and housing markets because of their asset positions, and somewhat less obviously because of linkages to their children. On the positive side, they have been relatively unaffected by unemployment. Furthermore, because of the importance of Social Security to the bottom half of the income distribution, many less-well-off older households were unaffected directly by the crisis. The older preretirement population has also accumulated equity and, because of the transition from defined benefit (DB) to defined contribution (DC) pensions, their sources of retirement income security are subject to capital market risk. On the other hand, because of relatively high rates of labor force participation, they are vulnerable to unemployment. When they lost jobs, they had little time to recover from those losses. In contrast to the retired population, those of working age at the lower end of the income distribution were particularly vulnerable to unemployment. Another consideration is how housing values behaved. After appreciating for some time, the housing market reached its maximum in May 2006 and then began a long downward slide. While stocks have recovered somewhat since then, the housing market has not.

This chapter studies the effects of the financial crisis on the population aged 55+, drawing on longitudinal data from the Health and Retirement Study (HRS), a household dataset containing observations from the time before the economic crisis began until it was well underway, with the latest available data point in 2009. The HRS data, collected every two years since 1992, span this period. Especially when combined with supplemental data collections, the HRS provides very rich information for the study of the effects of the financial crisis on older households. Specifically, in 2001, the HRS began collecting longitudinal data on household spending: this effort is repeated every two years. In 2009, much of the HRS Internet study content was dedicated to eliciting information relevant to measuring the effects of the financial crisis. In what follows, we analyze changes in consumption associated with the crisis and examine housing, expectations, and retirement among older Americans.[1]

Data sources

The analysis focuses on the HRS from the 2006 and 2008 core surveys, as well as from two supplemental studies: the Consumption and Activities Mail Survey (CAMS) and the HRS Internet study. The HRS is a biennial panel first conducted in 1992, with the cohorts born between 1931 and 1941 as the target population (Juster and Suzman, 1995). Additional cohorts were added in 1993 and 1998, so that in 2000 the HRS represented the population from the cohorts of 1947 and earlier. In 2004, new cohorts were again added, making the HRS representative of the population aged 51+. In September 2001, CAMS Wave 1 was mailed to 5,000 households selected at random from households that had participated in HRS 2000. In couples' households, it was sent to one of the two spouses at random. The fact that the CAMS sample was drawn directly from the HRS 2000 sample offered an important advantage: it allowed the CAMS data to be linked to the vast amount of information collected in prior waves of the HRS on those participating in the core longitudinal survey. In 2003, 2005, 2007, and 2009, CAMS Waves 2–5 were sent to these same 5,000 households.[2] To facilitate panel analysis, the structure of the questionnaire was almost the same in each of these waves (Hurd and Rohwedder, 2006).

CAMS asked respondents about their spending in each of the thirty-two categories which cover almost all spending according to the Consumer Expenditure Survey (CEX). Rates of item nonresponse were small. Some values could be imputed to zero with considerable confidence, due to the information in the linked HRS core data.[3] The 2009 HRS Internet survey is the third wave in a series of Internet surveys of a subset of HRS respondents. Eligibility to participate in the 2009 wave was determined by whether, in the 2008 core HRS survey, a respondent reported regularly using the Internet, and about 7,000 respondents qualified.[4] The resulting sample tends to overrepresent those with higher education, but this bias is less for those aged 65 or younger in the HRS; in this age group, Internet usage is more common throughout the distribution of both education and wealth.[5] The field period was March 2009–August 2009. For the purposes of this chapter, we will refer to the data collection as having taken place in May 2009.

The HRS Internet survey has a module on the economic effects of the crisis on individual households, as well as modules on health and life satisfaction. To measure responses about the crisis's economic effects, broadly our approach is to find within-person changes in important outcomes that have resulted from the crisis.

Effects of the crisis on the economic circumstances of HRS households

A broad gauge of the scale of the impact of the economic crisis is the simple response to a question about whether a respondent has been affected. About 28 percent of respondents reported that they had been affected a lot, about 46 percent said they had been affected a little, and just 26 percent reported not having been affected.

Effects on consumption

Economists deem consumption a better measure of economic well-being than income or wealth. To judge whether households reduced consumption in response to the crisis, the HRS Internet survey asked respondents how their spending compared with a year earlier. In May 2008, prices in the housing market had begun to decline, but the stock market was still at a relatively high level (the large declines in stocks began later in the year). Unemployment was at 5.4 percent, although it had been increasing. Accordingly, from the typical household's point of view, the economic crisis was still in the future.

Table 4.1 shows the percentages of respondents indicating in May 2009 that their spending had increased, decreased, or remained the same, compared with a year earlier. In normal times, we would expect that for

TABLE 4.1 Household spending 2011 compared to a year ago (%)

Age (years)	Increased	About the same	Decreased
55–64	14.7	52.7	32.6
65–74	19.2	56.7	24.1
75+	23.9	59.3	16.8
Total	17.1	54.5	28.5

Source: Authors' calculations from weighted HRS data.

TABLE 4.2 Important reasons for spending decline by age: percent stating very or somewhat important

Age (years)	Needed to reduce debt	Lower income	Worse employment	Stocks down	Lower house value	Worried about economic future
55–64	74.5	76.4	53.7	56.3	53.4	86.4
65–74	63.6	71.8	36.9	65.7	48.9	82.1
75+	46.5	59	14.2	64.6	42.2	80
Total	69.9	74.1	47.2	59.2	51.6	84.9

Source: Authors' calculations from weighted HRS data.

the younger age groups, spending would increase over time, and this is what we observe in cross-section spending data. But among respondents in their 50s, more than 30 percent said their spending had decreased, whereas only about 15 percent said it had increased. For those aged 65+, however, the pattern reverses, which is the first indicator that the older population was relatively better protected from the effects of the crisis.

The Internet survey contained follow-up questions to assess more directly the importance of various reasons for any changes in spending for respondents reporting having lowered their spending. Table 4.2 shows the percent that indicated that a specific reason for reducing spending was very important or somewhat important. Averaged over all ages, 85 percent of respondents indicated that being worried about the economic future was an important factor. Although the differences by age are not large, in the oldest age group this percentage was somewhat lower. There is disagreement in the literature about whether households will change their spending in response to movements in asset prices such as stocks or housing. In the HRS, about half of respondents who had decreased spending attributed their actions to declines in asset prices (stocks and housing). With regard to the other reasons, there is a clear age gradient: the older population was less likely to have reduced spending because of the need to reduce debt, having a lower income, or worse employment prospects.

TABLE 4.3 Important reasons for spending increase by age: percent stating very or somewhat important

Age (years)	Wealth increased	Better employment	Higher mortgage payment	Increased spending needs	More optimistic
55–64	42.8	32.2	31.4	92.3	42.7
65–74	36.9	15.4	27.8	96.2	63.9
75+	20.8	7	11.6	96	51.6
Total	37.4	23	27.2	94.2	51.1

Source: Authors' calculations from weighted HRS data.

The Internet survey also asked those respondents who said their spending had increased to indicate the importance of various reasons. Broadly speaking, a household's spending might increase due to an increase in the household's economic resources (a positive reason) or due to an increase in the household's needs (possibly a negative reason), such as higher mortgage payments, for example. Table 4.3 shows the distribution of responses among those who said spending had increased. Almost all respondents cited increased spending needs. About half of the respondents were optimistic about their economic future, in sharp contrast to those who had reduced spending (Table 4.2). It is notable, however, that among those aged 55–64, fewer had increased spending because of optimism. Because just 15 percent of this group had increased their spending (Table 4.1), the fraction of the total population aged 55–64 that spent more because of optimism is only about 6 percent.

About one-third of the 55–64-year-olds cited better employment as a reason for increasing spending, compared with a negligible percentage in the 75+ age group which is mostly retired. About 30 percent of those aged 55–64 attributed more spending to higher mortgage payments. This is in line with rising housing debt (which we will examine directly below), and possibly with balloon mortgages that were a frequent financing instrument during the housing-market bubble.

These changes in consumption observed in the Internet survey are self-assessed. While respondents may have good qualitative knowledge of the changes they have made, they are considerably less likely to have a good quantitative assessment. Accordingly, to quantify the magnitude of spending declines, we use CAMS to compare two-year panel transitions in spending in 'normal' times, with two-year panel transitions during the economic crisis. We define 'normal' times to be 2001–7, and the time of the economic crisis to be 2007–9. We average three panel transitions in spending (2001–3, 2003–5, and 2005–7) so as to smooth out noise in the data and average out other macro shocks. We disaggregate by age band because the older population may have been better protected, as suggested by the self-assessed differences in changes in spending shown in Table 4.1.

Table 4.4 shows changes in mean and median spending, both overall and for nondurables, adjusted for price changes.[6] Among those aged 50–64, mean total spending declined by about 2.1 percent every two years, averaged over the period 2001–7. This reduction is likely due to a number of reasons, such as changes in household composition or parental support for children's education.[7] The decline in mean nondurable spending among this age group was about 1 percent per two-year period. Among those aged 65+, reductions were much greater, amounting to 6.3 percent in mean total spending and 4.9 percent in mean nondurable spending. These reductions are likely life cycle effects. During the economic crisis, consumption fell at a much greater rate: almost 10 percent for the younger age group and 9 percent for the older one. The levels and changes in the medians are smaller, but the patterns are the same.

We summarize and compare the results for the two age groups in Table 4.5. Among those aged 50–64, mean spending declined between 2007 and 2009 by 7.6 percentage points more than between 2001 and

TABLE 4.4 Two-year change in real consumption: 2001–7 and 2007–9

	Percent change in means		Percent change in medians	
	2001–7	2007–9	2001–7	2007–9
Age 50–64				
Total consumption	−2.1	−9.9	−2.3	−7.5
Nondurable consumption	−1	−8.6	−0.6	−7.3
Age 65+				
Total consumption	−6.3	−9.1	−3.3	−5.9
Nondurable consumption	−4.9	−8.3	−3	−6.4

Source: Authors' calculations from weighted HRS data.

TABLE 4.5 Summary of two-year change in nondurable spending (%)

	Means		Medians	
	50–64	65+	50–64	65+
2001–7	−1	−4.9	−0.6	−3
2007–9	−8.6	−8.3	−7.3	−6.4
2007–9 change minus average of two-year changes from 2001 to 2007	−7.6	−3.4	−6.7	−3.4

Source: Authors' calculations from weighted HRS data.

2007. Among those aged 65+, spending declined by 3.4 percentage points more in the later period than the earlier. Our interpretation is that, indeed, spending declined in response to the economic crisis, and that the comparisons of actual measured spending are consistent with the self-assessments in Table 4.1. Furthermore, spending by the older population declined less during the crisis than spending by the younger population, in keeping with our expectations that the older population was better protected against the economic crisis and the self-reports of Table 4.1.

Effects on housing

Whether homeowners were affected by the large drops in home values, and how seriously they were affected, depends on where they live and when they live. According to the Case–Shiller twenty-city average,[8] prices peaked in May 2006 at about 50 percent above the level at which they had been at the beginning of 2003, but this average conceals substantial intercity variation. In Denver, there was a moderate increase in housing prices, followed by a small decline. In Los Angeles and Phoenix, prices peaked at more than 100 percent above their 2003 value and declined thereafter by more than half. Thus, a family living in Denver would be relatively unaffected by price changes, while a family living in Los Angeles or Phoenix might be affected depending on its purchase date, method of financing, and the family's overall economic situation. For example, a family that bought a house in 2003 and took on a mortgage that was reasonable in relation to family income could have sound finances today, even though the value of the home dropped below its 2006 peak. However, if a family bought at the top of the market with a small percentage downpayment and a balloon loan, that family would now find itself with substantial negative home equity and increased mortgage costs that it might not be able to afford.

The HRS asks respondents about the value of their houses, both in the core survey and the Internet study. These data have the advantages of being reports on the same house over time and being nationally representative. Other commonly used data sources are based on recent actual property sales (possibly including refinanced properties) or on the Case–Shiller index, confined to twenty large cities.

Over several waves of the HRS, the longitudinal rate of homeownership has remained constant at almost 90 percent. Table 4.6 shows mean and median house values, and mean and median housing debt, as reported by HRS respondents in 2006, 2008, and 2009, converted to 2010 dollars. Mean house values declined between 2006 and 2008 by about 7 percent real per year, and the median declined by about 4 percent real over the same time period.[9] Between 2008 and the HRS Internet survey, on average about nine

TABLE 4.6 Home values and housing debt balances ($000, 2010)

Year	Home value		Housing debt	
	Mean	Median	Mean	Median
2006	358.6	248.8	81.7	32.4
2008	309.9	227.9	74.8	30.4
2009	282.5	203.3	80.4	30.5

Notes: Only households who report owning a home in all three years are included and for whom there is no missing information on whether they have a mortgage and on whether they have other home loans. Housing debt includes the value of any mortgages and other home loans on the primary residence. Input values allowed on amount. Constant weights used for all statistics (2008 household weights) to ensure that variation in statistics across waves is not due to cross-wave variation in weights.

Source: Authors' calculations from weighted HRS data; $N = 2{,}630$.

months later, the decline was about 9 percent real, and the decline in the median was about 11 percent real. These are, of course, very substantial reductions in the most important asset of most Americans. The mean value of housing debt (mortgage balances plus other outstanding home loans) expressed in 2010 dollars dropped by about 4 percent per year between 2006 and 2008, and the median dropped by about 3 percent per year over the same period. Note that in nominal dollars the mean was almost constant between 2006 and 2008, and the median did not change, implying that at the population level there was almost no net pay-off of mortgage balances over that period. However, in just the short period between the 2008 HRS core interview and the HRS Internet interview, the mean value of housing debt increased by about $6,000 or 7.5 percent, while the median remained unchanged. The increase in the mean could be due to equity extraction, which may have made households more vulnerable to other economic shocks, such as unemployment. When combined with the reduction in house prices, the debt-to-value ratio increased between 2008 and the Internet survey.

Table 4.6 is calculated over all households that reported owning a home in all three surveys.[10] It also includes some who did not fully report actual values for house prices and for their mortgages or other home loans; most of the nonreporters reported a bracket. Thus, Table 4.7 excludes anyone with an imputed value because we want to report the fraction of households with negative housing equity: the imputation of a value even within a bracket could falsely classify some as having more mortgage than house value. A comparison of Table 4.7 with Table 4.6 shows that excluding respondents with incomplete reports does not materially affect the conclusions we make about the trends in home value and housing debt on average.[11] The table shows that in 2006 and 2008, about 1.1–1.4 percent

TABLE 4.7 Home values, housing debt, and negative home equity ($000, 2010)

Year	Home value ($)		Housing debt ($)		Negative home equity (%)	
	Mean	Median	Mean	Median	All homeowners	Only households with housing debt[a]
2006	361.9	270.4	86.2	40	1.1	1.8
2008	320.1	243.1	77.7	32.4	1.4	2.4
2009	292.2	223.6	84.1	30.5	3.9	6.7

[a] Number of households with housing debt varies across waves: 1,187 in 2006; 1,128 in 2008; 1,111 in 2009.

Notes: Same sample as in Table 4.6, but imposing the additional restriction that none of the amounts are imputed. $N = 2{,}106$. Constant weights used for all statistics (2008 household weights) to ensure that variation in statistics across waves is not due to cross-wave variation in weights.

Source: Authors' calculations from weighted HRS data.

of homeowners owed more than their house was worth.[12] Among homeowners with a mortgage, 1.8–2.4 percent had negative equity. But by 2009, 3.9 percent of all homeowners had negative equity and 6.7 percent of those with a mortgage had negative equity.

House price expectations

As reported in Table 4.2, an important reason for a reduction in spending was worries about the economic future. We assess one component of expectations about the economic future—house price expectations. Respondents were asked about expectations that their own home would appreciate in price, in the form of a subjective probability as follows:

> On a scale from 0 percent to 100 percent where 0 means that you think there is no chance and 100 means that you think the event is absolutely sure to happen, what do you think are the chances that by next year at this time your home will be worth more than it is today?

In follow-up questions, respondents were asked about additional price targets, such as an increase in value of 10 or 20 percent or a decrease in value of 10 or 20 percent. Respondents were also asked the same question with a time horizon of five years.

Table 4.8 shows the average of those subjective probabilities. The average subjective probability that respondents expected their houses to be worth more in a year than they were at the interview date was just 32 percent. This indicates that individuals were very pessimistic about the housing market, and these expectations were very much different from historical trends. For

TABLE 4.8 House price expectations, one year and five years ahead

	1 year from now	5 years from now
Any increase	32.3	53.5
Increase by 10% or more	21.3	47
Increase by 20% or more	10.6	28
Decrease by 10% or more	18.5	13.7
Decrease by 20% or more	11	9.2
N	1,820	1,723

Source: Authors' calculations from weighted HRS data.

instance, housing price data show that in 88 percent of one-year intervals between 1991 and 2009, housing prices increased.[13] Individuals are somewhat more optimistic over the five-year horizon. There, the average subjective probability is about 54 percent. But the discrepancy with the historical record is even greater, as in every five-year interval between 1991 and 2009, US actual housing prices increased.[14] Most likely, such pessimistic expectations are a partial explanation for the decline in spending reported in Tables 4.1 and 4.4.

Stock market expectations

Using the same format as for house price expectations, respondents were asked about the chances the stock market would be higher in a year. This question was asked in both HRS 2008 and in the HRS Internet survey, so we can make a direct comparison of the same people over time. Figure 4.1 shows the cumulative distribution of reported subjective probabilities of a gain. The distribution for 2009 is shifted to the left of the 2008 distribution, showing a reduction in the average expectation of a gain. Indeed, the average subjective probability declined from 52 percent probability in 2008 to 41 percent probability in the HRS Internet survey. The decline was particularly striking at the lower part of the distribution: at the 25th percentile, the subjective probability was 40 percent in 2008, but it was just 20 percent in 2009. As with housing prices, such pessimistic expectations may explain some of the spending decline.

Subjective bequest probabilities

Using the same format, the HRS asked respondents about the probability they would leave a bequest greater than $10,000. If this reported probability was positive, the question was repeated with a target of $100,000 and

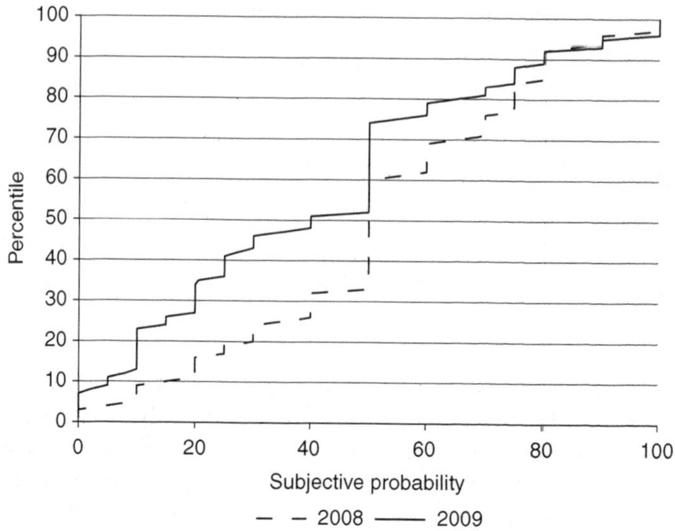

Figure 4.1 Cumulative distribution of the reported subjective probability of a stock market gain one year ahead

Source: Authors' calculations.

then with a target of $500,000. In cross-section, these subjective bequest probabilities varied positively with wealth, which increases our confidence that they are predictive of actual bequests. We expect some of the losses of assets between 2008 and 2009 would result in lower bequests, as well as lower consumption. Table 4.9 shows the implied distribution of probability mass in the population in each of the wealth intervals. Averaging over all responses, the probability of a bequest less than $10,000 was 16.2 percent and the probability of a bequest between $10,000 and $100,000 was 19.8 percent. It is clear that between 2008 and 2009, the probability mass shifted toward the lower wealth bands, reflecting wealth losses.

We calculate expected bequests by multiplying the expected bequest within a wealth band by the probability of a bequest in that interval and then summing over all intervals. The expected bequest within an interval is calculated from the observed distribution of wealth in that interval in the 2008 HRS. The average wealth in the interval 0 to $10,000 was $1,831, and the expected contribution to bequests from that interval was $296. Summing over all intervals, we find that expected bequests declined from $542,364 in 2008 to $441,571 in the HRS Internet survey. This reduction is entirely dominated by the top interval, which is a result of the highly skewed distribution of wealth.

TABLE 4.9 Bequest probabilities and expected bequests ($ 2010), weighted

Wealth band	Average bequest probability (%)		Average wealth ($)	Expected bequests ($)	
	2008	2009	In 2008	Using 2008 probabilities	Using 2009 probabilities
0 to <$10k	16.2	23.9	1,831	296	438
$10k to <$100k	19.8	20.2	52,792	10,448	10,684
$100k to <$500k	35.2	33.4	275,134	96,921	92,005
$500k or more	28.8	22.4	1,508,899	434,699	338,445
All	100	100	715,417	542,364	441,571

Note: N = 3,061.

Source: Authors' calculations from weighted HRS data.

Effects on retirement

The interval between the HRS 2008 interview and the 2009 Internet interview was too short to observe many actual retirements. But, over many waves, the HRS has asked workers about retirement expectations (in the form of the subjective probability of working past ages 62 and 65). We call these subjective probabilities *P*62 and *P*65. Earlier work has shown that they are predictive of actual retirement (Hurd and Rohwedder, 2009), and that they have an advantage over data on actual retirement because changes in the subjective probabilities control for individual fixed effects, such as unmeasured permanent taste differences. Such fixed effects are difficult to control for when using data on actual retirement. We expect that the financial crisis would have had two opposing effects on retirement. The declines in stock and possibly housing values should have delayed retirement because of the unexpected loss of wealth. Yet the worsening of the labor market and increased risk of unemployment should have led to earlier expected retirement, because the older population often has more difficulty in finding a job. The net effect is an empirical matter.

Table 4.10 shows averages of *P*62 for the population of workers in HRS 2008 who were respondents in the Internet interview.[15] The average increased from 58.2 to 61.7 percent, a large increase over a short time period (a little more than a year for some respondents and less than six months for others). To put that change in perspective, the labor force participation rate of the older population has risen during the 1990s, and particularly in the 2000s. In 2003, the rate among those aged 60–64 was 51 percent, and was 54.1 percent in 2008.[16] The increase over five years

TABLE 4.10 Average subjective probability (%) of working past age 62 among those working in 2008: ages 51–61

	All	Work status in 2009	
		Working	Not working
HRS 2008	58.2	60.9	44.7
HRS 2009 Internet	61.7	65.9	40.3
N	1,062	917	145

Notes: Average for 'all' is not equal to the weighted average of 'working' and 'not working' when the weights are the sample sizes. The average for 'all' uses the HRS person weight adjusted for the Internet interview.

Source: Authors' calculations from weighted HRS data.

was 3.1 percentage points, about the same as the increase in *P*62 over six to twelve months. If future actual labor force participation is well predicted by *P*62, these data suggest an acceleration of the trend toward deferred retirement.

We note, however, that the stock market reached its low in March 2009—just a month before the HRS Internet survey was initially fielded. Since then, it has recouped some of its earlier losses, so possibly some of the negative effect of the stock market decline on wealth has dissipated. Also, the unemployment rate today is slightly higher than during the Internet survey. But most importantly, any expectations among respondents at the time of the survey that the unemployment rate would recover quickly were not realized. Instead, the mood about the labor market is likely worse today than it was in May 2009.

The table shows *P*62 both in HRS 2008 and 2009 according to work status in the 2009 Internet survey. There are 145 individuals who were working in 2008 and so were asked about *P*62, but who were not working at the time of the Internet survey. When they were working in 2008, their average *P*62 was just 44.7 percent. That low value compared with *P*62 among those who were still working in 2009 shows the power of *P*62 to predict future labor force participation. But a striking comparison is between the changes in *P*62 across the two groups. Among those who continued to work, *P*62 increased by 5 percentage points; among those who stopped working, *P*62 declined by 4.4 percentage points. This difference in the change may well reflect the differing effects of the stock and housing market losses and of the worsening of the labor market.

Table 4.11 offers similar statistics with respect to working past age 65. Qualitatively, we find the same patterns as for *P*62: an overall increase in *P*65 driven by increases among those working in 2008 and 2009, which offsets declines among those not working in 2009. Yet the magnitude of the increase was remarkably larger for *P*65, a little over double the increase

TABLE 4.11 Average subjective probability (%) of working past age 65 among those working in 2008: ages 51–61

	All	Work status in 2009	
		Working	Not working
HRS 2008	38.6	39.6	33.4
HRS 2009 Internet	46.4	49.5	30.8
N	1,056	911	145

Notes: Average for 'all' is not equal to the weighted average of 'working' and 'not working' when the weights are the sample sizes. The average for 'all' uses the HRS person weight adjusted for the Internet interview.

Source: Authors' calculations from weighted HRS data.

observed in *P*62 (for an increase of 7.8 percentage points, from 38.6 to 46.4). Putting it in historical perspective, according to CPS statistics (see note 15), the labor force participation rate among those aged 65–69 was 23 percent in 1999. By 2008, it had risen to 30.7 percent—a change of 7.7 percent. Thus, the increase in the predicted labor force participation rate in just nine months of the economic crisis was about the same magnitude as the actual increase over nine years. Even if respondents have revised their expectations about working past age 65 since May 2009 when the HRS Internet interview was fielded—possibly due to increases in the stock market and worsening of the labor market since then—it is unlikely that *P*65 will have returned to its 2008 levels. That would suggest that the economic crisis will accelerate the trend of the past two decades of increased labor force participation among the older population. The stratification by work status in 2009 reveals another difference with *P*62: the levels of *P*65 in 2008 were much more comparable (just a 6 percentage-point difference for *P*65, compared to a 16 percentage-point difference in P62).

Conclusion

The 2007–9 recession imposed substantial losses in stocks and housing on the older US population, and these losses particularly affected the retirement security of those at or nearing retirement. While stock values have recovered somewhat since March 2009, house prices have not. For the majority of older households, housing is the most important asset. In May 2009, HRS respondents were pessimistic that house and stock prices would recover any time soon (in next year). Both actual losses and this pessimism led many households to reduce spending, with a stronger effect on households aged 50–64. Those aged 65+ were less affected, due to having more home equity and Social Security. With wealth positions substantially reduced, it may be that households will pass on less wealth to the next generation. According to respondents' subjective beliefs, this will be the case, and the reductions may be sizeable (about 20 percent on average). The median older household will not see much change because the bequest effect is concentrated among households with high wealth. The economic downturn also appears to have accelerated the increase in deferred retirement seen over the past twenty years. This accelerated trend will relieve some of the financial pressures facing Social Security and Medicare programs, since both programs will benefit from additional tax revenues when people work longer.

In sum, the economic crisis has caused households in and near retirement to respond in several ways: they reduced spending, saved more, and believed they will work longer. They also will pass on less to their children. Future work will assess whether these intentions come true.

Acknowledgments

The authors are grateful for funding from the US Social Security Administration (SSA) via the Michigan Retirement Research Center (UM10-06). The opinions and conclusions expressed are solely those of the author(s) and do not represent the opinions or policy of SSA or any agency of the Federal Government.

Endnotes

1. Related studies in this volume include Butrica et al. (2012), Chai et al. (2012), and Coronado and Dynan (2012).
2. The CAMS 2005 also included a subsample of the Early Baby Boomer cohort recruited into the HRS sample in 2004.
3. For example, some homeowners (as recorded in the HRS core) did not report a value in CAMS for 'rent'; we impute rents of $0 for these cases. Resulting spending levels are close to totals from the Consumer Expenditure Survey (www.bls.gov/cex) for the age groups 55–74. The CEX collects the most detailed and comprehensive information on total spending by households. CAMS shows higher levels of spending than the CEX among those aged 75 or over. There is no obvious reason that this difference should show in this age group, but not in the younger age group. However, we believe that the higher CAMS totals are more accurate than those in the CEX because they better match observed rates of wealth decumulation at older ages. When compared with after-tax income in the HRS, the lower levels of spending in CEX imply that single persons accumulate wealth, whereas in panel, they decumulate wealth (Hurd and Rohwedder, 2009).
4. Unit response rates in the first two HRS Internet surveys (conditional on being invited to participate) were 70 percent.

5. We have rich background information from the HRS core survey for those who did not participate in the HRS Internet survey, and this information can be used to reweight any results from the Internet survey.
6. The changes in Table 4.4 are derived from the ratios of mean and median spending. The mean of household-level spending change is not a good indicator of population spending change because observation error causes bias in the ratio.
7. On average, the two-year changes in household size among the 50–64-year-old households show a decline of 6 percent for the period 2001–7.
8. Accessed on August 18, 2011 at http://www.standardandpoors.com/indices/sp-case-shiller-home-price-indices/en/us/?indexId=spusa-cashpidff–p-us——
9. These price changes are not directly comparable with the Case–Shiller index, which is confined to twenty large cities.
10. In defining the sample, we do not include imputed information on home ownership, nor whether the household has any mortgage or other home loans.
11. Note that median housing debt shows a decline between 2006 and later years in Table 4.7, which is not observed in Table 4.6. We place more weight on the evidence in Table 4.6 as it is based on a larger sample (Table 4.6 includes observations with incomplete reports for amounts which are imputed, while Table 4.7 excludes these observations).
12. These percentages of homeowners with negative equity are more representative of the population than those obtained from sources such as lenders or property records which are either incomplete or outdated.
13. Calculated as the percentage of twelve-month intervals over which the housing price index increased between January 1, 1991 and November 1, 2009.
14. Calculated as the percentage of five-year intervals over which the housing price index increased from January 1, 1991 to November 1, 2009. See note 12.
15. In HRS 2008, *P62* was only asked of workers younger than age 62. In the Internet survey, the question was asked irrespective of labor force status, so we have responses from people who had stopped working between the two surveys, as well as from those who were still working.
16. See ftp.bls.gov/pub/special.requests/lf/aa2003/aat3.txt and ftp.bls.gov/pub/special.requests/lf/aa2008/aat3.txt, accessed August 18, 2011.

References

Butrica, B. A., R. W. Johnson, and K. E. Smith (2012). "The Potential Impact of the Great Recession on Future Retirement Incomes", in R. Maurer, O. S. Mitchell, and M. J. Warshawsky, eds., *Reshaping Retirement Security: Lessons from the Global Financial Crisis.* Oxford, UK: Oxford University Press.

Chai, J., R. Maurer, O. S. Mitchell, and R. Rogalla (2012). "Lifecycle Impacts of the Financial Crisis on Optimal Consumption—Portfolio Choices and Labor Supply", in R. Maurer, O. S. Mitchell, and M. J. Warshawsky, eds., *Reshaping Retirement Security: Lessons from the Global Financial Crisis.* Oxford: Oxford University Press.

Coronado, J. and K. Dynan (2012). "Changing Retirement Behavior in the Wake of the Financial Crisis", in R. Maurer, O. S. Mitchell, and M. J. Warshawsky, eds., *Reshaping Retirement Security: Lessons from the Global Financial Crisis.* Oxford, UK: Oxford University Press.

Hurd, M. and S. Rohwedder (2006). "Economic Well-Being at Older Ages: Income- and Consumption-based Poverty Measures in the HRS", RAND Working Paper No. WR-410. Santa Monica, CA: RAND Corporation.

—— and —— (2009). "Wealth Change and Active Saving at Older Ages", RAND report. Presented at the Annual AEA Meeting, San Francisco, January 2009.

Juster, F. T. and R. Suzman (1995). "An Overview of the Health and Retirement Study", *Journal of Human Resources,* 30(5): S7–S56.

Chapter 5

Retirement Behavior and the Global Financial Crisis

Jason J. Fichtner, John W. R. Phillips, and Barbara A. Smith

The financial crisis that began in 2008 resulted in a great and unanticipated loss of wealth for millions of Americans. The US stock market, as measured by the broad S&P 500 index, fell 56.7 percent from a peak on October 10, 2007 to a bottom on March 9, 2009.[1] Housing prices plummeted and unemployment rose quickly to double digits. General confidence in the financial system was greatly weakened. Though the broad stock market has recovered much of its losses, housing prices remain low. Unemployment is still high, with unemployment rates for workers aged 55–64 averaging 7 percent for the years 2009–10, compared to 3 percent for the period 2005–8 (BLS, 2011). Survey research suggests financial wealth declined by 15 percent for the median household as a result of the 2008 financial crisis (Shapiro, 2010).

These economic conditions have vastly changed the retirement landscape for millions of Americans, and have likely influenced retirement behavior. This chapter begins by providing a survey of the current literature on the influence of employment and wealth shocks on retirement.[2] Next, we analyze administrative records from the Social Security Administration (SSA) on benefit applications at age 62 to document the changes in retirement patterns resulting from the recent economic downturn and to consider implications for retirement security. Given the importance that Social Security benefits play in the retirement security of millions of Americans, and the possibility that the financial crisis is affecting retirement decisions, the chapter then addresses how SSA helps Americans prepare for retirement.

The effects of wealth shocks and employment on retirement behavior

The global financial crisis that began in 2008 and the resulting recession were notable for the speed at which the decline in financial markets, housing, and employment occurred. Also notable was the widespread nature of the economic crisis, affecting a range of ages and income levels. According to data from the Health and Retirement Study (HRS),[3] about 28 percent of HRS households reported that they had been affected 'a lot' by the financial crisis, 46 percent responded they had been affected 'a little', and only 26 percent reported not having been affected (Hurd and Rohwedder, 2010).

A sudden and unplanned drop in wealth and income can have significant effects on retirement behavior. Younger or middle-aged workers have more than a decade before retirement, and so they still have time to recover financial losses. A financial shock, such as steep drops in the value of stock prices, investment portfolios, and housing assets, might cause a delay in retirement plans,[4] with workers remaining in the workforce longer than planned to rebuild retirement savings (Bosworth and Burtless, 2010). Those near or postretirement are more limited in their ability to attain or maintain a secure retirement. For those near retirement, a financial crisis might also change the timing of retirement.[5] For current retirees, sudden declines in wealth from housing assets and financial portfolios might force immediate changes in consumption.

Research using the HRS data for 2008 and 2009 highlights the immediate impact of the financial crisis on retirement behavior (Hurd and Rohwedder, 2010).[6] For those working in 2008, the authors compared data between the two survey years and found that in the 2009 HRS Internet survey, 61.7 percent of the 2009 respondents expected to work past age 62, up from 58.2 percent in the 2008 HRS.[7] For those working in 2008, 46.4 percent of 2009 respondents expected to work past age 65, compared to 38.6 percent in the 2008 HRS.[8] Thus, these results suggest that many are planning on working longer and retiring later as a result of the financial crisis. Hurd and Rohwedder conclude that '...the economic crisis has caused households in and near retirement to suffer sizeable losses in assets. These households responded in several ways: they reduced spending and with that increased saving, they intend to work longer, and anticipate bequeathing less.'[9] Data from the Federal Reserve support Hurd and Rohwedder's finding, reporting that since the financial crisis the personal saving rate has trended upward from around 1 percent to around 6 percent (Glick and Lansing, 2011). All else equal, a reduction in wealth from a negative financial shock often results in workers near retirement increasing income and saving by remaining in the workforce or reducing planned consumption in retirement.[10]

The loss of a job can also affect retirement behavior. As Bosworth and Burtless (2010) note, 'At ages past 60 and especially past 65...reduced employment levels caused by a weak job market very quickly translate into reduced labor force participation rates.' An employment shock, such as a sudden loss of a job and a labor market with high unemployment might hasten the decision on both when to retire and when to begin receiving Social Security benefits. As noted earlier, the unemployment rate for workers aged 55–64 has more than doubled during the recent recession. Also, older workers who lose their jobs are likely to have longer durations of unemployment than are younger workers. According to recent data from the US Bureau of Labor Statistics (BLS), 49 percent of unemployed workers aged 55 or older had been unemployed for 27 weeks or longer, compared with 28 percent of unemployed workers aged 16–24 and 41 percent of unemployed workers aged 25–54 (BLS, 2010). A Congressional Research Service (CRS, 2007) study found that older workers who are unemployed have a higher incidence of withdrawing from the labor market. When they do so, they replace earnings with obvious sources of income, such as pensions and Social Security benefits. According to some studies, unemployment among older workers contributes significantly to the probability of retirement. All of these impacts will be amplified in the current recession. Though the decision to start receiving Social Security benefits can be contemporaneous with retirement, electing to receive benefits is not necessarily a predictor of leaving the workforce (Bosworth and Burtless, 2010). In actuality, the decision on whether to stop work can be completely independent from the decision to begin collecting Social Security benefits. For example, a worker might choose to stop working but delay receipt of Social Security benefits, to take advantage of higher monthly benefit amounts that accrue the later one waits to claim (up to age 70). Or a worker might decide to elect retirement benefits as early as 62, receiving a permanently reduced monthly benefit,[11] yet continue to work full- or part-time for continued income support.[12]

The net effect of a financial crisis and recession on retirement behavior is ambiguous. While some workers will delay retirement, others will exit the workforce earlier due to job loss. Thus, the decision to begin Social Security retirement benefits is intuitively correlated with leaving the workforce, but not necessarily. Accordingly, we might expect recessions to lead to an increase in those electing to begin receiving Social Security retirement benefits earlier.

Researchers have long recognized the role Social Security benefits play in a secure retirement.[13] Social Security retirement benefits provide income security for millions of Americans, with 64 percent of all aged beneficiary units[14] relying on Social Security for 50 percent or more of their income, and 34 percent relying on Social Security for 90 percent or more of their income (SSA, 2010*b*). Yet, because households at the lower end of the income and wealth distribution receive a larger share of their income from Social Security benefits, the financial crisis has affected these retirees less (Hurd and Rohwedder, 2010).

Data to study the retirement and saving effects due to the global financial crisis that began in 2008 are just beginning to become available, so additional research is necessary to fully understand how retirement behavior has changed because of the shocks to wealth and employment of the past few years.

Are people electing to receive Social Security benefits early due to the financial crisis? A preliminary look at trends

Over time, there has been a relatively stable percentage of workers who elect to claim Social Security retirement benefits as soon as they become available (Muldoon and Kopcke, 2008). Annual data published by SSA show that between 1985 and 2009 the percentage of those claiming retirement benefits at age 62 has gradually declined in the case of women, while remaining relatively constant in the case of men (SSA, 2010*a*) (see Figure 5.1).

But these data do not accurately reflect the trends in claiming behavior by age (Muldoon and Kopcke, 2008), since they present claiming by calendar year, not by birth year or cohort. A more accurate way of assessing claiming behavior of 62-year-olds is to look at the percentage of each birth cohort that claims at age 62 (e.g. the percent of people born in 1946, who claim benefits at age 62 when first becoming eligible in 2008). Using cohort data, comparisons can be made across birth years to see if those born in the 1920s have

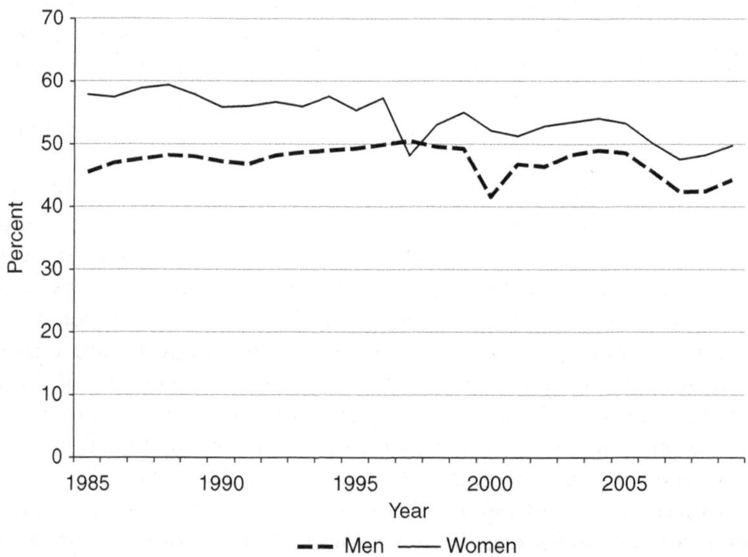

Figure 5.1 Percent of OASDI benefits awarded at age 62

Source: Derived from Table 6.B5 (SSA, 2010*a*).

different claiming behaviors than those born in the 1930s and early 1940s. Using the Continuous Work History Sample (CWHS),[15] we calculated claiming patterns at age 62 for cohorts born between 1913 and 1947, including only those who are fully insured for benefits.[16] Note, those born in 1913 first become eligible for reduced Social Security retirement benefits at age 62 in 1975, while those born in 1947 become eligible in 2009. These calculations are shown in Figure 5.2 and Appendix Table 5.1A.

For both men and women, there is a clear decrease in the percentage claiming at age 62 beginning in 1997, for the cohort born in 1935. As the number of women in the paid labor force increased, the percentage of those claiming benefits at 62 began to decline steadily, reaching a low of 36.3 percent in 2007 at the peak of the last economic expansion.

Men, who have traditionally had more consistent employment patterns, display a time series increase in benefit receipt at age 62. For men born in 1920, 41.1 percent elected to receive benefits when they turned age 62 in 1982. A pronounced 3 percentage-point increase occurred in 1983, as 44.2 percent of men born in 1921 elected to start receiving retirement benefits at age 62. The fraction of men taking early retirement benefits then trended upward from 1983 through 1993, reaching a peak of 49.1 percent. Beginning in 1997, the trend started to reverse, with a decline in the

Figure 5.2 Percent of fully insured workers who claim at age 62: cohorts born 1913–48 (by sex)

Source: Authors' calculation based on SSA administrative data, Continuous Work History Sample.

percentage of men claiming at age 62, reaching a new trough of 33.5 percent in 2007 (those born in 1945).

Did the financial crisis of 2008 result in an increase in those electing to receive early retirement benefits at age 62? While correlation is not causation, a preliminary analysis of the data do support the thesis that, in response to financial shocks and increases in unemployment, more people elected to begin taking Social Security retirement benefits as soon as they were eligible. In 2007, the year before the recession, 33.5 percent of fully insured men chose to begin retirement benefits at age 62, while 36.3 percent of fully insured women began benefits at age 62. These figures increased for the 1947 birth cohort who turned 62 in 2009 when the recession hit a low point, as 35.8 percent of fully insured men started receiving benefits and 38.9 percent of fully insured women followed suit. Similar patterns exist when the data is disaggregated by race, as shown in Figure 5.3.[17]

We conducted a similar analysis by state, to test whether states with higher unemployment rates also exhibited higher percentages of early claiming behavior at age 62. We used BLS data on state-level unemployment in 2009 and claiming information from the CWHS. The national unemployment rate was about 9.2 percent in 2009, and in that year, state-level unemployment varied from 4 percent in North Dakota to 13 percent in Michigan. As Figures 5.4 and 5.5 show, higher unemployment in a state

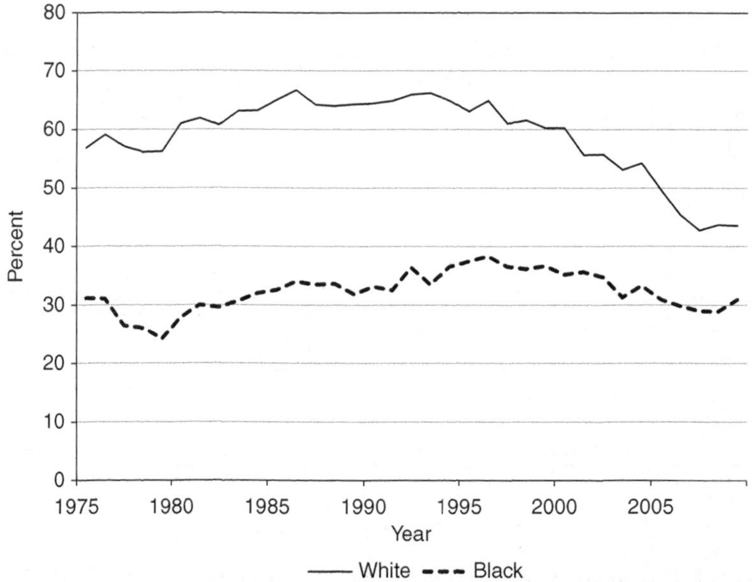

Figure 5.3 Percent of fully insured workers who claim at age 62: cohorts born 1913–48 (by race)

Source: Authors' calculation based on SSA administrative data, Continuous Work History Sample.

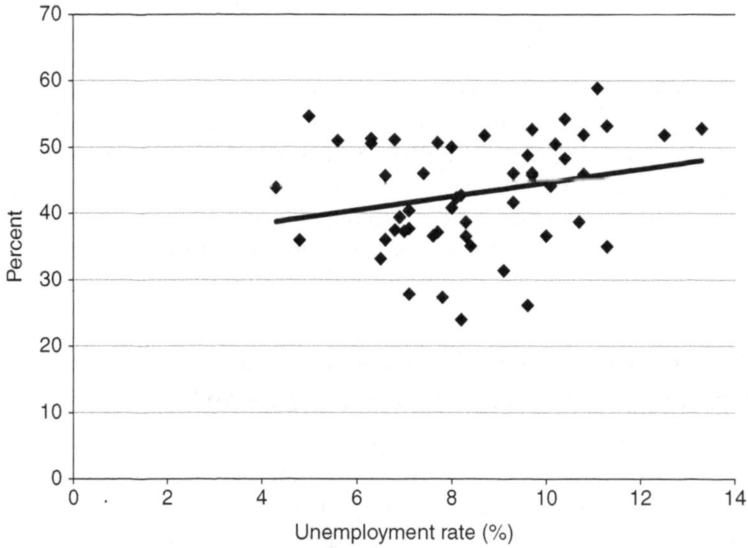

Figure 5.4 Unemployment rates and percent claiming at age 62 by state (2009)

Note: Percent claiming based on population aged 62.

Source: Authors' calculation based on SSA administrative data, Continuous Work History Sample.

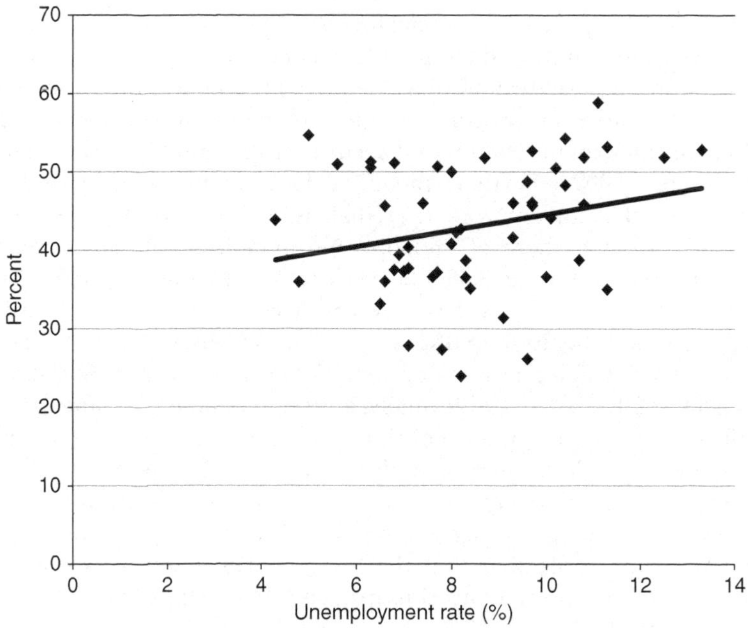

Figure 5.5 Unemployment rates and percent claiming at age 62 across states (2009)

Note: Percent claiming based on estimates of fully insured at age 62.

Source: Authors' calculation based on SSA administrative data, Continuous Work History Sample.

was correlated with a higher incidence of claiming at age 62 in 2009. We present the information two ways: first by showing the age-eligible population for claiming benefits, and second, by limiting the age-eligible population to only those fully insured for benefits. In both figures, a simple linear regression shows a positive relationship between unemployment and age 62 retirement claims (see Appendix Table 5.2A).[18]

How the Social Security Administration helps Americans prepare for retirement

A preliminary analysis of the data supports the thesis that more people will elect to begin taking Social Security retirement benefits as soon as eligible, due to financial shocks and increases in unemployment because of the global financial crisis. SSA plays a unique role in the financial security of millions of Americans, and in helping people better prepare for retirement in a postfinancial crisis world. Therefore, in 2009, the Agency undertook a special initiative to develop and refine print, web, and other products to better inform the public about retirement planning options and the importance personal savings contribute to a financially secure retirement (SSA, 2011*a*).

SSA decided to promote financial literacy in part because research found differences between how much people expect to receive in Social Security benefits when they retire, and what they actually receive. For example, only 19 percent of workers can correctly identify the age at which they will be eligible for full benefits from Social Security (EBRI and Mathew Greenwald & Associates, 2007). Further, the 2011 Retirement Confidence Survey (RCS) found that current workers are half as likely to expect Social Security to provide a major share of their income in retirement (33 percent) as current retirees are to say Social Security makes up a major share of their income (68 percent).[19] However, research conducted by the Employee Benefit Research Institute (EBRI) found that 60 percent of those aged 65 or older received at least three-quarters of their income from Social Security in 2009 (EBRI, 2010). Additionally, although people are living longer, a significant fraction of workers continues to take Social Security benefits at age 62, even though this permanently reduces monthly benefits for the rest of their life. Also influencing SSA's decision to move forward with a special initiative to encourage saving was research linking financial literacy and saving behavior, indicating that the less financially literate are also less likely to plan for retirement (Lusardi and Mitchell, 2006, 2007, 2008, 2009; Lusardi, 2011).

SSA's first undertaking was to improve the Social Security Statement with modest changes to the content and language. Specifically, the agency changed the order in which benefit projections were displayed, to focus attention on the full retirement age instead of the early retirement age (age 62). The Statement was sent to all US workers age 25 or over, and it provided a personal record of their earnings and taxes paid, along with an estimated benefit of what the worker might receive in the future. Approximately 150 million Statements were mailed in 2010. Research has shown that the introduction of the Statement in 1995 had a significant impact on increasing workers' knowledge about Social Security benefits (Mastrobuoni, 2009).[20] Surveys commissioned by SSA also found that those respondents who stated they had received a Statement were better informed than those who did not recall receiving one. Additionally, the Social Security Advisory Board (SSAB) recognized that the Statement is the 'most direct and important means of communicating with the public' about Social Security benefits (SSAB, 2009).

Along with the modest content and language changes in the Statement (SSAB, 2009), SSA also created two one-page, double-sided inserts to accompany the Statement. The first insert entitled 'Thinking of Retiring?' was included in Statements sent to workers aged 55+, beginning in October 2000. It addressed important topics, including the reduction in benefits that occurs if one elects to begin benefits before full retirement age, the role of survivor and spousal benefits, and the fact that the decisions to stop work and begin collecting benefits can be made independent of one another. The insert also provided information on how workers could go to the SSA's website and use online tools to estimate retirement benefits.

The second insert entitled 'What Young Workers Should Know About Social Security and Saving' was issued in February 2009 and was designed for workers aged 25–35. It informed younger workers that Social Security is a form of social insurance that provides disability and retirement benefits, while stressing the importance of personal savings for a financially secure retirement. Additionally, the insert informed its young readers that Social Security benefits are designed to replace approximately 40 percent of income in retirement, but financial planners suggest that retirees will need to replace 70–80 percent of preretirement income for a secure retirement. Accordingly, individuals will need to make up the difference with personal saving or pensions.

An additional one-page, double-sided information pamphlet was also created to address one of the most important questions people ask SSA, namely 'What is the best age to start receiving retirement benefits?' The document entitled 'When to Start Receiving Retirement Benefits' stresses that when to begin benefits is a very personal decision and that no simple answer is correct for everyone. This document indicated that monthly benefits vary substantially, depending on the age one begins receiving benefits. It also noted that retirement may be longer than most people expect, and it highlighted that one's decision about when to begin benefits might also affect the benefits a person's family is eligible to receive. Finally, it also explained the rules regarding working and receiving benefits. This document was distributed to all SSA field offices (approximately 1,300) and it is available on the agency's website.[21]

The SSA also supported an extramural program of research on retirement, including several interdisciplinary projects on financial literacy, decision-making, and behavior change. The research goals were to learn the most effective ways to help foster retirement and other saving strategies at all stages of the life cycle, to help low- and moderate-income populations successfully plan and save for retirement and other life events, and to improve understanding of Social Security's programs. The goal was to have the findings inform Social Security's efforts (statement, web, program design, etc.) as well as spillover to other relevant areas, such as employer-sponsored retirement programs.

Several of the financial literacy projects have produced promising results. For example, an innovative study used the American Life Panel to experiment with different ways of framing monthly benefit information (Brown et al., 2010). The authors held constant the factual information presented, but varied on how the information was presented to highlight the financial gains of delaying or claiming. That study found that framing information strongly shaped respondents' expected claiming ages.

Due to the tightening of federal budgets in 2011, the SSA curtailed its efforts in the financial literacy domain. Moreover, the agency suspended the mailing of the Statement to workers, and limited research expenditures for financial literacy projects.[22]

Conclusion

The financial crisis that began in 2008 resulted in substantial and unanticipated job loss and loss of wealth for millions of people. Many Americans responded by reducing consumption and increasing saving. Moreover, based on a preliminary analysis of the data, it also seems that some will elect to receive retirement benefits at age 62, reversing the precrisis trend to file at later ages. Further research will be required to confirm this trend.

Appendix

APPENDIX TABLE 5.A1 Beneficiary claiming rates, by birth cohort

Birth cohort	Year at age 62	Beneficiary claiming rates at age 62 (%)	
		Male	Female
1913	1975	37.0	50.2
1914	1976	39.9	50.9
1915	1977	36.9	49.6
1916	1978	37.0	47.3
1917	1979	36.2	48.2
1918	1980	41.2	50.4
1919	1981	42.4	50.7
1920	1982	41.1	50.5
1921	1983	44.2	50.9
1922	1984	44.4	51.2
1923	1985	46.4	51.8
1924	1986	48.2	52.2
1925	1987	46.4	50.6
1926	1988	46.5	50.0
1927	1989	47.1	49.7
1928	1990	48.0	49.2
1929	1991	48.3	49.4
1930	1992	48.8	51.6
1931	1993	49.1	51.1
1932	1994	48.4	52.2
1933	1995	47.6	49.5
1934	1996	48.4	51.5
1935	1997	46.5	47.7
1936	1998	46.5	48.7
1937	1999	45.3	48.2
1938	2000	45.1	48.7
1939	2001	43.4	43.9
1940	2002	42.7	45.2
1941	2003	40.1	43.3
1942	2004	40.6	44.9
1943	2005	38.5	40.1
1944	2006	34.6	37.9
1945	2007	33.5	36.3
1946	2008	35.1	38.3
1947	2009	35.8	38.9
1948	2010	35.3	36.6

Source: Authors' calculations based on SSA administrative data, Continuous Work History Sample.

Appendix Table 5.A2 Unemployment rates and percentage claiming at age 62 across states (2009)

State	Number of beneficiaries aged 62 in 2009 (1947 birth cohort) (hundreds)	(Total no. of fully insured at age 62 in 2009) × (state population/US population)	State population/ US population aged 62	Population aged 62 in 2009	Unemployment rate in 2009	Beneficiaries as a % of population aged 62	Beneficiaries as a % of estimate of fully insured
AL	205	44,478.5	0.01593	57,144	9.7	35.9	46.1
AK	16	5,845.5	0.00209	7,510	7.8	21.3	27.4
AZ	293	55,619.9	0.01992	71,458	9.7	41.0	52.7
AR	128	27,826.3	0.00997	35,750	7.4	35.8	46.0
CA	1,047	298,828.7	0.10703	383,922	11.3	27.3	35.0
CO	174	44,969.6	0.01611	57,775	8.3	30.1	38.7
CT	128	35,010.5	0.01254	44,980	8.3	28.5	36.6
DE	44	8,799.3	0.00315	11,305	8	38.9	50.0
DC	14	5,351.2	0.00192	6,875	9.6	20.4	26.2
FL	899	178,050.9	0.06377	228,752	10.2	39.3	50.5
GA	378	82,601.7	0.02959	106,123	9.7	35.6	45.8
HI	59	11,532.9	0.00413	14,817	6.8	39.8	51.2
ID	67	13,222.0	0.00474	16,987	7.7	39.4	50.7
IL	414	112,966.2	0.04046	145,134	10	28.5	36.6
IN	285	58,991.0	0.02113	75,789	10.4	37.6	48.3
IA	143	28,046.6	0.01005	36,033	5.6	39.7	51.0
KS	102	25,230.5	0.00904	32,415	7.1	31.5	40.4
KY	163	42,062.5	0.01507	54,040	10.7	30.2	38.8
LA	146	40,492.5	0.01450	52,023	6.6	28.1	36.1
ME	64	14,980.3	0.00537	19,246	8.2	33.3	42.7
MD	150	53,835.1	0.01928	69,165	7.1	21.7	27.9
MA	156	65,027.9	0.02329	83,545	8.2	18.7	24.0
MI	513	97,105.6	0.03478	124,757	13.3	41.1	52.8
MN	199	47,005.0	0.01684	60,390	8.1	33.0	42.3
MS	128	26,250.1	0.00940	33,725	9.6	38.0	48.8

MO	260	56,458.2	0.02022	72,535	9.3	35.8	46.1
MT	50	9,886.7	0.00354	12,702	6.3	39.4	50.6
NE	56	15,556.3	0.00557	19,986	4.8	28.0	36.0
NV	124	23,913.5	0.00857	30,723	12.5	40.4	51.9
NH	72	14,037.7	0.00503	18,035	6.3	39.9	51.3
NJ	260	82,716.1	0.02963	106,270	9.1	24.5	31.4
NM	69	18,493.0	0.00662	23,759	7	29.0	37.3
NY	649	184,802.4	0.06619	237,426	8.4	27.3	35.1
NC	454	87,542.7	0.03135	112,471	10.8	40.4	51.9
ND	24	5,468.0	0.00196	7,025	4.3	34.2	43.9
OH	505	114,418.6	0.04098	147,000	10.1	34.4	44.1
OK	155	33,933.3	0.01215	43,596	6.6	35.6	45.7
OR	232	39,404.4	0.01411	50,625	11.1	45.8	58.9
PA	521	127,503.6	0.04567	163,811	8	31.8	40.9
RI	48	10,459.6	0.00375	13,438	10.8	35.7	45.9
SC	241	45,298.1	0.01622	58,197	11.3	41.4	53.2
SD	39	7,136.0	0.00256	9,168	5	42.5	54.7
TN	333	61,367.3	0.02198	78,842	10.4	42.2	54.3
TX	693	189,256.9	0.06779	243,149	7.6	28.5	36.6
UT	67	17,762.1	0.00636	22,820	7.1	29.4	37.7
VT	27	6,842.5	0.00245	8,791	6.9	30.7	39.5
VA	278	74,087.2	0.02654	95,184	6.8	29.2	37.5
WA	267	64,081.4	0.02295	82,329	9.3	32.4	41.7
WV	75	20,174.3	0.00723	25,919	7.7	28.9	37.2
WI	270	52,147.6	0.01868	66,997	8.7	40.3	51.8
WY	17	5,122.4	0.00183	6,581	6.5	25.8	33.2

Notes: Total US population aged 62 in 2009 = 3,587,039; total fully insured population at age 62 in 2009 = 2,792,000.

Source: Authors' calculations based on SSA administrative data, Continuous Work History Sample (BLS, 2011).

Endnotes

1. Data available from Yahoo! Finance. S&P 500 index value at market close on October 10, 2007 was 1,562.47. Index value at close on March 9, 2009 was 676.53. The National Bureau of Economic Research, the arbiter of the start and end dates of a recession, determined that the recession that began in December 2007 ended in June 2009, roughly coinciding with the peak and trough dates of the S&P 500 index.
2. Retirement in this paper refers to withdrawal from the labor force. Thus, retirement as defined here does not necessarily coincide with benefit claiming.
3. The HRS is a longitudinal survey of health, retirement, and aging that has been conducted every two years since 1992 and interviews more than 22,000 Americans over the age of 50. For more information on the HRS, see http://hrsonline.isr.umich.edu.
4. In this context, 'retirement plans' refers to peoples' goals, strategies, and behaviors, not to defined contribution or defined benefit retirement plans.
5. The timing of retirement can be affected by more than age, including accumulated savings, the availability of an employer-provided pension, the willingness or ability to continue working part-time in retirement, personal health, access to health coverage, and general economic conditions.
6. Although the time between the 2008 HRS interview and a subsequent 2009 HRS Internet survey was insufficient to observe actual behavior, the data nonetheless can be used to shed light on retirement expectations (Hurd and Rohwedder, 2010).
7. What is described here are the expectations of working past either age 62 or age 65. Hurd et al. (2005) have found that these retirement expectations are predictive of actual retirement.
8. See Hurd and Rohwedder (2010: 20, tables 10 and 11).
9. See Hurd and Rohwedder (2010: 11).
10. For a theoretical model of this behavior, see Chai et al. (2012) (this volume).
11. Social Security benefits taken between ages 62 and the full retirement age (FRA), currently 65 or 66 depending upon birth year, are actuarially reduced so that the expected value of total lifetime benefits received is approximately the same, regardless of when benefits are claimed.
12. Income earned by individuals who claim benefits prior to attaining the FRA is subject to the retirement earnings test. There are two different exempt amounts, depending upon when the individuals attain FRA. For individuals claiming benefits and working in 2011 but attaining FRA in 2012 or later, the annual exempt amount in 2011 is $14,160. For those individuals attaining FRA in 2011, the exempt amount is $37,680 and applies only to income earned in the months prior to attaining FRA. After attaining FRA, individuals are no longer subject to the earnings test. SSA withholds $1 in benefits for every $2 in earnings in excess of the lower exempt amount and $1 in benefits for every $3 of earnings in excess of the higher exempt amount.
13. For a summary of research work on this area, see Burkhauser et al. (2009).
14. An aged unit is either a married couple living together or an unmarried person, which also includes persons who are separated or married but not living

together. A married couple's age is defined as the age of the husband—unless he is under age 55 and the wife is 55 or older, in which case it is the age of the wife. The example in the paper refers to aged units that are 65 years of age or older. In this case, the age of the married couple is the age of the husband if he is 65 or older; if the husband is younger than 55 and the wife is aged 65 or older, the age of the married couple is the age of the wife. See https://www.socialsecurity.gov/policy/docs/statcomps/income_pop55/2008/incpop08.pdf.

15. The CWHS is the oldest major longitudinal sample data source in the federal statistical system. It contains demographic, earnings, and benefit data. For more information about the CWHS, see 'The Social Security Administration's Continuous Work History Sample': www.ssa.gov/policy/docs/ssb/v52n10/v52n10p20.pdf.
16. Individuals must be insured under the Social Security program before retirement, survivors, or disability benefits can be paid to workers or their spouses and dependents. Social Security considers the number of quarters of coverage earned to determine insured status. A quarter of coverage (QC)—also called a 'credit'—is earned for a certain amount of work covered under Social Security, but no more than four QCs can be earned in a given year. Generally, a person needs to be 'fully insured' to receive Social Security benefits, but other requirements may also apply. To be fully insured, a person needs at least one QC for each calendar year after turning 21 and the earliest of the following: (*a*) the year before age 62; (*b*) the year before death; or (*c*) the year of becoming disabled. For more information, see http://www.socialsecurity.gov/OACT/ProgData/insured.html.
17. We include the results disaggregated by race because we thought that a natural question to ask would be whether our findings hold for different demographic subgroups. Our future research will analyze in more depth changes in claiming behavior in subgroups of the population.
18. Using a simple linear regression of state-level unemployment and age-62 claiming, the relationship is significant at the 9 percent level.
19. The percentages in parentheses refer to the fraction of respondents reporting the stated response.
20. Prior to 2000, the Social Security Statement was known as the Personal Earnings and Benefit Estimate Statement (PEBES).
21. For a copy of this document, see www.ssa.gov/pubs/10147.pdf.
22. In recent testimony, the SSA Commissioner stated that to conserve funds, the agency would suspend the current contract to mail out the Statement (SSA, 2011*c*).

References

Bosworth, G. and G. Burtless (2010). "Recessions, Wealth Destruction, and the Timing of Retirement", CRR Working Paper No. 2010–22. Chestnut Hill, MA: Center for Retirement Research at Boston College.

Brown, J., A. Kapteyn, and O. S. Mitchell (2010). "Framing Effects and Social Security Claiming Behavior", Working Paper WR-793-SSA. RAND Corporation Financial Literacy Center.

Bureau of Labor Statistics (BLS) (2010). *Issues in Labor Statistics*, Summary 10-04. Washington, DC: US Department of Labor. www.bls.gov/opub/ils//summary_10_04/older_workers.htm

—— (2011). *Labor Force Statistics from the Current Population Survey*. Washington, DC: US Department of Labor. www.bls.gov/data/#unemployment

Burkhauser, R., A. Gustman, J. Laitner, O. S. Mitchell, and A. Sonnega (2009). "Social Security Research at the Michigan Retirement Research Center," *Social Security Bulletin*, 69(4): 51–64.

Chai, J., R. Maurer, O. S. Mitchell, and R. Rogalla (2012). "Lifecycle Impacts of the Financial and Economic Crisis on Household Optimal Consumption, Portfolio Choice, and Labor Supply", in R. Maurer, O. S. Mitchell, and M. J. Warshawsky, eds., *Reshaping Retirement Security: Lessons from the Global Financial Crisis*. Oxford, UK: Oxford University Press.

Congressional Research Service (CRS) (2007). CRS Report for Congress, *Unemployment and Older Workers*. Washington, DC: United States Congress.

Employee Benefit Research Institute (EBRI) (2010). *EBRI Databook on Employee Benefits*, Chapter 7, Updated October 2010. Accessed March 20, 2011. http://ebri.org/pdf/publications/books/databook/DB.Chapter%2007.pdf

EBRI and Mathew Greenwald & Associates, Inc. (2007). *Retirement Confidence Survey*. http://www.ebri.org/surveys/rcs/

—— and —— (2011). *Retirement Confidence Survey*. http://www.ebri.org/surveys/rcs/

Glick, R. and K. J. Lansing (2011). "Consumers and the Economy, Part I: Household Credit and Personal Saving", *FRBSF Economic Letter*, Number 2011-01. San Francisco, CA: Federal Reserve Board of San Francisco.

Hurd, M. and S. Rohwedder (2010). "The Effects of the Economic Crisis on the Older Population", MRRC Working Paper No. 2010-231. Ann Arbor, MI: Michigan Retirement Research Center.

——, M. Renti, and S. Rohwedder (2005). *The Effect of Large Capital Gains or Losses on Retirement*. http://www.nber.org/books_in_progress/boulders05/hurd-et-al8-9-06.pdf.

Lusardi, A. (2011). "Americans' Financial Capability", PRC Working Paper No. WP2011-02. Philadelphia, PA: Pension Research Council, The Wharton School, University of Pennsylvania.

—— and O. S. Mitchell (2006). "Financial Literacy and Planning: Implications for Retirement Wellbeing", MRRC Working Paper No. 2006-114. Ann Arbor, MI: Michigan Retirement Research Center.

—— and —— (2007). "Baby Boomer Retirement Security: The Role of Planning, Financial Literacy, and Housing Wealth", *Journal of Monetary Economics*, 54: 205–24.

—— and —— (2008). "Planning and Financial Literacy: How Do Women Fare?", *American Economic Review*, 98: 413–17.

—— and —— (2009). "How Ordinary Consumers Make Complex Economic Decisions: Financial Literacy and Retirement Readiness", NBER Working Paper No. 15350. Cambridge, MA: National Bureau of Economic Research.

Mastrobuoni, G. (2009). "The Role of Information for Retirement Behavior: Evidence Based on the Stepwise Introduction of the Social Security Statement", CRR Working Paper No. 2009-23. Chestnut Hill, MA: Center for Retirement Research at Boston College.

Muldoon, D. and R. W. Kopcke (2008). "Are People Claiming Social Security Benefits Later?", CRR Issue Brief Number 8-7. Chestnut Hill, MA: Center for Retirement Research at Boston College.

Shapiro, M. D. (2010). "The Effects of the Financial Crisis on the Well-Being of Older Americans: Evidence from the Cognitive Economics Study", MRRC Working Paper No. 228. Ann Arbor, MI: Michigan Retirement Research Center.

Social Security Administration (SSA) (2010*a*). "Table 6.B5", *Annual Statistical Supplement, 2010.* Washington, DC: SSA.

—— (2010*b*). "Relative Importance of Social Security, 2008", *Fast Facts & Figures,* August. Washington, DC: SSA. Accessed March 20, 2011. http://www.ssa.gov/policy/docs/chartbooks/fast_facts/2010/fast_facts10.html#agedpop

—— (2011*a*). *Agency Strategic Plan Fiscal Years 2008–2013.* Washington, DC: SSA. http://www.socialsecurity.gov/asp/plan-2008-2013.html

—— (2011*b*). "Understanding the Benefits," SSA Publication No. 05-10024. Washington, DC: SSA. http://www.socialsecurity.gov/pubs/10024.html

—— (2011*c*). *Statement for the Record,* Testimony of Commissioner Michael J. Astrue before the Subcommittee on Labor, Health and Human Services, Education, and Related Agencies, Committee on Appropriations, United States Senate, March 9, 2011.

Social Security Advisory Board (SSAB) (2009). *The Social Security Statement: How It can be Improved.* Washington, DC: SSAB.

Part II

Rethinking the Resilience of Defined Contribution Plans

Chapter 6

Trading in 401(k) Plans during the Financial Crisis

Ning Tang, Olivia S. Mitchell, and Stephen P. Utkus

Defined contribution (DC) or 401(k) plans are now the dominant form of US retirement accounts. They cover over 65 million American employees and encompass some $3 trillion in assets, with approximately two-thirds of those assets invested in equities.[1] During the financial crisis of 2008–9, retirement plan participants were confronted with one of the most dramatic downturns in stock prices, and one of the sharpest increases in market volatility, since the Great Depression. While only one-quarter of participants chose to trade in their accounts over our analysis period, in response to the crisis there was a sharp increase in the number of participants trading[2] and the fraction of portfolios shifted away from equities rose by nearly eight times. In this chapter, we trace how 401(k) plan participants as investors behaved in this exceptional market environment and identify whether and how trading patterns during the peak months of the financial crisis differed from trading during less volatile times.

We consider three separate explanations for heightened portfolio trading activity during the crisis. First, we evaluate the motivation for trading—whether 401(k) plan participants acted as momentum investors, simply selling equities as markets fell, or whether they were reacting to increased volatility of returns. Second, we consider the impact of prior trading experience on behavior during the crisis, comparing first-time traders during the crisis with those who were more experienced. Third, our analysis examines whether the salience of information on retirement wealth—as represented by the receipt of quarterly statements during certain months of the crisis—has an independent effect on trading behavior.

Prior research in household finance has shown that employees in 401(k) plans (DC plans) are often characterized by inertia, rarely altering their investment portfolios during normal market cycles. Only a minority trades at all and very active traders realize reduced returns.[3] There have also been studies indicating that holders of low-cost brokerage accounts are more active traders; here too, very active traders realize lower net returns.[4] Both sets of studies suggest the dominance of behavioral factors in driving household investment patterns: inertia broadly, with overconfidence among a small group of active traders. Yet the literature to date focuses on relatively calm financial markets. Our goal in this chapter is to examine 401(k) participant behavior from January 2006 to March 2009, to explore how retirement plan investors behaved when confronted with an extraordinary financial crisis.

Drawing on a large sample of 401(k) plans administered by Vanguard, we show that only a minority of 401(k) investors traded in their accounts, either before or during the crisis. Nevertheless, behavior did change for those who traded: the proportion of participants trading each month rose by nearly one-quarter, from 2.4 to 2.9 percent, and the mean portfolio fraction shifted away from equities rose almost eightfold during the crisis. We also show that this equity-selling pattern was in part due to increased sensitivity to volatility during the crisis. For instance, precrisis, a two standard deviation rise in market volatility (uncertainty) was associated with a 4 percent shift away from equities, while during the crisis it induced a 10 percent shift away. Responsiveness to returns also changed: 401(k) traders shifted from a momentum strategy during the precrisis period to a contrarian strategy during the turmoil. Thus, a sharp market decline (measured by a two standard deviation drop in the prior month's equity–bond spread) was associated with a 5 percent momentum shift *out* of equities precrisis, but during the crisis it elicited a 5 percent contrarian shift *toward* equities. In effect, an anticipated increase in investor reaction to volatility during the crisis period was partly offset by a contrarian 'buy on the dips' reaction to returns.

We also discover that prior trading experience played a paradoxical role in these dynamics: the most experienced active traders were less sensitive to market volatility and least contrarian during the crisis. But the least experienced trader group, first-time traders during the crisis, reacted much more negatively to rising volatility; these individuals were also more contrarian in their reactions to returns. Moreover, first-time traders were on average younger, more likely to be female, lower paid, and less wealthy than the experienced group, suggesting some degree of financial naiveté or illiteracy. Their tendency to react strongly to volatility fits this characterization; their tendency to act as contrarian investors during the crisis does not. These results suggest that 401(k) trading is more nuanced than previously imagined, and that 401(k) traders cannot be easily characterized as inexperienced, momentum investors. Finally, we find that making account wealth more salient during the crisis period had a surprising ameliorating effect. Prior to the crisis, participant trading patterns exhibited no measurable response when participants' quarterly statements were received from plan sponsors. In contrast, receiving such information during the turmoil led traders to independently boost equity holdings by 2 percent.

In what follows, we briefly review prior research on portfolio trading behavior. Next, we describe our data, including a description of participant trading patterns and characteristics. Our empirical strategy involves comparisons of trading patterns prior to and during the crisis, and we also detail how trading patterns varied by prior trading experience. A final section concludes.

Background

Prior research has offered competing views about why investors might trade in their investment portfolios. Early economic models suggested that investors would maintain constant portfolio allocations over the life cycle barring new information (cf. Aumann, 1976; Milgrom and Stokey, 1982). Subsequently, some have proposed that trading will occur to take advantage of tax strategies and reduce search costs, as well as for life cycle reasons (cf. Sirri and Tufano, 1998; Grinblatt and Keloharju, 2001; Bergstresser and Poterba, 2002). The neoclassical life cycle mode has also been extended to take into account labor income and consumption shocks as drivers of portfolio trading (cf. Horneff et al., 2009; Chai et al., 2010). From a less neoclassical vantage point, other researchers have proposed 'behavioral' explanations for trading, including the disposition effect, where traders are unwilling to sell losers (cf. Shefrin and Statman, 1985); overconfidence leading to excess turnover, and an inability to understand trading costs (Odean, 1998, 1999; Barber and Odean, 2000, 2001); and increasing trading volumes with high market volatility (cf. Epps and Epps, 1976; Cornell, 1981; Karpoff, 1987).

Relatively few empirical studies have examined trading in the context of DC retirement accounts. An analysis of a single large 401(k) plan found very limited trading, and what trading there was seemed to be momentum or return-chasing (Agnew et al., 2003). Additionally, extreme negative returns were seen as necessary to motivate plan participants to trade (Agnew, 2004). Using a much larger set of DC plans and participants, and analyzing a period of relatively calm markets, Mitchell et al. (2006) also found little evidence of portfolio churning in 401(k) accounts. Participants who did trade during those relatively calm markets were older, better-paid, and wealthier men. Moreover, as in studies on brokerage account traders, the active 401(k) traders also earned lower returns.[5]

One issue not yet examined in detail is how US investors responded to the market shock of 2008–9, whether in retirement or personal investment accounts. In what follows, we explore whether and how 401(k) participant trading responded, and what these patterns tell us about theories of investor behavior.

An overview of trading patterns in DC pension accounts

We assess 401(k) trading activity over the period January 2006–March 2009. In this time frame, US and global stock prices at first rose through October 2007; thereafter, they began to fall as the mortgage finance crisis accelerated and macroeconomic conditions deteriorated. Returns on US stocks relative to US taxable bonds, measured by the spread between the monthly return on the S&P 500 Index and the Barclay's US Aggregate Bond Index, widened and became increasingly negative. Market volatility rose early in 2008 as the US mortgage financing crisis deepened, and in September 2008, investment bank Lehman Brothers collapsed and insurer AIG was rescued by the federal government. These events marked the beginning of an accelerated decline in stock prices and an extraordinary increase in stock price volatility, with stocks underperforming bonds in the worst months by −14 percent (October 2008), −10 percent (November 2008), and −10 percent (February 2009).

To examine the impact of this market shock on 401(k) trading patterns, we draw on administrative records for active 401(k) participants in nearly 1,900 DC plans observed over the thirty-nine-month period.[6] On average, 65,000 of the 2.25 million 401(k) participants observed traded or moved money between investment options in their plans.[7] The dataset provides extensive information on individual plan participants, including their age, sex, account balances, plan tenure, indicators of nonretirement-plan wealth and homeownership, and whether the participants were registered for web account access.[8] We also observe each person's trade date, as well as the amount, source, and destination of funds traded, summarized on a monthly basis. The trading dataset is augmented with information on monthly returns of all investment options in each plan.

Our goal is to compare observed trading patterns *precrisis*, or January 2006–August 2008, with trading activity *during the crisis*, defined as September 2008–March 2009. We select the latter to define the crisis period due to the extreme return and volatility characteristics of US stocks over that seven-month span.[9] Comparing these two periods, Table 6.1 and Figure 6.1 show that the fraction of participants trading in a given month rose from 2.4 to 2.9 percent, an increase of 23 percent, and the mean number of participants trading jumped nearly one third, from just over 61,000 precrisis to more than 81,000 during the crisis.[10] As a measure of trading intentions, we calculate each trader's net flow to equities, defined as the participant's monthly flow to equities less his monthly flow to fixed income assets, as a fraction of his prior month-end account balance.[11,12] Prior to the crisis, during which time stocks underperformed bonds by 0.1 percent per month on average, the average trader shifted 1.2 percent of his balance

TABLE 6.1 Incidence of 401(k) trading

	Entire period (1/06–3/09)	Precrisis (1/06–8/08)	Crisis (9/08–3/09)	*Change* (crisis–precrisis) (%)
No. of traders (thousands)	64.80	61.25	81.11	*32*
No. of participants (millions)	2.25	2.23	2.38	*7*
Participants trading (%)	2.5	2.4	2.9	*23*
Net flow to equities (%)	−3.5	−1.2	−11.1	*789*
Benchmarks				
Equity–bond spread (%)	−1.69	−0.17	−6.89	*3,921*
Equity market volatility (%)	1.53	0.93	3.59	*286*

Note: Derived from a panel of 1,886 401(k) plans observed January 2006–March 2009. Participants are currently employed and eligible to contribute to the plan in months observed. Traders are participants who exchanged (traded) between one or more investment options in their plans in a given month. Values are monthly averages over the periods indicated.

Source: Authors' calculations (rows 1–4); and WRDS (https://wrds-web.wharton.upenn.edu/wrds/).

away from equities in a typical month; during the crisis, when stocks underperformed by 6.5 percent per month, the average trader shifted 11.1 percent of his balance away from equities. Equity market volatility, defined as the standard deviation of daily stock index changes in a given month, also rose, from under 1 percent precrisis to 3.6 percent during the crisis.

Types of traders

Trader characteristics are summarized in Table 6.2, Panel A, for the entire period (Column 1), as well as separately in the precrisis (Column 2) and crisis periods (Column 3). As we have found before, 401(k) plans traders tend to be male, affluent, and relatively long tenured;[13] the average trader was a 46-year-old man with an account balance of nearly $115,000 and plan tenure of over ten years. During the crisis, however, trader characteristics changed somewhat: they became more female, with shorter tenure and lower account balances (by about 12 percent), and with less nonretirement wealth. Inasmuch as these individuals are also those having lower levels of financial literacy (cf. Lusardi et al., 2010), it suggests that the financial meltdown prompted less financially sophisticated/knowledgeable individuals to trade.

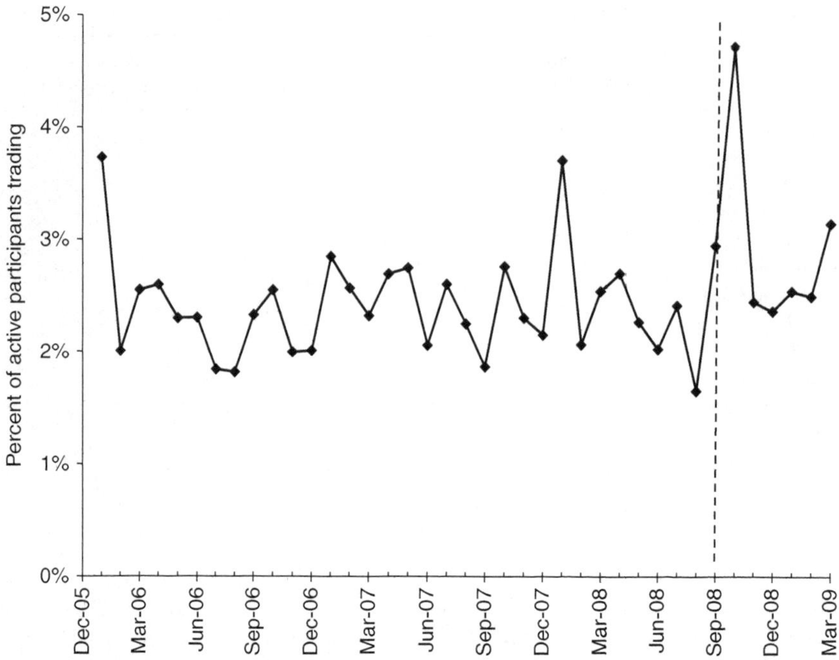

Figure 6.1 Proportion of 401(k) participants trading over time

Note: The vertical line indicates the onset of the crisis period.

Source: Authors' calculations; see text.

We are also interested in whether prior experience with trading influenced trading patterns during the crisis. Figure 6.2 depicts the distribution of number of trades over several time periods. We define *active traders* as those who had traded at least three times precrisis; this group accounts for 31 percent of all traders precrisis. *Infrequent traders* were the remaining 69 percent of precrisis traders, and they traded only one to two times precrisis. We also identify *first-time crisis traders* as those first observed trading during the crisis period.[14] Panel B compares these three groups and shows that active traders were wealthier (in terms of 401(k) account balance and nonretirement wealth), more male, and longer tenured than other traders. For example, the mean account balance of active traders, at around $157,000, was more than $50,000 above average balances for infrequent trader, and nearly $88,000 above first-time crisis trader balances. Infrequent traders tended to be less wealthy, more female, and less tenured than active traders, and first-time crisis traders even more so. Again, these characteristics are associated with lower levels of financial literacy.

TABLE 6.2 Demographic characteristics of traders as of September 2008

Panel A. All traders

	(1) Entire period	(2) Precrisis	(3) Crisis	(4) Diff: crisis–precrisis (3-2)
Age (mean years)	46.2	46.5	46.6	0.1***
% Male	63	64	62	−2***
Average account balance ($)	$114,765	$123,849	$108,863	−$14,986***
Plan tenure (years)	10.8	11.2	10.5	−0.7***
% Rich	31	31	29	−2***
% Poor	34	33	35	2***
% Homeowner	75	76	73	−3***
% Web-registered	86	88	84	−4***
N	683,399	569,488	320,520	

Panel B. Traders by type

	(5) Active traders, precrisis	(6) Infrequent traders, precrisis	(7) First-time crisis traders	*(8) Diff: active–infrequent traders (5)–(6)*	*(9) Diff: active–first-time crisis traders (5)–(7)*
Age (mean years)	47.7	46	45.1	2***	3***
% Male	69	62	57	7***	13***
Average account balance ($)	$157,150	$106,968	$69,348	$50,183***	$87,802 ***
Plan tenure (years)	12.4	10.5	8.6	1.9 ***	3.8***
% Rich	32	31	26	1***	6***
% Poor	32	34	38	−1***	−6***
% Homeowner	79	75	66	4***	13***
% Web-registered	90	87	77	3***	13***
N	191,572	377,916	113,911		

Note: See Table 6.1 for period definitions. Participant characteristics measured as of September 2008. Active traders traded more than three times precrisis (31 percent) and infrequent traders had one to two trades precrisis (69 percent). First-time crisis traders did not trade precrisis but did trade for the first time during the crisis. Average monthly account balance refers to the average balance in months where the trader had a balance. Wealth indicators are as follows: 'poor' refers to nonretirement wealth <$7,280; 'rich' >$61,289; with the reference category omitted. Panel A (Column 4) versus Panel B (Columns 8 and 9) differences indicated via *t*-tests (*** indicates 1% significance level).

Source: Authors' calculations.

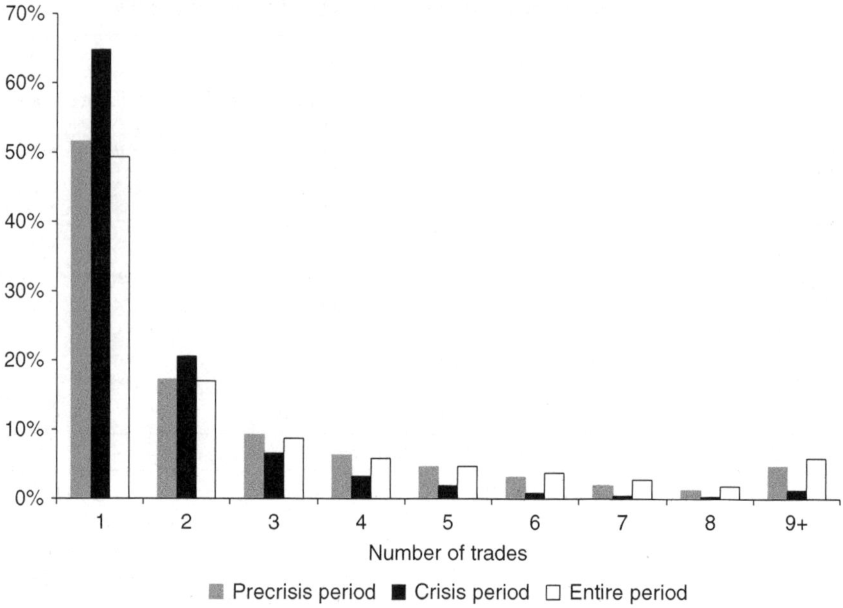

Figure 6.2 Distribution of the number of trades: precrisis, crisis, and entire period
Source: Authors' calculations; see text.

A comparison of portfolio and trading characteristics for the three trader types is presented in Table 6.3. All three groups shifted money out of equities during the crisis, with active traders shifting the least (−5 percent) and first-time traders the most (−20 percent). All three had similar equity exposure before the crisis (71–72 percent), but first-time traders moved to the lowest equity position during the crisis (50 percent) versus other traders (60–61 percent), due to their larger shift out of stocks. Active traders had more complex portfolios in terms of number of funds, and they traded more frequently per month; nevertheless, when they traded, they moved a smaller fraction of their portfolios (22 percent) than did infrequent traders (36 percent) or first-time crisis traders (46 percent). Overall, active traders accounted for about two-thirds of trading volume during the entire period, versus 31 percent for infrequent traders and 5 percent for first-time traders. During the crisis, first-time crisis traders accounted for over one-quarter of all trading volume.[15]

Multivariate analysis of trading patterns

As noted above, the fraction of 401(k) traders' portfolios shifted out of equities rose by nearly a factor of eight during the crisis period. Several possible explanations for this pattern come to mind. One is a 'fear factor'

TABLE 6.3 Portfolio and trading characteristics

	Entire period (1/06–3/09)	Precrisis (1/06–8/08)	Crisis (9/08–3/09)
Net flow to equities (%)			
Active traders	−2	−1	−5
Infrequent traders	−5	−3	−12
First-time crisis traders	−20	NA	−20
All traders	−4	−2	−11
Portfolio in equities (%)			
Active traders	69	72	60
Infrequent traders	69	71	61
First-time crisis traders	66	71	50
All traders	69	71	61
Number of funds held			
Active traders	5.8	5.8	5.6
Infrequent traders	4.6	4.6	4.7
First-time crisis traders	4.1	4.1	4.0
All traders	5.3	5.4	4.9
Mean number of trades per month			
Active traders	1.2	1.2	2.4
Infrequent traders	1.0	1.0	1.6
First-time crisis traders	1.1	NA	1.1
All traders	1.1	1.1	1.8
Mean portfolio traded (%)			
Active traders	22	22	20
Infrequent traders	36	36	34
First-time crisis traders	46	NA	46
All traders	28	27	31
Dollar trading volume (%)			
Active traders	64	68	49
Infrequent traders	31	32	25
First-time crisis traders	5	NA	26
All traders	100	100	100

Note: See Tables 6.1 and 6.2 for variable definitions. Percent of portfolio trade is calculated as the sum of total inflows and outflows divided by 2 and divided by the prior month's balance. Equities include equity funds and the equity portfolio of balances funds, estimated at 60 percent of balanced fund assets.

Source: Authors' calculations.

hypothesis: that is, traders might have sold stocks due to concern over rising market volatility.[16] In other words, the crisis could have induced some to think that markets were riskier than they had previously believed, and so they responded by reducing equity exposure. From this perspective, selling equities represented adaptive learning to new knowledge about equity market 'tail risk'. A second hypothesis is a 'performance chasing' or momentum hypothesis: 401(k) traders might buy equities in response to rising markets but sell equities in falling markets. Because many 401(k) participants are arguably unsophisticated investors, they might be hypothesized to pursue a naive momentum strategy, rather than a 'buy on the dips' contrarian strategy.[17] A third hypothesis is that investors' trading patterns may be influenced by the salience of financial information.[18] In our dataset, we know the month in which participants received their account statements and so we use the delivery of paper statements as a measure of refreshed information regarding one's wealth.[19] Holding all other factors constant, receiving the quarterly statement might have reminded traders of their losses and possibly elicited a separate trading response, independent of market volatility and momentum effects.

We test these hypotheses using the following multivariate model, estimated using OLS with controls for clustering at the plan and individual levels:

$$\begin{aligned}\text{NET\_FLOW\_PCT}_{i,j,t} &= \beta_0 + \beta_1 \text{TRADING}_t + \beta_2 \text{TRADING}_t \\ &\quad \times \text{CRISIS}_t + \beta_3 \text{DEMO}_{i,t} + \beta_4 \text{PLAN}_{j,t} + \varepsilon_{i,j,t}\end{aligned} \qquad (1)$$

Here, $\text{NET\_FLOW\_PCT}_{i,j,t}$ represents the *i*th participant's fractional net flow to equities in the *j*th plan in month *t*. TRADING is a vector of variables testing our trading hypotheses. For the volatility test, we include the standard deviation of changes in the daily Standard & Poor's price index for the current month *t*. For the momentum/contrarian hypothesis, we include the spread between equity and bond returns for the current month, as well as two lagged months.[20] For the report effect, we include a control indicating whether the participant received his statement in month *t*. CRISIS refers to a dummy time variable flagging the crisis period, September 2008–March 2009. DEMO includes a vector of participant demographic controls[21] and PLAN factors represent the firm's industrial sector.[22] All regressions also incorporate the key interaction term of interest, TRADING × CRISIS, indicating the marginal effects of the controls during the crisis versus the precrisis period.[23]

Coefficient estimates of equation (1) appear in Table 6.4. The 'fear factor' hypothesis cannot be rejected, judging from increased trader sensitivity to volatility during the crisis: a 1 percent increase in monthly price volatility was associated with a 1.7 percent shift away from equities precrisis,

TABLE 6.4 Determinants of net flows to equities for 401(k) plan traders: precrisis versus crisis periods

	Mean	σ	(1) Precrisis (marginal) (1/06–8/08)	(2) Crisis (marginal) (9/08–3/09)	(3) Total crisis effect
I. Market shock test					
Equity market volatility month t (%)	1.53	1.27	−1.68***	−2.12***	−3.80***
II. Momentum/contrarian test					
Equity–bond spread month t (%)	−1.69	5.28	0.33***	−0.32***	0.01***
Equity–bond spread month t - 1	−1.80	4.60	0.53***	−1.06***	−0.53***
Equity–bond spread month t - 2	−1.25	4.34	0.37***	−0.16***	0.21***
III. Information salience test					
Report month (=1)	0.39	0.48	−0.07*	2.24***	2.16***
N			2,131,938		
R^2			0.05		

Note: The dependent variable in this ordinary least squares regression is participant net flow to equities (monthly mean value of −3.18 percent); explanatory variables are as listed, as well as a control for the crisis period. The model includes plan and participant-level controls: male indicators, age home ownership, account balance, web access, year dummies, industry sector indicator, and missing value indicator. Column 1 reports coefficients for the precrisis period; Column 2 reports additional effects for the crisis period; and Column 3 provides total effects for the crisis period.

*** indicates 1% significance level.

Source: Authors' calculations.

but the effect more than doubled to 3.8 percent during the crisis period. In standardized terms, a two standard deviation increase in month volatility would mean a shift away from equities of 4.3 percent precrisis, but a 9.7 percent shift away from equities during the crisis.

Regarding the momentum hypothesis, trader responsiveness to recent returns seemed to follow the momentum approach precrisis, but it moved to a more contrarian strategy during the crisis months. Focusing on the largest effect, a 1 percentage point rise in the prior month equity–bond spread was associated with a shift precrisis *toward* equities of 0.5 percent (Column 1), which is a momentum-based strategy; during the crisis (Column 3), the effect was contrarian, with a shift *away* from equities of 0.5 percent. As another example, consider a two standard deviation decline in the prior month equity–bond spread: precrisis, it would have meant a 4.9 percent move away from stocks, and during the crisis period, a 4.8 percent move into stocks for a 'buy on the dips' strategy.[24]

Regarding the salience of information, it would appear that quarterly statements had little impact on movements into or out of equities in the precrisis period; however, during the crisis period, the receipt of quarterly statements was associated with a separate 2 percent shift into equities. In other words, the information had a net contrarian or stabilizing effect during the crisis months when stock prices were falling, after controlling for declining stock prices and increased volatility.

Differences by trader type

Next, we consider whether experienced traders behaved differently from inexperienced ones, by incorporating TYPE, a variable indicating the individual's prior experience trading in his account. As noted above, active traders had three or more trades precrisis; infrequent traders had one to two trades precrisis; and first-time crisis traders engaged in trading for the first time during the crisis. We also include an interaction of TRADING × CRISIS with TYPE to measure marginal effects of active and first-time crisis traders:

$$\begin{aligned} \text{NET\_FLOW\_PCT}_{i,j,t} = \beta_0 &+ \beta_1 \text{TRADING}_t + \beta_2 \text{TRADING}_t \times \text{CRISIS}_t \\ &+ \beta_3 \text{TRADING}_t \times \text{CRISIS}_t \times \text{TYPE}_i \qquad (2) \\ &+ \beta_4 \text{DEMO}_{i,t} + \beta_5 \text{PLAN}_{j,t} + \varepsilon_{i,j,t} \end{aligned}$$

Table 6.5 reports results, with marginal effects in Panel A and total effects given in Panel B. Column 1 (in both panels) focuses on the precrisis period and results are virtually identical to the precrisis effects reported previously. During the crisis, active traders reacted to volatility similar to all traders precrisis; for this group, a 1 percent rise in monthly market volatility during the crisis was associated with a 1.69 percent portfolio shift away from equities. But infrequent traders and first-time crisis traders reacted much more strongly to changes in volatility during the crisis: the same 1 percent increase in volatility prompted infrequent traders to shift 4.4 percent of their portfolio out of equities (Panel B, Column 3), while first-time crisis traders shifted 6.8 percent (Panel B, Column 4). Put differently, a two standard deviation increase in volatility would be expected to induce active traders to shift 4.3 percent of their portfolios out of equities, while infrequent investors and first-time crisis traders would move 11.2 and 17.3 percent, respectively. Hence, the market volatility or 'fear factor' response seems more prevalent among the inexperienced.

In terms of the momentum test, there was a clear shift from momentum to contrarian behavior during the crisis for all three trader types based on the prior month's equity–bond spread (Panel B of Table 6.5). But first-time investors became even more contrarian than did infrequent investors, who

TABLE 6.5 Determinants of net flows to equities for 401(k) plan traders by type of trader: precrisis versus net flow to equities

	Mean	σ	(1) Precrisis (1/06–8/08)	(2) Crisis (9/08–3/09)	(3) Crisis: active traders (9/08–3/09)	(4) Crisis: first-time traders (9/08–3/09)
Panel A. Marginal effects						
I. Market shock test						
Equity market volatility month *t* (%)	1.53	1.27	−1.85***	−2.57***	2.73***	−2.37***
II. Momentum/contrarian test						
Equity–bond spread month *t* (%)	−1.69	5.28	0.32***	−0.26***	0.04*	−0.08***
Equity–bond spread month *t*–1	−1.80	4.60	0.53***	−1.23***	0.30***	−0.13***
Equity–bond spread month *t*–2	−1.25	4.34	0.36***	−0.08***	0.00	0.10***
III. Information salience test						
Report month (=1)	0.39	0.48	−0.11***	4.11***	−1.21***	−1.15***
N			2,131,938			
R^2			0.06			
Panel B. Total effects						
I. Market shock test						
Equity market volatility month *t* (%)	1.53	1.27	−1.85***	−1.69***	−4.42***	−6.80***
II. Momentum/contrarian test						
Equity–bond spread month *t* (%)	−1.69	5.28	0.32***	0.09*	0.06***	−0.03***
Equity–bond spread month *t*–1	−1.80	4.60	0.53***	−0.40***	−0.70***	−0.84***
Equity–bond spread month *t*–2	−1.25	4.34	0.36***	0.29	0.29***	0.39***
III. Information salience test						
Report month (=1)	0.39	0.48	−0.11***	2.79***	4.00***	2.85***

Continued

TABLE 6.5 Continued

	Mean	σ	(1) Precrisis (1/06–8/08)	(2) Crisis (9/08–3/09)	(3) Crisis: active traders (9/08–3/09)	(4) Crisis: first-time traders (9/08–3/09)
N			2,131,938			
R^2			0.06			

Note: See Table 6.4. The regression also includes interaction terms for the crisis, and for active and first-time traders during the crisis (infrequent traders are the reference group). The model includes plan and participant-level controls: male indicators, age, home ownership, account balance, web access, year dummies, industry sector indicator, and missing value indicator. Panel A, Column 1 reports coefficients for the precrisis period; Column 2: additional effects for the crisis period (also the additional effect for infrequent traders, the reference group); Column 3: additional effects for active traders during the crisis; and Column 4: additional effect for first-time traders during the crisis. Panel B summarizes total effects for the precrisis period and for the three types of traders in the crisis.
*** indicates 1% significance level.

Source: Authors' calculations.

in turn were more contrarian than active investors. Thus, a two standard deviation decline in the equity–bond spread during the crisis would have been associated with a 7.7 percent movement among first-time crisis investors, 6.5 percent for infrequent investors, and 3.7 percent for active traders. We also note that the information salience effect from quarterly statements was positive for all three types of investors, but for reasons that are not entirely clear, infrequent traders were the most responsive (with a 4 percent effect in Column 3, Panel B) versus active traders and first-time crisis traders (2.79 and 2.85 percent, respectively).

Conclusion

The financial crisis of 2008–9 produced some of the largest drops in stock returns and largest increases in market volatility ever experienced in the United States since the Great Crash. Although most 401(k) plan participants did not trade in response to these events over the past few years, some investment patterns did change. The number of participants trading rose, and, most notably, the fraction of portfolios shifted out of stocks increased by nearly a factor of eight, rising from 1.2 percent in the month prior to the crisis to 11.1 percent during the crisis.

Overall, the 401(k) traders examined here exhibited a rather nuanced set of behaviors during the crisis. As anticipated, there was a heightened sensitivity to market volatility, which contributed to larger sales of equities. We interpret this as an adaptive learning response, with some investors becoming aware of the true 'tail risk' associated with equities and hence reducing their holdings during the crisis. As might also be expected, this heightened sensitivity was most acute among the least experienced trading group, first-time crisis traders. These first-time traders have demographic characteristics often associated with lower levels of financial literacy, and so they might have been anticipated to respond more negatively to a sharp increase in stock market volatility. Yet at the same time, 401(k) traders became more contrarian in their response to falling markets during the crisis. Therefore, the increased sensitivity to market volatility was offset, in part, by a tendency to 'buy on the dips' in response to falling markets. What is more, first-time crisis traders were more likely to be contrarian during the crisis than active traders.

This leads to the paradoxical conclusion that 401(k) participants with characteristics typically associated with less investment experience may have overreacted to market volatility, while still in aggregate engaging in a more sophisticated contrarian strategy than their active-trading counterparts. We also found surprising the fact that those who received their quarterly account statements during the crisis tended to move *into*, rather than out of, equities during the crisis. Perhaps the provision of account information had an independent stabilizing, rather than destabilizing, effect during the financial crisis.

Overall, these patterns belie a simplistic view that 401(k) participants are, in aggregate, naïve investors who pursue momentum or return-chasing in falling markets, selling equities even to the point of liquidating their entire equity positions. It is true that the less experienced plan traders, those who may have been less financially sophisticated, did react more strongly to abnormally high stock market volatility than did experienced traders. Yet their contrarian 'buy on the dips' countervailing response to returns indicates more complex dynamics than might have been expected.

Many 401(k) plans today impose trading restrictions designed to counteract frequent market-timing behavior by active traders, yet few (if any) impose 'circuit breakers' prohibiting participants from fleeing to safety in response to market shocks, or precluding employees from piling into equities when conditions improve. This research suggests that such restrictions would be unlikely to alter behavior of many 401(k) participants, even during a period of financial upheaval such as that recently experienced by participants.

In future work, we hope to examine individual trader behavior in more detail in an effort to further disentangle momentum and contrarian trading. For example, active traders might include some performance-chasing active traders and other active traders who dynamically alter their strategy over time. People fleeing equity might comprise both inexperienced investors and more experienced individuals taking a strong contrarian approach. The deeper question remains as to why so few participants trade, either for rebalancing or other reasons, and on the prevalence of inertia among majority of 401(k) participants.

Acknowledgments

The authors thank Peter Brady, Gregory Nini, Nicholas Souleles, Mark J. Warshawsky, and seminar participants at the University of Pennsylvania for helpful comments; they are also grateful to Vanguard for the provision of recordkeeping data under restricted access conditions. For research support, they acknowledge the Pension Research Council at the Wharton School, the Bradley Foundation, and Vanguard.

Endnotes

1. DOL (2010) reports that private profit sharing and thrift plans covered over 62 million active participants as of 2008. ICI (2011) reports that 401(k) and similar DC plan assets reached $3 trillion as of September 2010. Vanguard (2010) reports that the average equity allocation of its DC plans was approximately two-thirds.
2. In our dataset, the number of participants trading per month rose from 2.23 million precrisis to 2.38 million during the turmoil period.
3. See among others, Agnew et al. (2003), Tang et al. (2010), Yamaguchi et al. (2007), and Young and Utkus (2011).
4. See Odean (1999) and Barber and Odean (2000).
5. Tang et al. (2010) also show that most 401(k) participants do not invest particularly efficiently in noncrisis times, despite having a well-designed investment menu.
6. The dataset is drawn from Vanguard's recordkeeper information under restricted access conditions.
7. The dataset only includes trading consciously conducted by the 401(k) participants. It does not include the rebalancing by portfolio managers.
8. Using zip codes of individual participants, we impute their nonretirement wealth and homeownership provided by IXI Corporation.
9. We confirm this definition by checking whether the daily S&P 500 returns are within one standard deviation of the mean and if monthly S&P 500 volatilities are within one standard deviation of volatility mean (the monthly volatility is derived from S&P 500 daily return data from January 2008 through March 2009). Over this period, the only months with more than half of daily returns and monthly volatilities outside one standard deviation are September 2008–February 2009.

10. The trading dataset is not a balanced panel; that is, while many participants are in the dataset over the entire period, we also include participants who arrived in or departed from their DC plan over the period. These individuals appear in the analysis only for months when observed. As noted in Table 6.1, the total number of participants in the sample grew by 7 percent, which includes both new entrants and well as those leaving the plan. We do not exclude new entrants or those leaving the plan in order to avoid a tenure-biased sample.
11. Equity assets include both domestic and international funds and company stocks, as well as the equity portion of balanced funds such as target date, static allocation, and traditional balanced funds (where the equity position is assumed to be 60 percent of the fund's balance). Fixed-income assets include bond funds, money-market funds, and contract funds.
12. In this chapter, we concentrate on participant-driven trading in existing balances, as these represent the bulk of retirement assets; changes in future contributions are usually tiny compared to balances.
13. Participant characteristics are collected as of September 2008.
14. First-time traders can include long-tenured participants who participated in the DC plan prior to January 2006 but simply did not trade until the crisis period; they can also include new participants entering their DC plan after January 2006 or even during the crisis period itself, and then trading in the crisis months.
15. Note that trading population varies over time and so these monthly statistics cannot be simply annualized. For instance, first-time traders on average moved 20 percent of their balance to equities during the crisis period and traded 1.1 times per month, but one cannot extrapolate this figure to infer that first-time traders sold out of equities entirely (a 20 percent per month shift over seven months) or traded eight times (1.1 over seven months). This is because even among traders, trading is infrequent, and so the composition of the trading group varies from month to month.
16. Other research on aggregate investment flows has suggested that trading volume generally rises with market volatility. See Epps and Epps (1976), Cornell (1981), and Karpoff (1987).
17. However, evidence on this point is mixed: for instance, Grinblatt and Keloharju (2001) report that Finnish households display contrarian behavior.
18. A related phenomenon is the 'ostrich effect', where investors are more likely to look at their wealth holdings online in rising markets versus falling markets (Karlsson et al., 2009).
19. Paper statements are generally sent quarterly.
20. Correlations between current month equity volatility and the spreads between equity and bond returns for the three time lags are negative in precrisis and the crisis periods, as well as over the entire period.
21. Participant control variables include indicators for male, age, tenure, home ownership, account balance, and web access. We also include year dummies. For a robustness check, we also included tenure in the regressions to check whether new entrants and leavers behaved differently; results were quantitatively similar. The same robustness check for regression (2) in the following section also produced the same coefficient pattern as without tenure.

22. Multivariate analysis below also controls for the plan's industry sector (agriculture/mining/construction; transportation/communication/utilities; manufacturing; media/entertainment/leisure; trade; finance/insurance/real estate; professional/nonprofit services; education/health; and government services).
23. Standard errors are also adjusted for heteroskedasticity due to plan clustering of participant data.
24. Effects for the current month and two-month lagged spread show a similar contrarian effect; on a net basis, however, there was a small momentum effect for the lagged spread during the crisis period.

References

Agnew, J. (2004). "An Analysis of How Individuals React to Market Returns in One 401(k) Plan", Center for Retirement Research at Boston College WP#2004-13.

——, P. Balduzzi, and A. Sunden (2003). "Portfolio Choice and Trading in a Large 401(k) Plan", *The American Economic Review*, 93(1): 193–215.

Aumann, R. (1976). "Agreeing to Disagree", *Annals of Statistics*, 4: 1236–9.

Barber, B. and T. Odean (2000). "Trading is Hazardous to your Wealth: The Common Stock Investment Performance of Individual Investors", *Journal of Finance*, 55(2): 773–806.

—— and —— (2001). "Boys Will Be Boys: Gender, Overconfidence, and Common Stock Investment", *Quarterly Journal of Economics*, 116(1): 261–92.

Bergstresser, D. and J. Poterba (2002). "Do After-Tax Returns Affect Mutual Fund Inflows?", *Journal of Financial Economics*, 63(3): 381–414.

Chai, J., W. Horneff, R. Maurer, and O. S. Mitchell (2010). "Extending Life Cycle Models of Optimal Portfolio Choice: Integrating Flexible Work, Endogenous Retirement, and Investment Decisions with Lifetime Payouts." NBER WP 15682 (January).

Cornell, B. (1981). "The Relationship between Volume and Price Variability in Futures Markets", *Journal of Futures Markets*, 1: 303–16.

Epps, T. and M. L. Epps (1976). "The Stochastic Dependence of Security Price Changes and Transaction Volumes: Implications for the Mixture-of-Distribution Hypothesis." *Econometrica*, 44: 305–21.

Grinblatt, M. and M. Keloharju (2001). "What Makes Investors Trade?", *The Journal of Finance*, 56(2): 589–616.

Horneff, W., R. Maurer, O. S. Mitchell, and M. Stamos (2009). "Asset Allocation and Location over the Life Cycle with Survival-Contingent Payouts", *Journal of Banking and Finance*, 33(9 September): 1688–99.

Investment Company Institute (ICI) (2011). *The US Retirement Market: Third Quarter 2010.* Washington, DC: Investment Company Institute.

Karlsson, N., G. Loewenstein, and D. Seppi (2009). "The Ostrich Effect: Selective Attention to Information", *Journal of Risk and Uncertainty*, 38: 95–115.

Karpoff, J. (1987). "The Relation between Price Changes and Trading Volume: A Survey", *Journal of Financial and Quantitative Analysis*, 22: 109–26.

Lusardi, A., O. S. Mitchell, and V. Curto (2010). "Financial Literacy among the Young: Evidence and Implications for Consumer Policy", *Journal of Consumer Affairs*, 44(2): 358–80.

Milgrom, P. and N. Stokey (1982). "Information, Trade, and Common Knowledge", *Journal of Economic Theory*, 26: 17–27.

Mitchell, O. S., G. Mottola, S. P. Utkus, and T. Yamaguchi (2006). "The Inattentive Participant: Portfolio Trading Behavior in 401(k) Plans", Pension Research Council Working Paper No. 2006-05. Philadelphia, PA: Pension Research Council.

Odean, T. (1998). "Are Investors Reluctant to Realize Their Losses?", *Journal of Finance*, 53: 1775–98.

—— (1999). "Do Investors Trade Too Much?", *American Economic Review*, 89(5): 1278–98.

Shefrin, H. and M. Statman (1985). "The Disposition to Sell Winners Too Early and Ride Losers too Long", *Journal of Finance*, 40: 777–90.

Sirri, E. and P. Tufano (1998). "Costly Search and Mutual Fund Flows", *The Journal of Finance*, 53(5): 1589–622.

Tang, N., O. S. Mitchell, G. Mottola, and S. P. Utkus (2010). "The Efficiency of Sponsor and Participant Portfolio Choices in 401(k) Plans", *Journal of Public Economics*, 94(11–12): 1073–85.

US Department of Labor (DOL) (2010). *Private Pension Plan Bulletin: Abstract of 2008 Form 5500 Annual Reports.* Washington, DC: Employee Benefit Security Administration, US Department of Labor.

Vanguard (2010). *How America Saves 2010: A Report on Vanguard 2009 Defined Contribution Plan Data.* Malvern, PA: Vanguard Center for Retirement Research.

Yamaguchi, T., O. S. Mitchell, G. Mottola, and S. P. Utkus (2007). "Winners and Losers: 401(k) Trading and Portfolio Performance", Pension Research Council Working Paper No. 2006-26. Philadelphia, PA: Pension Research Council.

Young, J. A. and S. P. Utkus (2011). *The Great Recession and DC Participant Behavior.* Malvern, PA: Vanguard Center for Retirement Research.

Chapter 7

Life Cycle Impacts of the Financial Crisis on Optimal Consumption—Portfolio Choices and Labor Supply

Jingjing Chai, Raimond Maurer, Olivia S. Mitchell, and Ralph Rogalla

Workers are increasingly required to invest in investment-based defined contribution (DC) accounts, and then during their golden years, draw down their pension assets in an orderly fashion. Such accounts can help augment and partially replace public pension benefits, as aging economies move toward better-funded old-age systems. Yet the recent financial crisis has raised fresh concerns regarding the extent to which workers are exposed to capital market shocks in these pension systems: for instance, in 2008, US private pension fund assets declined by one-quarter or about US$ 2.7 trillion (OECD, 2009; Whitehouse, 2010). Moreover, the subsequent economic crisis generated rising unemployment and falling labor earnings, with the unfortunate effect of reducing worker contributions to both Social Security and many private pension schemes. Indeed, the US unemployment rate of 10 percent in 2009 was double that in 2007, with similar high jobless rates elsewhere. These combined capital and labor market shocks have made it much more difficult for retirement systems to deliver anticipated old-age benefits. This chapter examines how households may be affected by the dual financial and economic crisis such as the one recently experienced.

In particular, we explore how people might react to these shocks, by adjusting their consumption–saving patterns, investment–annuitization paths, work hours, and retirement patterns. Because actual responses are both short- and long-term in nature, some of these will not be observable for several decades to come; furthermore, responses are likely to be heterogeneous. That is, some younger workers may not react much, since they have several decades to adjust before they retire, whereas workers on the verge of retirement have little time to adjust their saving, work, and portfolios to offset potential capital and labor market losses. Furthermore, Baby Boomers' reactions are likely to differ according to individuals' financial wealth and human capital levels. To investigate possible outcomes, we develop a life cycle model with optimal investment, work hours, retirement, and annuitization decisions, allowing for shifts in the investment opportunity set and labor income dynamics.

We build on two strands of literature in our analysis. One strand studies how financial market downturns influence older workers' consumption decisions and retirement behavior. Hurd and Rohwedder (2012) as well as Shapiro (2010) point out that the recent financial and economic crisis significantly affected near-retirement households, which seem to have reacted by reducing consumption and working longer. Yet Gustman et al. (2010) estimate that retirement will only be postponed by 1.5 months on average, given their simulations of a structural retirement model. Nevertheless, due to lack of data, these studies have focused primarily on older persons near retirement and their short-run responses to the recent crises. Thus, they do not explore the long-term impact of the crisis on younger age groups, nor do they evaluate consequent changes in asset allocation behavior. Our chapter examines these points as we seek to understand how different age groups may adapt along several dimensions, as they react to stock market downturns and unemployment risk.

A second relevant literature has explored household portfolio choice in a discrete time life cycle model with risky capital market returns and uninsurable labor income risk, asking how such uncertainty influences saving, consumption, and asset allocation (Cocco et al., 2005). This literature was extended by Gomes et al. (2008) to include flexible hours; subsequent work by Chai et al. (2011) also incorporated flexible retirement and Social Security, as well as the option to annuitize one's wealth. A key lesson from this research is that well-being is greatly enhanced when labor effort is adjustable. Nevertheless, these papers assumed that permanent labor income shocks and risky asset returns were independently and identically distributed over time, while there is now clear empirical evidence refuting this assumption. For instance, Guidolin and Timmerman (2008) show that expected stock market returns and volatility vary both over time and across bull–bear states. That is, in some periods, equity returns are characterized by persistently low volatility/high expected returns, whereas in other periods, they are characterized by persistently high volatility/low expected returns. Instead of focusing on stock returns, Carroll and Dunn (1997) and Storesletten et al. (2004) estimate a regime-switching model of labor market earnings; they find that the volatility of labor income increases in recessions and falls in expansions.

In what follows, we combine the labor and stock market strands by modeling both time-varying and persistent stock market and labor income processes governed by a Markov chain for the business cycle. Here, some of the time, asset returns are characterized by persistent regimes with an expansive capital market having low volatility/high expected return; in other periods, a contractionary market is characterized by high volatility/low expected returns. In addition, we model the countercyclical dynamics of risky labor income using time-varying shocks on wage rates dynamics and unemployment probabilities driven by the same regime-switching process. Such a setting allows us to explore the situation where a financial sector crisis may also produce an economic crisis (with a time lag), driving high unemployment and lower earnings. In this way, we seek to show how these simultaneous shocks alter retirement, work hours, and consumption trajectories; asset allocation patterns; and annuity purchases of younger and elder households. In addition, we can cleanly illustrate the long-term impact of the financial and economic crisis on behavior well into the future. While it is too soon to actually observe how the crisis will alter long-term behaviors, our model provides a useful set of predictions for policy purposes.

Our results indicate that some will be able to hedge adverse capital market developments they face in the crisis, not only by altering their asset allocations but also by altering their work hours and retirement ages. In particular, we find that when hit by a financial and economic crisis, households near retirement must cut their consumption both in the short-term and also over the long-term. Moreover, they will have to increase their work effort and postpone retirement. These short-term results correspond to the recent empirical findings noted above. For young cohorts, short-term effects differ from those in the long run. During the first five years after the onset of the crisis, young households will reduce work hours, saving, and equity exposure, and suffer from a drop in consumption. In the long run, however, they will work more, retire later, invest more in stocks, consume less, save more, and spend less on private annuities. These predictions illustrate the key dimensions along which economic adjustment are likely to occur, in response to the most severe recession since the Great Depression.

The framework

Labor and capital markets

We take as a starting point the presence of dual regimes in capital and labor market dynamics driven by the business cycle. Accordingly, stock returns and labor earnings are modeled as subject to a business cycle governed by a Markov chain process that, following the NBER classification, has two states: expansion and contraction. The variable s_t indicates whether at time t the economy is in a state of expansion ($s_t = 0$) or contraction ($s_t = 1$). Transition probabilities between the two business cycle (BC) states are constant over time and defined as $\pi_{i,j}^{BC} := P(s_{t+1} = j|s_t = i)$ (i.e. $\pi_{i,j}^{BC}$ denotes the probability that at time $t+1$ the economy will be in state j, given that the economy is in state i at time t). Hence, $\pi_{0,1}^{BC}$ represents the probability that state 0 (expansion) will be followed by state 1 (contraction). The unconditional probability for state expansion ($s_t = 0$) is given by $(1 - \pi_{0,0}^{BC})/(2 - \pi_{0,0}^{BC} - \pi_{1,1}^{BC})$ and for contraction ($s_t = 1$) by $(1 - \pi_{1,1}^{BC})/(2 - \pi_{0,0}^{BC} - \pi_{1,1}^{BC})$, respectively. In what follows, we assume that investors can observe s_t and know the state transition probabilities $\pi_{i,j}^{BC}$ at time t.

Next, we characterize what we mean by regime shifts in the labor income process, allowing for unemployment risk and state-dependent wage rate dynamics. The worker faces a risk of being unemployed in the period $[t, t+1]$, where the probability of unemployment π_s^U is state-dependent and specified as:

$$\pi_s^U := (\pi_{[t,t+1]}^U | s_t = i) = \begin{cases} \pi_i^U & \text{with probability} \; \pi_{i,j}^{BC} \\ \pi_j^U & \phantom{\text{with probability}} \; \pi_{i,i}^{BC} \end{cases}$$

The unemployment probability is lower in expansionary than in contractionary times (i.e. $\pi_0^U < \pi_1^U$). At time t, the worker must decide what fraction of time ($1-L_t$) to devote to employment. L_t stands for leisure and is measured as a percentage of available time. In each period, if the individual is not unemployed, he receives an after-tax disposable labor income of

$$Y_{s,t+1}^E = (1 - q_{t+1})(1 - t^1) \times WR_{s,t+1}(1 - L_t) \tag{1}$$

at time $t+1$, where q_{t+1} is the age-dependent deterministic tax-deductible fraction of labor income spent on housing and other durable goods, t^1 is a proportional tax rate on labor income, and $WR_{s_t,t+1}$ is the state-dependent wage rate at time $t+1$ (i.e. the income per hour of work effort). The wage rate dynamic process consists of three components as follows:

$$WR_{s,t+1} = \exp(w_{t+1}) E_{s,t+1} U_{t+1} \tag{2}$$

Here, w_{t+1} is a deterministic age-dependent function of wage rates that allows us to capture the shape of various empirically observed earnings profiles,[1] and U_{t+1} is a state-independent transitory income shock whose logarithm is independent and identically distributed (i.i.d.), normally distributed with mean zero and standard deviation σ_U. In addition, $E_{s,t+1} = E_{s,t} n_{s,t+1}$ is a permanent labor earnings component. The logarithm of the permanent income shock $n_{s,t+1}$ is drawn from a Gaussian mixture distribution, with mean zero and standard deviation $\sigma_{n,s}$ changing across the two phases of the business cycle. Formally:

$$\ln(n_{s,t+1}) := \left(\ln(n_{t+1})|s_t = i\right) \sim \begin{cases} N(0, \sigma_{n,i}) \\ N(0, \sigma_{n,j}) \end{cases} \text{with probability} \begin{matrix} \pi^{BC}_{i,i} \\ \pi^{BC}_{i,j} \end{matrix}.$$

To capture countercyclical labor income risk, we set $\sigma_{n,0} < \sigma_{n,1}$ such that the volatility in an expansion ($s_t = 0$) is lower than in a contractionary period ($s_t = 1$).[2] We also allow for unemployment compensation payments at time $t+1$ worth a specific fraction $\upsilon \in (0;1)$ of labor income (i.e. $Y^U_{s,t+1} = \upsilon \times Y^E_{s,t+1}$).

In later life, we take the US Social Security system into account and allow for a flexible retirement age. According to Social Security Administration (SSA) rules, the worker may elect to claim Social Security benefits in the window [62, 70] bounded by the 'early' retirement age (*ERA*) and the late retirement age (*LRA*). The actual normal retirement age (*NRA*) is set for this chapter at age 65. If the worker claims prior to the NRA, he receives a permanently reduced benefit. Otherwise, the Social Security benefit is increased by the delayed retirement credit. To capture this feature, we calculate the after-tax Social Security benefits as in Chai et al. (2011):

$$Y_t = (1 - q_t)(1 - t^r)\left[\sum_{t=1}^{K}(1 - \bar{L})\exp(w(t))/\text{k}\right]E_K\zeta F_{\tau,\text{NRA}} \tag{3}$$

where $F_{\tau,\text{NRA}} = \exp(-g_1(\text{NRA} - \tau))I_{(\tau \leq \text{NRA})} + \exp(-g_2(\text{NRA} - \tau))I_{(\tau > \text{NRA})}$. Here, we assume that when people claim retirement benefits they also consume full leisure simultaneously (as in Chai et al., 2011).[3] In this way, τ is the endogenous retirement age and ζ is the Social Security replacement rate based on lifetime average earnings, and $1 - \bar{L}$ stands for the average fraction of available time worked during the work life. The worker's average lifetime earnings level is approximated by $\sum_{t=1}^{K}(1 - \bar{L})\exp(w(t))/KE_K$, where K denotes when the individual attains her normal retirement age under the Social Security rules (NRA). Retirement benefits are taxed at a rate t^r. I is an indicator function identifying whether the individual retires at/prior to the NRA, or later. $F_{\tau,\text{NRA}}$ is a factor which depends on the NRA and the endogenous retirement age τ. g_1 and g_2 are positive constants.

Capital markets include two liquid assets—riskless bonds and risky stocks—and illiquid deferred and immediate fixed payout life annuities. The real bond gross return R_f is state-independent and constant over time, while there is a time-varying investment opportunity set in the stock market. Given a specific state $s_t = i$ at time t, the risky real log-return on stocks $\ln(R_{s,t+1})$ over the period $[t, t+1]$ is drawn from Gaussian mixture distribution with state-dependent mean μ_s and standard deviation σ_s, formally:

$$\ln(R_{s,t+1}) := \left(\ln(R_{[t,t+1]})|s_t = i\right) \sim \begin{cases} N(\mu_i, \sigma_i) \\ N(\mu_j, \sigma_j) \end{cases} \text{with probability } \begin{matrix} \pi^{BC}_{i,i} \\ \pi^{BC}_{i,j} \end{matrix}. \quad (4)$$

Each period, investors can observe the state of the economy at time t, but the actual probability distribution of returns on stock investments in each period depends on the (unknown) state of the economy at time $t+1$. The (state-dependent) correlation between shocks to permanent earnings and stock market returns is denoted by ϕ_s.

In addition to stocks and bonds, the investor can, prior to the NRA, purchase fixed payout deferred annuities that provide lifelong payments commencing at the NRA. From that point onward, she can purchase additional immediate life annuities. Annuity prices are calculated based on actuarial principles. For a deferred life annuity paying yearly benefits of one from NRA on, the premium is calculated as

$$h_t = (1+\delta)\left(\prod_{u=t}^{NRA-2} p^a_u\right) R_f^{-(NRA-1-t)} \sum_{m=1}^{T-NRA} \left(\prod_{u=K-1}^{NRA-1+m} p^a_u\right) R_f^{-m}, t < NRA \quad (5)$$

where p^a_u are the survival probabilities based on the insurer's annuitant mortality table and δ is the expense loading factor. Accordingly, the premium for an additional immediate life annuity purchased after the NRA is given by

$$h_t = (1+\delta) \sum_{m=1}^{T-1} \left(\prod_{u=t}^{t+m} p^a_u\right) R_f^{-m}, t \geq NRA \quad (6)$$

To account for adverse selection, the survival probabilities p^a_u used in pricing the annuities are typically higher than those of the overall population.

The consumer's life cycle problem

To explore how households might respond to these financial/economic and individual crises, we integrate the decisions to optimally select consumption and saving, asset allocation, work effort and retirement age, and annuitization paths over the life cycle. We posit that our individual faces an uncertain life span and can live for a maximum of T years. Her preferences are characterized by a time-additive CRRA utility function $u(C_t, L_t) = [1/(1-\rho)](C_t L_t^{\alpha})^{1-\rho}$ defined over the level of nondurable consumption C_t and leisure L_t at time t. After retirement, work hours are equal to 0 and leisure is equal to 1. The value function is given by

$$V_t = \frac{(C_t L_t^{\alpha})^{1-\rho}}{1-\rho} + \beta E_t(p_t^p V_{t+1}) \tag{7}$$

with terminal utility $V_T = (C_T L_T^{\alpha})^{1-\rho}/(1-\rho)$. The parameter p_t^p denotes the subjective probability of surviving to time $t + 1$, given the consumer is alive at t. The parameter ρ is the coefficient of relative risk aversion, and $\beta < 1$ is the time preference. Leisure preferences are governed by the parameter α.

Each period, the consumer decides how to allocate her cash on hand W_t to bonds B_t, stocks S_t, annuity purchases A_t, and consumption C_t. Her budget constraint is therefore:

$$W_t = S_t + B_t + A_t + C_t \tag{8}$$

and next period's wealth $W_t + 1$ is given by

$$W_{t+1} = \begin{cases} (S_t R_{s,t+1} + B_t R_f)(1-t^c) + t^c(B_t + S_t) + Y_{t+1} & t < NRA \\ (S_t R_{s,t+1} + B_t R_f)(1-t^c) + t^c(B_t + S_t) + P_{t+1} + Y_{t+1} & t \geq NRA. \end{cases} \tag{9}$$

Here, P_{t+1} is the sum of annuity income received from any previously purchased annuities. Before retirement, Y_{t+1} represents labor income, and afterwards, it represents Social Security benefits. The recursive evolution equation for the sum of after-tax payout claims at time t from all previous annuities purchased can be written as:[4]

$$P_{t+1}^{\geq NRA} = \left[P_t + \frac{A_t}{h_t}\right] \frac{(R_f - 1)(1 - t^c) + 1}{R_f}$$

where A_t/h_t refers to the additional annuity payment purchased in t.[5] We prevent households from borrowing against human capital and from selling annuities. These restrictions are binding, because otherwise households would engage in highly leveraged stock positions financed by short positions in bonds and/or annuities in order to compensate for their overinvestment in human capital when young. Thus, in every year, the optimal policy has to satisfy $C_t, S_t, B_t, A_t \geq 0$. Moreover, we posit that in order to participate in the stock market, the household has to be willing and able to invest a minimum amount in stocks (as in Smetters and Chen, 2010). This amount is set to 10 percent of the permanent labor income after taxes and housing expenditures.

The individual's optimization problem is now to maximize utility as in equation (7) with respect to her asset allocation between liquid bonds and stocks, illiquid annuities, consumption, work hours, and the retirement decision:

$$\max_{C_t, L_t, S_t, B_t, A_t, \tau \in [62,63,\ldots,70]} V_t \tag{10}$$

Assuming that the consumer knows about the regimes governing the business cycle, there are six state variables: cash on hand W_t, annuity payouts from previously purchased annuities P_t, the permanent labor earnings level E_t, retirement age τ, the business cycle state s, and age t. To reduce the problem by one state variable, we normalize the continuous state variables cash on hand with the permanent labor earnings component. Next, we discretize the (normalized) continuous state variables and solve the optimization problem by backward induction.[6]

Model calibration

For the base case, preference parameters are set to standard values in the life cycle literature: the coefficient of relative risk aversion is $\rho = 5$ and the discount factor $\beta = 0.97$. The leisure preference value α is set to 1.3. As shown in Chai et al. (2011), this set of preference parameters is able to reproduce central empirical facts, including the hump-shaped pattern of work hours, the two peaks in retirement rates, the sizeable decline in consumption at retirement, and low annuity take-ups of older households. The one-period survival rates p_t^p entering the utility function are taken from the US 1996 RP-2000 population tables for females; the life span is modeled from age 20 to 100 ($T = 81$). To estimate the business cycle transition matrix, we take US Gross National Product (GNP) growth from the Bureau of Economic Analysis (BEA) for 1929–2006 with Datastream data for the years 2007–8.[7] A contraction (expansion) state occurs when the GNP growth rate was less than (greater than) its sample period mean (as in Storesletten et al., 2004). In this way, we estimate the transition matrix to be of the following form: $\begin{bmatrix} 0.68 & 0.32 \\ 0.32 & 0.68 \end{bmatrix}$.[8] A process with such a transition matrix is more likely to stay in the same state, rather than to move to the other state, since probabilities $p_{1,1}$ and $p_{0,0}$ are greater than 0.5. The deterministic component of the wage rate process follows Fehr et al. (2006), reflecting middle-income households, and it is scaled to generate an average gross labor income of \$20,000 at age 20. In what follows, we assume an available time of 100 waking hours per week and set the minimum leisure time to $L_{\min} = 1/3$; in other words, the maximal labor supply is two-thirds of available time. The average labor supply $1 - \bar{L}$ used to calculate Social Security benefits is equal to 0.4, which corresponds with an average lifetime work effort of 40 hours per week.

We follow Storesletten et al. (2004) and set the cyclical dynamic labor market risk $\sigma_{n,0}(\sigma_{n,1})$ to 8.4 percent (15.9 percent) and the corresponding volatility of the transitory shock σ_u to 32.9 percent.[9] The unemployment probability in expansion (contraction) periods $\pi_0^U (\pi_1^U)$ is set to 5 percent (10 percent). The parameter for unemployment compensation payments is set to υ = 60 percent. The Social Security benefit structure is similar to that in effect in the United States. The benefit replacement rate ζ is set to 0.52 (as per Mitchell and Phillips, 2006); the actuarial reduction rate for early retirement benefits is g_1 = 0.0713; the delayed retirement crediting rate is g_2 = 0.077; and the normal retirement age is 65, as in Buchinsky et al. (2000) and Chai et al. (2011). Social Security benefits are taxed at a rate of 15 percent as in Gomes et al. (2008).[10] Housing-related expenditures q_t are modeled, as in Gomes and Michaelides (2005).

The annual real value-weighted market index portfolio returns on the NYSE, AMEX, and NASDAQ (from CRSP) from 1950 to 2008[11] are classified into two states which are identified by the GNP growth rate. Then the regime-dependent parameters specifying the normal distribution of log gross return are given as follows: μ_0 = 6.84 percent, σ_0 = 11.21 percent, μ_1 = 2.12 percent, and σ_1 = 20.77 percent,[12,13] equivalent to a yearly expected gross real return of 1.0775 and standard deviation of 12.12 percent in the expansion period, and 1.0437 and 21.91 percent in the contraction phase. Here, the expansion–contraction economy tends to coincide with a low/high-volatility, high/low-mean regime in the stock market. This evidence is also be found in Gordon and St-Amour (2000), Ang and Bekaert (2002), Kim and Lee (2007) and Guidolin and Timmermann (2008). The correlation between stock returns and permanent and transitory earnings shocks ϕ for both cases is set to zero, consistent with empirical evidence provided by Cocco et al. (2005). The real riskless gross return for bond investments is R_f = 1.02. To price the life annuities, future benefits are discounted with the riskless return. The conditional survival probabilities p_t^a are taken from the US 1996 female annuitant RP-2000 mortality table to account for potential adverse selection in the voluntary annuity market. The expense loading factor δ is set to 2.38 percent, a number in line with industry leaders such as Vanguard. Returns on assets are assumed to be taxed at 20 percent; labor earnings are taxed at 30 percent following Gomes et al. (2008).

For the average household aged 55, we estimate a wealth-to-income ratio of 9, which approximately represents the median of the wealth distribution. To this end, we draw on wealth data from Gustman et al. (2010), and income data from the SSA. Specifically, we employed the distribution of assets by wealth deciles in 2006 for households with at least one member born from 1948 to 1953, defining wealth as total wealth net of Social Security and defined benefit pension wealth. To estimate median labor income for households aged 55, we use SSA data on the median income of nonmarried persons aged 65–69 in the year 2006. We match labor income profiles estimated by Storesletten et al. (2004) to this income data and calculate the income at age 55 based on those profiles. Moreover, we assume that households aged 55 have not yet purchased any annuities.

Results

Having solved the life cycle problem for the optimal policies (consumption, asset allocation, work hours, saving, and retirement behavior), next we evaluate the distribution of decision variables based on a Monte Carlo simulation of 100,000 life cycle trajectories, differentiating between two general economic and financial scenarios: crisis and normalcy.

Identifying the tails of the financial/economic distribution

Here, we characterize a *financial/economic crisis* as one where the economy is in the contraction state for four years in a row, and in addition, in the first year the stock return is a −30 percent. By contrast, a *normal* financial and economic environment, which we treat as the baseline scenario, is defined as one in which no additional exogenous restrictions are imposed on the state of the business cycle or the stock market performance. Hence, the initial state of the business cycle is determined by the (unconditional) long-run state probabilities and the states in subsequent periods by the conditional state transition probabilities, while stock market returns are governed by the business cycle, state-specific distributions as described above.

In addition to this general analysis using the whole simulation sample, we are also keenly interested in the distributional tails. We examine these by analyzing subsamples of those 100,000 life cycles, as not all households may be affected similarly by the business cycle; some perform exceptionally well, while others who experience unemployment and persistent wage shocks fare far worse. Accordingly, we stipulate that an individual suffers from a '*triple whammy*' if he/she experiences a financial/economic crisis at the beginning of the analysis, is unemployed in at least two of the first four years thereafter, and also suffers from below-first-quartile cumulated stock market returns until age 62, when he becomes eligible for Social Security benefits. By contrast, we define a *doubly fortunate* individual as someone that never experiences a financial/economic crisis, is never unemployed to age 62, and experiences above-average capital market returns to age 62 with cumulated stock returns in the top 25 percentile.

In what follows, we differentiate between the short- and long-term effects of the financial/economic crisis on households' behavior and well-being. While short-term effects can be studied using already available empirical data, sample data on the crisis' long-term effects will obviously not be available for several decades. For this reason, model simulations are the only way to make predictions about what future outcomes might be. Of particular interest in this context is how different cohorts are influenced by, and react to, the economic/financial crisis. While over the short run both younger and elder cohorts could be substantially affected by the crisis, due to their longer remaining period of economic activity, younger people might suffer less in the long run than do elder generations. To explore this outcome, we conduct our analyses for households that are hit by a financial/economic crisis at ages 20 and 55. For the cohort aged 20 (55), out of the 100,000 sample paths, we identify 933 (979) that qualify for the *double fortune* scenario and 1,321 (1,355) that comply with the *triple whammy* scenario.

Short-term effects

We next turn our attention to the impacts of and the reaction to an economic/financial crisis over the short run, which in this study we define to cover a period of a decade. Figures 7.1 and 7.2 depict the effects for households initially aged 20 or 55 on key decision variables: expected work hours (Panel A), consumption (Panel B), saving/withdrawal (i.e. labor income/Social Security benefits after taxes and housing expenditures minus consumption, Panel C), and stock investment (Panel D). Here, the solid black line presents absolute values for the normal scenario (left axis), while the bars show relative deviations from the base case results for three alternative scenarios: crisis (black), double fortune (pattern), and triple whammy (white) on the right axis.

Short-term effects for the younger cohort

In the base case scenario, the work effort of a young individual exceeds 40 hours per week, with average work effort starting at 47 hours per week at age 20 and then rising further to above 51 hours in the mid-20s (Figure 7.1, Panel A). Long and rising work hours, combined with a wage rate increasing with age and experience, generate high and rising labor income. This allows the individual to increase consumption from $9,000 at age 20 to about $14,000 in the mid-20s (Panel B). At the same time, periodic savings more than double from $1,600 to about $3,700 (Panel C). At age 20, the household will on average invest about 65 percent of liquid funds accumulated in stocks and increase this fraction over the following six years to almost 100 percent (Panel D). The young household seeks high stock fractions due to the rather bond-like nature of labor income. Yet the minimum required investment amount for participating in the stock market results in stock fractions falling short of 100 percent early in the life cycle, as sufficient funds must first be accumulated. Once a sufficient amount of liquid assets has been saved, the investor then maximizes equity exposure. With wage rates increasing even further and invested funds starting to generate measurable returns, the individual can afford to enjoy more leisure by already slightly reducing work hours in his late 20s, initiating the oft-cited hump shape in work effort. Both consumption and periodic saving increase further to about $17,400 and $4,100 by age 30.

When we compare this baseline to a young household experiencing a financial and economic crisis at age 20, work effort proves to be virtually identical as a result of two offsetting effects. The crisis lowers wage rates resulting from higher unemployment probabilities, leaving the individual less inclined to work and more likely to consume leisure (by the substitution effect). Yet, lower income provides less consumption opportunity, which induces greater work effort (by the income effect). As work effort does not rise beyond base case, the individual compensates for his income drop by reducing both consumption and saving. Moreover, these reductions persist over the next decade even if the economy eventually recovers; consumption drops by 2 percent and periodic saving by 2–3 percent compared to the normal scenario. Not yet having accumulated financial assets, the young individual does not suffer from the 30 percent downturn in the stock market at the beginning of the financial and economic crisis, so his stock holdings are hardly affected, only dropping slightly (2.5 percent) in the first two years.

By comparison, a young worker hit by a *triple whammy* will substantially reduce work effort. His hours worked per week drop by almost 10 percent in the first two years, compared to the base case, after which they slowly rise again. The corresponding drop in income drives a consumption decline of about 15 percent over the first four years. Periodic saving is even more affected, dropping by more than 60 percent for a worker in his early 20s. Having so few liquid assets, the worker cannot afford to participate in the stock market, and overall stock fractions drop by 10–20 percent during the first five years (from a low base). After four years' time, as the initial crisis wanes, the individual strives to recover by increasing work effort above that in the base case over the second half of the decade. While consumption again converges toward the base case level, even at age 30, it remains about 2 percent less than in the normal scenario. At the same time, the household seeks to replenish accumulated funds by saving between 10 and 20 percent more than the baseline investor from the mid- through late-20s. Once sufficient funds have been built up again, the household can then afford to invest in equities, and stock holdings converge to those in the normal scenario from the mid-20s.

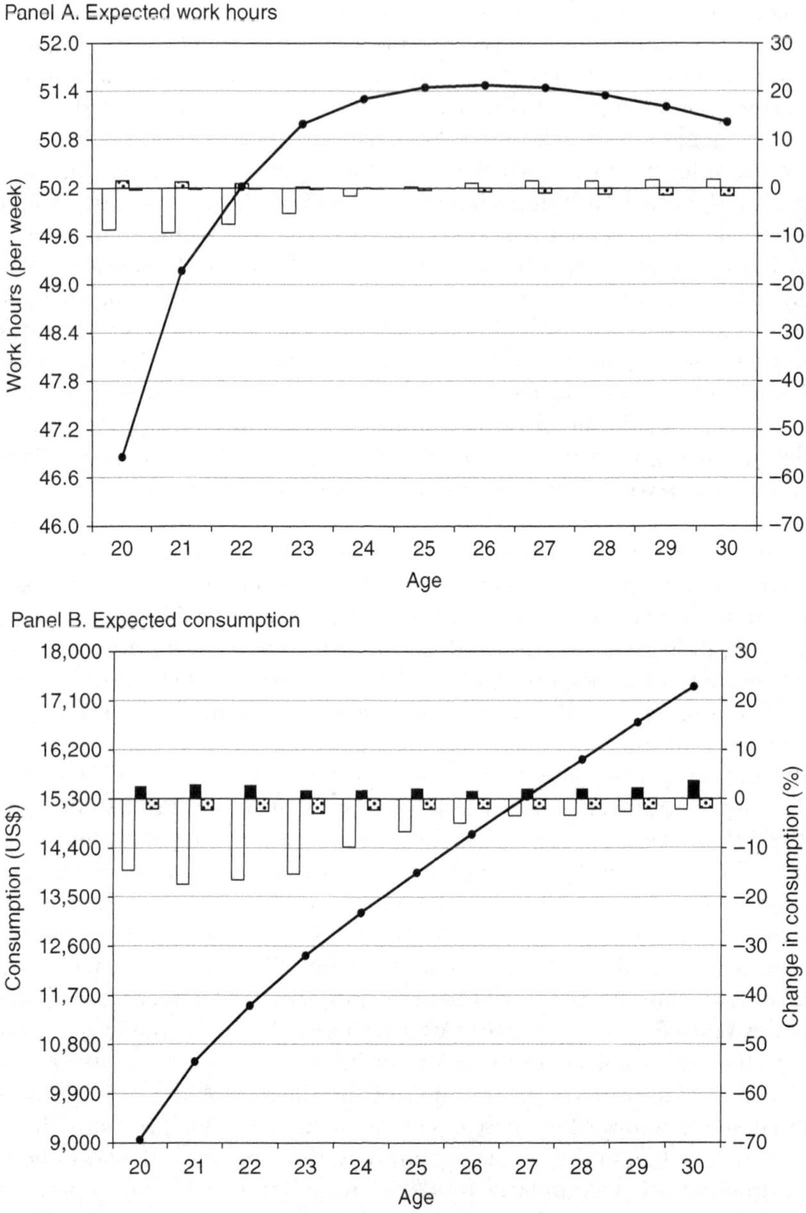

Figure 7.1 Short-term effects of financial/economic crises on young cohort (age 20). Panel (A): expected work hours; Panel (B): expected consumption; Panel (C): expected saving/withdrawal; Panel (D): expected stock investment

Notes: Panel C: labor income/Social Security benefits after taxes and housing expenditures minus consumption. Solid black line (left axis): absolute values under normal scenario. Bars (right axis): relative deviations from normal case for alternative scenarios: crisis (black), double fortune (pattern), triple whammy (white).

Source: Authors' calculations.

Panel C. Expected saving/withdrawal

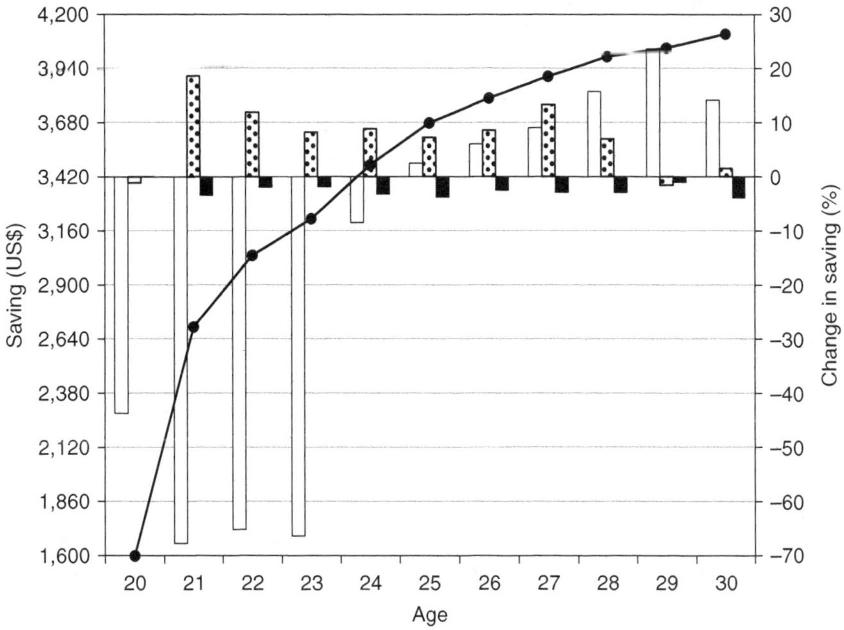

Panel D. Expected stock investment

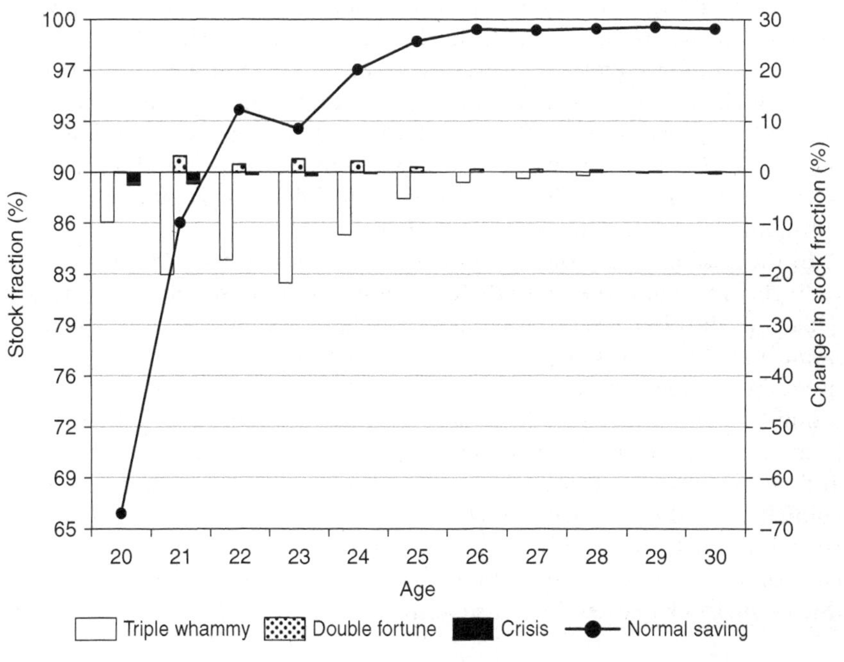

Finally, the *doubly fortunate* are even inclined to work slightly more in the early 20s than our baseline households, which enables them to consume about 2–3 percent more; this is the result of never being unemployed and not confronting a financial/economic crisis. Additionally, these individuals save substantially more, which increases their ability to early invest in stocks. With above-average labor income and capital market performance, they can reduce their work effort even more than the baseline households in their late 20s, while still being able to afford 2–3 percent higher consumption.

Short-term effects for the near-retirement cohort

Next, we turn to our attention to the cohort looking ahead to retirement, initially age 55. In the baseline scenario, people reduce their work effort into their late 50s and early 60s, following the conventional hump-shape work pattern. At age 55, on average, they still engage in near full-time employment, but work hours per week gradually taper to 20 by age 65 (Figure 7.2, Panel A). As in the case of the younger cohorts, older people who experience the financial/economic crisis maintain a virtually identical work effort path.

The picture changes, however, when looking at households hit by the triple whammy. The near-retirement cohort—with a shorter period of economic activity remaining—must compensate for reductions in wage rates and wealth by immediately increasing work hours. (It will be recalled that the younger cohort can work less, counting on a longer time horizon over which it can recover income losses.) Consequently, older persons' work effort rises by around 10 percent relative to the base case, and in their 60s, the difference is greater, about 25 percent. Sensibly, the doubly fortunate workers cash in on their luck in both the labor and capital markets by substantially reducing work effort sooner.

In the base case, the older cohort consumes about $30,000 per year on average, or two to three times the consumption of households in their 20s. This consumption level is financed, to a large extent, by drawing down liquid financial assets (Figure 7.2, Panels B and C). Those older persons beset by a financial/economic crisis reduce annual consumption by around 4 percent per year from age 55 to 65, and annual withdrawals fall by about 2–3 percent. Those hit by a triple whammy experience substantial and persistent reductions in annual consumption of about 10 percent compared to the base case. Early in the crisis, workers seek to maintain consumption by withdrawing almost 30 percent more from liquid assets, compared to the base case. As financial wealth was already heavily battered due to the stock market downturn at the beginning of the crisis, these high withdrawals can only be maintained over a short period. Subsequently, withdrawals must be reduced by 30 percent more than the base case between the late 50s and mid-60s. Consumption can only be maintained by substantially increasing work effort.

In our base case, as is typical in life cycle models, the fraction of financial wealth invested in stocks, around 80 percent in the mid-50s, is below that early in working life, but it slightly increases again toward retirement age as the worker's exposure to labor market shocks declines. Given a financial/economic crisis, equity exposure falls short of the base case value by over 20 percent during the first four years; thereafter, after the initial crisis is over, stock fractions again converge. For those hit by the triple whammy, the change in the stock fraction compared to the base case traces out an S-shape. Early in the crisis, stock allocations drop by about 10 percent, but from the late 50s it exceeds that of base case households by about 10 percent. Anticipating a high probability of poor stock market performance in the following period, the household is less inclined to hold equities over the first years of the crisis. Later, the remaining low financial wealth provides incentives to gamble and invest more in the stock market. Finally, doubly fortunate workers have persistently lower stock fractions over the entire period under scrutiny. Having accumulated high financial wealth allows the household to invest more conservatively.

In sum, for both younger and older cohorts, the financial/economic crisis has hardly any short-term impact on work effort on average. But a subset of people fares far worse, including near-retirees hit by a triple whammy who face a hostile labor market environment and also suffer substantial losses in financial wealth. Since they only have a few work years available to adjust to these shocks, they must immediately and significantly increase their work effort after being unemployed. By contrast, those hit at the beginning of their work lives must optimally reduce work hours in the less favorable labor market environment. The same conclusion holds for consumption on average: the impact of the financial/economic crisis is comparable for younger versus older cohorts. Yet, older households hit by the triple whammy experience persistent consumption shortfalls, which are mitigated for the younger cohort where consumption converges to the base case level in time. The same holds for saving at young ages and withdrawals near retirement. And most striking is the difference in household allocations to stocks. Near-retirees have already accumulated financial wealth, and hence are more vulnerable to equity fluctuations, while the young have accumulated little in the way of financial assets. For this reason, the financial/economic crisis has little impact on the young, but near-retirees will optimally cut their equity exposure by over 20 percent during the crisis. This depends on the

Panel A. Expected work hours

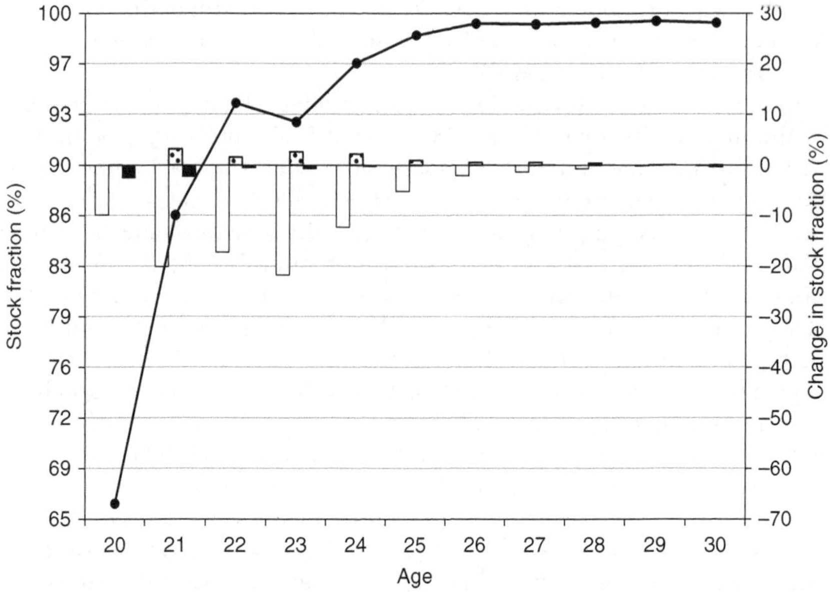

Panel B. Expected consumption

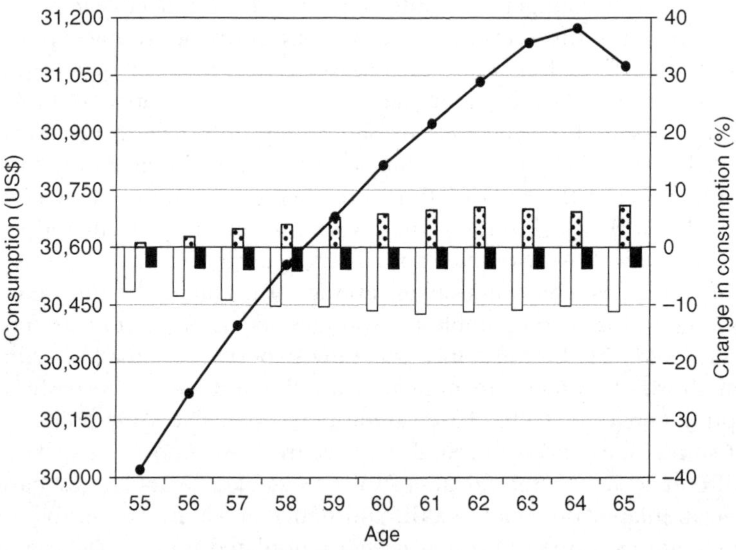

Figure 7.2 Short-term effects of financial/economic crises on near-retirement cohort (age 55). Panel (A): expected work hours; Panel (B): expected consumption; Panel (C): expected saving/withdrawal; Panel (D): expected stock investment

Notes: Panel (C): labor income/Social Security benefits after taxes and housing expenditures minus consumption. Solid black line (left axis): absolute values under normal scenario. Bars (right axis): relative deviations from normal case for alternative scenarios: crisis (black), double fortune (pattern), triple whammy (white).

Source: Authors' calculations.

Panel C. Expected saving/withdrawal

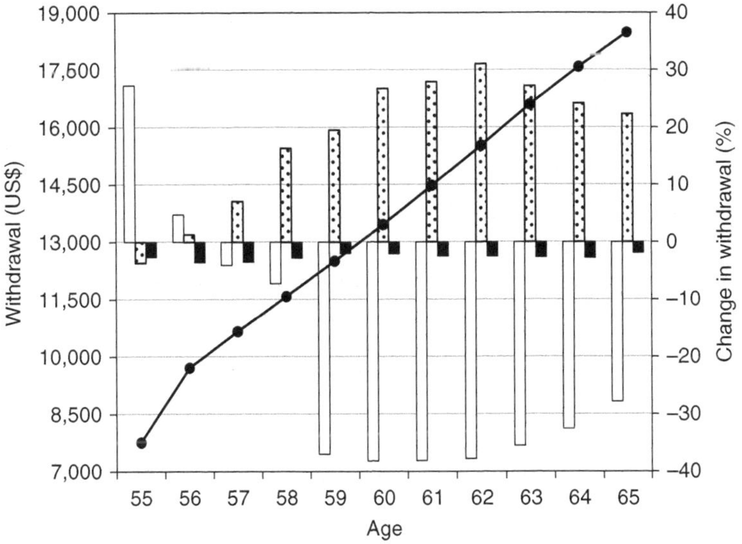

Panel D. Expected stock investment

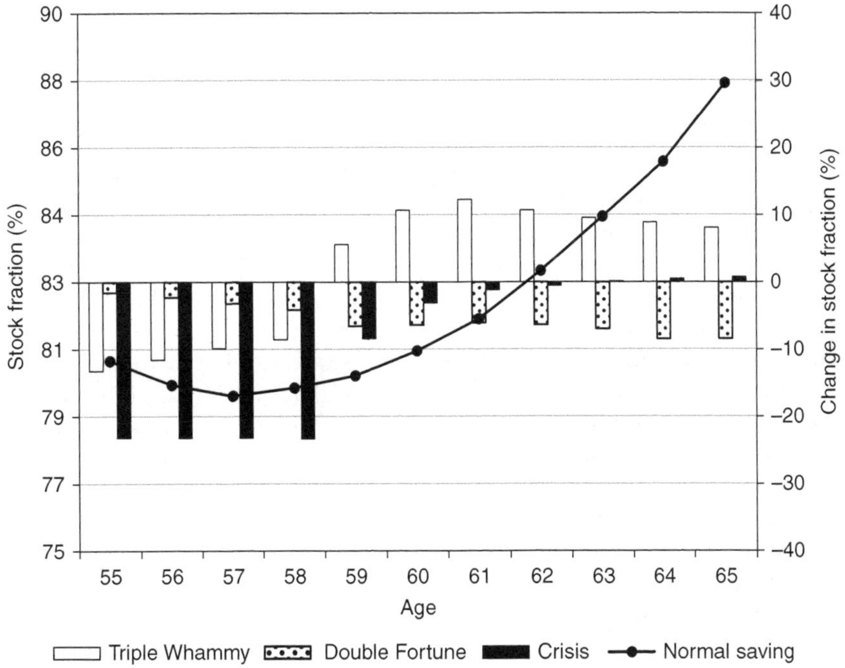

nature of the shock, however, since near-retirees hit by the triple whammy will invest more in stock, hoping to hit high returns.

Long-term effects

Next, we turn our attention to the impacts of and the reaction to an economic/financial crisis in the long run (i.e. over the remaining lifecycle). Findings are presented in Figures 7.3 and 7.4 and Tables 7.1–7.4. Figure 7.3 depicts expected work hours (Panel A), consumption (Panel B), and saving/withdrawal (i.e. labor income/Social Security benefits after taxes and housing expenditures minus consumption, Panel C) for the younger cohort. Again, the black line presents absolute values for the baseline or normal scenario (left axis), while the bars show relative deviations from the base case for the alternative scenarios (right axis): crisis (black), double fortune (pattern), and triple whammy (white). Panel C distinguishes between saving (solid black line) and withdrawal (i.e. negative saving dashed black line). Figure 7.4 presents consumption (Panel A) and withdrawal (Panel B) for the near-retirement cohort. Work hours for this cohort are omitted as households in this cohort will all have retired over the longer run. Tables 7.1 and 7.2 show retirement behavior for both cohorts and Tables 7.3 and 7.4 present their long-term asset allocations.

Long-term effects for the younger cohort

Looking at the cohort of persons first experiencing a shock at age 20, it is clear that patterns that already emerged in the later years of our short-term analysis of work effort continue to persist over the longer run (Figure 7.3, Panel A). Our base case household in a normal scenario will gradually reduce weekly work hours from about 50 at age 30, to around 25 by age 60. As in the short-term case, the long-term effects of the financial/economic crisis on work effort are negligible. By contrast, doubly fortunate households reduce their level of work effort below that of base case households, by about 10 percent at age 45, and 20 percent at age 55. Those hit by the triple whammy, however, must boost work hours substantially compared to the base case, by about 10 percent at age 50, and 20 percent at age 60. Hence, work effort at these ages is still as high as that of base case households that are five years younger.

Turning to lifetime effects on consumption (Panel B, Figure 7.3), we find that under the normal scenario, consumption grows to age 60 and peaks at an annual $30,500. Subsequently, households start to retire and substitute less goods consumption with more leisure time consumption.[14] Doubly fortunate households can substantially increase their consumption level relative to the normal scenario, by 17 percent during their 70s and still by 15 percent at age 90. Crisis households, however, experience a persistent consumption reduction of 2 percent, and those going through a triple whammy have 3 percent shortfalls over their work lives. Though the latter are surely financially worse off, due to poor capital market performance, they can maintain much of their consumption by working more. Later in life, however, they lose this flexibility and hence suffer from higher consumption shortfalls, of around 10 percent at age 70.

Wealth patterns are also different. Base case households continue to build up financial wealth until their 40s (Figure 7.3, Panel C); from their 50s onward, they begin drawing down assets to pay for high and still increasing consumption while already reducing work effort. Apparently, as consumption reaches its peak at age 60, so do withdrawals with a maximum value of $12,500 per annum. A worker who started his work life crisis will save about 4 percent less than base case households by age 30; over the next decade, he must boost saving to ensure sufficient financial reserves for the withdrawal phase, so by age 40, saving exceeds that of base case households by about 5 percent. Later in the life cycle, withdrawals are similar to the normal scenario. Doubly fortunate households can afford to save less and withdraw more than the base case household due to their above-average labor and capital market performance. For those experiencing the triple whammy, obviously, the opposite is true and they have to save more and invest less.

Table 7.1 depicts how the younger cohort allocates financial wealth to liquid stocks and bonds, as well as to illiquid life annuities over the life cycle. First, in the normal scenario, we see a typical stock fraction path over the life cycle. The young household is almost fully invested in stocks by age 30, and over time he reduces equity exposure near retirement to well below 80 percent. Initially, stocks are substituted by bonds which make up about 20 percent of the portfolio by age 50. As the survival credit and, hence, the excess return of annuities over bonds increases with household age, annuities start to crowd out bonds, making up about 14 percent of the portfolio by age 70. At older ages, the individual gradually depletes his liquid financial wealth and lowers his stock fraction to 34 percent by age 80; the share of annuities in the allocation of overall financial wealth increases to about half. Even at age 80, the investor optimally holds over 16 percent of financial wealth in bonds, despite the fact that annuities substantially outperform liquid bond holdings. The reason is that, as liquid assets are consumed, it becomes more and more difficult for the household to meet the minimum requirement on stock investments. Accordingly, bonds increasingly represent the only sensible liquid asset held by the household.

Comparing the crisis setting to our base case scenario, we find hardly any differences, indicating that the long-term effects of the crisis on workers'

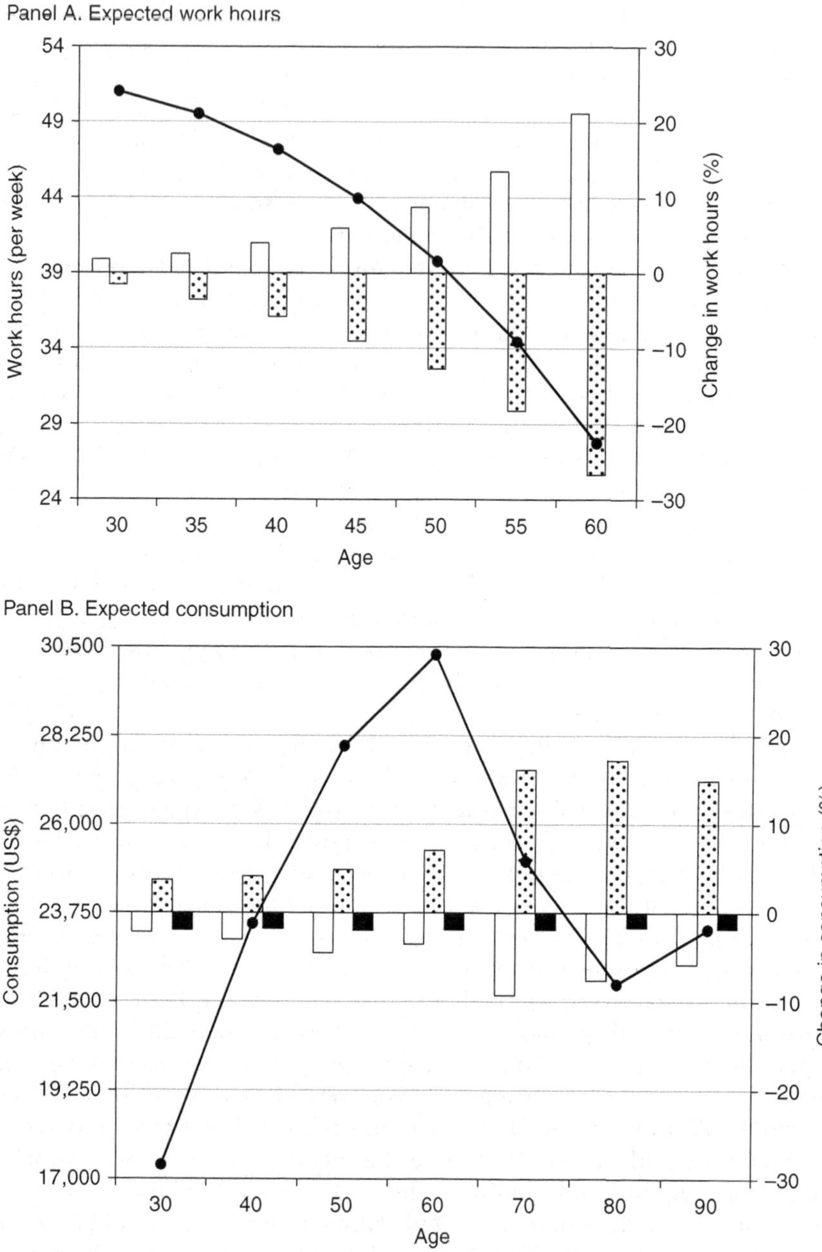

Figure 7.3 Long-term effects of financial/economic crises on young cohort (age 20). Panel (A): expected work hours; Panel (B): expected consumption; Panel (C): expected saving/withdrawal

Notes: Panel (C): labor income/Social Security benefits after taxes and housing expenditures minus consumption. Solid black line (axis on the left): absolute values under normal scenario. Bars (axis on the right): relative deviations from normal case for alternative scenarios: crisis (black), double fortune (pattern), triple whammy (white).

Source: Authors' calculations.

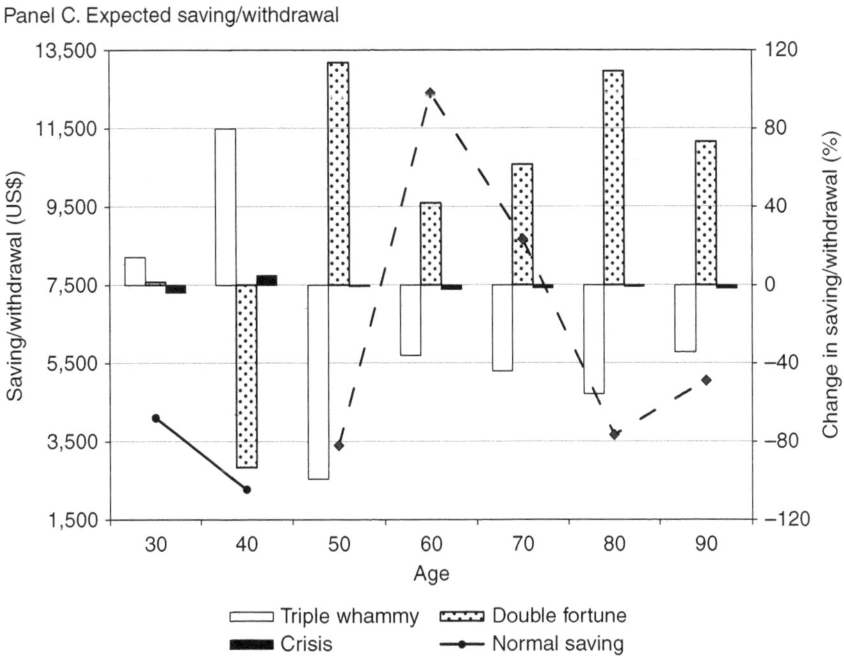

asset allocations are negligible when the impact strikes young, as these individuals lack financial assets. By contrast, experiencing the triple whammy young does have a lifelong impact. Young workers with very low financial wealth have only one major asset, their bond-like human capital, so they are much more likely to hold more stock over their lifetimes. In their 60s, for example, they still invest over 85 percent of financial wealth in equities. The opposite is true for the doubly fortunate households, who invest less in equity over the whole life cycle. Their bond-like labor income makes up a smaller part of their overall wealth, leading them to diversify by shifting a higher share of financial wealth into less risky assets (i.e. bonds earlier in life and later, annuities).

It is also of interest to ask how the crisis shapes retirement behavior. Table 7.2 presents the fraction of households that retire from age 62 to 70 (retiring is defined by reducing work effort to below 20 hours per week). The base case setting exhibits the empirically well-documented two-peaked distribution: over one-quarter of households retires at the early retirement age of 62, while around half retire later, at ages 66 and 67. By age 68, all households have retired, and on average, retirement occurs at age 64.8. Workers struck by the crisis at a young age have several decades to adjust, and they make retirement timing decisions virtually identical to those of

TABLE 7.1 Long-term impacts of crisis on asset allocation of young cohort (age 20)

Age (years)	Asset allocation (%)			
	Average		Tails	
	Normal	Crisis	Double fortune	Triple whammy
	Stocks			
30	99.3	99.3	99.0	99.2
40	90.0	90.0	84.3	94.5
50	79.5	79.5	69.3	87.1
60	77.3	77.3	66.3	86.7
70	79.5	79.3	63.6	85.8
80	34.1	34.2	21.1	41.1
	Bonds			
30	0.6	0.7	1.0	0.7
40	10.0	9.9	15.5	5.5
50	19.3	19.3	25.7	12.7
60	18.7	18.6	20.4	12.5
70	6.7	6.7	6.0	8.1
80	16.5	16.5	11.3	23.1
	Annuities			
30	0.0	0.0	0.0	0.1
40	0.1	0.1	0.2	0.0
50	1.2	1.2	5.0	0.2
60	4.1	4.1	13.4	0.8
70	13.8	14.0	30.3	6.1
80	49.4	49.3	67.6	35.8

Source: Authors' calculations.

base case households (resulting in the same average retirement age). By contrast, young workers experiencing a triple whammy when young must work longer to make up the shortfall: three-quarters postpone retirement beyond the normal retirement age, and on average they retire one year later than the base case scenario, at age 65.8. Not surprisingly, half of the doubly fortunate group retires as early as possible; 70 percent leave work prior to normal retirement age, twice as high as in the base case, which drives down the average retirement age by more than a year (to 63.5).

Long-term effects for the older cohort

Our base case households in the normal scenario consume about $31,000 at age 65 on average, and reduce their spending over the following two decades to around $22,000. After that, consumption increases again (Figure 7.4, Panel A). Being exposed to a financial/economic crisis leaves

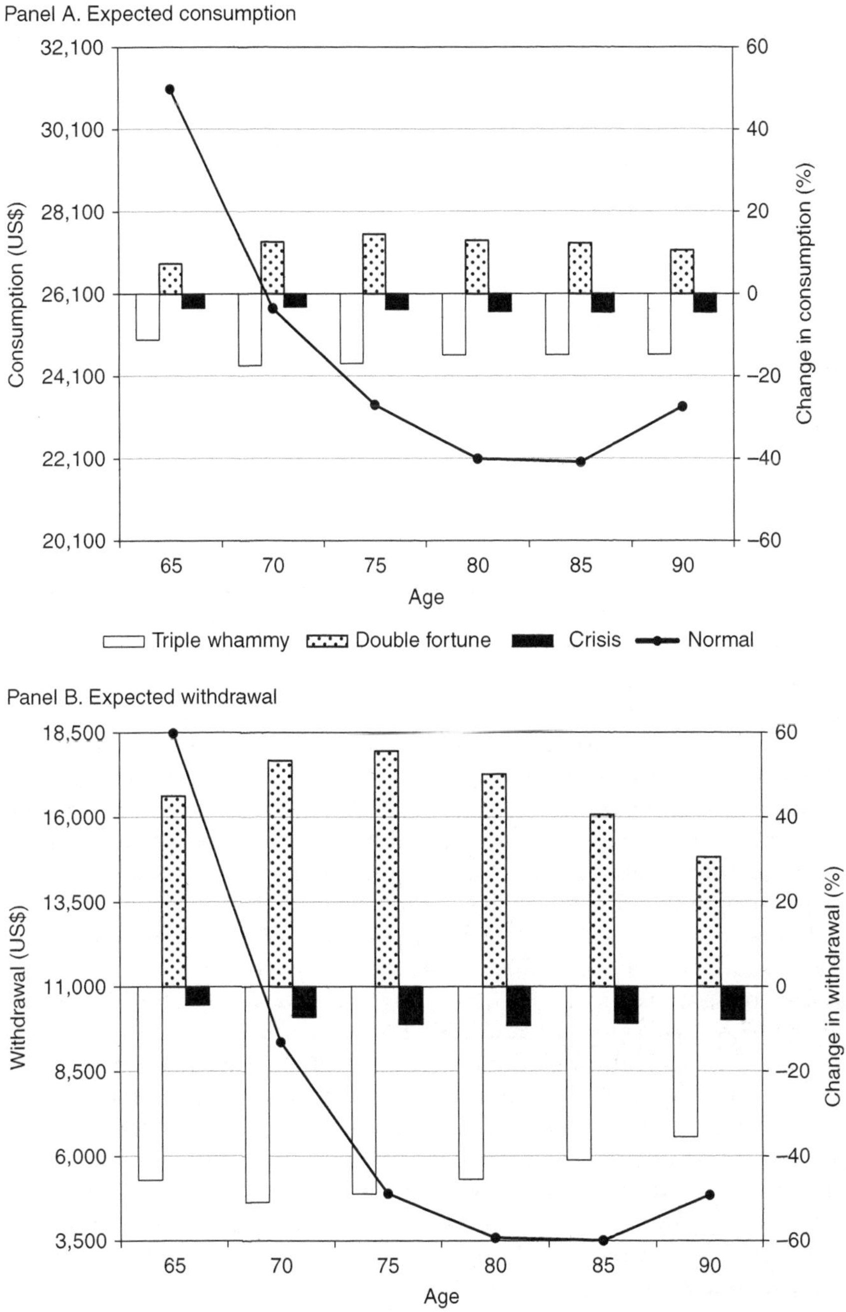

Figure 7.4 Long-term effects of financial/economic crises on near-retirement cohort (age 55). Panel (A): expected consumption; Panel (B): expected withdrawal

Notes: Panel (B): labor income/Social Security benefits after taxes and housing expenditures minus consumption. Solid black line (axis on the left): absolute values under normal scenario. Bars (axis on the right): relative deviations from normal case for alternative scenarios: crisis (black), double fortune (pattern), triple whammy (white).

Source: Authors' calculations.

TABLE 7.2 Crisis impact on retirement behavior of young cohort (age 20)

Age (years)	Retirement ratio (%)			
	Average		Tails	
	Normal	Crisis	Double fortune	Triple whammy
62	27.4	27.4	53.9	8.0
63	6.3	6.2	8.8	3.6
64	6.6	6.5	7.3	5.5
65	8.2	8.2	5.1	8.8
66	24.6	24.5	12.6	36.3
67	22.3	22.3	9.9	32.7
68	4.7	4.8	2.1	5.1
69	0.0	0.0	0.2	0.1
70	0.0	0.0	0.0	0.0
Average retirement age	64.8	64.8	63.5	65.8

Source: Authors' calculations.

households with lower financial wealth as well as lower Social Security income. Consequently, retirement consumption falls short of that of base case households by 4 percent per year. Households hit by the triple whammy close to retirement suffer dramatically over the remaining lifetime, as consumption persistently drops by 11–18 percent. By contrast, doubly fortunate households enjoy consumption that exceeds base case levels by 8–15 percent. Consumption is predominantly financed through constant Social Security income, to about 80 percent from age 75 on. The remainder must be supported by withdrawals from financial wealth that, consequently, exhibit the same temporal pattern as consumption, yet with higher magnitude due to the base effect (Figure 7.4, Panel B).

Long-term asset allocation patterns for the older cohort appear in Table 7.3. Under all scenarios, stock fractions decrease over time as the household gradually depletes liquid financial wealth, from 80–95 percent at age 65 to 24–38 percent at age 85. Bond fractions decline through the 60s, increase again through the 70s, and peak in the early 80s, when due to diminishing liquid wealth, households increasingly face difficulties to finance the minimum amount required to participate in the stock market. To take advantage of the increasing survival credit, households gradually shift financial wealth from liquid assets into annuities. When combined with the depletion of liquid assets due to consumption-financing withdrawals, this drives annuity fractions up from 0.2–5 percent at age 65 to 45–64 percent at age 85. In general, compared to the base case calibration, the allocation to liquid assets is marginally higher under the crisis scenario and substantially higher for triple whammy households. The asset allocation of

TABLE 7.3 Long-term impacts of crisis on asset allocation of near-retirement cohort (age 55)

Age (years)	Asset allocation (%)			
	Average		Tails	
	Normal	Crisis	Double fortune	Triple whammy
	Stocks			
30	99.3	99.3	99.0	99.2
40	90.0	90.0	84.3	94.5
50	79.5	79.5	69.3	87.1
60	77.3	77.3	66.3	86.7
70	79.5	79.3	63.6	85.8
80	34.1	34.2	21.1	41.1
	Bonds			
30	0.6	0.7	1.0	0.7
40	10.0	9.9	15.5	5.5
50	19.3	19.3	25.7	12.7
60	18.7	18.6	20.4	12.5
70	6.7	6.7	6.0	8.1
80	16.5	16.5	11.3	23.1
	Annuities			
30	0.0	0.0	0.0	0.1
40	0.1	0.1	0.2	0.0
50	1.2	1.2	5.0	0.2
60	4.1	4.1	13.4	0.8
70	13.8	14.0	30.3	6.1
80	49.4	49.3	67.6	35.8

Source: Authors' calculations.

TABLE 7.4 Crisis impact on retirement behavior of near-retirement cohort (age 55)

Age (years)	Retirement ratio (%)			
	Average		Tails	
	Normal	Crisis	Double fortune	Triple whammy
62	20.6	18.2	40.6	4.4
63	7.0	7.4	9.3	3.3
64	7.0	8.1	9.1	3.2
65	9.0	9.5	8.7	10.2
66	26.8	26.8	16.6	38.2
67	24.4	24.7	13.0	33.2
68	5.1	5.4	2.8	7.5
69	0.0	0.0	0.0	0.0
70	0.0	0.0	0.0	0.0
Average retirement age	65.08	65.15	64.02	66.04

Note: Fractions of households that retire at specific age. Definition of retirement: work effort reduced to below 20 hours per week.

Source: Authors' calculations.

doubly fortunate households, on the other hand, is characterized by lower stock and higher annuity fractions.

Finally, Table 7.4 summarizes the impact of the financial/economic crisis on retirement patterns of the older cohort. In the baseline case, the average retirement age is 65.1; one-fifth of all households (20.6 percent) retire at the early retirement age 62; about half (51 percent) at age 66–67; and the remainder (5.1 percent) at age 68. In the crisis scenario, the fraction of households retiring at the early retirement age drops by 2.4 percent, and that of households retiring prior to the normal retirement age of 65 drops by a mere 0.4 percent; this produces a tiny increase in the average retirement age of only 0.07 years (a little less than a month). Things are very different for those individuals who experienced the triple whammy: almost 90 percent cannot afford to retire before the normal retirement age, which drives up the average retirement age by one year compared to the normal scenario. Two of five doubly fortunate households retire at the early retirement age, and three of five retire prior to the normal retirement age; consequently, the average retirement age falls by about one year compared to the base case scenario. Under all scenarios, the latest retirement age is 68.

Conclusion

Our goal was to investigate the short- and long-term impacts of a combined financial and economic crisis on households at different stages in their life cycles. To this end, we have developed a life cycle model that allows for optimal consumption, work effort, retirement, asset allocation, and annuitization decisions, incorporating countercyclical labor income and unemployment risk, as well as regime shifts in the investment opportunity set. We show that for young households, the financial/economic crisis will have little impact on either work effort or retirement behavior, though they do suffer from a long-term decline in annual consumption accompanied by lower saving. Stock fractions are marginally lower at the onset of the crisis, but over the remaining life cycle, asset allocation does not change much.

Young households hit particularly badly by the financial/economic crisis do have more response, reducing their work effort during the crisis by up to 10 percent; later in life, they must boost work hours substantially—over 20 percent at age 60 compared to the noncrisis scenario, and must defer retirement by one year on average. Lifetime consumption is also lower: in their early 20s, it is about 15 percent less, and 5 percent less even after age 70. The other effect is that young households must save substantially more than noncrisis households later in life, to build up at least some financial wealth. Low savings early in life go hand in hand with low stock investment; thereafter, from about age 40 on, equity exposure is continuously higher than that of noncrisis households, while both bond investments and annuity purchases are reduced.

When older persons are hit by a combined financial and economic crisis, they are predicted to boost work effort slightly, around 0.3–1.3 percent, over the rest of their work lives. Moreover, their average retirement age rises slightly as well (less than one month). The crisis is felt, instead, in more marked declines in annual consumption, both short- and long-term. Compared to a noncrisis scenario, consumption drops by 3.5 percent before retirement and by around 4.5 percent after age 80. Households reduce their asset withdrawals by about 2.5 percent over the short run and by about 9 percent later in life. During the immediate crisis, households reduce their equity exposure by more than 20 percent, on average, in favor of risk-free bonds. Over the longer run, however, investors have a marginally higher appetite for liquid assets, both stocks and bonds, than investors in a noncrisis scenario. Consequently, the level of annuitization decreases.

Those older households hit especially badly by unemployment and stock market shocks must substantially boost their work effort, by over 20 percent in their early 60s. Moreover, they cannot afford to retire early and must postpone retirement by about one year, on average.[15] Yet, they still experience consumption losses of about 10 percent in the short-term and about 15 percent later in life. While they are able to dampen the immediate impacts of the crisis through an increase in withdrawal of financial assets (about 30 percent at age 55), the corresponding drop in financial wealth results in substantial cuts in withdrawals later in life (more than 40 percent from age 70). These households reduce their equity exposure only by 10 percent early in the crisis. Over the remaining life cycle, allocation to stocks is substantially higher than that of households in the noncrisis scenarios.

Our predictions that older households must curtail their consumption, boost work effort, and defer retirement correspond to recent evidence on short-term effects of the crisis on older individuals (Gustman et al., 2010; Shapiro, 2010; Hurd and Rohwedder, 2012). For younger cohorts, on the other hand, there are (to the best of our knowledge) no empirical studies on how they are responding to the crisis in the short term. And for obvious reasons, it will take years to trace out how the crisis will influence long-term work, saving, consumption, and investment behavior. Our research offers a valuable means for informing policymakers about how such crises can differentially influence household responses to economic shocks, as they deploy the adjustment mechanisms at their disposal. Based on the framework provided, subsequent work can evaluate how policy changes might enhance well-being in the face of such crises; for instance, by making the retirement process more versus less flexible, supporting annuitization of retirement assets, or by changing retirement ages under Social Security.

Acknowledgments

The research reported herein was performed pursuant to a grant from the US Social Security Administration to the Michigan Retirement Research Center (MRRC) as part of the Retirement Research Consortium. Additional research support was provided by Netspar, the German Investment and Asset Management Association (BVI), the Pension Research Council at The Wharton School of the University of Pennsylvania, the German Science Foundation (DFG), and the Metzler Bank Exchange Professorship. Helpful comments were provided by Peter Brady, Susann Rohwedder, Mark J. Warshawsky, and participants at the 2011 Pension Research Council Conference. This research is part of the NBER programs on Aging, Public Economics, and Labor Studies. Opinions and errors are solely those of the authors and not of the institutions with whom the authors are affiliated.

Endnotes

1. Bosworth et al. (2000) report that middle-class workers are likely to have hump-shaped earnings profiles.
2. Carroll and Dunn (1997) and Storesletten et al. (2004) show that permanent labor income risk is strongly countercyclical.
3. Coile et al. (2001) show that a vast majority of workers claim and also stop working at the same juncture. In what follows, we abstract from other Social Security rules such as the earnings test for a retiree who returns to work before the normal retirement age, but after claiming benefits.
4. We assume that the annuities are held in nontax-qualified accounts and interest earnings are taxed as capital gains. Chai et al. (2011) show that this is a reasonable approximation to the exclusion ratio approach implemented by the US tax authority, and we adopt it here for greater computational tractability (also following Brown et al., 1999).
5. Prior to the retirement period, this state variable records the amount of payouts starting from the normal retirement age (NRA), from all previously purchased deferred annuities. After the NRA, this state variable denotes the sum of payouts from previously purchased immediate and deferred annuities.
6. For computations, we use a grid of dimension $40(W) \times 30(P) \times 2(s) \times 42(t)$ before and $40(W) \times 30(P) \times 2(s) \times 39(t) \times 9(\tau)$ after the ERA. For each grid point, we evaluate the policy and value functions using Gaussian quadrature integration and cubic-splines interpolation.
7. See http://www.bea.gov/national/index.htm
8. Storesletten et al. (2004) use the same transition matrix.
9. The volatility of the transitory shock is estimated by averaging the fixed effect and measurement error from Storesletten et al. (2004).
10. Future work can explore alternative tax structures in more detail; see also Smetters and Chen (2010).

11. The US Consumer Price Index (CPI) from Datastream for the years 1950–2008 is used to get the real number.
12. Over our sample period, the average realized equity premium was 5.73 percent. As this is perceived to be too high (a result known as the equity premium puzzle), we reduce the historical mean return estimate by 1.73 percent and calculate with an equity premium of 4 percent, which is a standard value in the literature on life cycle line portfolio choice.
13. A Jarque–Bera test is applied to test the normal distribution at each observable regime. The null hypothesis of normal distribution cannot be rejected at a 5 percent significance level. The critical values are computed using Monte Carlo simulation for small sample sizes.
14. This accords with empirical evidence regarding pre/postconsumption patterns in Aguiar and Hurst (2005).
15. This is in line with the simulations developed by Brady (2009).

References

Aguiar, M. and E. Hurst (2005). "Consumption vs. Expenditure", *Journal of Political Economy,* 113(5) (October): 919–48.

Ang, A. and G. Bekaert (2002). "International Asset Allocation with Regime Shifts", *Review of Financial Studies,* 15: 1137–87.

Bosworth, B., G. Burtless, and G. Steuerle (2000). "Lifetime Earnings Patterns, the Distribution of Future Social Security Benefits, and the Impact of Pension Reform", *Social Security Bulletin,* 63(4): 74–98.

Brady, P. (2009). "What Does the Market Crash Mean for the Ability of 401(k) Plans to Provide Retirement Income?", *National Tax Journal,* 52(3): 455–76.

Brown, J., O. S. Mitchell, J. Poterba, and M. J. Warshawsky (1999). "Taxing Retirement Income: Nonqualified Annuities and Distributions from Qualified Accounts", *National Tax Journal,* 52(3): 563–92.

Buchinsky, M, J. Rust, and H. Benítez-Silva (2000). "Dynamic Structural Models of Retirement and Disability", Yale University Department of Economics Working Paper. New Haven, CT: Yale University.

Carroll, C. D., and W. E. Dunn (1997). 'Unemployment Expectations, Jumping (S,s) Triggers, and Household Balance Sheets,' in B. S. Bernanke and J. J. Rotemberg, eds., *NBER Macroeconomics Annual 1997, vol. 12.* Cambridge, MA: MIT Press, pp. 165–230.

Chai, J., W. Horneff, R. Maurer, and O. S. Mitchell (2011). "Optimal Portfolio Choice over the Life-Cycle with Flexible Work, Endogenous Retirement, and Lifetime Payouts", *Review of Finance,* 15(4): 875–907.

Cocco, J., F. Gomes, and P. Maenhout (2005). "Consumption and Portfolio Choice over the Life Cycle," *Review of Financial Studies,* 18: 491–533.

Coile, C., P. Diamond, J. Gruber, and A. Jousten (2001). "Delays in Claiming Social Security Benefits," *Journal of Public Economics,* 84: 357–85.

Fehr, H., S. Jokisch, and L. J. Kotlikoff (2006). "Will China Eat our Lunch or Take Us Out to Dinner? Simulating the Transition Paths of the US, EU, Japan and

China", in T. Ito and A.K. Rose, eds., *Fiscal Policy and Management in East Asia.* Chicago, IL: University of Chicago Press, pp. 133–98.

Gomes, F. and A. Michaelides (2005). "Optimal Life-Cycle Asset Allocation: Understanding the Empirical Evidence", *Journal of Finance,* 60: 869–904.

——, L. Kotlikoff, and L. M. Viceira (2008). "Optimal Life-Cycle Investing with Flexible Labor Supply: A Welfare Analysis of Life-Cycle Funds", *American Economic Review: Papers & Proceedings,* 98: 297–303.

Gordon, S. and P. St-Amour (2000). "A Preference Regime Model of Bull and Bear Markets", *American Economic Review,* 90: 1019–33.

Guidolin, M. and A. Timmermann (2008). "International Asset Allocation under Regime Switching, Skew, and Kurtosis Preferences", *Review of Financial Studies,* 2: 889–935.

Gustman, A. L., T. L. Steinmeier, and N. Tabatabai (2010). "What the Stock Market Decline Means for the Financial Security and Retirement Choices of the Near-Retirement Population", *Journal of Economic Perspectives,* 24(1): 161–82.

Hurd, M. and S. Rohwedder (2012). "The Effects of the Economic Crisis on the Older Population", in R. Maurer, O. S. Mitchell, and M. J. Warshawsky, eds., *Reshaping Retirement Security: Lessons from the Global Financial Crisis.* Oxford, UK: Oxford University Press.

Kim, S. and B. Lee (2007). "Stock Returns, Asymmetric Volatility, Risk Aversion, and Business Cycle: Some New Evidence", *Economic Inquiry,* 46: 131–48.

Mitchell, O. S. and J. Phillips (2006). "Social Security Replacement Rates for Alternative Earnings Benchmarks", *Benefits Quarterly,* 4: 37–47.

OECD (2009). *Pensions at a Glance: Retirement-Income Systems in OECD Countries.* Paris, France: OECD.

Shapiro, M. D. (2010). "The Effects of the Financial Crisis on the Well-Being of Older Americans: Evidence from the Cognitive Economics Study", MRRC Working Paper 2010-228. Ann Arbor, MI: MRRC.

Smetters, K. and Y. Chen (2010). "Optimal Portfolio Choice over the Life Cycle with Social Security", Wharton School Working Paper. Philadelphia, PA: The Wharton School.

Storesletten, K., C. I. Telmer, and A. Yaron (2004). "Cyclical Dynamics in Idiosyncratic Labor Market Risk", *Journal of Political Economy,* 112: 695–717.

Whitehouse, E. (2010). *Pensions During the Crisis: Impact on Retirement-Income Systems and Policy Responses.* Geneva: OECD.

Chapter 8

A Stress Test for the Private Employer Defined Contribution System

David Wray

Beginning in the late 1980s, defined contribution (DC) plans began to emerge as the preferred employer-sponsored retirement vehicle in the United States. The trend from defined benefit (DB) to DC plans was welcomed by some, while others worried that a sharp fall in asset values might produce the collapse of the DC system. Some hypothesized that a dramatic decline in the value of DC plan assets might induce plan participants to stop contributing and expose employers to litigation regarding plan menu construction.

The year 2006 was a good one for private employer-sponsored DC plans in the United States. Key indicators of growth for the system were positive, with rising numbers of plans offered, increases in active participants, escalating employer and employee contributions, and improvements in total assets. In addition, the Pension Protection Act of 2006 made permanent several regulatory changes removing impediments restraining the use of automatic enrollment. But shortly thereafter, global financial markets crashed and virtually every asset class lost value. Over the next year, many 401(k) participants were exposed to the largest market downturn they had ever experienced.

In what follows, we examine initial data on the impact of the financial crisis on the DC system, focusing on plan sponsor and participant choices. Though we have no crystal ball, we conclude that many plans did well, resulting in little change in employer sponsorship and employee participation. Moreover, account balances and contributions have recovered, boding well for the future of the DC system.

Responses to the crisis: plan sponsors

Despite the financial market downturn of 2008–9, private sector employers by and large retained their plans and continued to make company contributions. Some adjusted plan design, and others changed how plan assets were invested.

In terms of numbers of plans, the private DC system continued to grow. According to the US Department of Labor (DOL, 2010), there were 669,156 private employer plans in 2008, up from 658,805 in 2007 and 645,971 in 2006. While 2009–10 data are not yet available, it appears that in 2009 there were few plan terminations, except in the case of bankruptcies, mergers, and acquisitions. The same data reports contributions by plan sponsors to DC retirement plans rose from 2006 to 2008. Firms contributed $120,267 million in 2008, up 19 percent from 2006. Moreover, according to Profit Sharing/401k Council of America (PSCA, 2010*a*) survey data, most plan sponsors in 2009 maintained their matching and other plan contributions; nevertheless, some 15 percent did suspend their 401(k) matches, 4 percent reduced matching contributions, and 27 percent suspended or reduced their profit-sharing/other nonmatching company contributions, declines somewhat offset by the 5 percent of plan sponsors that initiated a match or increased their match.

By 2010, according to PSCA (2010*b*) survey data, some firms began to restore their plan contributions: 39 percent of those who had suspended their matching contribution reestablished them, and 30 percent of those who had reduced their match returned to normal levels. Also, 4 percent of plan sponsors increased or initiated a matching contribution and 3 percent of companies increased or initiated a nonmatching contribution. Moreover, 19 percent of companies suspending or reducing their nonmatching company contributions restored them. Working in the other direction, 2 percent of companies reduced matching contributions (Figure 8.1).

All employees are not necessarily eligible to make contributions, nor are they immediately eligible for company contributions as soon as they begin working. According to PSCA survey data, prior to 1998, it was standard practice to limit employee participation in a plan after one year of service and attaining age 21. Since that year, service requirements for eligibility were reduced and the trend continued through 2010. Short-service requirements (fewer than three months of service) are now common for participant contributions. In 1998, only about one-quarter of DC plans allowed new hires to begin contributing immediately; by 2010, 60 percent of all plans permitted immediate participation, and in 78 percent of plans, employees could participate within three months of employment. Forty-four percent of plans have no minimum age requirement for elective deferrals; the usual minimum age requirement, if there is one, is still age 21.

There has also been a continued trend toward immediate plan eligibility for employer contributions, and twice as many plans provide immediate eligibility for matching as for nonmatching contributions. Within three

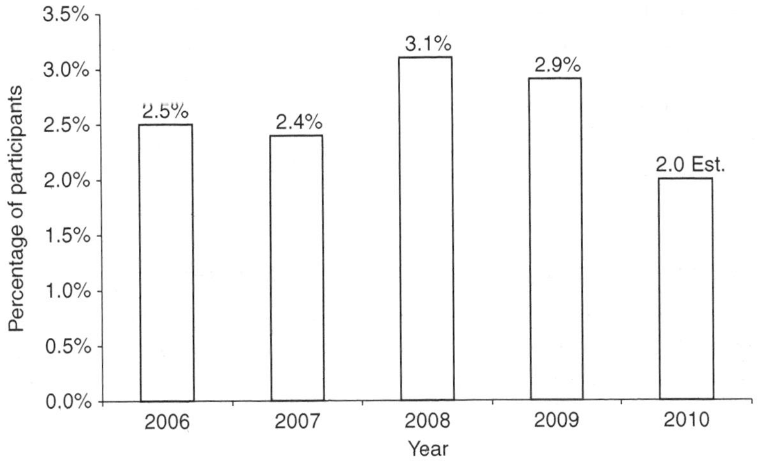

Figure 8.1 Percentage of participants contributing to plans that ceased making contributions by the year end: 2006–10

Source: Author's calculations.

months of employment, 60 percent of plans make employees eligible for matching contributions and 32 percent provide eligibility for nonmatching contributions. Thirty percent of companies require one year of service or longer for matching contribution eligibility, while over half of employers require one year or more of service to be eligible for nonmatching company contributions according to PSCA survey data.

In many DC plans, employers enroll new hires as soon as the employees are eligible; after that participant contributions are automatically deducted from employee pay unless an employee instructs the employer otherwise. According to Fidelity Investments (2011), automatic enrollment has spread in the DC environment, from 10 percent of plans in 2006 to 24 percent of plans by 2010.

In large firms with 5,000+ participants, automatic enrollment stood at 54 percent in 2009, up from 41 percent in 2006 (PSCA, 2009). Many employers will also select an investment portfolio to use as a 'default', absent investment guidance provided by the participant. Such investment patterns have changed substantially over time. In 2001, 48 percent of plans used either a stable value or money market fund as the default portfolio; by 2009, only 3 percent of plans used these funds (PSCA, 2010*a*). In their place, the defaults are now target retirement date funds, with over half (57 percent) using them in 2009.

When a DC plan permits participants to contribute after-tax dollars to a 401(k), under certain conditions, participants may take tax-free distributions of investment earnings. These are known as Roth 401(k) plans. Previously, only after-tax participant contributions were allowed, with investment earnings growing tax-deferred and taxable on distribution. The trend to Roth 401(k) plans has been impressive: in 2006, only 18 percent of firms allowed participants to make Roth after-tax contributions, while in 2009 the rate had more than doubled to 41 percent (PSCA, 2010*b*).

Education, plan support, and investment offerings

From the onset of the financial crisis, volatility in the financial markets bred concern that employees might cease participating in their plans and/or reallocate their account balances to risk-free investments. Consequently, many employers with DC sought to enhance employee education and provide participant support when needed. In 2008–9, over half (54 percent) of plan sponsors increased plan education and communication efforts (PSCA, 2010*a*, 2010*b*). Moreover, providers added to their call centers to handle participant inquiries and ran numerous workshops.

Also during this period, plan sponsors recognized that some participants needed far more than education, and many now help participants with their investment allocation decisions with target-date funds, investment advice, and professionally managed investment options. For example, almost two-thirds (62 percent) of sponsors in 2010 offered target-date funds, up from about one-third (35 percent) four years earlier (PSCA, 2010*a*, 2010*b*). Investment advice was offered in 60 percent of plans in 2009, up from 45 percent in 2006. Almost a third (31 percent) of plans offered participants a managed account option in 2009, allowing participants to delegate plan allocations to professional managers selected by the plan sponsor. In 2009, 19 percent of plans made all three of these options available and only 9 percent of plans did not provide at least one (see Table 8.1).

Many companies also increased the frequency with which they monitor plan investment offerings, and a majority changed plan menus. For

TABLE 8.1 Percentage of DC plans offering target-date funds, professionally managed accounts, and/or investment advice to participants

Offers	% of plans
Offers all three options	18.6
Offers two of the three	35.8
Offers one of the three	36.5
Does not offer any	9.1

Source: PSCA (2010*a*, 2010*b*).

instance, almost two-thirds (64 percent) of sponsors reviewed plan investment menus quarterly, up from about half (53 percent) in 2006. The fraction undertaking a review annually fell from 27 to 18 over the same period. Fifty-six percent of plan sponsors changed plan investments lineups in 2010 (PSCA, 2010*a*, 2010*b*).

Responses to the crisis: participant behavior

As shown elsewhere in this volume (Tang et al., 2012), the vast majority of 401(k) participants showed substantial resilience in the face of stock market volatility, falling housing prices, and overall economic uncertainty. Most continued saving in their plans, maintained their saving rates, and continued to hold diversified portfolios with the majority of the assets in equities. They have been rewarded with increases in both median and average account balances by the end of 2010 according to Vanguard (2011).

Participant contributions

Federal law limits the amount highly compensated employees (HCEs) can contribute to their plans, compared to the nonhighly compensated. Evidence suggests that the nonhighly compensated participants more or less maintained their DC contributions despite the crisis. Thus, as a percentage of pay, average contributions for nonHCEs eligible to participate (including noncontributors), stood at 5.4 percent of pay in 2006, 5.6 percent in 2007, 5.5 percent in 2008, and 5.2 percent in 2009 (PSCA, 2010*a*). One reason for the bump down is probably that some plans suspended employer matching contributions, making employee participation less attractive.

Distributions

Some 87 percent of private employer-sponsored DC plans permit their participants to borrow from their accounts: federal rules limit the loans to 50 percent of their account balances or $50,000, whichever is less. It is generally thought that sponsors include this plan provision to encourage participation and higher contribution rates, and to avoid hardship withdrawals. Available evidence suggests that plan loan rates were virtually unchanged over the period. As of 2006, 24 percent of participants had a loan outstanding, given that they could borrow; as of 2009, the fraction was 23 percent. (Average loan amounts did rise from $7,766 to $8,760 according to PSCA survey data.)

A majority of plans, 86 percent, allow hardship withdrawals; common reasons for permitting these include purchase of a primary residence, to prevent eviction or foreclosure, for medical expenses, and to cover post-secondary education expenses. The fraction of plan participants taking hardship distributions has increased, but remains small: it was 1.5 percent of eligible participants in 2006 and 2.2 percent in 2010 according to Vanguard (2011).

Another way in which funds can leave DC plans is via lump-sum distributions. When a participant leaves an employer with an account balance, this balance can be preserved by leaving the amount accumulated in the former employer's plan, rolling it over into a new employer's plan, or rolling it into an individual retirement account (IRA). Alternatively, the former employee may also elect to take a lump-sum distribution, which will be subject to income tax, as well as a 10 percent early withdrawal penalty (if under the age of 59.5). Over the period under observation, there was little change in participant behavior regarding distributions: for instance, in 2006, 72 percent of terminated vested participants did not cash out plan assets, so that 93 percent of the available assets were retained in the system (Vanguard, 2011). By 2010, the percentage declined only slightly: 70 percent of terminating employees preserved their saving in a tax-qualified program, amounting to 92 percent of available assets.

Balances and trading activity

Total assets in private sector DC plans increased from $3.55 trillion at the end of 2006 to a historic high of $3.86 trillion by the end of 2010 (FRB, 2011). The median participant account across all eligible participants grew from $25,953 in 2006 to $26,926 in 2010; the median account balance for participants with an account in 2007 increased by 31 percent by the end of 2010. Average participant account balances grew from $75,791 in 2006 to $79,077 in 2010 (Vanguard, 2011).

Most participants do not actively trade their DC plan portfolios. In 2006, only fourteen of the participants made at least one trade or exchange; this number rose slightly to 16 percent in 2008 and then fell back to 12 percent in 2009 and 2010 (Vanguard, 2011). Moreover, the fraction of new contributions going to equities in these plans remained relatively steady over the period: in 2006, 72 percent of new contributions to DC plans went to equities; in 2007, it was 74 percent; in 2009, it was 68 percent; and it rebounded to 70 percent by 2010 (Vanguard, 2011). The commitment to equities stood at 73 percent of the DC balances 2006–7, reaching a low of 61 percent in 2008 with the market shock. As the market rallied in 2009 and 2010, the percentage of plan assets in equities rebounded to finish at 68 percent in 2010 (Vanguard, 2011). These trends resulted from several factors, including the fact that employees continued to contribute new money to equities, as well as the rebounding stock market.

Another look at the long-term trend is taken from private retirement plan asset data reported by the Federal Reserve (2011). Here DC plans' asset allocation has remained virtually unchanged from 2006 to 2010. Additionally, private DC plan assets rose by 8.8 percent over the relevant time frame.

Conclusion

Without a doubt, the past few years have been an unusually difficult period for plan sponsors and participants in the DC arena. Nevertheless, most private sector employers who had DC plans continued their sponsorship, and the majority of employees and firms continued to contribute. It now seems clear that the employer-sponsored DC system performed well in difficult times, with little permanent decline in employer sponsorship or employee participation. This permitted account balances and contribution levels to recover as the economy improved.

References

Board of Governors of the Federal Reserve System (FRB) (2011). *Flow of Funds Accounts of the United States.* Statistical Release Z.1. Washington, DC: FRB.

Fidelity Investments (2011). *Debunking Five Key Myths about Defined Contribution Plans.* Boston, MA: Fidelity Investments.

Profit Sharing/401k Council of America (PSCA) (2001–2010). *45th–53rd Annual Surveys of Profit Sharing and 401(k) Plans.* Chicago, IL: PSCA.

—— (2009). *Impact of Economic Conditions on 401(k) and Profit Sharing Plans.* Chicago, IL: PSCA.

—— (2010*a*). *401(k) and Profit Sharing Plan Response to Current Conditions.* Chicago, IL: PSCA.

—— (2010*b*). *401(k) and Profit Sharing Plan Eligibility Survey 2010.* Chicago, IL: PSCA.

Tang, N., O. S. Mitchell, and S. P. Utkus (2012). "Trading in 401(k) Plans during the Financial Crisis", in R. Maurer, O. S. Mitchell, and M. J. Warshawsky, eds., *Reshaping Retirement Security: Lessons from the Global Financial Crisis.* Oxford, UK: Oxford University Press.

US Department of Labor (DoL) (2008). *Private Pension Plan Bulletin Historical Tables and Graphs Abstract of 2006 Form 5500 Annual Reports.* Washington, DC: Employee Benefits Security Administration.

—— (2009). *Private Pension Plan Bulletin Historical Tables and Graphs Abstract of 2007 Form 5500 Annual Reports.* Washington, DC: Employee Benefits Security Administration.

—— (2010). *Private Pension Plan Bulletin Historical Tables and Graphs Abstract of 2008 Form 5500 Annual Reports.* Washington, DC: Employee Benefits Security Administration.

Vanguard (2011). *The Great Recession and 401(k) Plan Participant Behavior.* Center for Retirement Research. Valley Forge, PA: Vanguard.

Part III

How Defined Benefit Plans Handled the Financial Crisis

Chapter 9

Defined Benefit Pension Plans and the Financial Crisis: Impact and Sponsors and Government Reactions

Mark J. Warshawsky

The dramatic events of the global financial crisis and the great recession of 2008–9 affected many aspects of world economies, and corporate defined benefit (DB) plans in the United States were no exception. The most obvious and immediate impact showed up in plan funding rates: there was a dramatic decline and then a more gradual rise in equity prices, along with an initial large rise and then a gradual decline in corporate bond yields. As yields fell, plan liabilities increased. The finances of the government insurer of DB plans, the Pension Benefit Guaranty Corporation (PBGC), also worsened. But the longer-term impact of the global financial crisis is likely to be in the deeper appreciation of the high levels of risk inherent in the external economic environment. In turn, this will shape the long-term decision-making of corporate DB plan sponsors pertinent to investment policies, contributions, and plan sponsorship and design, as well as decisions by the federal government, including temporary funding relief to plan sponsors.

This chapter discusses how corporate DB plans fared during the global financial crisis, and how the main actors reacted. We begin with a detailed time line of legislative and regulatory temporary funding relief. We also review a reform proposal that arose out of this environment and experience recommending a new type of retirement plan and other changes in government policies.

Background

To illustrate the backdrop against which this analysis unfolds, Figure 9.1 shows monthly and annual returns of the S&P500 for the period 2007–10, a period that bookends the great recession that began in December 2007 and ended in June 2009. The global financial crisis was most intense from

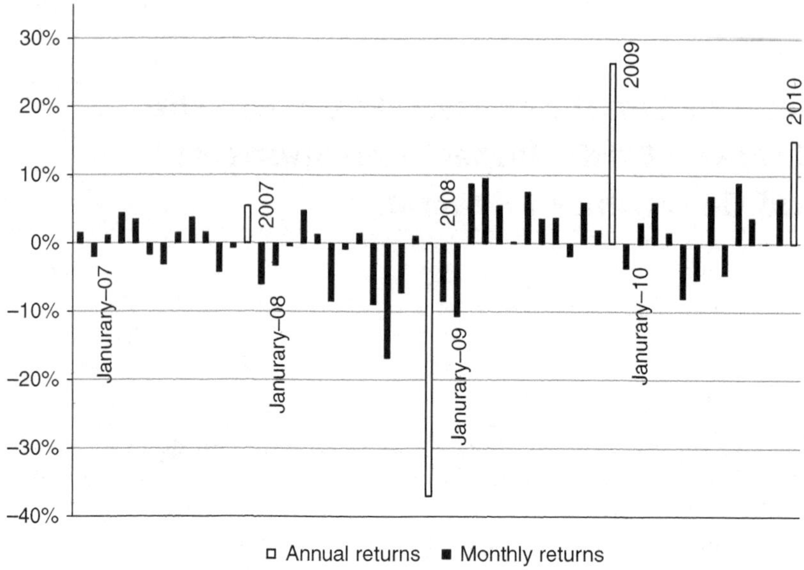

Figure 9.1 Total index monthly and annual returns, S&P 500 (%): 2007–10

Source: Author's computations using data from Haver DLX database, including monthly returns for the S&P from the years of 2007 to the end of 2010.

September 2008 through March 2009. Equity securities, represented by the S&P500, are a major asset class for pension funds; because of their generally high return, they also embody more risk. Figure 9.2 reports yields on high-grade corporate bonds at month ends, again for 2007–10. The series shown from the Internal Revenue Service (IRS) reflects a composite of rates on high-grade corporate bonds fairly representative of rates pension sponsors use for the purposes of financial accounting (and, within a range, for legal funding requirements in calculating their pension liabilities).

As the figures show, while equity returns were volatile in 2007, they were modestly positive. Beginning in 2008, however, larger losses began to accrue and September through November saw extremely large declines in prices. For the year, losses reached nearly 40 percent. January and February 2009 saw continued large losses, but then confidence was restored in the financial markets and, overall, the equity market in 2009 had a gain of more than 25 percent. There was continued volatility in 2010, but, on net, there was again a gain at over 15 percent.

Yields on high-grade corporate bonds generally follow those on long-maturity Treasury bonds, and were increasing through mid-year 2007 and

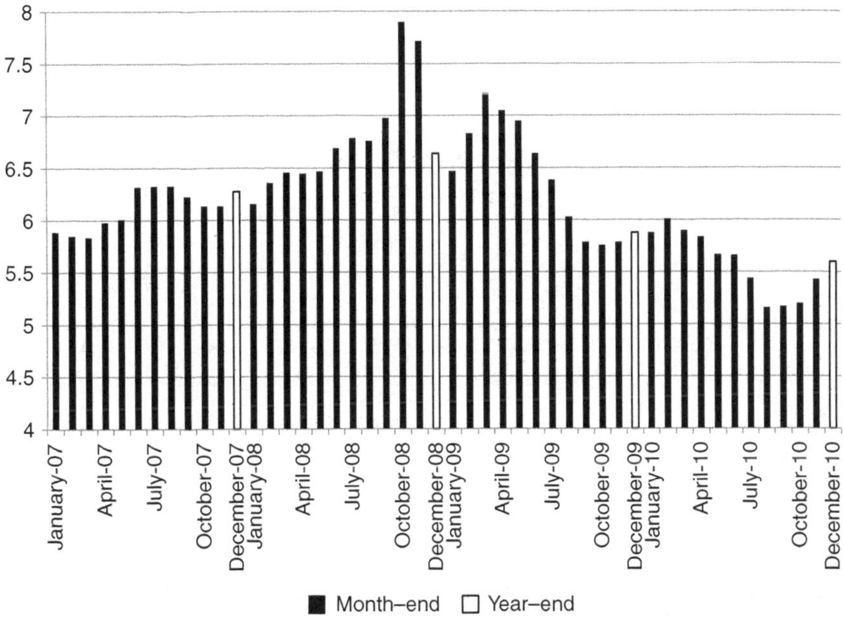

Figure 9.2 Composite Corporate Bond Rate (%): month-end, 2007–10

Source: Author's computation from the Internal Revenue Service (2011).

then began to decline with the onset of the recession. In 2008, however, that relationship broke, as spreads widened dramatically. Treasury bond yields fell while corporate bond yields rose dramatically in the depth of the financial crisis to nearly 8 percent (end of October 2008): during this period, investors doubted the creditworthiness of even the highest rated corporate issuers. Thereafter, corporate yields declined (although there was a bump-up in March 2009) until they were below 6 percent at the end of 2009 and around 5.5 percent at the end of 2010. Spreads with Treasury securities also narrowed significantly.

Impact on corporate pension-funding status

The funding status of DB plans is calculated as the ratio of the market value of plan assets to liabilities (formally, the projected benefit obligation or PBO) for financial accounting year-end disclosures. This is the most immediate and sensitive summary measure of the plan's benefit security level, and it is widely cited and used. Figure 9.3 shows the history of the funding

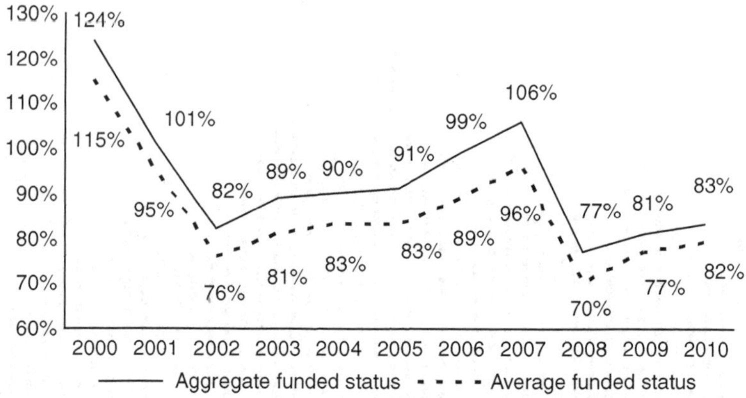

Figure 9.3 Pension funding status for Fortune 1000 companies: percentage per year 2000–10

Source: Author's computations using data from Towers Watson; see text.

status of the DB plans of Fortune 1000 companies 2000–10, on an aggregate basis (total of all plan assets divided by total of all plan liabilities) and also as a simple average across the companies (average of individual company pension asset–liability ratios). In 2000, the overall funding status was quite high at 124 percent, but it dropped during the dot-com bust, and the ensuing recession saw a low of 82 percent in 2002. Thereafter, there was a slow climb through 2007 when most plans were fully funded, only to experience the dramatic falloff in 2008 to an aggregate funding status of 77 percent and an average status of 70 percent. The years 2009 and 2010 saw some modest improvement. Though discount rates fell which boosted liabilities, there was also an increase in asset values; the estimated aggregate status was 83 percent in 2010 and average was 82 percent. Note that when the aggregate funding measure was uniformly higher than the average, it meant that larger plans were better funded than smaller plans.

A somewhat brighter view of the 2009–10 experience results from examining funding patterns across companies for fiscal years 2008 through 2010 (Figure 9.4). In 2008, almost one-quarter of companies had pension plans with a funding status of under 60 percent; by 2009, this share had declined to 10 percent, and in 2010 it declined further to 7 percent. On the other end of the spectrum, only 4 percent of companies had overfunded DB plans in 2008; by 2009, the percentage of overfunded plans improved a bit, to over 5 percent, and in 2010, it jumped to 10 percent.

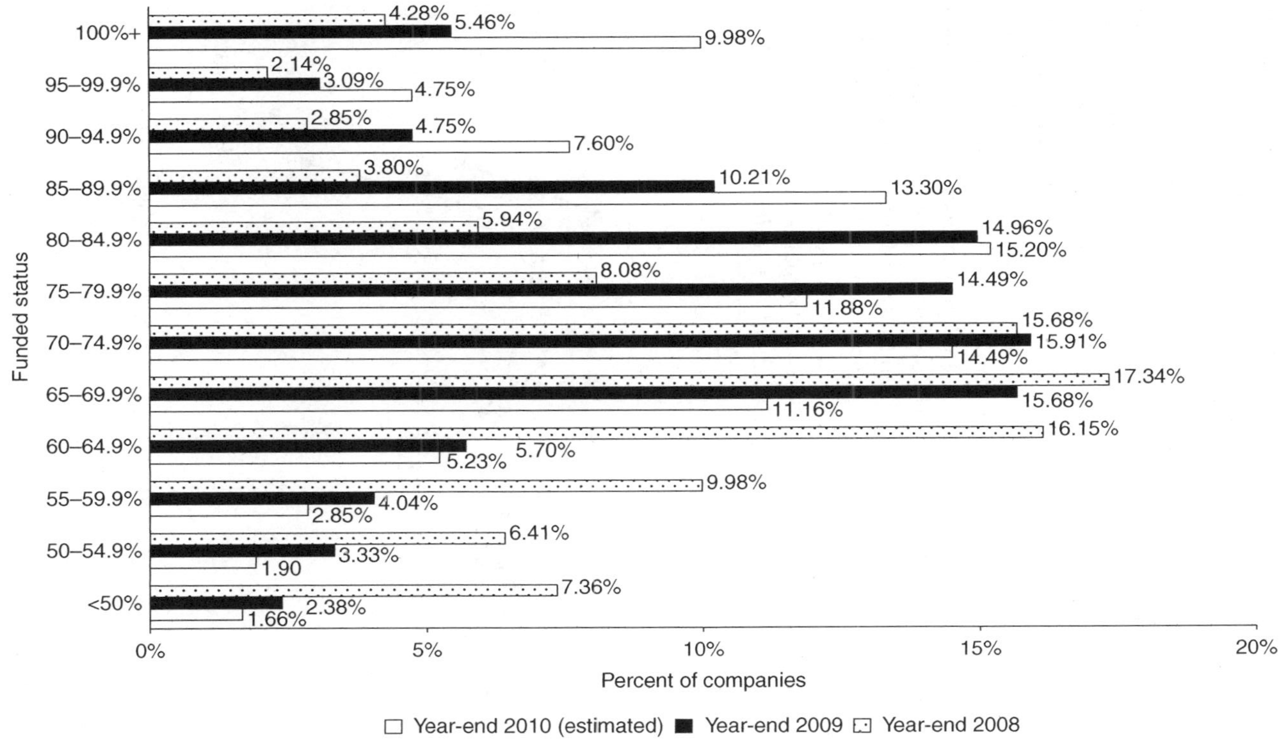

Figure 9.4 Funding status of defined benefit pensions offered by Fortune 1000 companies: 2008–10

Source: Author's computations from data from Towers Watson; see text.

Pension plan investments

Perhaps the easiest and most direct way for a plan to control cost and risk in its DB plan is through asset allocation. A higher allocation to equities not only lowers the plan sponsor's expected cost but also increases its risk, especially in the sense of more volatile required cash contributions. When DB plans are active and growing, equity investments make particularly good sense, as assets that increase with economic growth match liabilities that likewise increase with growth (more workers and higher wages). When DB plans are no longer growing or are closed or frozen—and mainly pay out benefits—many experts say that a better match is obtained when debt securities are the primary investment. These considerations should hold regardless of whether there is a bull or bear stock market. Even sophisticated professional and institutional investors, however, might be influenced by unusual realizations of risk, such as that which occurred during the global financial crisis. Overall, as we shall see, there has been a movement away from equity investments for DB plans. This pattern was apparent before the crisis, but it was deepened as a result.

Figure 9.5 shows the equity share for private DB plans from 1995 through 2010 taken from the Flow of Funds Accounts;[1] the equity share for private

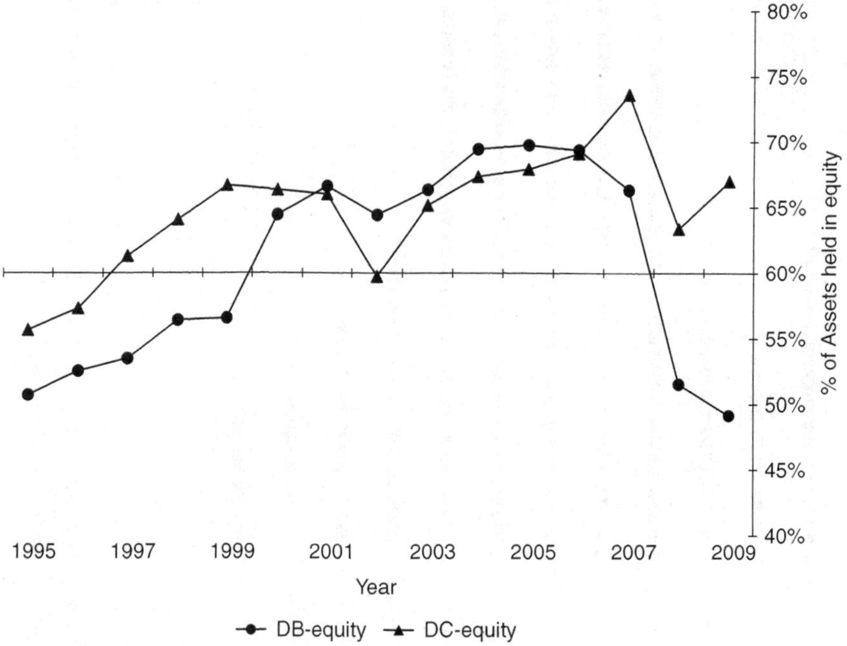

Figure 9.5 Equity shares for private DB and DC plan assets: 1995–2009
Source: FRB (2011).

defined contribution (DC) plans is also shown for comparison purposes. The DB equity share rose steadily from about 52 percent in 1995 to nearly 70 percent in 2005. There was a slight decline in 2002, likely reflective of equity price declines. Then, in 2006, the equity share for DB plans began to decline, more significantly in 2007, dramatically in 2008, and again in 2009, to only about 48 percent. In 2010, it declined again to 45 percent. While the decline in 2008 may be attributed at least in part to the massive and sudden meltdown in the stock market in the fourth quarter, the continued decline in share in 2009 and 2010 likely represents a conscious decision to reduce risk-taking, as equity prices rose in most of 2009 and 2010. The different behavior seen for DC plans makes this interpretation of a conscious move away from equities by DB plans more certain. While asset allocation mutual funds like target-date and balance funds are popular and growing, these still represent a distinct minority of assets and investors in DC plans. And it appears that most DC plan participants were passive investors and did not automatically rebalance their allocations. Indeed, the equity share in DC plans followed stock market movements closely over time, with some hint of an upward secular trend in the equity share. Overall, the equity share of DC plans has generally been higher than for DB plans, and in 2010, it was almost 20 percentage points higher than for DB plans.

Figure 9.6 shows a similar pattern based on data from large DB plan corporate sponsor annual reports.[2] In particular, the figure presents the aggregate average and the distribution of equity shares among plan sponsors 2005–9. Allocations to equity from 2005 to 2008 decreased from 62 to 44 percent, and they only recovered slightly to 45 percent in 2009. As further proof of the trend, fewer than 1 percent of large plan sponsors allocated less than 20 percent to equity in 2005, whereas more than 5 percent invested less than 20 percent in equities in 2008. Similarly, at nearly the other end of the spectrum, almost 9 percent of plan sponsors held 75–80 percent of plan assets in equities in 2005, but by 2009, fewer than 1 percent did so.

According to McFarland and Warshawsky (2010), other information sources indicate that equities have been a source of funding for both debt and alternative investments such as hedge funds and real estate in pension plans. More broadly, investment consultants in this field have been urging for some time that sponsors consider the liability structures of their plans and reduce risk, for example, through liability-directed investing, and this message is apparently getting through. Also, as McFarland and Warshawsky find, closed and frozen plans invest somewhat less in equities and more in debt securities; as such plans increase in number, aggregate allocations will also change in that direction.

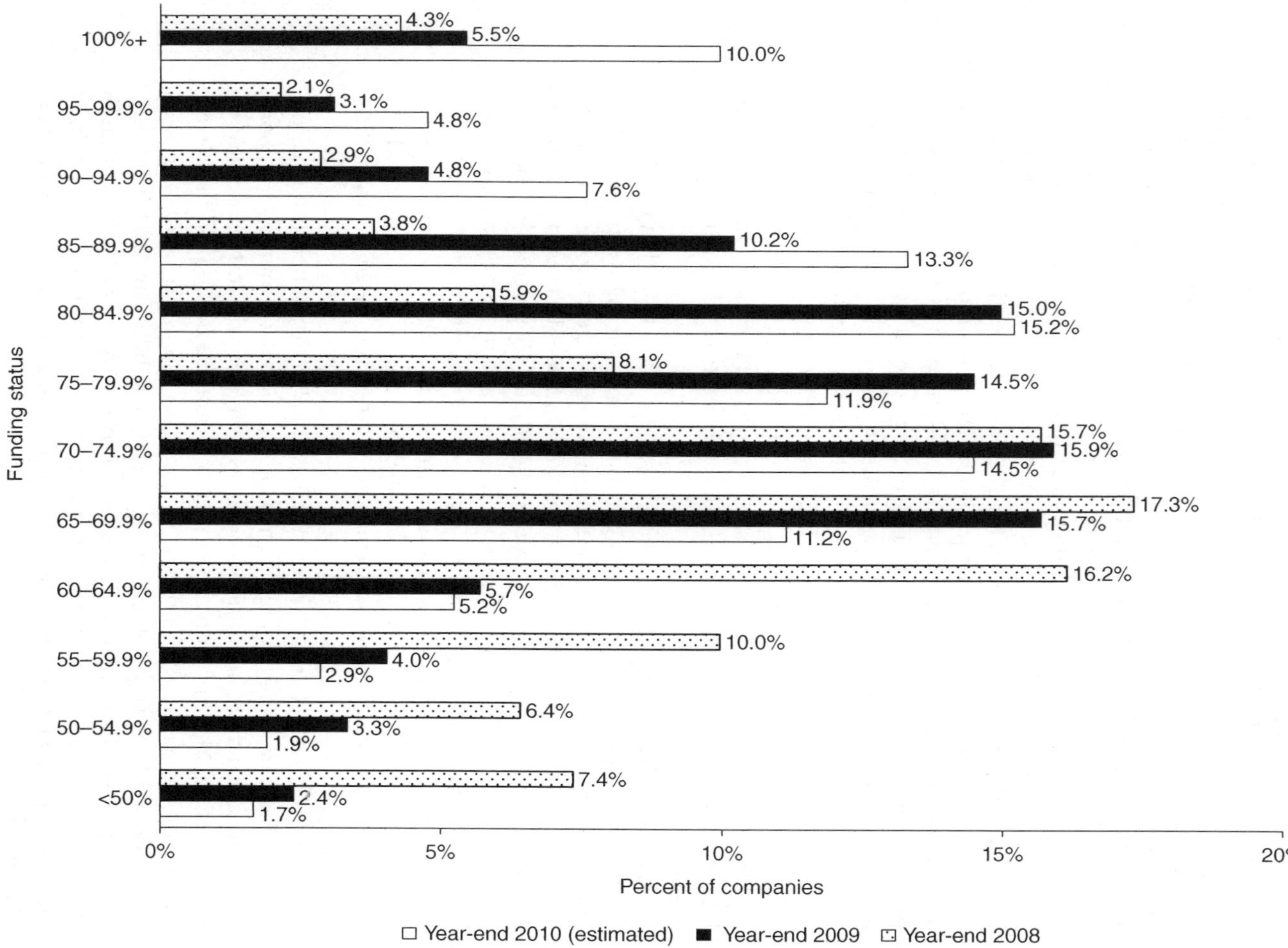

Figure 9.6 DB plan asset allocations to equities of Fortune 1000 companies: 2005–9

Source: Author's computations using data from Towers Watson; see text.

Contribution patterns

Another way in which DB sponsors can react to financial market developments is through employer contributions to help fund the plan. The federal government sets a lower bound to these contributions, which it moves from time to time (Warshawsky, 2007). In particular, the Pension Protection Act of 2006 (PPA) implemented a regime whereby market conditions were ultimately better reflected in plans' regulatory funded status, and minimum required contributions were linked more explicitly and quickly to that status than in the past. These requirements are quite complex, and during the global financial crisis, they were temporarily altered to reduce the otherwise large minimum contributions that would otherwise have been required. At the same time, plan sponsors can contribute more than the minimum if it fits their business strategy and financial wherewithal; one of the accomplishments of PPA was to allow these extra contributions on a tax-deductible basis to a much greater extent than did prior law. Contributions can be either cash or employer securities (the latter within legal limits), but in practice the vast majority of contributions are made in cash.[3] There is evidence that many plan sponsors do pursue the strategy of contributing more than the minimum required.

Table 9.1 shows employer DB plan contributions by Fortune 1000 companies. These are mainly for single-employer qualified DB plans in the United States (though they also include non-qualified executive DB plans and foreign DB plans). The advantage of this data series, compared to the Form 5500 filed by individual plans with the federal government, is that it is available more quickly. Here, we see that contributions do follow plans' current funded status. In 1999, plan sponsors only contributed about $11

TABLE 9.1 Employer contributions to corporate DB plans by Fortune 1000 companies: 1999–2009 ($000 nominal)

Fiscal year	
1999	$10,760,323
2000	$16,685,625
2001	$13,856,128
2002	$44,351,971
2003	$71,950,882
2004	$52,305,607
2005	$55,333,997
2006	$44,775,654
2007	$33,187,663
2008	$35,920,612
2009	$60,459,778

Source: Author's computations of data from Towers Watson.

billion, but by 2003, contributions rose to nearly $72 billion. Contributions then declined, and by 2007 had reached $33 billion. In 2008, they rose to $36 billion and in 2009 to more than $60 billion. As explained below, contribution levels in 2008 and 2009 are clearly above the minimum required by law.[4]

DB plan sponsorship and design

The long-term trend in sponsorship of active DB plans by large corporations represented here by the list of Fortune 100 companies from 1998 through May of 2011 appears in Table 9.2. These are, in turn, divided into traditional final-average-pay and career-average-pay plans on the one hand, and hybrid plans, mainly cash balance plans, on the other. Clearly, since 2004 the trend has been away from DB plans, particularly traditional plans. Although the trend continued and even accelerated in subsequent years, we do not sense that the global financial crisis per se caused that acceleration, despite the rapid drop-off in funded status in 2008 and increase in future funding obligations. Rather, it appears to be a continuation of a preexisting trend.

Pension plans in the United States are long-term commitments of the plan sponsor, by law and practice. Particularly for large corporations, they represent an important part of the compensation structure and a tool for workforce management, especially regarding turnover and retirement rates. Accordingly, there are many considerations when closing or freezing a DB plan, beyond the plan's current financial status. Moreover, because pension plans have a 'long tail' in terms of liabilities, even freezing all accruals immediately will not reduce a sponsor's risk exposure much for several years. Indeed, McFarland et al. (2009) showed that the announcement of a freeze or close generally led to slightly *lower* share prices for the plan sponsor, rather than an increase. Standard terminations of plans will take the risks off the books of plan sponsors, but they are expensive: the funding gaps must be made up immediately, and the extra charges by the insurer issuers of group annuity contracts to take on the accrued pension liabilities must be paid.

The obverse of risk exposure to the plan sponsor is risk protection for employees who better appreciate DB plans after a financial crisis (Towers Watson, 2010*a*). Moreover, once a decision has been made to move away from the DB plan, it may take several months or even years before it is implemented, owing to administrative, legal, and labor relations issues that must be managed. So there is reason to expect no sudden movements in DB plan sponsorship trends owing to the global financial crisis. Nevertheless, market events that highlight risk are likely to have an impact eventually. Prior to the financial crisis, plan sponsors said 'risk' was the most important reason given for a plan freeze or close (Watson Wyatt Worldwide,

TABLE 9.2 Retirement plans offered to newly hired employees by Fortune 100 firms: 1998–2011

	1998	1999	2000	2001	2002	2003	2004	2005	2006	2007	2008	2009	2010	May 2011
All DB pension plans	72	72	72	71	70	68	66	64	57	50	45	40	37	30
Traditional DB plan	64	59	58	53	47	40	37	36	33	29	22	20	17	13
Hybrid pension plan	8	13	14	18	23	29	29	28	24	21	23	20	20	17
DC plan only	28	28	28	29	30	31	34	36	43	50	55	60	63	70

Note: Sponsorship shown as the retirement plan offered to new hires at end of year through May 2011 (by the 2011 Fortune list of the 100 largest companies) and includes announcements for future plan changes 2011 and beyond.

Source: Author's computations of data from Towers Watson.

2008). By all accounts, the global financial crisis was a realization of risk far beyond normal expectations—considerably beyond one standard deviation. Accordingly, ways to reduce risk while keeping the essence of the DB plan are likely to be more seriously explored and perhaps adopted.

Plan design is yet another important option for risk management (Pang and Warshawsky, 2011*b*). Cash balance hybrid plans represent less risk to a plan sponsor than traditional DB plans, in that for the latter, liabilities fluctuate with salary increases and service years. Moreover, these liabilities are also highly sensitive to changes in interest rates. By contrast, liability variations are mitigated in cash balance plans by their accrual formulas: usually the cash balance benefits are expressed as account balances at retirement, and the pay credit rate is fixed (e.g. 6 percent of pay). Cash balance accruals do vary with new realizations of crediting interest rates; for instance, the thirty-year Treasury bond yield is a frequently used crediting rate. In addition, liabilities for cash balance accounts are typically less interest rate-sensitive because the duration is shorter (account balances are usually paid out as a lump sum upon termination or retirement) and because of the internal partial hedging of the benefit accrual (being dependent on interest rate levels) and the liability. For example, declines in discount rates will not only increase the computed liability of a cash balance plan, but also gradually reduce plan benefits through lower interest credits. Pang and Warshawsky conclude that the cash balance plan has less expected volatility than the traditional DB plan and only slightly higher average cost, for the same 60/40 equity/bond investment strategy.

This lower risk may explain why hybrid plans have maintained a steadier share of plan sponsorship than traditional DB plans for Fortune 100 companies. The legitimization of these plans by PPA, after years of legal and political controversy, undoubtedly also played a part in steadying the overall environment for their sponsorship (Clark et al., 2012).

Temporary funding relief from the government

As the depth and extent of the global financial crisis became apparent in late 2008, many policymakers, plan sponsors, pension community leaders, and analysts began to worry about the impact of the drop in equity values and interest rates on the funded status of single-employer DB plans.[5] In particular, at a time of massive layoffs, hiring freezes, and the big drop in corporate plant and equipment investment, they grew concerned about the call on corporate cash arising from the impact of the legal funding obligations under PPA requirements. These requirements, first imposed for 2008 plan years, require the plan sponsor to face a seven-year amortization period for measured funding losses. These funding losses, in turn, are broadly reflective of market conditions for both asset and liability values. There are, however, many transition rules, and special definitions, including some allowed smoothing of values and so on, that make an accurate picture of the actual law requirements quite complicated, as we shall see later. Indeed, this complexity is a key part of the story of how temporary funding relief was accomplished in various stages.

The first response to the crisis was to provide some limited relief as part of a legislative package of technical corrections to PPA, through the Worker, Retiree, and Employer Recovery Act of 2008 (WRERA, 2008). To avoid a cliff-like effect funding requirement, this new bill relaxed PPA's transition rule for phasing in liability targets, and it allowed a look back for the restriction on benefit accruals on severely underfunded plans. In addition, WRERA allowed plans to use twenty-five-month asset-smoothing with an assumed earnings rate to determine the actuarial value of assets, generally increasing values.[6] This technical change, while directly of relatively small consequence, did later allow regulators to grant significantly more temporary relief.

Pang and Warshawsky (2009*b*) estimated that for the 2008 plan year (for most plans, at the end of calendar year 2007), the average regulatory funded status was 97 percent and the aggregate of minimum required contributions was $38 billion. But this relatively benign situation was upended by the financial crisis: for the 2009 plan year, they projected that the average funded status had declined to 75 percent and contributions would increase dramatically to $125 billion under PPA. Some relief was provided by WRERA; because of it, required contributions were projected to be instead $108 billion. The 2010 plan year was likely to be extremely challenging, as the average funded status would only improve to 80 percent and required contributions to $103 billion.[7]

With the passage of WRERA, plan sponsors lobbied the IRS to allow for changes in valuation elections, arguing that (had they been aware of the law change) they would have made different elections in 2008.[8] These allowances for different valuation methodologies improved the average funded status to 94 percent in 2009 and reduced the required contribution to only $32 billion (Pang and Warshawsky, 2009*c*). In plan year 2010, it was anticipated that average funded status would be 84 percent and required contribution would be $89 billion. These figures, of course, represent considerable improvements and relief compared to the situation as projected in January 2009. Yet plan year 2010 still represented a large increase in required contributions, and plan year 2011 a massive increase. The average funded status was expected to fall to 77 percent and required contributions jump to $147 billion in 2011 (Pang and Warshawsky, 2009*c*).

This led plan sponsors and their trade groups to seek further temporary relief. Eventually, Congress assembled a package that was responsive to sponsor concerns, including extending the time period of relief, but it was still only limited and conditional. This legislation, called the Access to Care for Medicare Beneficiaries and Pension Relief Act of 2010 (ACMBPRA), was signed by President Obama in 2010. Under ACMBPRA, sponsors of underfunded DB plans may elect either a '2+7' rule or a fifteen-year amortization rule for losses incurred in any two plan years between 2008 and 2011. Under the 2+7 rule, the sponsor makes interest-only payments for two years, followed by the regular seven-year amortization schedule. Under the fifteen-year rule, the sponsor amortizes the funding shortfall over fifteen years. Also, the relief from freezing benefit accruals for severely underfunded plans was extended to the 2010 plan year. The legislation conditioned this relief, however, on a so-called cash flow rule, that is, relief recipients must make higher pension contributions if they pay 'excess' employee compensation, declare extraordinary dividends, or redeem company stock in excess of certain thresholds. The condition period is three years for the 2+7 rule and five years for the fifteen-year rule.

Models of the relief provisions using updated market conditions and assumptions suggested that if all underfunded plan sponsors chose the 2+7 rule for the 2010 and 2011 plan years, then required contributions would be only $66 billion in 2010 and $96 billion in 2011, a reduction of $47 billion for those two years compared to pre-ACMBPRA law (Pang and Warshawsky, 2010). By 2012, however, required contributions would jump to $147 billion in this scenario. By contrast, election of the fifteen-year amortization by all underfunded plans for the 2010 and 2011 plan years would provide lesser relief in 2010–11 but more through 2013—a $63 billion reduction in required contributions over the longer period. Subsequent surveys have indicated that the extent of utilization by plan sponsors of the latest legislative relief will be somewhat limited (Towers Watson, 2010*b*). Only about 30 percent of plans will use any relief, although the more severely underfunded plans are more likely to do so. Of those electing relief, most will use the fifteen-year amortization rule for the 2010 and 2011 plan years, which maximizes the longer-term relief but minimizes the immediate impact. The cash flow rule conditions are apparently discouraging some sponsors; with economic and financial conditions finally improving in late 2010 and early 2011, other plan sponsors preferred to bite the bullet and make extra contributions to improve funding status.

On updating the projections in January 2011, Pang and Warshawsky (2011*a*) included actual contributions in 2008 and 2009 (Table 9.3) and discovered that contributions were considerably in excess of the minimum required contributions. Nevertheless, declines in interest rates during 2010 worsened projected funding and increased required contributions compared to earlier projections. Indeed, in the 2011 plan year, required contributions increased to $163 billion, and to $175 billion in 2012, before declining to still high levels of $149 billion in 2013 and $136 billion in 2014,

TABLE 9.3 Estimates and projections of DB corporate plan funded status and required minimum contributions: 2008–14

	A. Pre-Relief Act without funding relief			B. Relief Act with estimated elections		
		Contribution ($b)			Contribution ($b)	
Plan year	Funded status (%)	Actual	Minimum	Funded status (%)	Actual	Minimum
2008	95.3	77.9	37.1	95.3	77.9	37.1
2009	94.6	92.1	24.7	94.6	92.1	24.7
2010	88.8		91.2	88.8		88.6
2011	77.5		163.0	77.4		155.3
2012	79.8		175.4	79.4		170.5
2013	87.1		148.5	86.5		147.3
2014	91.3		135.5	90.6		135.8

Note: Author's estimates of actual contributions based on Form 5500 and financial disclosure data.

Source: Author's computations of data from Towers Watson.

without considering funding relief (Panel A). Because of the limited take-up of any of the relief choices, the 2010 legislative relief is not projected to have much of an impact on these numbers (Panel B).[9]

The PBGC single-employer insurance program

The corporate DB pension sector in the United States is protected by the PBGC. For several reasons, it is to be expected that the global financial crisis would have hurt this entity's assets and liabilities, and also increased the number of terminated underfunded DB pension plans resulting from corporate bankruptcies. This did occur, but perhaps to a lesser extent than what one might have expected given the severity of losses in financial markets and the depth of the overall recession.

Table 9.4 shows the net position of the PBGC single-employer insurance program, defined as the difference between its total assets and total liabilities, from 2001 through 2010 (fiscal years). Assets are mainly investment funds controlled by the PBGC, amassed over the years from the assumption of corporate plans terminated in distress. Similarly, liabilities are mainly the present value of future benefits accumulated over the years from terminated plans. From 2007 to 2010, the net position of the program declined from −\$13.1 billion to −\$21.6 billion. This was indeed a worsening in the financial situation of the program to be sure, but not nearly the extent of decline as occurred from 2001 to 2004, from \$7.7 billion (a surplus!) to −\$23.3 billion, nor reaching as deep a level, even though the program's exposure rose over time due to growing corporate pension liabilities.

This cushioning of the PBGC financial situation in 2008 and 2009 can be explained in part by the extraordinary support given by the federal

TABLE 9.4 Pension Benefit Guaranty Corporation (PBGC) single-employer insurance program: net position, 2001–10 ($m)

Fiscal year	Total assets	Total liabilities	Net position
2001	$21,768	14,036	7,732
2002	$25,430	29,068	(3,638)
2003	$34,016	45,254	(11,238)
2004	$38,993	62,298	(23,305)
2005	$56,470	79,246	(22,776)
2006	$59,972	78,114	(18,142)
2007	$67,241	80,352	(13,111)
2008	$64,612	75,290	(10,678)
2009	$68,736	89,813	(21,077)
2010	$77,827	99,421	(21,594)

Source: Author's computations from PBGC Annual Reports (2001–10).

government and the Federal Reserve to specific financial and nonfinancial companies in severe distress during the recent global financial crisis. Assisted companies thereby avoided the need to turn over their underfunded pension plans to the PBGC. The entity's change in net position can be explained more specifically by the finances of annual operations shown in Table 9.5 for fiscal years 2007–10. Premiums plus investment income (or less losses) less actuarial charges (or plus credits) less losses from completed and probable terminations (or plus credits) less administrative and investment expenses equals the net income (loss) for the year; this is identical to the change in net position. Premium income, owing to a provision in PPA, now increases when the funded status of corporate pension plans deteriorates; this was evident in 2009 and 2010, when premiums paid to the PBGC nearly doubled. Investment income reflects the performance of the PBGC portfolio; as we will see in the next table, the portfolio does include equity holdings, as well as debt and cash, and therefore is subject to financial market fluctuations. Returns were negative in 2008 and positive in 2009 and 2010.

Actuarial charges should generally be positive, owing to the passage of time, but in fact they show big swings across the zero line over time, mainly caused by changes in the discount rate applied to the calculation of the present value of future benefits owed by the PBGC. This volatility was particularly evident in 2009, and losses from terminations were also substantial that year. It should be noted, however, that, complying with generally accepted accounting rules, the PBGC reflects probable terminations of underfunded plans on its books and sometimes reverses those entries when specific corporate financial situations turn around unexpectedly.

Table 9.6 provides us with some key indicators for the PBGC single-employer insurance program, including the number of underfunded plans newly terminated and the net loss in billions from actual plan terminations

TABLE 9.5 Pension Benefit Guaranty Corporation (PBGC) single-employer insurance: annual operations, 2007–10 ($m)

	Fiscal year			
	2010	2009	2008	2007
Premium and other income	$2,261	$1,838	$1,363	$1,531
Investment income (loss)	7,594	6,330	(4,164)	4,737
Actuarial charges and adjustments (credits)	9,421	13,901	(4,813)	346
Losses (credits) from completed and probable terminations	509	4,234	(826)	399
Administrative, investment, and other expenses	442	432	405	492
Net income (loss)	(517)	(10,399)	2,433	5,031

Source: Author's computations using data from PBGC (2007–10).

that year. These indicators clearly worsened in 2009–10. Another critical determinant is the interest rate factor used in valuing PBGC liabilities. As the interest rate factor declined from 6.66 percent in 2008 to 4.41 percent in 2010, the value of PBGC liabilities (which have long durations) increased substantially.

It should also be noted that the PBGC changed its valuation methodology during this period. Currently, the PBGC surveys life insurance industry group annuity indicated prices through the American Council of Life Insurers (ACLI) to obtain input needed to determine interest factors used in valuing pension liabilities and then derives interest factors that will best match the prices from the surveys. Despite its importance to the reported net position of the program, that survey apparently is not audited by the PBGC's accounting firm. Further, the prices from the survey are not necessarily reflective of actual market transactions, nor is the sample of companies surveyed necessarily large and consistent. Prior to 2009, the PBGC had also used an aggregate bond index in 'the mix' of its determination of interest factors, but it discontinued that practice because 'significant volatility in the bond markets led PBGC to research the relationship between quarterly bond yields and annuity prices' (PBGC, 2010: 67).

In January 2006, with a change in mortality tables (due to lower mortality rates), the PBGC increased its interest factors by 170 basis points. Comparing PBGC rates with corporate bond rates over the period 2001–10, two distinct periods are notable. During 2001–5, PBGC rates were lower but they were highly correlated ($R^2 = 0.9151$) with market rates measured by the Composite Corporate Bond Rate (CCBR). In the second period, however, the correlation with market rates is much lower ($R^2 = 0.6509$), while PBGC rates are still below the CCBR. Warshawsky (2009) has suggested that the PBGC should instead use the corporate bond yield curve calculated by the Treasury Department and employed by many corporate pension plans, as the basis for the calculation of its pension liabilities. This may be a more

TABLE 9.6 Pension Benefit Guaranty Corporation (PBGC) single-employer insurance program: key indicators

	Fiscal year		
	2010	2009	2008
New underfunded plans terminated	147	144	67
Net loss from terminations ($b)	1.44	5.83	0.27
Interest rate factor (%)	4.41	5.17	6.66
Return on investment portfolio (%)	12.1	13.2	6.5
Equity share in investment portfolio (%)	31.1	37.2	27

Source: Author's computations using data from PBGC (2008–10).

transparent and accurate methodology in the determination of interest rate factors underlying reasonable estimates of current group annuity prices.

As also seen in Figure 9.7, the return on the PBGC investment portfolio is somewhat volatile and reflects financial market conditions. During 2008–9, the PBGC increased its exposure to the equity market, but then in 2010 it brought that exposure back down. These changes reflect mainly changes in the PBGC Board's investment policy determined by its trustees, the Secretaries of Labor, Treasury and Commerce, and as suggested by the Executive Director.

The 2012 proposed federal government budget released by President Obama in February 2011 included a plan to increase PBGC premiums to make them reflect the riskiness of the pension plan and the plan sponsor, and to give the PBGC Board the authority to set the premium rate. The budget indicated that this proposal would raise $16 billion over ten years, although it would not start for two years. Assuming that the stated increase in revenues represented just an increase in premiums (no details were given), this would represent nearly a doubling in annual premiums from current levels.

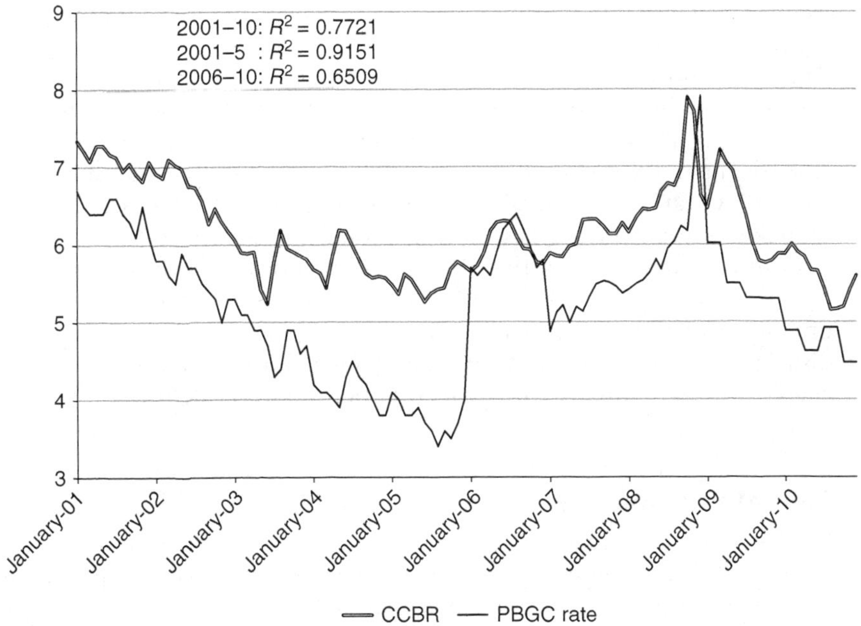

Figure 9.7 Composite Corporate Bond Rate (CCBR) and PBGC rates: 2001–10

Source: Author's computations from PBGC (2011).

Reform proposals

Another way to reduce risk imposed on plan sponsors is to change certain laws that currently constrain risk management in, and therefore increase the risk of, DB plans. Indeed, in light of the global financial crisis, several analysts have recently put forward reform proposals to better enable the management and sharing of risk between plan sponsors and participants. For example, the Society of Actuaries Retirement 20/20 initiative sponsored a conference in 2010 where several proposals were presented, emphasizing new third-party institutions and the DC approach (Kessler and Peterson, 2010).

Another such proposal offers a new type of single- or multiple-employer retirement plan, namely something called a *flexible structured* plan (Warshawsky, 2010). It has the basic features of a DB plan, but the plan sponsor can cut back benefits according to a specified legal rule if the plan funding falls severely, and it must increase benefits if plan funding rises significantly. No reversion of excess assets would be allowed here. This type of plan is intended to share investment risk and return between employers and employees. The proposal would also apply a uniform standard of benefit adequacy on plan design and operation based on certified retirement saving models, with appropriate differentiation for the different plan types, with the structure intended to encourage guaranteed benefits. Nondiscrimination requirements could then be eliminated as essentially redundant, according to the proposal. Other changes in plan rules and provisions include a reform of the reversion tax for DB (both traditional and hybrid) plans, intended to right the risk imbalance inherent in the sponsorship of these plans currently. Additionally, PBGC accounting for its liabilities would be revamped, to improve transparency. The various limits on benefits and contributions to plans would be indexed to wages, rather than prices—it is claimed that this is policy consistent with sensible plan design because plans are intended to replace preretirement wages, not prices, and because the relative position of plan limits in the income distribution is more likely to be maintained, rather than slowly erode, keeping the active interest of sponsor owners and executives.

Role of the employer

Unlike some other recent proposals, this proposal builds on the current employer-based system; accordingly, the current voluntary nature of the second-tier retirement system would continue. Retirement plan sponsorship would not be required by employers, nor would a plan need to be fully paid by employers. Accordingly, incentives under the proposal are designed to be consistent with the encouragement of plan sponsorship, as well as adequate and secure benefits; the goal is to produce a level playing field among plan types, while assuring plan participants and broader society that their needs and concerns are also addressed. An important consideration and even constraint for its success would be a continued sustainable interest by employers in retirement plans.

The *flexible structure plan* has the basic features of a DB plan and therefore the retirement benefits would be specified. The sponsor, however, would be allowed to implement certain specified benefit cutbacks, across the board in percentage terms, to all participants not currently receiving payments from the plan or not older than the plan's normal retirement age, from the currently indicated level of benefits, if the plan funding, specially defined, fell below certain thresholds. As a counterpart, plan improvements, again distributed evenly and proportionately across the board to participants not receiving benefits, would be required from the current benefit level if the plan funding increased above certain thresholds. No reversions of excess pension assets would be allowed for this plan type.

Any unilateral or bargained improvements in future benefit accruals for a flexible structure plan, unrelated to funding status, could be made proportionally among participants, not favoring any group, on a going-forward basis. Benefit improvements for past service, however, could only be made if they were funded fully. Benefit cutbacks would not be allowed except in response to declines in funding status.

For this purpose, funded status would be defined as the ratio of plan assets to plan liabilities, where the present value of benefits accrued to participants receiving payments or older than the plan's retirement age is subtracted from both the numerator and denominator. Plan assets and liabilities would otherwise follow the definitions and valuation requirements in current law.

The cutback–enhancement regime for this plan type has several elements. Within a corridor of funding statuses around the current plan liability (say, 80–120 percent), the current funding requirements operate; that is, normal cost must be covered, any shortfalls must be amortized over seven years, but no benefit improvements are required. The corridor provides stability of benefits to plan participants most of the time, while imposing only modest volatility on plan sponsors. If the funding status were to fall below the corridor, the benefit liability may be reduced, according to a rule considered below (flexible). Normal cost is still paid, and the corridor is reset around the new liability. Benefit reductions are limited: if the current liability falls below 50 percent of the initial liability, there can be no further cuts, and contributions must be made to amortize losses so that at least 50 percent of the initial liability will be paid to plan participants. Above the corridor, benefit improvements must be made, again according to one of the rules discussed below; the rules generally give symmetrical treatment to cuts and improvements. The new liability is calculated and the corridor is moved around it. Finally, normal cost relates to the current accruals of the plan, which are dependent on the plan's fixed design (structured) and not to its funding status. The plan would offer a life annuity as a distribution option.

Contributions would be made by the employer in the new plan type. Mandatory employee contributions would not be allowed because the participants do not control the plan investments. As a retirement instrument where the worker shares to some extent the results of the plan's performance, voluntary employee contributions to the plan would be allowed to purchase extra benefits, on a tax-deductible basis, comparable to the treatment of 401(k) plans.

This proposal considers alternative cutback–enhancement rules (regimes), with somewhat different risk-sharing properties. One possibility would set the corridor at 80–120 percent; if outside the corridor, cuts and increases in benefits would be made *pari-passu* with funding status changes below or above the corridor (i.e. according to the distance outside the corridor). For example, if the funding status fell to 75 percent of the current liability, a 5 percent cut could be made to the benefits, and the corridor would move downward around the new, lower benefit liability. Normal cost must be paid, as well as any amortizations of past losses. Cuts may continue to be made, as warranted by funding status changes, but benefits cannot fall below 50 percent of the initial promise. If the funding status rose to, say, 130 percent, a 10 percent 'permanent' increase to benefits must be made, and the corridor would move upward around the new benefit liability.[10] It is therefore argued that this change could reduce the risk inherent in the sponsorship of these plans currently, perhaps renewing the interest by plan sponsors in DB plans. In the context of the overall proposal, the change in excise tax is intended to help achieve 'an even playing field' in the costs, burdens, and advantages for sponsors and participants among the three plan types in the new, reformed, retirement system.

The team has also explored having the PBGC use market interest rates as the discount rate used to value its obligations (instead of the current practice of basing it on insurance industry surveys). Specifically, the idea is to use the high-grade corporate bond spot 'yield' curve calculated by the Treasury Department in a highly transparent manner, with appropriate adjustments for agency expenses, to arrive at good estimates of group annuity prices and to be used in calculating the finances of the PBGC, both income statement and balance sheet. The purpose of this change is to bring more transparency and accuracy to the accounting for the insurance program. And finally, the proposal posits that the indexation of the various limits on all types of qualified retirement plans should be made to the average wage computed by Social Security, rather than the consumer price index. In addition, levels should be increased as Social Security is reformed, presumably becoming even more progressive, to maintain a fair balance between public and private programs for retirement.

Conclusion

The global financial crisis hit corporate DB pension plans hard. Asset values declined dramatically as the stock market was shocked in late 2008 and early 2009. Interest rates used to value pension liabilities rose initially in late 2008, but then they declined steadily over the next two years. As a result, the funding status of plans declined quickly, from 106 percent in 2007 to 77 percent in 2008, before recovering somewhat to 83 percent in 2010. Plan sponsors curtailed their investment portfolio risk (moving away from equities), increased contributions (even above legal minimums), and froze and closed traditional DB plans, continuing trends already evident before the financial crisis. The federal government provided several types of funding relief, both legislative and regulatory. Some reforms were substantial, for the 2009 plan year in particular, in that even the high level of contributions actually made was below what would otherwise have been required. In any case, the relief was temporary, and required contributions will increase significantly in the foreseeable future unless discount rates rise significantly or asset markets boom.

Clearly, there remains much risk and fragility in financial markets and the economy, perhaps more than countenance prior to the global financial crisis. Plan sponsors are reluctant to bear the entire risk burden, yet workers and retirees still want structured benefits and desire guaranteed benefits. Accordingly, to encourage the activities of plan sponsors, and to better manage risk, fairly and efficiently, while still providing structured benefits to workers, it is useful to evaluate new plan designs that can more fairly and efficiently spread the risk burden between sponsors and workers. Ultimately, the goal would be to ensure that workers can retire at appropriate ages in reasonable comfort and at reasonable cost.

Acknowledgments

The author acknowledges Brendan McFarland and Gaobo Pang for their contributions included here, Vishal Apte for excellent research assistance, and Susie Farris for her help with document preparation. Opinions and conclusions are solely those of the author and do not reflect views of the institutions supporting the research, with whom the author is affiliated, or the Pension Research Council.

Endnotes

1. Two fairly ready and current sources of information exist on investment patterns of private DB (and defined contribution or DC) plans. The first, from the Flows of Funds Accounts of the Federal Reserve Board (FRB, 2011), provides data on flows and outstanding amounts, by asset classes, on a quarterly basis. As of this writing, the most recent data available is for third quarter 2010. A drawback to this source is that single-employer and multiemployer plans are reported together, although assets of single-employer plans generally represent more than three-quarters of the total for DB plans. Another drawback is that these data are estimated from various underlying sources; the estimates change for several quarters until no further revisions are made. The second information source, from disclosures in the annual financial reports of corporate plan sponsors, provides detailed data on asset holdings by class and valuation methodology on an annual basis. Recent changes in financial accounting standards made these disclosures more granular and accurate. Yet one drawback is that the data are reported and collected with a lag; another is that the collections do not represent the universe of single-employer plans. As of this writing, the most recent financial disclosure data are available for year-end 2009 for Fortune 1000 companies (collected by Towers Watson). Despite their differences, the two sources are largely consistent in the story they tell about trends, changes, and the influence of the global financial crisis on DB plan investments.
2. These are the Fortune 1000 companies with calendar-year financial statements for which Towers Watson has consistently obtained data.
3. Kummernuss et al. (2010) offer evidence that contributions of employer securities actually declined during the global financial crisis.
4. Data on contributions actually made on which we base our modeling of future funding obligations come from Schedule SB of the Form 5500 through 2008 for the universe of plans; for 2009, it is from the financial disclosure data for larger companies reported above, adjusted for average relationships with the Schedule SB data.
5. See Mazo and Greenblum (2012) for a discussion of the impact of the financial crisis on multiemployer pensions.
6. This smoothing is somewhat limited though, such that the assumed earnings rate cannot exceed the third segment rate mandated by PPA for valuing benefits starting in fifteen or more years, and overall computed values are subject to the asset corridor test; that is, that the actuarial asset value must fall within 90–110 percent of the fair market value.
7. Pang and Warshawsky (2009*b*) assume that most plan sponsors elected to use the market value of assets in their required funding calculation and a smoothed actuarial value of liabilities (as allowed by PPA), using three segment discount rates averaged over the past twenty-four months. This is because plan sponsors did not want to use the simple twenty-five-month average of past asset values without also gaining the ability to assume some expected investment return over the averaging period on the expectation that generally market prices, particularly of equities, tend to rise over time. So, according to the model, the WRERA provision allowing asset smoothing then had little direct impact on expected funding obligations, without an ability to switch valuation methodologies. If,

however, plan sponsors would switch their valuation elections to maximize asset values and minimize liability values, funding obligations for the 2009 plan year would be considerably reduced. In particular, smoothed asset values and market value of liabilities (using the temporarily high corporate bond yields as of October and November 2008) would provide considerable funding relief. Under law and regulation, sponsors are generally only allowed to change valuation elections once every five years without permission from the IRS; hence, Pang and Warshawsky initially assumed that plan sponsors would be reluctant to choose such a 'mismatched' valuation methodology, part smoothed and part market, and to be locked in to that choice. Choosing consistent valuations (all smoothed or all market, but mostly all smoothed), these methodologies were estimated to improve the average funded status to 80 percent in plan year 2009 and to 85 percent in plan year 2010, and to reduce required contributions to $91 billion in 2009 and to $84 billion in 2010.

8. In March 2009, the IRS announced that plans would be allowed to make a change, without the need to ask for permission from the IRS, so that 'for a calendar year plan with a January 1, 2009 valuation date, the IRS will not challenge the use of the monthly yield curve for January 2009, or any of the four months immediately preceding January 2009'. In September 24, 2009, the IRS said that regulations would provide for 'automatic approval for a new choice of interest rates for the first plan year beginning in 2010'. Hence, according to internal Watson Wyatt surveys, most plan sponsors felt comfortable in choosing a smoothed asset valuation and market liability valuation for the 2009 plan year, with the ability to switch again in 2010 or later.
9. It should also be noted that multiemployer plans were also subject to new PPA requirements and got considerable funding relief (Mazo and Greenblum, 2012).
10. A specific provision in the overall proposal intended to encourage the maintenance of guaranteed DB plans (not applied to flexible structured plans) is also modeled by Pang and Warshawsky (2009*a*), which would lower the excise tax rate to 20 percent (instead of the current 50 percent) and allow excess asset reversions to employers for DB plans funded at least at 120 percent of their liabilities. As in current law, sponsors would have to fully vest accrued benefits if they took reversions, though they would not have to terminate their plans. Also, the proposal includes a lower excise tax rate—15 percent—on asset reversions in bankruptcy, instead of the 20 percent under current law. The excise tax rate chosen reflects some past research that finds the rate needed to capture the corporate income tax otherwise avoided by the exclusion of pension fund investment income from taxation. Corporate income taxes would also need to be paid on the asset reversions. The model results indicate that a more moderate excise tax rate together with a reasonable funding threshold for asset reversions would enable sponsors to spend the excess funds on other corporate needs, thereby lowering the cost of sponsorship of DB plans. It would also open a considerable revenue source for the government, with only a small increase in bankruptcy cost for the PBGC.

References

Board of Governors of the Federal Reserve System (FRB) (2011). *FRB: Z.1 Release—Flow of Funds Accounts of the United States.* Washington, DC: FRB (June–July).

Clark, R., A. Glickstein, and T. Hill (2012). "Adopting Hybrid Pension Plans: Effects of Economic Crisis and Regulatory Reform", in R. Maurer, O. S. Mitchell, and M. J. Warshawsky, eds., *Reshaping Retirement Security: Lessons from the Global Financial Crisis.* Oxford, UK: Oxford University Press.

Internal Revenue Service (IRS) (2011). "Composite Corporate Bond Rate Table", 5 August. Washington, DC: IRS. http://www.irs.gov/retirement/article/0,,id=123229,00.html

Kessler, E. and A. Peterson (2010). "The Amazing Transformation of Ret I. Rement", *The Actuary*, October/November: 25–29.

Kummernuss, E, B. McFarland, and M. J. Warshawsky (2010). "Company Securities in Pension Plan Assets", *Towers Watson Insider*, n.p. New York, NY: Towers Watson (December).

Mazo, J. F. and E. Greenblum (2012). "Multiemployer Pension Plans in the Financial Crisis", in R. Maurer, O. S. Mitchell, and M. J. Warshawsky, eds., *Reshaping Retirement Security: Lessons from the Global Financial Crisis.* Oxford, UK: Oxford University Press.

McFarland, B. and M. J. Warshawsky (2010). "Asset Allocations of Corporate Pension Plans in 2009", *Towers Watson Insider*, 20(11): 1–6. New York, NY: Towers Watson (November).

——, G. Pang, and M. J. Warshawsky (2009). "Does Freezing a Defined-Benefit Pension Plan Increase Company Value? Empirical Evidence", *Financial Analysts Journal*, 65(4): 47–59.

Pang, G. and M. J. Warshawsky (2009*a*). "Reform of the Tax on Reversions of Excess Pension Assets", *Journal of Pension Economics and Finance*, 8(1): 107–30.

—— and —— (2009*b*). "The Future of DB Funding Under PPA, the Recovery Act and Relief Proposals", *Watson Wyatt Insider*, 19(1): 1–6 (January).

—— and —— (2009*c*). "Funding for DB Pension Plans in 2010 and 2011 Under Relief Proposals", *Watson Wyatt Insider*, 19(10): 1–4 (October).

—— and —— (2010). "Single-Employer DB Plan Funding Obligations Under 2010 Funding Relief", *Towers Watson Insider*, 20(7): 1–4. New York, NY: Towers Watson (July).

—— and —— (2011*a*). "Funding Obligations for Single-Employer DB Pension Plans: Updated Projections for 2011–2014", *Towers Watson Insider*, n.p. New York, NY: Towers Watson (March).

—— and —— (2011*b*). "Comparative Costs and Risks for Sponsors of Traditional Defined Benefit, Defined Contribution and Hybrid Plans", Towers Watson Working Paper. Washington, DC: Towers Watson (February).

Pension Benefit Guaranty Corporation (PBGC) (2001). *Annual Report.* Washington, DC: PBGC.

—— (2002). *Annual Report.* Washington, DC: PBGC.

—— (2003). *Annual Report.* Washington, DC: PBGC.

—— (2004). *Annual Report.* Washington, DC: PBGC.

—— (2005). *Annual Report.* Washington, DC: PBGC.

—— (2006). *Annual Report*. Washington, DC: PBGC.
—— (2007). *Annual Report*. Washington, DC: PBGC.
—— (2008). *Annual Report*. Washington, DC: PBGC.
—— (2009). *Annual Report*. Washington, DC: PBGC.
—— (2010). *Annual Report*. Washington, DC: PBGC.
—— (2011). *Interest Rate and Mortality Factors*. Washington, DC: PBGC (April).
Towers Watson (2010*a*). "Retirement Attitudes Survey, Part II, Attitudes Toward Risk", Towers Watson Report. Washington, DC: Towers Watson.
—— (2010*b*). "Towers Watson-Forbes Insights 2010 Pension Risk Survey: U.S. Executive Views", Towers Watson Report. Washington, DC: Towers Watson.
Warshawsky, M. J. (2007). "The New Pension Law and Defined Benefit Plans: A Surprisingly Good Match", *Journal of Pension Benefits*, 14(3): 14–27 (Spring).
—— (2009). "Funding Relief for Single-Employer Defined Benefit Pension Plans." Testimony before the Ways and Means Committee (October 1).
—— (2010). "A Proposal for Retirement Plan Reform", *Tax Notes*, 128(10): 1041–58 (September 6).
Watson Wyatt Worldwide (2008). *Retirement Plan Design: Past, Present and Future*. Washington, DC: Watson Wyatt.

Chapter 10

Multiemployer Pension Plans Respond to the Financial Crisis

Judith F. Mazo and Eli Greenblum

Multiemployer pension plans cover workers under collective bargaining agreements including one or more unions and at least two employers. Negotiated employer contributions to stand-alone trust funds are managed by boards of trustees, on which employers and employees are equally represented; almost all multiemployer plans are subject to the Taft-Hartley Act as well as the Employee Retirement Income Security Act (ERISA) and the Internal Revenue Code (IRC). These plans are distinctive both in terms of their administrative logistics and the extent to which covered employee preferences influence plan design and operations. This chapter offers a description of the plans themselves and the rules governing their financing. Next, we analyze the impact of the financial crisis on a subset of multiemployer plans—the 400+ plans whose actuarial valuations are handled by the Segal Company—with special focus on a subset of 107 plans classified as being in critical funding status for the 2010 plan year that had adopted rehabilitation plans by the time of the study.

We show that the Pension Protection Act of 2006 (PPA), as supplemented by temporary relief legislation in 2008 and 2010, resulted in an overall beneficial effect on these multiemployer plans and enabled most of them to navigate to a relatively secure financial position, as determined under the funding rules for multiemployer plans. The sacrifices made by employers and participants in these efforts suggest that multiemployer defined pension plans continue to enjoy support from those they cover, plus their employers' cooperation in keeping the plans going.

Methodology

The total number of multiemployer defined benefit (DB) plans in the United States has dropped from about 2,400 in 1980 to 1,600 in 2009, largely due to plan mergers. Yet over the same period, the number of participants in multiemployer plans has grown somewhat, reaching 10.4 million by 2008, but the demographics have also shifted dramatically. In 1980, 76 percent of multiemployer pension participants were active workers, a share that dropped to 45 percent by 2008, according to the Pension Benefit Guaranty Corporation (PBGC, 2010). As the largest actuarial and benefits consulting firm in the United States working with multiemployer plans, the Segal Company's clients represent about 25 percent of those plans, covering roughly 30 percent of multiemployer plan participants nationwide. The information provided below is based on published annual surveys of plans' funded status information as measured under PPA, completed by Segal Company actuaries in connection with the required annual certifications, as well as an unpublished in-depth survey of plans classified as critical for 2010.[1] The Segal Company's database covers virtually all types and sizes of multiemployer pension plans, in all geographic areas, industries, and levels of financial stability. The plans covered represent the broadest and most complete picture available of this country's multiemployer plans.[2] Our review of the data is supplemented by observations based on illustrative experiences of assorted plans with which we work.[3]

What are multiemployer plans and why do they have special rules?

The core definition of a multiemployer plan is straightforward: it is a plan to which two or more employers are required to contribute, under one or more collective bargaining agreements. Beyond that simple statement lie many variations. For example, these funds may range from 50 to 100 active workers and include two to four contributing employers in a locality to hundreds of thousands of participants and thousands of employers covering large geographic regions. Likewise, assets may range from $15 million to $20 billion; however, the typical size ranges from 1,000 to 5,000 participants, with assets of about $100–$500 million. In some industries, a fairly large number of employers may contribute under one or a few collective bargaining agreements to which they all subscribe, while in others there may be as many labor agreements as there are contributing employers, or even more (if companies contribute under separate agreements with respect to separate facilities). Some plans cover metropolitan areas, cities, or even smaller jurisdictions, while many are statewide. Beyond some very large regional plans (e.g. the Teamsters' Central States and Western Conference Pension Funds, the two largest multiemployer plans which together cover people in diverse industries working from the southeastern United States to the Pacific coast), many unions cosponsor national funds as well as those with more targeted coverage. Predictably, the size and shape of fund coverage reflect the size and shape of the industries in which the participants work and the evolution of union representation in those industries. Most multiemployer groups have DB plans, many also have defined contribution (DC) plans (called 'annuity funds'), and a fairly small subset of those include 401(k) arrangements. Many multiemployer pension plans facing financial problems have reduced future benefit accruals, but few have completely frozen accruals.

Ordinarily, covered workers are all represented by the same local union, or by locals affiliated with the same international union. Multiemployer plans are found throughout the economy, notably in the construction industry, entertainment, trucking and transportation, longshore, retail, mining and manufacturing, food service, hospitality, health care, building service, communications, and the garment trades. More than half of the nation's multiemployer funds are in the construction trades, whose funds cover roughly 35 percent of all multiemployer-plan participants. Multiemployer pension plans are usually paired with multiemployer funds that provide health coverage, life insurance, and other welfare-type benefits, which are also financed through fixed employer contributions.

Understanding that there are exceptions at each general point, commonly found general characteristics of multiemployer funds have led to the development of special rules to accommodate their special circumstances. Most notably, virtually all multiemployer plans are set up as trusts structured under the Taft-Hartley Act, operated by joint management–labor Boards of Trustees as stand-alone entities operationally independent of the contributing employers and the unions that represent their participants. The Trustees, as plan sponsors, have full responsibility for managing the assets and administering the benefits, including the duty to make sure the plan meets all applicable legal requirements. For the great majority of plans, they are also responsible for designing the benefit formulas.

Typically, participating employers contribute the amounts negotiated under their bargaining agreements, say $2 for each hour that participants work in covered service. The plan trustees, working with their professional advisors, determine and set the benefits, while the unions and employers independently negotiate over the flow of contributions. While the employers' most salient obligation is to contribute as defined in their labor contracts, because the plans promise participants a fixed benefit, these are classified as DB plans under ERISA and the IRC. Contributing employers are often small businesses that might not provide pension or health coverage on their own. Also, employees often work for short periods before moving on to similar jobs with different contributing employers. The employers compete with each other and with noncontributing companies for contracts and customers.

Without the intra-industry standardization and portable pension coverage that multiemployer plans provide, few of the participants would have access to a DB plan or the tenure with any one employer to earn reasonable pensions, given their transitory employment. Consistent with minimum standards set in ERISA and the IRC, most plans require a worker to have 1,000 hours of service with the employer sponsoring the plan during a twelve-month period (a year of service) to be eligible for plan coverage and vesting credit, and between 1,000 and 2,000 hours during a twelve-month period for a full-year's benefit credit.[4] A multiemployer plan participant may work for a single employer for 20, 50, or 150 hours during a given year, but will earn years of vesting and accrual credit by combining the service performed for all employers contributing to the same multiemployer plan. Regardless of which or how many employers a participant worked for, his or her pension is owed by the plan, backed by the industry. Contributing employers may come and go, but whoever is obliged to contribute in a given year will be funding a portion of the plan's accumulated liabilities to all of its participants over time, not just the benefits being earned by its own workers.

Retirement benefits in a multiemployer plan are rarely based on an employee's pay. Rather, the pension is usually a specified dollar amount per year of covered service (e.g. $80 per month times years of service), or a specified percentage of the total that employers are required to contribute based on the participant's work (e.g. a monthly benefit equal to 2 percent of total required contributions, so a participant with 1,500 hours of service in a given year at a $1.00 hourly contribution rate would accrue a $30 monthly benefit). Often the benefit formula is a combination, reflecting changes in the formula over time. For example, a plan may provide a monthly benefit that is the sum of $28 per year of service prior to 1980, $49 per year of service from 1980 through 2003, and 2 percent of contributions required from January 1, 2004. Some plans have a uniform benefit formula for all participants, while others offer a variety of benefit formulas that correspond, for example, to varying contribution rates under the different collective bargaining agreements.

Multiemployer pension plans hardly ever pay out benefits prior to early or normal retirement (except for death or disability), since 'termination of employment' other than for retirement is not a meaningful concept in these kinds of continuous-coverage group pension plans. Multiemployer pension plans generally pay pensions as life annuities: few of them offer lump-sum options, and those that do usually offer only a small portion of a participant's benefit as a lump sum. Retirees make up a relatively large proportion of the participant base for many multiemployer plans in part because the plans reserve most or all of the benefits earned for the provision of ongoing streams of retirement income.

Several pertinent points emerge from our overview. First, because multiemployer plans are the product of collective bargaining, the funding and other regulatory requirements must accommodate bargaining realities, where stability in pension and other costs is paramount.[5] Moreover, since employers cannot be compelled to contribute beyond what they have agreed to in collective bargaining, the required funding generally cannot change during the term of a collective bargaining agreement. Inasmuch as many plans have a multitude of bargaining agreements that expire and renew at varying times, and as the bargaining process cannot accommodate sharp or unanticipated expense shocks, predictability in pension-funding requirements is essential, over time, beyond the standard three- to four-year duration of a single bargaining agreement. When the parties negotiate pension contributions, the amounts are explicit alternatives to increases in wages, health contributions, or other elements of compensation, so the employees often view the contributions as 'their money'. If they do not believe the trade-off is worth it, they might reject the agreement, which could throw the plan's funding arrangements into disarray.

The fact that the plans are run for union-represented groups also means that policymakers have not worried that these plans might be used to maximize tax advantages for employers, especially since both the Taft-Hartley Act and ERISA bar employers from recovering surplus assets after a plan termination. Moreover, the plans are egalitarian, providing essentially the same benefits for all employees with the same patterns of service under the plan, so there is no question of discrimination in favor of the highly paid. Due to the Taft-Hartley structure, with an independent operation run by a Board on which the employers and the employees have equal representation, the entire cost of plan administration must be paid out of the plan's assets, with funds that would otherwise be dedicated to paying benefits.

In most cases, union trustees are also union officers elected by the membership to their union position, and as politicians they are highly sensitive to the will of the voting membership (which sometimes includes retired as well as active workers). Trustees, in turn, are alert to the fact that the employees and the employers can ultimately express their sentiments about how the plan is being run, by negotiating to reduce or cut off contributions.[6] Accordingly, multiemployer plan strategies tend to reflect their stakeholders' preferences subject to the demands of governing federal law.

In our judgment, the finances of multiemployer plans are typically more stable than those of single-employer plans sponsored by the kinds of small- and medium-sized employers because of the broader multiemployer contribution base. By definition, a multiemployer plan does not depend on the fortunes of one company. Often when a local multiemployer plan does begin to falter, it is merged into a larger, stronger plan covering people represented by the same international union. On the other hand, when a multiemployer plan actually fails, it tends to be because of the failure of the industry that has supported it, and the losses to participants and to the pension guarantee system can be large because they include liabilities accrued by the industry over time and not just by people working for the current cadre of contributing employers.

How do funding rules address multiemployer plans?

Distinctions for multiemployer plans have been part of the ERISA minimum-funding rules and termination insurance program since the start. As experience under ERISA has developed, the differences between the regimes governing single-employer and multiemployer plans have widened. That history can be instructive.

1974–80: the post-ERISA years

The US IRC has long included special rules to allow multiemployer plans to function as pools, rather than a cluster of individual employer plans, and to rely on negotiated contribution rates for funding and deduction purposes. Thus, among other things, IRC s. 413(b) provides that employer contributions are considered to be deductible if the amounts expected to be contributed would have been within the deduction limits. This protects the employers if, for example, there is more covered work than anticipated, resulting in the employers' contributing more to the plan, in the aggregate, than would normally be deductible.

When the pension plan termination insurance program was designed, Congress was initially uncertain whether it was needed by or appropriate for multiemployer plans. When ERISA was passed, no multiemployer plan had ever terminated, and, because of their broad contribution bases, these plans were expected to be able to cover all of the benefits they promised without government help. Accordingly, the initial multiemployer guarantee program was an experiment: from 1974 to 1977, the PBGC had the discretion to insure benefits under terminated multiemployer plans, and very little financing for it ($0.50/participant annual premiums vs $1.00/participant for single-employer plans).

Early experience

Rather soon after ERISA was passed, three multiemployer plans sought PBGC protection. These covered milkmen in New York, milkmen in New Jersey, and cap makers in St. Louis. This made clear that there was a role for a government guarantee of multiemployer pensions, and although it was rarely likely to be invoked, the aggregate pension claims could be large compared to claims then typical under terminating single-employer plans. Experience during that discretionary period also disclosed one of the most serious threats to these plans' survival and the guarantee program: like employers sponsoring single-employer plans, employers contributing to multiemployer plans could be liable to the PBGC for the underfunding of a terminated plan that PBGC took over. Accordingly, it was in an employer's interest to leave a multiemployer plan when plan funding first showed signs of weakening. This, of course, would aggravate the plan's problems as fewer and fewer employers would be left to carry the funding load. It would also stress established labor relations, as employers had only three ways to get out of a multiemployer plan: with the union's agreement (which was likely to mean an agreement to end pension coverage for that group and substitute a DC plan), by persuading the employees to oust the union, or by going out of business.

Early multiemployer funding reform

In 1977, Congress extended the discretionary coverage period to allow for the in-depth study of multiemployer pension plans that had not been done in the lead-up to the enactment of ERISA. It concluded that adapting the PBGC guarantee program to fit multiemployer plans would be futile unless the law also addressed the 'last-man-standing' psychology that was propelling employers to exit multiemployer plans or press for their termination. Ultimately, the Multiemployer Pension Plan Amendments Act of 1980 (MPPAA) introduced the concept of withdrawal liability. Complex and controversial, this law generally imposes liability on an employer that withdraws from a multiemployer plan for a *pro rata* share of the plan's underfunding. The more underfunded the plan is when the employer leaves, the higher its withdrawal liability is likely to be.

Withdrawal liability created a major incentive for employers to push to get their multiemployer plans well funded and to keep them there. MPPAA also revamped the pension guarantee program for those plans, making the PBGC the financier of very last resort. Instead of guaranteeing unfunded benefits when a multiemployer plan terminates, the PBGC does not step in with financial support until the plan becomes insolvent and lacks cash to pay currently due benefits at the guaranteed level. Just about all multiemployer plans terminate when there are no employers left to contribute, because all of them have either gone out of business or otherwise are no longer obligated to contribute to the plan.[7] When that happens, plan Trustees continue to administer the plan, collecting withdrawal liabilities, managing assets, and paying benefits, until the funds are used up. That is the point at which the plan can draw on PBGC for financial assistance.

The multiemployer benefit guarantees themselves were also redefined and reset at a low level. Initially, this was a maximum of $234/year per year of service, or an annual pension of $7,020 for a retiree who had worked under the plan for thirty years. This was not indexed for inflation. Congress has increased the guarantee level once, in 1999, and today the maximum is $429/year for each year of service, or $12,870 a year for someone with a thirty-year career under the plan. The other especially notable MPPAA change was the introduction of special funding rules for multiemployer plans nearing or at bankruptcy (IRC ss. 418–418E), which authorized benefit reductions and required that benefit payments be cut down to guaranteed levels. As it turns out, this plan reorganization concept hardly ever comes into play, mainly because it focuses on plans that do not have enough assets to cover their liabilities for current pensioners. While this may have been a concern in 1980 shortly after the ERISA funding requirements took effect, at this point, when multiemployer plans start running short of funds, it tends to be due to investment losses that erode the reserves being held for future retirees.

1980–2008: the Multiemployer Pension Plan Amendments Act

While funding and guarantee programs for single-employer plans were changed repeatedly over the next quarter-century, multiemployer rules stayed essentially the same. The 1976 ERISA rules continued to govern multiemployer plans' minimum funding requirements. Following a flurry of protest and litigation, including several trips to the US Supreme Court, employers adapted to withdrawal liability and learned to take it into account in business planning. Only a few small plans applied for PBGC financial assistance and the multiemployer guarantee fund consistently ran a surplus. During the 1990s, most plans faced the challenge of overfunding, and looked for ways to be sure the employers could take a tax deduction for their pension contribution. The MPPAA helped establish this period of repose. After the intensity of the 1979–80 legislative battles, neither Congress nor the Administrations had much appetite for reigniting the withdrawal liability controversy, so multiemployer plans were routinely exempted from whatever funding changes were enacted. But the real reason why the MPPAA reforms seemed to work so well was that multiemployer plans were prominent among those benefiting from the general prosperity of the 1990s. By and large, plan investments did well, there was plenty of work for participants, and employers made profits, so withdrawal liability and statutory minimum funding requirements drew little attention.

During the 1990s, negotiated contributions generally kept rolling in to multiemployer pension plans even when the new money was not needed for plan funding. Some plans allowed unions and employers to negotiate short-term 'contribution holidays', and in some cases the bargaining agreements redirected the flow of contributions to the health plan or the annuity fund. But unions were typically reluctant to propose or agree to interrupt the rhythm of continuous pension contributions because restarting them at a later date would be costly from a negotiating perspective: the union would have to trade other benefits just to reestablish the practice of employer contributions. Most plans were amended during that period to increase benefits, sometimes repeatedly, in order to absorb the additional funds and assure that employers could deduct their plan contributions.

This era of general contentment and overabundance came to an abrupt end when the investment markets crashed in 2000–2. Mature multiemployer plans with many retirees and declining numbers of active participants had become highly leveraged, living off the earnings from the very considerable reserves they had built up. When those investment gains turned into losses, funding levels declined and withdrawal liability flared back up, reawakening employer suspicions. The median investment performance of multiemployer plans in the Segal Advisors Multiemployer Universe was 3.5 percent in 2000, −3.4 percent in 2001, and −8.2 percent in 2002.[8] Since the plans' typical actuarial earnings assumption was 7–7.5 percent, this translated into actuarial losses ranging from 4 percent in 2000 to 15.2 percent in 2002. Some plans saw funding deficiencies looming and turned to IRS for help under ERISA relief provisions (mainly amortization extensions), but the agency was swamped with funding-waiver pleas from troubled single-employer plans and those relatively unfamiliar with the intricacies of multiemployer funding. In fact, the IRS did not start acting on multiemployer plan relief requests until 2005.

The Pension Funding Equity Act of 2004 provided a little breathing room for single-employer plans but not for multiemployer plans. By mid-2004, most multiemployer plans seemed to be treading water well enough to avoid the catastrophic terminations that workers and the PBGC had faced in the airline and steel industries, so the multiemployer sector did not command policymaker attention. Nevertheless, some plans were significantly damaged and were facing imminent minimum funding crises. In 2005, several major employers and employer associations, unions, and multiemployer plans banded together to advocate for a substantive update to the multiemployer funding rules that would be compatible with the character of the plans and the industries that support them. This coalition's work with Congress led to the development of the multiemployer provisions of the PPA of 2006.

2008–present: the Pension Protection Act

Enacted in the summer of 2006, the PPA funding rules took effect with the start of the 2008 plan year. This Act made a few changes in the mechanics of the ERISA funding standard account and related rules, which continued to apply to multiemployer plans. New benefits and benefit increases are now amortized over fifteen rather than thirty years, and any short-term benefit increases must be funded as quickly as they will be paid.[9] Unlike single-employer plans, multiemployer pension plans can continue to use long-term investment return assumptions chosen by their actuaries and employ traditional actuarial methods of smoothing changes in asset values to temper the impact of investment market fluctuations. PPA also increased the limits on deductible contributions, to help pension plans build reserves without penalizing contributing employers.

Longer term perspectives: the zones

For multiemployer plans, the principal PPA innovation was to require trustees and bargaining parties to look past the plan's financial status as of a given valuation date, to take a measure of where it is headed. If the funding is projected to deteriorate to specified levels over a seven-year horizon, the trustees must adopt a formal corrective plan with annual monitoring and adjustments specified to stay on course. The law provides new tools to help trustees bring plan liabilities and assets into balance. Additional reporting to participants and employers, as well as to the government, provides extra transparency and accountability.

Specifically, the law characterizes a multiemployer plan as 'endangered' if its funding percentage (ratio of assets to liabilities, both measured on an actuarial basis) is below 80 percent, or if it is projected to have an accumulated funding deficiency in the funding standard account within seven years (as established under the ERISA rules, with the PPA modifications noted above). If both are true, the plan is considered 'seriously endangered'. 'Critical status' indicates more serious problems: a projected funding deficiency within four or five years or pending near-term cash-flow difficulties. Colloquially, endangered status is called the 'yellow zone' and critical status is the 'red zone'. Following the Homeland Security theme, a plan that is neither endangered nor critical is said to be in the 'green zone', although there is no official classification for a plan that looks healthy according to these metrics.

When a plan goes into the yellow zone, contribution reductions and benefit increases are restricted. The trustees must come up with a Funding Improvement Plan ('FIP') designed to close the underfunding gap by at least one-third over a ten-year period (for most seriously endangered plans, the goal is a 20 percent improvement over fifteen years). This must include schedules of benefit changes and, if necessary, contribution increases, to be presented to the employers and unions so they can choose a solution for their group through collective bargaining. The FIP must be reevaluated each year by the trustees, and adjusted if needed to stay on schedule.

A plan in the red zone must be addressed with more serious solutions. When a plan goes into the red zone, in addition to enforcing restrictions on reducing contributions and increasing benefits, the plan must stop paying lump sums and similar front-loaded benefits to new retirees. Trustees must adopt a rehabilitation plan that aims at getting the fund out of critical status within a ten-year period. This includes offering the bargaining parties schedules of benefit cuts and contribution increases that are calibrated to achieve this improvement, for them to select through bargaining. To give parties a full opportunity to deal with the plan's financial challenges through bargaining, the law starts the funding improvement and rehabilitation periods at the beginning of the plan year following the expiration of the bargaining agreements covering 75 percent of the active participants. As a practical matter, this often gives plans an extra two or three years to recover. Also, the Workers, Retirees, and Employers Relief Act of 2008 allowed multiemployer plans that were in endangered or critical status in 2009 to extend their recovery periods by three additional years.

Benefit reductions under a rehabilitation plan can include the reduction or elimination of 'adjustable benefits' that are ordinarily protected from cutback, including recent benefit increases, early retirement subsidies, and other benefit features—but not the accrued benefit payable at normal retirement age. Moreover, these benefit reductions are ignored when computing withdrawal liability. For active workers, future accrual rates cannot be cut below 1 percent of contributions unless the union and employers negotiate a deeper reduction as part of a package that is acceptable to the trustees. Employers that contribute to a red-zone plan are subject to a contribution surcharge (initially 5 percent, going up to 10 percent after the first plan year) until they agree to an acceptable schedule of contributions and related benefit adjustments under the rehabilitation plan. However, there are no penalties on employers if a red-zone plan actually has a funding deficiency, as long as the parties are living up to their red-zone obligations and the fund makes progress as expected under the rehabilitation plan. The rehabilitation plan benchmarks can be revised if it turns out that the original program was too ambitious, but the ultimate goal remains the same: emergence from critical status by the end of the rehabilitation period.

If the trustees determine that, after exhausting all reasonable measures, a multiemployer plan will not be able to recover within the statutory period, they must adopt a recovery program that may take longer but is likely to work. If they believe that they cannot reasonably turn the situation around even with extra time, they must design a plan to forestall insolvency. The statutory provision authorizing these alternative approaches is often called the 'safety valve'.

The PPA goes into effect

The PPA funding rules first took effect as of the start of the 2008 plan year. The first round of zone certifications was delivered on or before March 29, 2008 deadline for multiemployer plans whose plan year coincides with the calendar year. Results were about what had been expected (Segal, 2008, 2009*a*, 2009*b*, 2010, 2011*a*, 2011*b*, 2011*c*). After all, the PPA was enacted because the stock market plunge at the start of the century had knocked a number of pension plans back on their heels. Many of the plans had already taken action by reducing future accrual rates, recommending contribution increases, or both. Enactment of the PPA added an additional incentive during 2007, as some boards reined in benefits and pressed the bargaining parties for contribution increases so that their plans could avoid a certification of yellow or red. In the survey of plan-year 2008 results, 78 percent of the plans were 'green'; that is, neither endangered nor critical (Segal, 2008). That meant that, at a minimum, they were more than 80 percent funded and were not faced with an imminent minimum funding deficiency. Twelve percent of the plans were classified as yellow, usually because they were on their way out of danger but had to continue exercising contribution and benefit discipline in order to avoid going into a troubled zone.

In that first year, fewer than 20 percent of the multiemployer plans had funding ratios below the 80 percent funding mark. In many cases, the yellow-zone plans only needed what were called 'no-action' FIPs. The discipline they had imposed in the prior few years was projected to be enough to carry them out of endangered status within the statutory time frame, without the need for additional special action. Plans that were classified as red were usually expecting it. After PPA was enacted, most of the plans in that initial group had been alerted to what they were facing, and many had already started planning for it well before the law took effect (Segal, 2008).

Plans are not allowed to reduce adjustable benefits of participants who retire before they are given notice that their pension plan is in the red zone and warned that benefits may be cut. Because the law was passed in 2006 and the zone rules did not take effect until 2008, plans whose financial struggles were widely known were concerned that the advance-notice requirement could trigger a run for the door, with participants retiring at their earliest opportunity to avoid possible cutbacks. Accordingly, PPA authorized plans that believed they would be in critical status to give the warning early. Ultimately, only a handful of plans took advantage of this opportunity. The funds certified as critical initially were generally plans that were overloaded with retirees and terminated vested participants, which had been grappling with funding challenges for years. For the 2008 plan year, 10 percent of the surveyed plans were in the red zone (Segal, 2008).

The market crashes: 2008–9

Stock values had already begun to fall in the spring of 2008, with losses picking up speed over the summer; in late September, both the equity and bond markets plunged and the nation's financial system was in turmoil. The sudden, severe drop took a heavy toll on many pension plans. Even though multiemployer plans had funding rules that provided mechanisms to smooth out volatility, the impact of the asset crash on plans' zone classification was immediate and dramatic because the asset plunge was so severe. With typical portfolio losses in the 20–25 percent range, this resulted in actuarial losses of roughly 25–30 percent. Bleak employment projections used in the zone status determination process exacerbated the decline in the number of green-zone plans.

The Worker, Retiree, and Employer Recovery Act of 2008

Employers grew concerned about the pension claims on their cash flows attributable to the combined asset drop and unfunded liability spike. Moreover, multiemployer plan sponsors worried about the disruption to their industries that could be triggered by the drastic cuts in benefits and increases in contributions that the PPA rules might force them to adopt. Benefit cuts and contribution hikes might also become unnecessarily severe if the crisis proved to be short-lived and would be difficult to unwind once bargaining agreements had been amended and benefit reductions had been put into place.

Before the official start of the rehabilitation or funding improvement period, during what the law labels the funding improvement or rehab plan 'adoption period', benefit increases are not allowed. During the formal correction period, plan amendments increasing benefits are allowed only if they are funded with new money and do not slow down the plan's recovery process. Also during the adoption periods, negotiated contribution rates cannot be reduced, directly or indirectly; this restriction continues to apply to yellow-zone plans throughout the funding improvement period.

Congress responded to these concerns by passing the Worker, Retiree, and Employer Recovery Act ('WRERA') in December of 2008. For multiemployer plans, the intent and effect of the WRERA relief provisions was to give trustees and bargaining parties some breathing room, to take stock of what had happened and come up with a strategy for repairing the damage. Under WRERA, multiemployer plan trustees had additional options for the 2009 plan year.[10] Regardless of their actual status in 2009, they could stay in the zone status in which they had been classified for 2008 (the 'freeze'). If they were in the yellow or red zone in 2009 and chose to accept that status, rather than to freeze at a higher 2008 level, they could add three years to their statutory recovery periods. That meant that, instead of aiming to get out of the red or yellow zone by, for instance, 2019, their deadline would be 2022. This might enable them to use less drastic corrective measures in the early years. Also, if they had been in the red or yellow zone for 2008 and they chose the freeze, they could skip the otherwise-required annual update to their Funding Improvement or Rehabilitation Plan and wait to adapt their remedial program until they had a clearer picture of the plan's and the employers' financial situation.

Where multiemployer plans ended up

Indeed, the plan classifications did shift dramatically from 2008 to 2009. As measured by the actuaries, the share of plans whose funded status put them in the red zone jumped from 10 to 30 percent, while 32 percent of the plans met the tests for endangered, or yellow-zone, status. For 2009, plans in the green zone still represented a plurality, but their share of the total dropped by more than half, to 38 percent (from 78 percent in 2008). These were classifications based solely on the statutory tests for endangered and critical status.[11] For more than 150 plans (or almost half of those that had been green in the 2008 database), the indicators of zone status had deteriorated to the point that they dropped to yellow or even red for 2009. Yet, WRERA gave the trustees the opportunity to freeze their 2008 status and stay in the green zone for one more year, and 88 percent of those plans elected to do so. As a result, the final *official* zone count for the 2009 plan year, taking into account trustees' freeze elections, was 75 percent green, 11 percent yellow, and 14 percent red. In addition, 40 percent of the plans in the yellow or red zone in 2009 chose to accept the offer under WRERA and take three extra years to recover, and roughly 75 percent of the plans classified as endangered or critical in 2008 chose the WRERA freeze for 2009, to avoid imposing deeper benefit cuts or requests for higher contributions.

Toward recovery

As investment markets started to rebound in 2010, the funded classification of multiemployer pension plans generally followed suit. The zone line-up for the 2010 plan year reflected the country's tentative economic recovery. When compared to the 2009 status (as determined by the actuaries and ignoring the WRERA freezes): 53 percent green, 18 percent yellow, 29 percent red (see Table 10.1). Notably, nearly all of the improvement from 2009 to 2010 in the share of green-zone plans seems to be due to the recovery of plans that had been labeled endangered (yellow zone) the prior year. By contrast, there was little change in the proportion still in critical condition, which dropped 1 percentage point from the 30 percent level in 2009.

We believe that this is largely due to three factors. First, since a plan can be assigned to the yellow zone based solely on its funded percentage, it is easier to flip into and out of endangered status due to transient events than it is to enter and exit the red zone. This suggests that mechanical metrics do not necessarily reveal much about a plan's financial vigor—the extent to which its income stream is keeping up with its benefit payment commitments, and whether that outlook is improving or declining—so the yellow-zone tests can yield a fairly large proportion of false positives or false negatives. The funded percentage used in these tests is based on the plan asset values used by the actuary for plan funding. The asset smoothing process (spreading out recognition of the impact of actual performance) and the ability to switch smoothing methods also contribute to the variances between plans' financial outlook and how they score on the yellow-zone tests.

Second, the law deliberately makes it hard to get out of the red zone. Instead of just reversing the triggers that put it into critical status, a plan cannot emerge from the red zone unless its actuary projects that it will meet the minimum funding standards for at least ten years. The goal was to keep plans from bouncing into and out of the red zone and having to start and stop the rehabilitation process repeatedly. And the third factor

Table 10.1 Breakdown of multiemployer plans by certified zone status by percentage of plans in each: 2008–10 zone

Zone	2008	2009	2010
Red zone	9	30	29
Yellow zone	11	32	18
Green zone	80	38	53

Source: Authors' computations from Segal (2008–2011*a*, 2011*b*, 2011*c*); see text.

distinguishing the red zone is more important: in addition to other negative financial indicators, by definition, plans in the red zone are facing either a funding deficiency or insolvency within the next ten years. This is about more than fluctuations in asset values that can put a plan's funded ratio a few percentage points on one side or the other of a fixed cutoff point. The economic disruption of 2008 had abiding consequences for many of the industries supporting multiemployer plans, beyond driving down plan assets. Of greater concern has been the relentless recession and corresponding plunge in the availability of work for so many multiemployer plan participants, especially in the construction industry.

When employers have enough business, they hire covered workers and contribute to their pension plans based on measures of covered work as set out in their bargaining agreements (usually on a per work-hour or work-week basis). As covered hours have fallen substantially, however, year-to-year improvements in the plans' equity portfolios may not be sufficient to propel troubled plans back to financial health. For example, since 2008, some multiemployer plans have reported employment declines of 30 percent or more, especially in the construction industry, which represents roughly half of the plans. This feeds back into the zone certification via the trustees' projections of future industry activity, which the actuary looks to in projecting the possibility of a funding deficiency or insolvency in the coming years. Regardless of the performance of plan assets, in a number of instances, trustees are projecting a slow recovery to pre-2008 levels, if they expect an industry recovery at all.

Multiemployer plans in critical status for the 2010 plan year

Of the 373 multiemployer plans for which 2010 financial and zone-related data had been tabulated as of the date of this writing, 107 critical status plans had formally adopted rehabilitation plans by the end of that year. The principal purpose of the special multiemployer PPA rules was to identify struggling plans, give their sponsors tools and flexibility to fix them, and make them responsible for doing so. Here, we look at how the rules are working for this subgroup of multiemployer plans.

Plan characteristics

Like the universe of surveyed plans, these red-zone plans are distributed throughout the country, range in size from very small to very large, and cover people working in a broad range of industries (Tables 10.2 and 10.3). Of these, 21 percent had been in critical status in 2008 when PPA went into

TABLE 10.2 Geographical and industry distribution of red-zone and bright-red-zone multiemployer plans in 2010

	No. of multiemployer plans	
	Red zone	Bright red zone
Region		
New England	10	10
Midwest	26	15
New York	28	18
West	22	11
Mid-Atlantic	12	7
South	9	6
Total	107	67
Industry		
Construction	48	41
Entertainment	3	
Manufacturing	8	3
Printing	9	1
Retail	7	5
Services	10	9
Transport	21	7
Other	1	1
Total	107	67

Source: Authors' computations from Segal (2010); see text.

effect, and 63 percent were in fact in the green zone for that year. For sixty-two of the plans, 2010 was the first year that their status was officially red. This was generally because they took the WRERA option to retain their 2008 green or yellow zone status for 2009. Two-thirds of these otherwise red-zone plans elected the freeze. Moreover, a few were surprisingly well funded, including one that was more than 100 percent funded (Table 10.3). This is another example of the shortcomings of using the ratio of assets to liabilities as of a given date as an indicator of plan strength.

Red-zone plans

While the law identifies a subcategory of endangered plans deemed to have multiple problems but not yet in the critical category, labeling them 'seriously endangered' (colloquially, 'deep yellow' or 'orange'), and subjects them to somewhat different requirements,[12] there is no such formal ranking among critical status plans. In fact, there is some sorting among those in the red zone, as the trustees make decisions about fashioning a rehabilitation plan, which is due roughly eight months after a plan's initial certification as critical. The *de facto* subcategories are plans that believe they can recover within the specified time frame (called here 'bright red'); plans

TABLE 10.3 Funded percentage distribution of red-zone and bright-red-zone multiemployer plans in 2010

Funded %*	No. of multiemployer plans	
	Red zone	Bright red zone
20–30	1	0
30–40	0	0
40–50	6	5
50–60	13	6
60–70	30	17
70–80	38	24
80–90	15	11
90–100	3	3
100–110	1	1
Total	107	67

Note: *Assets as % of accrued benefits.

Source: Authors' computations from Segal (2010); see text.

that expect to emerge from red over a somewhat longer period ('dark red'); and those ('rusty red') plans that have basically given up and are focused on forestalling insolvency, which is the minimum required by PPA'06. The statutory provision directing trustees of red-zone plans to pursue alternative goals if they determine that, after 'exhausting all reasonable measures', their plans could not recover within the standard time frame—or at all—is referred to as 'the safety valve'. Of the red-zone plans described here, roughly 63 percent have created rehabilitation plans that, in the view of the trustees and bargaining parties, should enable the plans to exit the red zone by or before the end of the standard ten-year (or thirteen-year, if that option was chosen under WRERA) rehabilitation period. Four of these have the so-called 'do-nothing' rehabilitation plans; that is, no additional contribution increases or benefit reductions are needed, beyond what was already agreed to in the bargaining agreements before the plans went into critical status, to carry them out of the red zone.

Many critical-status plans that are aiming to recover try to get thoroughly out of red and into the green zone, because advancing just to endangered status—the yellow zone—means they would have to recapitulate the whole process of notices, formal planning, and monitoring, and they would have even less flexibility in managing their plan benefits and contribution rates than they do in critical status. Also, they are required under PPA to develop a decent margin of protection from slipping back into red in the near future, and they usually want to do whatever they can to avoid a restart of the red-zone ordeal in case there is another reversal of the fortunes of the plan or the industry. Like the critical status plans generally, the plans on track to get out of the red zone within the standard twelve to fifteen years do not fit any particular profile in terms of size, industry, or geographic area. As Tables 10.2 and 10.3 indicate, there is a surprising variety in their funded percentages, which range from 40 to 108 percent, averaging 71 percent. Fifteen of these plans were funded at 80 percent or better.

Virtually all of the plans in this group that were eligible to do so chose to add the extra three years to their rehabilitation periods. Excluding the four 'do-nothing' plans, 85 percent offered the bargaining parties at least one optional package of benefit reductions and contribution increases in addition to the mandatory default schedule, which emphasizes benefit reductions. In most cases (63 percent), the choice was between the default schedule and one preferred option. Some offered two or even three alternatives to the default, and one rehabilitation plan had as many as fourteen options from which the parties could select in bargaining. Particularly with plans maintained under a small number of bargaining agreements, positions taken by the employer and union representatives on the boards of trustees can be a good preview of the reactions of the bargaining parties. The expectation is that the parties will elect the preferred option, which may have been informally pre-negotiated before the trustees officially settled on schedules. In the more typical situation, trustee-level discussions supported by actuarial modeling can address questions from the employer and union perspectives so that less time is needed for the official collective-bargaining process. This phenomenon also appears where there may be numerous contracts but a few dominant employers or employer associations. Prompt adoption of an acceptable schedule enables the employers to avoid or minimize the contribution surcharges that go into effect roughly shortly after a plan's red-zone status is certified.

In considering the interaction of trustee decision-making and collective bargaining, it is worth recalling that plan trustees and bargaining parties are often the same people wearing different hats. The fact that, as trustees, they reach decisions that are designed to be acceptable to both sides in their labor-relations capacity is the rationale for the 'two-hat' concept under ERISA and the Taft-Hartley Act. Plans would soon fail if their trustees had to ignore the practical effects of plan benefits and costs on the employers and workers whose support is necessary to keep the plans going. The standard approach is for the trustees to work their way to a few consensus solutions. In many industries, the default plan may be too extreme to be acceptable to either side, but it put together at the end of the process because the law requires that it be offered. Sometimes the parties take special steps to make the default plan especially unappealing, with deep benefit cuts and a sharp first-year contribution increase, in order to assure widespread agreement on the preferred schedule. For example, in one case, contributions were required to increase in the first year by

23 percent under the preferred schedule but 186 percent under the default. The differential was due in part to the fact that the default required the full increase to go into effect the first year, while the preferred allowed it to be phased in over a number of bargaining cycles. (All of the groups bargaining with regard to that plan accepted the preferred schedule.)

If a plan's funded positions and the industry's financial positions were static, phased-in contribution increases would end up with a higher eventual rate, as compared to an earlier but higher increase—like paying the same dollar amount of debt in long-term or short-term installments. But, of course, these real-life circumstances will vary from time to time and the bright-red plans, by definition, are expected to recover—perhaps before the higher contribution rates would fully phase in.

The rehabilitation plans that these boards of trustees designed (again, other than the 'no-action' ones) 'mix-and-match' contribution increases and benefit reductions in a wide variety of combinations, corresponding to the wide variety of circumstances in which the different plans must make their way back to financial stability. The preferred schedules called for contribution increases in the first year ranging from 4.4 to 97 percent, averaging 23 percent, but most of the increases are clustered in the 6–15 percent range. All of the preferred schedules for these plans cut adjustable benefits—primarily early retirement subsidies—for the then-current active participants and all future retirees. In addition, roughly 30 percent of the bright-red plans would reduce future accrual rates as part of the preferred schedules under their rehabilitation plans. These benefit reductions ranged from 7 to 75 percent, with a high degree of variation.

Reductions in future benefit accrual rates are more common among multiemployer plans wrestling with funding issues than these figures show, since this type of benefit cut is often made outside of the rehabilitation plan. In the four years before going into critical status, one-third of the bright-red plans had cut future accrual rates, either directly or by a plan amendment, excluding recent contribution increases from the benefit formula.

The default schedules for these plans also displayed wide variation. Only 28 percent of the default schedules called for no initial increase in contribution rates, because—as required by PPA—the remedial plan could be fashioned solely based on benefit reductions. For the other bright-red plans, the initial year default contribution rate increases for bright-red plans ranged from 1 to 186 percent, with an average increase of 37 percent (the 'interquartile range' was 10–50 percent, meaning half of the plans required a default increase in that range, while one-quarter each were above and below).

For some 30 percent of the bright-red-zone plans, the default schedule required a higher contribution rate increase than the preferred alternative, for the reasons discussed above. For four of them, the preferred schedule cut future accruals more deeply than the default schedule. That may have been due to the 1 percent floor on permitted default-schedule reductions in future accrual rates. Thirteen of the sixty-seven bright-red plans, including all those with 'do-nothing' rehabilitation plans, offered only one schedule, the default. Four of those plans aim to repair their funding positions without contribution rate increases, relying instead on reductions in adjustable benefits and future accrual rates. Three of these plans offer only the default schedule, both to preserve their tradition of providing a uniform benefit formula for all participants (a strong incentive for many plans, both to maintain equity among bargaining groups and to simplify administration, especially where employees move from employer to employer) and to avoid provoking influential employers who have expressed opposition to the DB format.

'Dark-red' plans: safety-value plans with extended red-zone exit goals

Twelve of the plans in the sample—about 11 percent of those in critical status for 2010—have determined that, even after 'exhausting all reasonable measures', they could not emerge from that status within the time allotted by the statute. Rather than forcing the plan into the standard mold to the point that, in their trustees' judgment, their plans or industries would be severely damaged, those plans have set a longer-range goal for their rehabilitation. Seven of them have set target emergence dates in 14–19 years, two in 21–28 years, and three in 30 or more years. Seven of these dark-red plans are in the transportation industry, three in construction, and two in retail trade. One is quite small, with only $6 million in assets; four are fairly small, with $23–$77 million in assets; and the remaining seven are standard size for local/regional multiemployer plans, with assets ranging from $133 to $272 million. On average, their funding ratio as measured for this purpose is 67 percent, with the actual percentages running from 56 to 78 percent. All have adopted rehabilitation plans that call for a combination of benefit reductions, including adjustable benefit cuts for active and retiring participants, and contribution rate increases. One of these plans offers only the default schedule, nine offer the default plus one option, and two of the plans offer two alternatives to the default. For two of the plans, the default schedule calls for a significantly higher initial contribution rate increase than the alternatives, while in six plans the initial default and preferred schedule contribution increases are the same or fairly close (within 1 percentage point). In six cases, the rehabilitation plan does not call for cuts in future accruals, either under the default or the preferred schedule. In the others, the accrual-rate cuts are either the same or deeper under the default schedule.

'Rusty-red' plans: critical plans aiming to forestall insolvency

Finally, there is a cluster of plans whose trustees—unquestionably in consultation with bargaining parties—have concluded that there is no way their plans could recover, at least without demanding unreasonable sacrifices from the parties, which they believe would probably hasten the plans' failure. These rusty-red plans are stretching to try to forestall eventual insolvency, which would force a reduction in benefit payments to PBGC-guaranteed levels. There are twenty-eight such plans (26 percent of all of the rehabilitation plans in the sample) in a range of industries, most of which are dying or severely impaired, at least in the regions where the plans operate. These include eight in the printing/newspaper industries, seven in transportation, five in manufacturing, only four in construction, three in entertainment (two of which cover people working in local movie theaters), and one in services. Only two expect to become insolvent within five years, another five before ten years, seventeen more within twenty years, and the remaining four expect that it will be thirty or more years until they run out of funds to pay benefits. At least one plan has set up its rehabilitation program to theoretically—and just barely—avoid ever running out of money.

These plans have undertaken several changes in their structure of late. All but one imposed adjustable benefit cuts; eight have preferred schedules that severely cut the benefit accrual rate (by at least 20 percent), while eleven others had already slashed benefits prior to the rehab process. The average first-year contribution rate increase is 21 percent in the default schedule, and 19 percent in the preferred, but this is heavily influenced by a few outliers. For the majority, these increases are in the 10–17 percent range. For those that apply these increases on a compounded basis over several years (as is generally the case in the preferred schedule when emergence is planned), this can amount to enormous increases over time. For example, if the rehabilitation plan schedule calls for a 10 percent contribution-rate increase every year during the rehabilitation period, a bargaining agreement calling for a $2 hourly contribution rate for 2010 would have to be renegotiated to provide for a $3.22 rate by 2015, and ultimately a contribution of $5.19 per hour starting in 2020. The average funding ratio is 67 percent, and only two were below 50 percent for 2010. Four have a funding ratio above 80 percent. As to asset size, four have less than $10 million remaining, twelve others have less than $80 million, eight more have between $80 and $400 million, and four had at least $600 million at the beginning of the 2010 Plan Year.

Whether all of these plans will inevitably proceed to fail is an open question. It is possible that some may recover with an industry turnaround, or that the more viable groups will be spun off and merged with plans in their industry whose prospects are better. Others may find that a mass withdrawal is more affordable for their participants and employers than a slow and hopeless decline. Currently, there is a gap in the law between the MPPAA plan reorganization/insolvency rules and the PPA zone rules. For plans that are drifting into insolvency, with or without a mass withdrawal along the way, statutory amendments are needed to make the processes work together seamlessly. In the course of reexamining the end-of-life rules for multiemployer plans, Congress may also consider updating the level of the multiemployer benefit guarantees, as some multiemployer advocates have requested.[13]

A mass withdrawal typically requires union cooperation, unless all of the employers are going out of business. Negotiated withdrawals usually include a replacement retirement plan of some kind. This may be a DC plan but, if the employer has a very well funded single-employer plan for the rest of its workforce, might include coverage under that plan. So the decision on a mass withdrawal is likely to be a mutual one, with both parties weighing the ultimate costs they would face. On the other hand, in some situations a plan that is on the ropes might have a chance at resurrection. While the rapid recovery hopes of a few construction funds in the Chicago area were dashed when the city lost its bid for the 2016 Olympics, the announcement of a different large-scale project—say, the licensing of a nuclear power plant or building of the long-awaited third regional airport—could have the opposite effect.

Coda: funding relief and 2011 funded status results

Following up on WRERA, in late June of 2010, Congress passed the Pension Relief Act ('PRA'),[14] which (among other things) softened the recovery burden for multiemployer plans with reasonable expectations of moving into the green zone and stabilizing their ongoing funding status. It gave plans the option to amortize the 2008–9 asset losses over twenty-nine rather than fifteen years[15] and to extend the smoothing period over which those losses are recognized in their actuarial value of assets. A plan is not eligible to use these tools unless it is projected to be solvent over the period that the relief would be in effect, based on contribution levels already bargained, so few of the 'safety-valve' red-zone plans are likely to qualify. For other plans, the relief will enable them to improve their zone status or to impose less drastic recovery measures because it will not be as difficult to avoid a funding deficiency. Still other plans hope to use the relief as an opportunity to stabilize their finances, by adding margins to absorb adverse future experience (Table 10.4).

Depending on the situation, in practical terms, this could permit a plan to avoid the need for additional remedial actions, to preclude a plan from

TABLE 10.4 Average funded percentage and market value of assets of red-zone and bright-red-zone multiemployer plans in 2010

Zone	Average funded %	Average market value of assets ($m)
Bright red (67)	71	467
Dark red (12)	67	132
Rusty red (28)	67	190
All plans in rehabilitation (107)	70	357

Source: Authors' computations from Segal (2010); see text.

dropping back into the yellow or red zones and starting the rehabilitation process all over again, or, for plans that have always been green, to strengthen their buffer against endangered or critical status. At this point, it is too early to analyze the effect of that funding relief on the plans and on their zone status. The initial phase of the 2011 Segal survey covers 234 calendar-year multiemployer plans, for which 2011 zone certifications were completed by March 31. Of these, 66 percent (154 plans) elected some or all of the PRA funding relief. Coupled with continued favorable investment results, the plans appear to be continuing their climb back to a more comfortable financial status. Sixty-five percent of them are now in the green zone, 11 percent are in the yellow zone, and the share in the red zone has dropped to 24 percent (Segal, 2011*c*).

Conclusion

The PPA of 2006 challenges the trustees, employers, and unions that manage and fund multiemployer pension plans to look at their plans' finances—not just as of the start of each year but also over a longer period, to project where the plans are headed. If the intermediate outlook does not look good, the parties must act to correct the trajectory based on metrics prescribed in ERISA and the IRC. PPA also gave trustees and bargaining parties flexibility to accomplish this, including the authority to cut early retirement subsidies and other protected benefits in order to bring plan assets and liabilities into a better balance. PPA provides a structure that enables trustees to devise plan remedies that fit within the industry- and labor-relations framework on which the plan depends. Shortly after the provisions became effective, the financial crisis forced trustees and bargaining parties for most plans to confront this challenge in a meaningful way.

The experience of the multiemployer plans analyzed here indicates that PPA is doing the job for which it was designed, for those plans. Even in the face of the dramatic investment losses experienced in 2008–9, followed by the depressed level of employment in the construction and other industries where multiemployer plans are prevalent, a large majority of the plans appears to be succeeding. This might not have been possible under PPA as enacted, and it appears that the temporary extra help that Congress provided in WRERA and the PRA was essential. Nevertheless, one in four of the red-zone plans—between 5 and 10 percent of all multiemployer plans—has concluded that it is unlikely to recover, a conclusion that many would probably not yet have reached if PPA had not spurred them to confront their futures. It is possible that having the opportunity to plan for an orderly decline will enable the parties responsible for those plans to provide more retirement security for their participants than they would have had without that clear and inescapable warning that catastrophe was looming.

The PPA special multiemployer zone rules are set to expire ('sunset') at the end of the 2014 plan year, but they will remain in effect for plans that are in endangered or critical status at that point until they complete the course of their recovery. The law also calls on the Departments of Treasury and Labor and the PBGC to make a comprehensive study of the multiemployer funding rules—with particular attention to their impact on small employers—by the end of 2011. Congress will then have three more years to consider whether to extend the zone approach, introduce a different funding regime for multiemployer plans, or just let the basic ERISA rules go back into effect. (Presumably, the 2011 tri-agency funding study will be just the start of its fact-finding and policy deliberation on this subject.) Perhaps the most important innovation in the zone concepts is the reintroduction of risks to participants' existing benefits when a multiemployer pension plan starts to falter. The notion that it is appropriate for the participants to bear some of the risk of adverse investment and other experience, even in a DB plan, appears to have been useful to many plans in developing their recovery path, and the possibility of going a step further is starting to gain some currency among policy experts. Proposals for formal mechanisms for rolling back participants' accrued benefits when a DB plan comes under severe financial stress have been floated in various quarters, as a way to moderate employers' financial exposure and thus revive their interest in sponsoring DB plans (Warshawsky, 2012). The experience of red-zone multiemployer plans, as it develops, may provide some insights into how this kind of sacrifice affects participants' willingness to support the pension plan and whether it is an effective way to stabilize pension plans in the long run.

Acknowledgments

The authors express their appreciation to The Segal Company for data on which this analysis is based. Findings and conclusions expressed are solely those of the authors and do not reflect views of the institution supporting research, with whom the authors are affiliated, or the Pension Research Council.

Endnotes

1. Four years of zone status information appears in Segal (2011*a*, 2011*b*, 2011*c*). The zone surveys for all years starting with 2007 (the first of which reports on projected zone status for 2008) are available on request through http://www.segalco.com/publications/surveysandstudies.
2. One client, the Central States Pension Fund, is so large and so distinctive that it is omitted from the database for the surveys to avoid distorting the results. Accordingly, its experience is not reflected in this analysis.
3. Because of client privacy commitments, we cannot identify the specific plans on which these analyses are based.
4. In addition, many plans for salaried workers use the 'elapsed time method' to determine eligibility, vesting, and accrual credit. This enables them to avoid counting individual hours, if they credit a person with a year of service if he or she is employed by the employer at the beginning and end of a stated twelve-month period. As with hours-based methods, employees whose jobs change frequently and who are likely to be working for different companies at the beginning and end of a year can fall between the cracks under this system even with substantial longevity in the industry.
5. To date, multiemployer plans have generally not used liability-driven investments or similar strategies to avoid potential funding volatility. One reason is that funding rules for multiemployer plans do not require trustees to trade off higher returns on the participants' assets in favor of stability in funding demands. The 2006 redesign of the single-employer funding rules, with the emphasis on market-based asset and liability measures and drastically reduced role for credit balances, sparked the current interest among corporate plan sponsors in using investment strategy as a buffer against volatility.
6. One notable example of this occurred in late 2006, when UPS negotiated with the Teamsters to exit the Central States Fund and cover its workers in a single-employer plan.
7. This is called a termination by mass withdrawal. Although the law recognizes multiemployer-plan terminations that are initiated by the trustees through plan amendments, this rarely (if ever) happens.
8. As of December 2010, the funds in the Segal Advisors Multiemployer Universe represented $65 billion. The average multiemployer investment allocation is 44 percent domestic equity, 25 percent fixed income, 11 percent international equity, 5 percent real estate, and 15 percent other, such as cash or non-real-estate alternatives. Typical policy constraints are 40–70 percent to equities.

9. In prosperous times, multiemployer plans are frequently amended to provide '13th checks'—a one-time, ad hoc extra payment to retirees. These now must be fully funded in the year they are paid out.
10. The relief was actually available for the first plan year beginning on and after October 1, 2008, to include plans whose plan year began in the last quarter of 2008, which would be among the hardest hit by the market decline.
11. Although the law only prescribes tests for endangered and critical status, IRS rules also require multiemployer plans' actuaries to certify if the plan is not in either category.
12. In some ways, this distinction looks more important than it turns out to be in practice, as these seriously endangered plans usually drop into the red zone in short order.
13. By contrast with the multiemployer guarantee levels, which can only be changed by Congressional action, the single-employer benefit guarantees are indexed to inflation on the same basis as Social Security benefits.
14. Officially, this is the 'Preservation of Access to Care for Medicare Beneficiaries and Pension Relief Act of 2010'.
15. The bill's proponents intended to provide for a thirty-year extended amortization period, but it ended up at twenty-nine years because of an apparent drafting error.

References

Pension Benefit Guaranty Corporation (PBGC) (2010). *Pension Insurance Data Book, 2009.* PBGC (Summer).

Segal (2008). *Survey of Multiemployer Pension Plans' Anticipated Zone Status and Funded Percentage under PPA'06.* The Segal Group (Winter).

——(2009*a*). *Final Survey of Plans' 2008 Zone Status.* The Segal Group (Spring).

——(2009*b*). *Survey of Plans' 2008 Zone Status.* The Segal Group (Winter).

——(2010). *Survey of Plans' 2009 Zone Status.* The Segal Group (Winter).

——(2011*a*). *Report of Results of the Survey of Calendar-Year Plans' 2011 Zone Status.* The Segal Group (Spring).

——(2011*b*). *Survey of Calendar-Year Plans' 2011 Zone Status.* The Segal Group (Winter).

——(2011*c*). *Survey of Plans' 2010 Zone Status.* The Segal Group (Winter).

Warshawsky, M. J. (2012). "Corporate Defined Benefit Pension Plans and the Financial Crisis: Impact and Sponsor and Government Reactions", in R. Maurer, O. S. Mitchell, and M. J. Warshawsky, eds., *Reshaping Retirement Security: Lessons from the Global Financial Crisis.* Oxford, UK: Oxford University Press.

Chapter 11

Adopting Hybrid Pension Plans: Effects of Economic Crisis and Regulatory Reform

Robert L. Clark, Alan Glickstein, and Tomeka Hill

Beginning in the mid-1980s, many large US employers began converting traditional defined benefit (DB) pension plans to hybrid plans, primarily cash balance plans. While legally these are DB plans, hybrids have important characteristics that mimic defined contribution (DC) plans.[1] The first hybrid plan was created by BankAmerica in 1985, and over the next few years, only a few companies adopted hybrid plans. But the 1990s saw a surge in hybrid plan adoptions and by May 1999, there were at least 325 hybrid plans (*Pensions and Investments*, 1999). Adoptions of hybrid pension plans continued through 2003, before coming to a relative standstill, primarily due to concerns about the legal status of some of the plan characteristics.

Prior research has sought to explain the attraction of hybrid plans and to identify the primary reasons that US employers converted traditional DB to hybrids prior to 2003. Clark and Schieber (2002) describe the conversion to hybrid plans as an effective method of moving away from the incentives for early retirement (i.e. prior to age 65) imbedded in most traditional DB plans. Clark and Schieber (2004) provide an early history of the adoption of hybrid plans and an assessment of the key factors driving firms away from traditional DB plans and toward the adoption of hybrid plans. They point to changing accounting rules, increasing preferences by workers for more mobile pensions, shifts in compensation packages that reduced resources allocated to retirement plans, and the overfunded status of some of the traditional plans. Clark et al. (2001) also highlighted the importance of effective communication concerning the value of retirement benefits and noted that the basic characteristics of hybrid plans are easier for workers to understand.[2]

IBM's conversion to a cash balance plan in 1999 caused considerable controversy and resulted in a series of lawsuits and Congressional hearings, raising questions about whether hybrid plans might be in violation of Employee Retirement Income Security Act (ERISA) and age discrimination standards. McGill et al. (2010) summarize key aspects of the controversy over hybrid plans, their legal status, and their impact on employee benefits and firm costs. The legal uncertainty surrounding these plans resulted in a sharp decline in plan conversions between 2004 and 2006. This chapter first discusses the legal controversy over conversions to hybrid plans and then explains how the Pension Protection Act of 2006 (PPA) resolved these issues. We then review how the economic crisis impacted pension funding and influenced the ways in which sponsors redesigned their retirement plans. Next, we examine the trend in plan conversions since 2000. Using pension data from Form 5500 datafiles and financial as well as other information on Fortune 1000 companies, we examine the determinants of plan conversions and consider the impact of legislation confirming the legal status of hybrid plans and the impact of the economic crisis.

Legal status of hybrid plans and the Pension Protection Act

As noted above, a long period of regulatory uncertainty in the United States suppressed the rate of adoption of hybrid plans, especially when the legal status of these plans was being challenged in the courts. Three primary issues posed questions about their legal status. First, opponents argued that hybrid plans were age discriminatory, because younger participants received more interest credits than those near retirement. Under the law at that time, a benefit payable from a DB plan was normally described as a benefit payable at retirement age. For example, if a 25-year-old employee and a 60-year-old employee both began accruing a hybrid plan benefit at the same time, when they reached retirement age, say age 65, the 25-year-old would have a larger benefit because he had forty years to accrue, compared to the 60-year-old, who only had five years to accrue. Thus, stated as a retirement-age benefit, the younger employee's benefit was much larger than the older employee's benefit—suggesting to some that hybrid plans appeared age discriminatory.

Second, the method of conversion from a traditional DB plan benefit to a hybrid plan also became controversial. Under a common conversion technique, a hybrid plan participant was credited with an initial hypothetical or 'notional' account. For some participants, this opening balance was less than the present value of the accrued benefit under the traditional DB plan at the point of conversion. As a result, that participant would not accrue any additional future benefits from the plan until the hybrid plan benefit caught up to the value of the traditional DB plan benefit at the time of conversion resulting in what became known as 'wear-away'. For some participants, the net effect of the wear-away was that benefit accruals were temporarily frozen and this freeze would sometimes last for years. Some argued that this violated the rules against backloading benefits.

Third, plan sponsors were worried about what was termed a 'whipsaw effect'. This occurred because plans were required by the Internal Revenue Service (IRS) to calculate a participant's actual benefit payment by projecting the participant's hypothetical notional account balance to normal retirement age using the plan's interest crediting rate, converting that amount to an annuity payable at normal retirement age, and then discounting it back to a present value amount based on statutory defined interest rates. The greater of the resulting calculation or the notional account balance was then paid. This often resulted in a benefit payment greater than the participant's hypothetical account balance, which plan sponsors did not like as it was contrary to what the plan communicated and intended to pay and was not expected by the plan participants.

Eventually, the US federal circuit courts determined that hybrid plans were not age discriminatory and Congress further clarified the legal status of hybrid plans in 2006 when it signed the PPA.[3] The PPA addressed various issues regarding retirement plans, but a subset of PPA provisions dealing with certain selected design aspects of hybrid plans provided plan sponsors some guidance on how to administer the new regulations.[4] For the first time, the PPA provided an age discrimination safe harbor for hybrid plans encompassing essentially all existing designs (Hill et al., 2010). The Act also stated that the participant's total accrued benefit cannot be less than the participant's accrued benefit for years of service before the effective date of the amendment plus the participant's accrued benefit for years of service after the effective date of the amendment. This essentially eliminated 'wear-away'. The PPA further provided a path to eliminate the notion of 'whipsaw' by providing rules under which plans could simply pay the account balance out to participants, if a lump-sum payment is chosen, upon termination of employment.

In addition, the Act imposed a new requirement on hybrid plans—the notion of a market rate of interest. Interest credits under cash balance plans cannot exceed the (unspecified in the law) market rate of interest, generally from 2008. The law also required faster vesting for cash balance plans. While the elimination of these key uncertainties is a welcome development, as of this writing, critical final regulations implementing the principles of PPA have still not been issued in several key areas, notably the market rate of return requirement. So the true impact on plan conversions reflecting the regulatory clarity provided by PPA may not be seen for some time. Thus, one can only speculate on the actual number of conversions that might have occurred had this uncertainty been resolved more quickly. Many of the plan sponsors who chose to terminate their DB plan and adopt a DC plan instead of converting the existing DB plan to a hybrid plan during the long period of regulatory uncertainty probably will not consider reestablishing a DB plan in the near future.

The economic crisis changed how companies looked at retirement plan design

When the PPA passed in 2006, many policymakers and economists were optimistic that the new guidance it provided on hybrid plans would lead more employers to consider hybrid plans as an option, and, indeed, the number of conversions rose in the last part of that decade. Yet the motivations for converting to a hybrid plan were starkly different than the earlier part of the decade due to the economic crisis. As noted earlier, employers converted to hybrid plans in the early part of the decade, in part, as a way of eliminating early-retirement subsidies, in response to changing demographics and related cost pressures, to shift to compensation packages that reduced dollars allocated to DB retirement plans, and to have access to assets that were in overfunded traditional DB plans. Other motivations included the popularity of lump sums and the desire for greater portability of benefits. When the economic crisis hit, however, employers began to look at their pension plans in a different way.

The economic crisis led to a huge drop in the value of equities, causing many pensions to experience a decline in funding. This was exacerbated by a drop in long-term interest rates used to discount plan liabilities. From end 2007 to end 2008, total assets in US DB pensions dropped 23 percent (from $2.6 trillion to $2.0 trillion; DOL, 2010). When corporate pension plans are underfunded, companies are required by IRS regulations to invest fresh capital into the funds to correct the imbalance in the forthcoming years. Thus, many firms were required to increase their contribution rates. Moreover, the timing of this crisis was coupled with new PPA funding rules, shortening the amount of time during which funding shortfalls need to be made up. As a result, many plan sponsors found it difficult to come up with the increased contributions needed to improve their DB funding levels.

Some firms had to make several drastic changes regarding their pensions and overall cost structure. First, many employers began laying off workers and, in some cases, offering early-retirement windows to help reduce their overall compensation costs. Second, some employers sought ways to reduce their benefit obligations, redesigning programs to reduce benefits, including temporary measures such as suspending matching contributions to 401(k) plans. In the later part of the decade, plan sponsors continued to move away from traditional DB plans and more toward offering hybrid plans and offering DC-only designs. Fortunately, the advent of the PPA gave plan sponsors an enhanced option to use hybrid plans when redesigning their retirement programs, and there was some increase in hybrid plan conversions. The timeline for making major changes to a pension program is significant (typically more than a year), and, as noted above, there remain regulatory uncertainties which still inhibit some cash balance conversions. So it remains to be seen what long-term impact the financial crisis will have on pension design generally and cash balance conversions specifically.

Hybrid plans: 2000–9

Since their creation, hybrid pension plans were mainly adopted by large employers in the United States. For the most part, hybrid plans result from plan sponsors having had traditional DB plans and then converting them to hybrid plans. In this sense, relatively few firms have selected hybrid plans as their initial pension structure. To examine the growth of hybrid plans in the last decade, we rely on three datasets. First, we use Form 5500 datafiles (annual government filings required from all private employer retirement plan sponsors) for all plan sponsors with nonfrozen plans having over 1,000 total participants; these cover the period 2000–7 in accessible form and contain information about pensions at the plan level. Second, we employ the Towers Watson pension finance data source with information about Fortune 1000 companies offering at least one traditional DB plan for the period 2000–9. This source allows us to focus on large employers who initially offered a traditional DB retirement plan, and it allows us to determine which converted to hybrid plans; this file contains company-level financial information. Third, we integrate the Towers Watson pension finance data with all nonfrozen plans sponsored in the Form 5500 database, linking financial information for the Fortune 1000 companies and information about the pension plans they sponsor.

In constructing the first data source of all plans with 1,000+ participants from the Form 5500 datafiles, we include all plans having 1,000+ and some positive number of active participants in each year. The Form 5500 datafile has indicators identifying whether the pension plan is a DB plan, and if so, whether it is a hybrid. Responses to these indicators are used to separate traditional DB from hybrid plans.[5] The Towers Watson pension finance database is a collection of pension finance and company finance information for Fortune 1000 companies that sponsor a DB pension plan. The information comes from publicly available annual 10-K reports with detailed information about the company's business, finance, and management (filed with the Securities Exchange Commission (SEC)).

In order to integrate the Form 5500 and the Towers Watson pension finance datasets, information from the Towers Watson file was added to the

Form 5500 datafiles using Employer Identification Numbers (EINs). This database includes company-level information plus information about all the nonfrozen pension plans they sponsor (not just plans with 1,000+ participants). When developing the datafile using this method, we are unable to determine all traditional DB and hybrid plans sponsored by Fortune 1000 companies because some plans are sponsored by subsidiaries and the EINs for some of these subsidiaries are unknown. But we can match pension plans in the Form 5500 data with the company financial information for over 80 percent of the Fortune 1000 companies that have a pension in each year of the sample period.

Table 11.1 presents information from the Form 5500 on all nonfrozen pension plans with 1,000+ participants between 2000 and 2007. Four key measures of the importance of hybrid plans are shown: the number of hybrid plans with 1,000+ participants, the proportion of DB plans that are hybrid plans, the percentage of active participants in DB plans enrolled in hybrid plans, and the share of total DB assets held in hybrid plans. The number of hybrid plans grew rapidly from 446 in 2000 to 640 in 2005, but it fell slightly in 2007. The share of hybrid plans among all large DB plans grew from 11 percent in 2000 to 18 percent in 2007.

While the number of hybrid plans grew, the number of all nonfrozen DB plans dropped during the 2000s. The proportion of all active DB participants in hybrid plans increased from 18 to 29 percent from 2000 to 2007. As one might expect, given the increase in plans and participants, the share of total assets in hybrid plans also increased, rising from 21 to 33 percent. Comparing data on plans, participants, and assets, it appears that the largest DB plans were more likely to have switched to hybrid plans over the last decade.

TABLE 11.1 Hybrid plan share of all nonfrozen DB plans with 1,000+ participants: 2000–7

Plan year	No. of hybrid plans	Hybrid plans as a % of DB plans	Active participants in hybrid plans as % of active participants in DB plans	Assets in hybrid plans as % of assets in DB plans
2000	446	11	18	21
2001	510	13	18	21
2002	524	15	21	25
2003	614	16	25	29
2004	611	16	27	30
2005	640	17	27	30
2006	588	17	28	32
2007	583	18	29	33

Source: Authors' calculations from Form 5500 data (see text).

We repeat the analysis focusing only on DB plans with Form 5500 data, sponsored by Fortune 1000 companies for years 2000–7 in Table 11.2. The plans sponsored by the Fortune 1000 companies are even more likely to have been converted to hybrid plans, which is evident from all measures reported. The number of hybrid plans sponsored by Fortune 1000 companies rose from 134 in 2000 to 207 in 2005. In 2006, the number of hybrid plans sponsored dropped to 185 and rose to 195 in 2007. The proportion of DB pensions that are hybrid plans among Fortune 1000 companies increased from 13 percent in 2000 to 25 percent in 2007. Thus, the Fortune 1000 companies in 2007 are one-third more likely to have a hybrid plan compared to all plans with 1,000+ participants (25 versus 18 percent). As the share of hybrid plans increased, so did the percentage of active participants that are in hybrid plans. The percentage of active participants in hybrid plans increased from 27 to 46 percent, indicating that almost half of all DB participants were enrolled in hybrid plans. The share of total assets in hybrid plans also increased from 31 to 44 percent during the sample period.

The movement to hybrid plans varies considerably across the US industry, as indicated in Table 11.3 for 2007. We report the prevalence of hybrid plans in the Form 5500 dataset (1,000+ participants) for all nonfrozen pension plans and also for nonfrozen plans sponsored by the Fortune 1000 companies. Among Fortune 1000 companies, hybrid plans range from less than 10 percent of DB plans in the wholesale sector to approximately half of plans in the professional and business services sector. While there are only two health-care firms in the Fortune 1000, both of them sponsor a hybrid plan. In the property and construction sector, there are only five employers, and three of them sponsor a hybrid. There are also

TABLE 11.2 Hybrid plan share of all DB plans in Fortune 1000: 2000–7

Plan year	No. of hybrid plans	Hybrid plans as a % of DB plans	Active participants in hybrid plans as % of active participants in DB plans	Assets in hybrid plans as % of assets in DB plans
2000	134	13	27	31
2001	126	13	25	30
2002	163	17	29	34
2003	192	19	36	37
2004	189	20	39	39
2005	207	23	42	40
2006	185	23	40	39
2007	195	25	46	44

Source: Authors' calculations from Form 5500 and 10-K data (see text).

TABLE 11.3 Hybrid plans as percent of DB plans by industry: 2007

Industry	No. of hybrids in Form 5500	Large hybrid plans as % of all large DB plans in Form 5500	No. of hybrids sponsored by Fortune 1000	Hybrid plans as % of all DB plans sponsored by Fortune 1000
Aerospace and defense	11	23	5	28
Communications/ high technology	40	22	16	24
Energy/utilities/ natural resources	66	35	36	35
Financial services	91	21	25	39
Food services and beverages	23	11	13	16
Health care	113	23	2	100
Manufacturing	142	17	49	17
Pharmaceuticals	7	18	3	21
Professional and business services	30	23	7	47
Property and construction	18	6	3	60
Retail	8	15	6	46
Transportation and transportation equipment	28	12	10	23
Wholesale	13	14	2	8
Other	51	15	18	32

Source: Authors' calculations from Form 5500 Large Plans and Fortune 1000 companies (see text).

substantial differences by industry, depending on the two samples. In particular, hybrid plans are much more prevalent for Fortune 1000 companies compared to all plans with 1,000+ participants in retail, financial services, property and construction, and professional and business services industries. Industry differences in the adoption of hybrid plans likely reflect differences in labor market conditions, unionization, demographics, and turnover rates that vary among the different industry sectors.

To trace the adoption of hybrid plans over time, we constructed a sample of Fortune 1000 companies in the datafile 2000–9 and which sponsored a traditional DB plan in 2000. Some 153 companies offered at least one traditional DB plan in 2000 and remained on the Fortune 1000 list for all ten years. By 2009, 38 out of these 153 companies converted at least one of their

DB plans to a hybrid over the period (Figure 11.1). Most of these hybrid plan conversions were done early in the decade (twenty-nine occurred between 2000 and 2003); in 2004–6, only one of these companies converted. Eight additional conversions took place in the next three years, after the passage of PPA in 2006 and during the onset of the economic crisis.

Another way to trace the trend in plan conversions is to examine year-to-year changes from 2000 to 2009. Table 11.4 reports these year-by-year conversions and reveals the same time pattern of adoption of hybrid plans as shown in Figure 11.1. Panel A indicates that, between 2000 and 2003, there were forty-one plan conversions to hybrid plans among Fortune 1000 firms, but in the next three years there was only one conversion per year. Beginning in 2006, plan conversions resumed, although at a somewhat lower rate than in the earlier period. It is important to note that although there was a significant number of hybrid plan conversions among the Fortune 1000 during the early part of the decade, the number of Fortune 1000 companies offering *either* a traditional or a hybrid pension plan dropped 23 percent between 2001 and 2004 (451 to 348 companies).

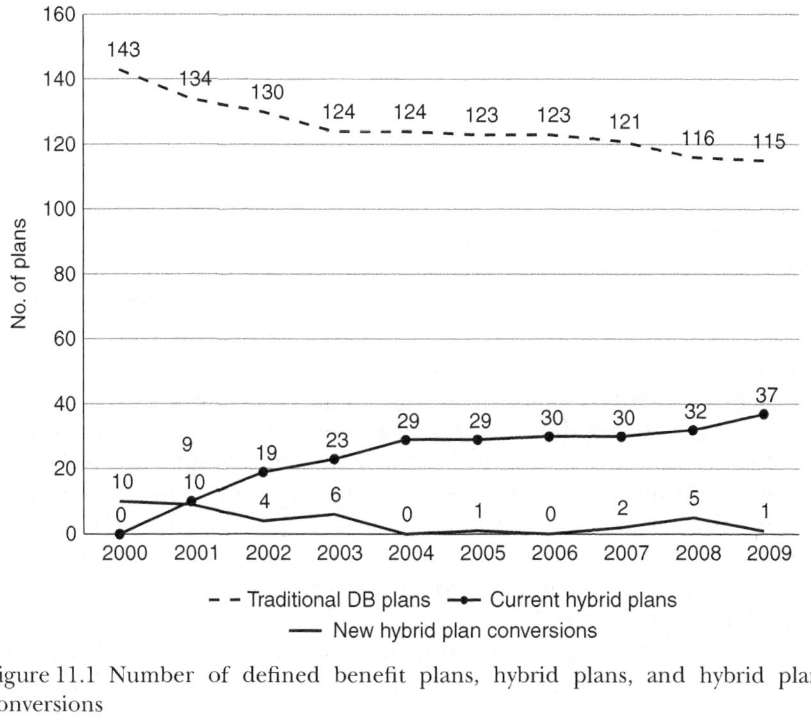

Figure 11.1 Number of defined benefit plans, hybrid plans, and hybrid plan conversions

Source: Authors' computations (see text).

TABLE 11.4 Pension plan conversions over time

Year	Number continued sponsoring traditional DB plan (active and closed DB plans)	Number converted to hybrid plan	Total number
Panel A. Fortune 1000 firms			
2000–1	433	18	451
2001–2	414	12	426
2002–3	395	11	406
2003–4	347	1	348
2004–5	313	1	314
2005–6	308	1	309
2006–7	288	5	293
2007–8	232	8	240
2008–9	219	2	221
Panel B. Form 5500 pension plans with 1,000+ participants			
2000–1	2,850	25	2,875
2001–2	2,661	37	2,698
2002–3	2,659	48	2,707
2003–4	2,993	18	3,011
2004–5	2,937	24	2,961
2005–6	2,618	15	2,633
2006–7	2,475	21	2,496

Source: Authors' calculations from Form 5500 data (see text).

During 2004–6, the fraction of Fortune 1000 companies offering a traditional or hybrid pension plan dropped 11 percent (348 to 309 companies). When PPA was passed in 2006, many assumed that more employers would consider converting to hybrid plans as an option when considering redesigning their retirement plan (even though some significant regulatory uncertainties remained). While the economic crisis did see an increase in the number of hybrid plan conversions, it also accelerated the number of companies dropping their traditional and hybrid pensions. Thus, Fortune 1000 companies converting to hybrid plans did rise after 2006, but the number offering either a traditional or hybrid plan dropped sharply by 28 percent in the period 2006–9 (309 to 221 companies). Hence, the number of nonfrozen DB plans has decreased among Fortune 1000 companies; of those continuing to offer DB plans, more are converting to hybrid formulas.

Turning to all DB plans appearing in consecutive years of the Form 5500 having 1,000+ participants, we can again ask about conversion rates by year. Panel B of Table 11.4 shows that 25 out of 2,850 plans converted from a traditional DB plan to a hybrid plan in 2001, 37 of 2,661 plans did so in

2002, and 48 of 2,659 plans did so in 2002. Once again there is a marked decline in conversion around 2003; however, the decline is not as stark nor is the rebound as large as in the other data that we have examined, nor is the trend away from traditional DB plans quite as defined.

We note five important observations from the data presented in this section. First, the recent history suggests a continued trend toward greater prevalence of hybrid plans that started in the 1990s. Second, the trend in greater use of hybrid plans was briefly interrupted between 2003 and 2006 as questions arose concerning the legal status of hybrid plans. Third, although there were a considerable number of conversions early in the decade and again in the latter part of the decade, the motivations for converting to hybrid plans were different. In the early part of the decade, converting to hybrid plans was motivated, in part, by assets in overfunded pensions and to meet the demand for workers who wanted mobile pensions. However, when the economic crisis began, the motivation for converting was primarily to cut costs. The passing of PPA in 2006 encouraged some sponsors to consider converting to hybrid plans as an option rather than not offering DB pensions altogether. Fourth, the adoption of these plans is greater among larger plans sponsored by the Fortune 1000 companies. Fifth, the adoption of hybrid plans is not uniform across industries. Next, we examine these patterns in more detail.

Explaining why firms adopt hybrid plans

Policymakers and analysts would benefit from a better understanding of why employers are converting traditional DB plans into hybrid plans. In this section, we explore a number of possible explanations.

The decision by plan sponsors to convert DB to hybrid plans is likely influenced by the plan's financial status as well as that of the plan sponsor, changes in the labor force and worker preferences, whether the plan is collectively bargained, plan size, and, of course, the regulatory environment. Nevertheless, it is difficult to obtain information on all of the determinants of plan conversions, so our empirical analysis is limited by data availability. Moreover, the time period for assessing plan conversions is relatively short, though we can capture the time series break coinciding with the legal uncertainty associated with hybrid plans. We are able to obtain several variables which can serve as proxies for plan and employer size, as well as the plan's and employer's financial status. The multivariate statistical analyses uses both datafiles described above.

Fortune 1000: DB in 2000, hybrid by 2009

To examine a plan sponsor's decision to convert from a traditional DB to a hybrid plan, we estimate a logit equation indicating whether each of the Fortune 1000 firms having a traditional plan in 2000 had converted to a hybrid plan by 2009. Potential determinants of plan choice include the measured pension benefit obligation and the plan's firm size. Accordingly, we evaluate the ten-year average of the company's End-of-Year (EOY) pension benefit obligation (PBO) divided by the company's market value (the latter is the market capitalization plus the market value of debt). We also subtract the EOY PBO from EOY plan assets divided by the market value of the company and include the ten-year average of this variable in the regression. We also control on the firm's average earnings per share (EPS) and the logarithm of average market value (in $ 2010). Variable means and medians distinguished by whether the plan was converted to a hybrid plan or not appear in Table 11.5, Panel A.

The PBO relative to market value is similar for companies that converted and companies that did not convert. The financial status of the pension plans relative to the market value shows that plans that were converted to a hybrid plan were similar to the financial status relative to the market value for those plans that were not converted; actually both groups had negative net assets. This may be some indication that large PBOs and overall poor financial health of pension plans may not be determinants of hybrid plan conversions. However, EPS and market share may be influential as the mean for both of these variables are higher for companies that converted compared with companies that did not convert.

Estimated logit coefficients from our model of plan conversions are derived from the following model:

$$\begin{aligned} y_i = \alpha + \beta \text{Average}(\text{PBO}/\text{MktVal21}_i + \beta \text{Average}\left((\text{Assets} - \text{PBO})/\text{MktVal}\right)_i \\ + \beta \text{Average}(\text{EPS})_i + \beta \log\left(\text{Average}(\text{MktVal})\right)_i + \beta \text{IndustryDummies}_i + \varepsilon_i \ldots \end{aligned} \quad (1)$$

where *i* represents the Fortune 1000 company. As Table 11.6 shows, neither financial measure of the pension plan or EPS have a significant impact on the conversion to a hybrid plan. Average market value during the sample period, by contrast, is significantly negatively associated with the probability of converting a traditional DB to a hybrid plan. Of the industry codes, only transportation is statistically significant.

Using the same year-by-year conversion data for Fortune 1000 companies as discussed previously, we estimated additional plan conversion equations with the addition of individual year dichotomous variables; here, the dependent variable indicates whether the sponsor switched from a DB to a hybrid plan each year during the period 2000–9.

TABLE 11.5 Plan features by conversion status: 2000–9

	Did not convert to hybrid plan		Converted to hybrid plan	
	Mean	Median	Mean	Median
Panel A. Fortune 1000 companies				
Avg PBO/Market Value ($)	0.29	0.16	0.25	0.16
Avg (Pension Assets —PBO)/MktValue ($)	−0.04	−0.02	−0.03	−0.02
Avg MktValue ($)	25,485,367	8,287,465	20,622,479	15,526,278
Avg EPS	6.77	2.37	19.60	2.79
Panel B. Form 5500 pension plans with 1,000+ participants: 2000–7				
% Funded	0.94	0.90	1.03	0.97
Actives/retirees	11.05	2.40	10.21	3.27
Total actives	4,168	1,350	7,185	2,945
Total participants	8,522	2,659	14,189	5,029
Total assets ($000)	429,136	102,661	1,060,625	219,522
Collectively bargained	45%	n/a	22%	n/a

Notes: Panel A: number that did not convert to hybrid = 115; number that did = 38. Panel B: number that did not convert to hybrid = 19,193; number that did = 118. All dollar values in $ 2010.

Source: Authors' calculations (see text).

TABLE 11.6 Logit regression analysis of the overall probability of hybrid plan conversion in Fortune 1000 companies: 2000–9

	Coefficients	Std error
Average PBO/market value	−0.289	0.630
Average (pension assets—PBO)/market value	2.22	3.75
Average EPS	−0.004	0.004
Ln(average market value)	−0.421***	0.111
Manufacturing	−0.059	0.394
Transportation	−0.751*	0.409*
Wholesale/retail	0.256	0.766
Finance, business services, and real estate	−0.045	0.419

Notes: * denotes significance at 10% level; *** denotes significance at 1% level.

Source: Authors' calculations (see text).

TABLE 11.7 Logit regression analysis of the annual probability of hybrid plan conversion in Fortune 1000 companies: 2000–9

	−1		−2		−3	
	Coefficients	Std error	Coefficients	Std error	Coefficients	Std error
PBO/market value	0.460***	0.165	0.445***	0.168	0.511***	0.178
(Pension assets—PBO)/market value	0.875**	0.390	0.890*	0.466	1.031**	0.484
EPS	0	0	−6E-05	0.0001	−7E-05	0.0001
Ln(market value)	−0.178***	0.050	−0.171***	0.050	−0.097*	0.055
Year controls	No		Yes		Yes	
Industry controls	No		No		Yes	
−2 log *L*	1,775.393		1,601.97		1,576.086	

Notes: N = 2,677; * denotes significance at 10% level; ** denotes significance at 5% level; *** denotes significance at 1% level.

Source: Authors' calculations using Fortune 1000 companies (see text).

$$y_{ij} = \alpha + \beta(\text{PBO}/\text{MktVal})_{ij} + \beta\big((\text{Assets} - \text{PBO})/\text{MaktVal}\big)_{ij} + \beta\text{EPS}.x_{ij} + \beta\log\big((\text{MktVal})\big)_{ij} + \beta\text{Dummies}_{ij} + \varepsilon_{ij} \quad (2)$$

We first present results without year and industry controls, while the second model includes both. The results are shown in Table 11.7. As above, the coefficients on EPS are not significant in all three models. Yet the financial status terms and benefit obligations are both significant and are positively associated; these estimates suggest that better-funded plans with larger total liabilities are more likely to be converted to hybrid plans. The logarithm of the firm's market value is negative and significant.

Form 5500 plans with 1,000+ participants

Using Form 5500 data for the period 2000–7 allows us to use more demographic and financial information specific to pension plans. Table 11.5, Panel B, reports means and medians in this sample, for key variables sorted again by whether the plans converted to hybrids. Variables include the number of active participants divided by the number of plan retirees, the number of active participants, the total number of participants, whether the plan was collective bargained, total plan assets, and the plan's funding level. The latter variable, funding level, is obtained by dividing the plan's actuarial value of assets by its current liability. The table shows that plans which converted to a hybrid plan were larger in terms of plan assets, as well as in active and total participants. Plans that converted to hybrid plans also had a higher median value for actives compared to retirees, and higher mean and median funding levels. Finally, plans which converted were also more likely not to be collectively bargained.

Whether the plan was converted in a specific year is used as a dependent variable by the logit model for this multivariate analysis. Again, we offer one set of estimates without year or industry controls; and a second includes both, as follows:

$$\begin{aligned} y_{ij} &= \alpha + \beta\text{Funding}_{ij} + \beta(\text{Actives/Retirees})_{ij} + \beta\text{TotalPart}_{ij} \\ &+\beta\log(\text{TotAssets})_{ij} + \beta\text{CollectiveBarg}_{ij} + \beta\text{Dummies}_{ij} + \varepsilon_{ij} \end{aligned} \tag{3}$$

where i represents the pension plan from the Form 5500 filings and j represents the year. The results in Table 11.8 for plan assets and being a collectively bargained plan are positively associated and significant in both specifications. Although previously we had seen a negative association between collectively bargained and plan conversions, the fact that these are larger firms may explain the positive association here. We also find that funding is insignificant, suggesting that plan financial health does not shape plan conversions.

TABLE 11.8 Logit regression analysis of the annual probability of hybrid plan conversion in Form 5500 plans with 1,000+ participants: 2000–7

	(1)		(2)	
	Coefficient	Std error	Coefficient	Std error
Funding	0.241	0.199	0.204	0.215
Actives/retirees	0.0001	0.0007	0.0002	0.0007
Total participants (000)	−0.003	0.003	−0.002	0.003
Ln(total assets)	0.414***	0.063	0.412***	0.065
Collective bargained plan	0.580***	0.090	0.557***	0.093
Year controls	No		Yes	
Industry controls	No		Yes	
−2 log L	1,951.864		1,898.965	

Notes: N = 18,907; * denotes significance at 10% level; ** denotes significance at 5% level; *** denotes significance at 1% level.

Source: Authors' calculations using Form 5500 plans with 1,000+ participants (see text).

Fortune 1000 companies with added pension information from Form 5500

Finally, we examine the sample of Fortune 1000 companies' pension plans found in the Form 5500 datafiles and the company and pension finance information from the Towers Watson database. We again look at Fortune 1000 companies that existed in consecutive years and determine whether or not they converted at least one of their traditional DB plans to a hybrid plan. To consolidate the plan-level pension data from the Form 5500 to the company-level information, we aggregated the pension plan information for each Fortune 1000 company. We calculated per-plan weighted averages of funding, total number of participants, and actives per retirees, using total plan assets as the weight. If the company had at least one plan in the Form 5500 data series identified as collectively bargained, we coded the company as having at least some collective bargaining coverage. We summed the number of nonfrozen plans that each Fortune 1000 company offered.

Table 11.9 demonstrates that companies which converted at least one plan to a hybrid plan tended to have larger plans, both in terms of total participants and asset size. The median market value for companies that converted at least one plan to a hybrid plan is larger than companies that did not convert any of their traditional DB plans. Interestingly, companies that converted at least one plan and companies that did not convert were equally likely to have at least one collectively bargained plan.

We next estimate logit models using the integrated Fortune 1000 financial and the Form 5500 database, with the dependent variable being equal to one if the plan was converted to a hybrid plan in the specified year. The independent variables used are weighted-average funding level, weighted average of actives divided by retirees, whether the company offers a collectively bargained plan or not, weighted average of total participants, average of plan assets, an indicator of whether the sponsor offers at least three plans, PBO and pension assets minus PBO both relative to market value, EPS, and logarithm of market value. The general regression is as follows:

$$\begin{aligned} y = {} & \beta \text{WeightedAvgFunding}_{ij} + \beta(\text{WeightedAvgActives/Retirees})_{ij} \\ & + \beta \text{CollBargInd}_{ij} + \beta \text{AvgTotalParticipants}_{ij} + \beta \log(\text{AvgPlanAssets})_{ij} \\ & + \beta \text{ThreePlanInd}_{ij} + \beta(\text{PBO/MktVal})_{ij} + \beta \text{EPS}_{ij} \log(\text{MktVal})_{ij} \\ & + \beta \text{Dummies}_{ij} + \varepsilon_{ij} \end{aligned} \tag{4}$$

where i represents the Fortune 1000 company and j represents the year. Table 11.10 shows one model that excludes year and industry controls, and a second model that includes both year and industry controls.

TABLE 11.9 Plan features by conversion status for Form 5500 pension plans sponsored by Fortune 1000 companies: 2000–7

	Did not convert to a hybrid plan		Converted to a hybrid plan	
	Mean	Median	Mean	Median
Weighted-average funding level	0.90	0.87	0.88	0.83
Weighted-average actives/retirees	6.58	2.08	12.93	1.90
1+ plan collectively bargained	0.35	0	0.46	0
Weighted-average total participants per plan	15,691	5,910	25,188	5,068
Average plan assets ($000)	1,162,491	334,329	3,527,991	543,750
No. of plans offered	1.42	1	1.61	1
PBO/market value	0.69	0.14	0.65	0.43
(Total pension assets—PBO)/market value	−0.10	−0.02	−0.10	−0.05
EPS	−21.94	1.83	1.55	1.56
Market value ($000)	21,298	5,793	13,564	6,149

Notes: Number that did not convert to hybrid = 1,347; number that did = 28. All dollar values in $ 2010.

Source: Authors' calculations (see text).

TABLE 11.10 Plan conversion logit regression results for Fortune 1000 companies with plans found in the Form 5500: 2000–7

	(1)		(2)	
	Coefficient	Std error	Coefficient	Std error
Weighted-average funding level	−0.511	0.796	0.704	0.666
Weighted-average actives/retirees	−0.001	0.004	−0.000	0.004
Plan collectively bargained	0.497***	0.166	0.464***	0.175
Weighted average total participants/ plan (000)	0.000	0.000	−0.006**	0.003
Ln(average % of plan assets)	0.079	0.147	0.168	0.157
3+ indicator	0.142	0.286	0.198	0.291
PBO/market value	2.334***	0.461	2.193***	0.487
(Total pension assets—PBO)/market value	3.167***	2.148	2.12	2.317
EPS	0.000	0.000	−0.000	0.000
Ln(market value)	−0.158	0.132	−0.123	0.139
Year controls	No		Yes	
Industry controls	No		Yes	
−2 log *L*	559.605		5,419.408	

Note: N = 1,375; * denotes significance at 10% level; ** denotes significance at 5% level; *** denotes significance at 1% level.

Source: Authors' calculations using Form 5500 plans with 1,000+ participants (see text).

In both models, coefficients on plan obligations and plan overall financial status (Assets minus PBO) are positively and significantly associated with converting at least one plan to a hybrid. Interestingly, having at least one plan that is collectively bargained is also positively and statistically significantly associated with converting to a hybrid plan. In the second regression, one more variable becomes significant.

Conclusion

This chapter examines the determinants of plan conversions from traditional DB plans to hybrid plans using three data sources, focusing particularly on firms on the Fortune 1000 lists from 2000 to 2009. From this set, we identify whether they sponsored a pension plan and if they converted at least one of their plans from a traditional DB to a hybrid plan. Company financial information in annual 10-K reports helps understand whether the firm's financial status and that of their pension plans played a role in converting to a hybrid plan. We conclude that the overall cost of pension plans and financial health of the pension plans was not associated with hybrid conversion. Nevertheless, the plan sponsor's market value, indicative of how well the overall company is doing, was strongly associated with the probability of converting to a hybrid plan. We also found that DB plans with better funding were more likely to be converted to hybrid plans, as were larger plans and those that were collectively bargained. These results suggest that companies did not convert to hybrid plans because the pension plans were not financially sound. Finally, the pension obligations relative to market share did influence the probability that firms converted at least one plan to a hybrid plan.

The detailed examination of these data sources showed a relatively high level of plan conversions until 2003, followed by three years of relatively few conversions. After the passage of the PPA in 2006, large employers have begun converting traditional DB plans to hybrid plans. We believe that the uncertain legal environment and changing regulatory status of hybrid plans has substantially affected the number of conversions. Finally, we speculate that the adverse economic climate of the past few years may have altered the desirability of DC plans for some workers, insofar as employees may now desire retirement benefits with a greater degree of certainty. Such changes in worker preferences may increase the demand for hybrid plans, relative to a move away from a DB toward a DC plan.

Endnotes

1. A detailed discussion of hybrid plans appears in Chapter 12 of McGill et al. (2010). Hill et al. (2010) describe the key characteristics of hybrid plans.
2. Cf. Brown et al. (2000) and Clark and Munzenmaier (2001) for additional discussion of early conversions to hybrid plans.
3. The PPA is a much broader bill that affects many aspects of plan design, management, and funding. Hill et al. (2010) cover how the PPA relates to hybrid plans.
4. Although the PPA offered some guidance, additional guidance was still needed. In October 2010, the Internal Revenue Service (IRS) issued final and proposed regulations on the Pension Protection Act of 2006 (PPA) provisions relating to hybrid pension plans, such as cash balance and pension equity plans (PEPs). The final regulations mostly firmed up the rules proposed in 2007; the 2010 proposed regulations focus on other issues, paying particular attention to interest-crediting rates that satisfy the market-rate-of-return standard.
5. Using the indicators to separate hybrid plans and traditional DB plans may yield a few misidentifications because some plans have a complicated plan design due to multiple structures and various transition provisions. Unfortunately, we are only able to remove plans that have no participants currently accruing benefits (i.e. frozen plans). We cannot identify plans that are closed (i.e. plans that have some participants who are not currently accruing further benefits because they did not meet service/age requirements or they were hired after a certain date).

References

Brown, K., G. Goodfellow, T. Hill, R. Joss, R. Luss, L. Miller, and S. Schieber (2000). *The Unfolding of a Predictable Surprise.* Bethesda: Watson Wyatt Worldwide.

Clark, R. and F. Munzenmaier (2001). "Impact of Replacing a Defined Benefit Pension with a Defined Contribution Plan or a Cash Balance Plan", *North American Actuarial Journal*, 5(1): 32–56.

——and S. Schieber (2002). "Taking the Subsidy Out of Early Retirement: Converting to Hybrid Pensions", in O. S. Mitchell, Z. Bodie, B. Hammond, and S. Zeldes, eds., *Innovations in Retirement Financing.* Philadelphia, PA: University of Pennsylvania Press, pp. 149–74.

——and S. Schieber (2004). "An Empirical Analysis of the Transition to Hybrid Pension Plans in the United States", in W. Gale, J. Shoven, and M. J. Warshawsky, eds., *Private Pensions and Public Policies.* Washington, DC: The Brookings Institution, pp. 11–42.

——, J. Haley, and S. Schieber (2001). "Adopting Hybrid Pension Plans: Financial and Communication Issues", *Benefits Quarterly*, 17(1): 7–17.

Hill, T., G. Pang, and M. J. Warshawsky (2010). "Hybrid Pension Plans: A Comprehensive Look at their History, Economics and Features", *Perspectives*, November: 1–28. New York: Towers Watson.

McGill, D., K. Brown, J. Haley, S. Schieber, and M. J. Warshawsky (2010). *Fundamentals of Private Pensions,* 9th edition. Oxford, UK: Oxford University Press.
Pensions and Investments (1999). "Special Report: Cash Balance Plans". May 31.
US Department of Labor (DOL) (2010). *Abstract of 2007 and 2008 Form 5500 Annual Reports.* Private Pension Plan Bulletins. Washington, DC: Employee Benefits Security Administration, DOL (March and December).

Chapter 12

Collective Pensions and the Global Financial Crisis: The Case of the Netherlands

Lans Bovenberg and Theo Nijman

The financial crisis has had a major impact on Dutch occupational pension schemes. The direct effect was that funding rates dropped dramatically, and indirectly the crisis revealed some weaknesses of the system and therefore led to various proposals for reforms. This chapter explores the impact of the crisis on the Dutch pension system and discusses various reform proposals.

In what follows, we first describe the Dutch pension system, followed by a discussion of the major strengths of the system compared to mainstream defined contribution (DC) schemes. The Dutch pension system is a rather unique pension system in the sense that it contains a large funded occupation pillar with forced participation and annuitization. Next, we investigate the impact of the financial crisis on the thinking about Dutch occupational pensions. We then turn to the main proposals for reform and discuss three kinds of pension rights that play a role in the current discussion. We discuss alternative pension reforms that have been proposed and end with conclusions.

Dutch occupational pensions

The Dutch pension system consists of three pillars. The first pillar is a pay-as-you-go public pension scheme. It provides a basic flat pension to all older residents at a level that is related to the minimum wage. Compared to other European Union (EU) countries, the state pension in the Netherlands provides only a relatively small part of pension income for those workers earning middle and higher incomes. If these workers want to maintain their standard of living in retirement, they need additional pension income. This is where the second pillar of occupational pensions comes in. The third pillar consists of voluntary personal savings, which are tax-favored up to a ceiling. This pillar can be used to tailor the pension portfolio to individual preferences and characteristics, and is especially important for self-employed individuals who lack occupation pension provisions.

Occupational pension schemes

Occupational pension schemes in the second pillar are funded. These schemes are earnings-related and supplement the flat public benefit for workers who earn more than the minimum wage. These schemes cover more than 90 percent of the labor force. The pension scheme is part of the labor contract, which is typically negotiated between unions and employers in collective labor agreements. Employees are thus obliged to participate in the negotiated pension scheme.

Dutch pension funds are independent trusts with their own governance and administrative structures. The governing board of pension funds consists of equal representatives of employers and unions. The value of assets in the second pillar amounts to about 800 billion euro (125 percent of GDP). Industry-wide pension funds are organized for workers in a specific sector of the economy. These sectoral funds own more than two-thirds of the assets in the second pillar and account for more than 80 percent of the active participants. A company can opt out of an industry fund only if it offers a better pension plan than the plan offered by the sectoral fund.[1] This mandatory participation of firms in sectoral arrangements explains the high coverage of supplementary pensions in the Netherlands.

Guarantees and ambitions

The occupational plans are run like defined benefit (DB) plans, which aim at a certain annuity level during retirement. Years of service and a reference wage typically determine the benefit entitlement. The reference wage used to be the final wage but in the past decade most funds have moved to career-average schemes. In these schemes, entitlements to deferred annuities accrue based on a percentage of the average wage level during the career. These schemes typically aim at an annuity level of about 80 percent of average pay (including the flat public benefit) after forty years of service. This corresponds to an accrual rate of about 2 percent per year. The goal is to index the deferred annuity to wage inflation during the accumulation phase. During the payout phase, some funds aim to index annuities to price inflation but others aspire to a link with the development of contractual wages.

The aspired annuity levels are ambitions rather than guarantees. In particular, the pension funds aim to index the pension rights to prices or wages, but this indexation is not guaranteed because indexation is conditional on the financial performance of the fund. One can in fact view the system as a hybrid system of guarantees and ambitions; nominal annuities are in principle guaranteed (but see below), but the degree to which pensions rise in line with prices and wages depends on the performance of the investments of the pension funds.

Through the shift from final-pay to career-average schemes with conditional indexation of nominal pension rights, pension funds have made indexation of the pension rights of workers conditional on the financial performance of the pension fund. Conditional indexation in these career-average schemes applies not only to the pension rights of the already retired members who are in the decumulation stage but also to the indexation of the pension rights of workers who are still in the accumulation stage. These reforms have thus strengthened the impact of the indexation instrument on the funding rate because this instrument now affects all accrued liabilities of the fund (including the entitlements of workers to deferred annuities). As a result of these reforms, those in the active working population absorb more risks in terms of their pension rights. Moreover, participants rather than employers have become the main risk-bearers of the fund.

More complete contracts

Several large sectoral pension funds now employ policy ladders—rules that state explicitly how both the extent of indexation of pension rights and a possible recovery premium (levied on top of the cost-based premia for the newly accumulated pension benefits) vary with the funding ratio. These policy ladders can be viewed as more complete contracts compared to the previous rather incomplete ones, which allowed for a great deal of discretion by the governing board. Indeed, in the past, funds would make only rather ambiguous statements that pension rights would be indexed as long as the financial position of the fund would allow it.

A policy ladder for a typical Dutch pension fund is shown in Figure 12.1, which is adapted from Ponds and van Riel (2009). The horizontal axis measures the assets of the pension fund. The nominal liabilities L_N corresponds to the value of nominal annuities, while L_R measures the value of indexed annuities. The values of these nominal and real annuities are calculated by using the nominal and real yield curve, respectively. The nominal curve is derived from prices of Government Bonds and published by the supervisor. The real curve can be derived from the nominal one using observed breakeven inflations in the (small) OTC (over-the-counter) market for inflation products.

The left vertical axis measures the actual extent of indexation of the pension rights. This actual indexation depends on comparing the actual

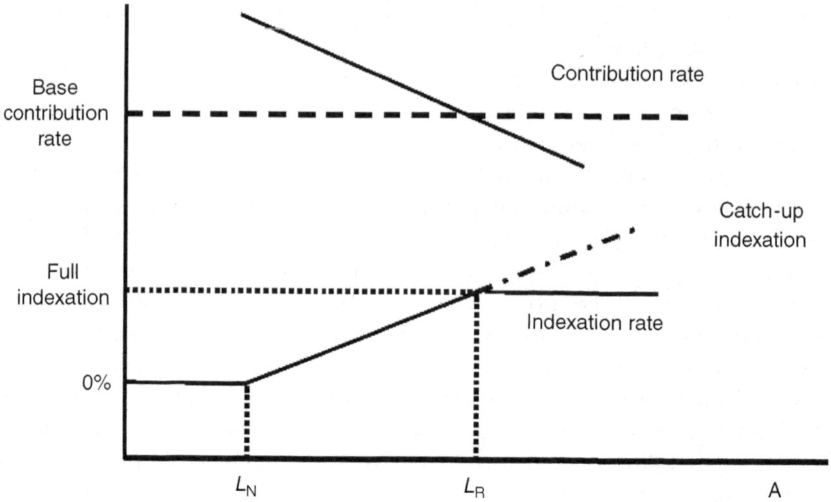

Figure 12.1 Conditional indexation and contribution mechanisms in the Dutch pension system

Source: Ponds and van Riel (2009).

indexation reserve $A - L_N$ to the indexation reserve that is required to fully meet the ambition to index the pension rights, $L_R - L_N$. If the actual indexation reserve is positive but less than the reserve needed to fully meet the aspirations (i.e. $L_N < A < L_E$ so that the nominal funding rate A/L_N exceeds 100 percent but the real funding rate A/L_R is lower than 100 percent), then actual indexation is provided in proportion to the actual indexation reserve $A - L_N$ as a share of the required indexation reserve $L_R - L_N$. If the actual indexation reserve exceeds the required reserve, then the pension fund provides the so-called catch-up indexation to make up for missed indexation in the past. The dotted line in Figure 12.1 depicts this possibility.

The collective buffer $A - L_N$ serves not only as an indexation reserve but also as a solvency buffer for the nominal annuities (i.e. the hard obligations of the fund). Solvency regulations stipulate that the solvency buffer should be so large that a year from now the nominal funding rate continues to exceed 100 percent in 97.5 percent of the cases. If this is not the case, the pension fund has a reserve shortage and should hand in a recovery plan to the supervisor. This plan should show how the fund will build up the required reserve on the expected path within fifteen years. For most pension funds, the critical level of the nominal funding rate below which they suffer from a reserve shortage is around 125 percent. If the nominal funding rate is below 105 percent, the fund is underfunded. If it features such a funding shortage, the fund must make a recovery plan that shows that the nominal funding rate will exceed 105 percent on the expected path in three years.

The left vertical axis of Figure 12.1 also measures the contribution rate. The base contribution rate is calculated as the market value of the hybrid pension claims that are acquired by the active participants (i.e. a nominal DB guarantee and a risky DC claim). An additional so-called recovery premium may be charged if the fund exhibits a funding shortage or a reserve shortage.

Strengths of Dutch occupation plans

This section discusses the main strengths of Dutch occupation pension schemes compared to mainstream DC schemes.

Advanced risk management

The Dutch occupational pension plans aim at achieving the ambition of a DB promise of an appropriate income level during retirement. In particular, the pension fund manages interest-rate risks and inflation risks so as to guarantee the nominal annuities and to realize its ambition to index these annuities to inflation. Hence, the hedge portfolio is defined in terms of income streams during retirement. Indeed, the main risks (e.g. investment risk, inflation risk, interest-rate risk, and longevity risk) are managed so as to hedge risks on behalf of households while at the same time exploiting the risk premia on various risk factors by optimizing the trade-off between return and risk (in terms of mismatch with portfolio hedging income risks).

Protection against behavioral biases

Cooperative pension plans allow individuals with scarce cognitive abilities to delegate complex saving, investment, and insurance decisions to professionals. Collective pension funds assist individuals in properly exploiting their long-run investment horizon and in gaining access to complex investment strategies provided by modern financial markets. More sophisticated life cycle investment by pension funds on behalf of long-term investors stabilizes financial markets and facilitates macroeconomic stability.

Low expenses, substantial buying power, and reduced selection

Cooperative pension funds with compulsory participation of members reduce marketing and other transaction costs. The board of trustees can contract out various financial services to insurance companies, hedge funds, or mutual funds. Accordingly, competition occurs on a wholesale level rather than a retail level. This tends to reduce transaction costs for individual members, who typically lack sufficient expertise to buy the various services that make up the pension product. Moreover, joining forces in a cooperative pension fund that is run professionally strengthens the buying power of individuals, exploits scale economies in buying complex financial products that are not available to individual investors, and helps to discipline commercial financial service providers to act in the interests of the members of the pension fund. Another advantage of forced risk pooling in a sectoral pension fund is that it reduces selection in longevity insurance. Also, this helps to reduce the costs of pension insurance.

Completion of financial markets and intergenerational risk sharing

Collective risk pooling not only combats selection in longevity insurance but also allows members to exchange risks that are not (yet) traded in financial markets. In particular, young members can share in longevity risks faced by older cohorts. To illustrate, if these cohorts live longer than expected, the resulting lower funding rate affects the indexation quality of the deferred annuities of the younger cohorts. In this way, the pension schemes help to fill the gaps of incomplete financial markets. Moreover, by linking pension benefits to the wages of workers, pension funds allow retirees to share in the wage risks of workers. Furthermore, young workers can share in financial market risks faced by the older members through the so-called recovery contributions. In fact, the risky pension contributions produced by the mismatch risk allow the young to transform their human capital into an asset with exposure to financial risks (Beetsma and Bovenberg, 2009).

In principle, one can share financial-market shocks not only between currently living generations but also with generations that are not yet participating in the pension scheme when the shocks actually materialize. In fact, the pension fund buys risk-bearing assets on behalf of future generations by, in effect, borrowing from older generations. From an ex ante point of view, this internal trade is actually welfare-improving because financial shocks are shared even more broadly, namely not only with the currently participating generations but also with future generations (Teulings and de Vries, 2006).

The impact of the crisis

Figure 12.2 displays the development of the nominal funding rates of Dutch pension funds in the past few years.[2] Before the onset of the financial crisis in 2007, the average nominal funding rate amounted to about 145 percent. A buffer of 45 percent of liabilities looks robust at first sight. However, a nominal funding rate of 145 percent translates into a real funding rate of close to 100 percent.[3] Moreover, funding rates differed across funds. About 35 percent of the pension funds exhibited a funding rate below 130 percent, close to the level below which funds feature a reserve shortage.[4]

The crisis caused the average funding ratio to decrease substantially from 145 percent before the crisis to a trough of about 90 percent in the first quarter of 2009.[5] In view of the underfunding, most pension funds have handed in a recovery plan in the beginning of 2009. Currently, the average funding rate is about 105 percent—the critical level for a funding shortage.

Three main factors contributed to the fall of funding rates since 2007. First of all, the worldwide collapse of share prices played a major role in the immediate aftermath of the financial crisis. Second, a sharp decline in

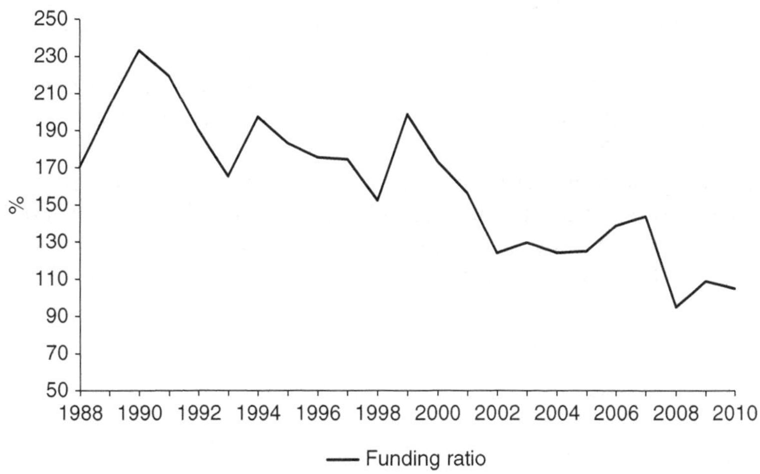

Figure 12.2 Average nominal funding rate of Dutch pension funds: 1988–2010

Source: Authors' calculations.

nominal interest rates increased the present value of nominal pension liabilities. The rise in liabilities was not insufficiently compensated by the increase in the value of bonds (or interest derivatives) on the asset side of the balance sheet because assets did not match nominal liabilities: not only were bond holdings (and derivatives hedging nominal interest-rate risk) much smaller than nominal pension liabilities, but also the duration of the bonds owned by pension funds was typically substantially shorter than that of pension liabilities. Most of the decline in the funding rate between 2007 and 2011 can be attributed to the lower nominal interest rates. The final factor behind the drop in funding rates is lower mortality. Following major health-care reforms in 2001, mortality rates for retirees have dropped more substantially than anticipated earlier. Upward revisions of life expectancy have depressed average funding rates by about 5 percentage points.

The financial crisis has had a major impact on thinking about Dutch occupational pensions. The main impacts are taken up next.

Participants become more aware that they are risk-bearers

The financial crisis revealed to participants that they have become a major risk-bearer in the pension system. In part, as a result of the move from a final-pay to a career-average system, occupation pension systems are no longer pure DB systems, but have been moving in the direction of collective DC systems in which participants rather than employers are the main risk-bearers. Indeed, pension funds are relying increasingly on the indexation instrument and less on the instrument of fluctuating recovery pension contributions to absorb risk. Table 12.1 shows how actual indexation to retirees has lagged indexation ambitions in recent years.

The main reason why participants are becoming the main risk-bearer is that aging and the maturation of pension funds makes recovery contributions a less effective instrument to maintain the solvency of pension funds. With a rising ratio of pensioners to workers, pension liabilities are increasing compared to wages, so that large changes in contributions are required to contain fluctuations in liabilities pension benefits. Indeed, for many companies, financial and actuarial risks of pension guarantees start to

TABLE 12.1 Actual increases in nominal pensions paid to retirees, compared to the indexation ambition: 2005–11

	2005	2006	2007	2008	2009	2010	2011
Indexation ambition	0.49	0.85	2.33	1.84	3.76	1.66	1.2
Actual indexation	0.3	0.82	2.14	2.91	0.17	0.42	0.02

Source: De Nederlandsche Bank (2010).

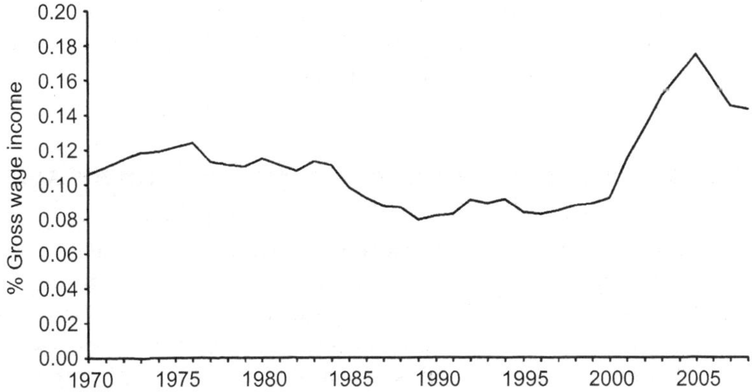

Figure 12.3 Average pension contribution rates as percentage of gross wage income: 1970 – 2008

Source: Authors' calculations.

dominate those of the core business for many companies. They therefore no longer underwrite the risks of their pension funds. Whereas volatile financial markets and increasing pension liabilities have increased financial risks of pension funds, employers are thus supplying less risk-bearing capital to these pension funds. As a direct consequence, participants must supply more risk-bearing capital through pension rights that fluctuate with financial shocks.

Another reason why contributions can no longer absorb shocks is that contribution rates to Dutch occupational pensions have reached rather high levels (see Figure 12.3). The costs of volatile contributions are increasingly being recognized in terms of adverse demand- and-supply side-effects. In particular, fluctuating recovery premia are likely to affect the demand side of the economy in a pro-cyclical fashion. As regards the supply side, the fluctuating pension contributions distort the labor market. Indeed, higher pension contributions aimed at correcting funding deficits act as an implicit tax on labor.

Lack of risk-bearing capital

The financial crisis has also shown that the indexation instrument may not be strong enough to stabilize funding rates in times of economic stress. Indeed, the volatility of financial markets is large compared to the steering capacity of the indexation instrument. The evaluation of the Dutch government of its solvency regulations has revealed that these regulations have tended to underestimate financial risks (including liquidity risk). Whereas financial risks have increased, risk-bearing capital in pension funds has declined as a result of high contribution levels and a premium base that is declining compared to pension liabilities.

Declining mortality rates requires higher retirement age

Mortality rates in the Netherlands have been rather flat in the past two decades of the twentieth century. Moreover, increases in pension costs due to lower mortality could easily be financed on account of booming financial markets, resulting in high funding rates in the 1990s. Since 2002, however, mortality rates of pensioners have started to drop substantially. It gradually became clear that this involved a structural development so that pension funds had to revise their mortality projections downward. In the face of the financial crisis and the high level of contribution rates, the associated higher structural pension costs could no longer be financed out of higher-than-expected returns or increased higher contribution rates.

More and more stakeholders became convinced that longer life expectancy must go together with a higher retirement age. The rule of automatically linking pensions to life expectancy avoids the political costs of discretionary decisions to limit eligibility to public pensions and tax benefits if longevity increases further. Agreeing on a risk-sharing rule ex ante also reduces the political risks associated with collective discretionary decision-making. Moreover, it allows individuals and firms to gradually adapt to a longer working life by better maintaining human capital and adjusting the organization of work. An increase in spending on disability pensions and unemployment benefits is thereby avoided.

By reducing output levels, the financial crisis worsened the public finances, which were already burdened by rising health-care costs. To restore the sustainability of the public finances, the Dutch government proposed to increase the eligibility age for the public pension from 65 to 67. These proposals also include tightening the tax regime for supplementary pensions so that the retirement age of the occupation pensions rise in line with the higher retirement age for the public pension.

Ambiguous status of nominal guarantees

The low nominal funding rates caused by the financial crisis have complicated the investment policy of the funds. Do they defend nominal guarantees by matching these nominal obligations and de-risking their investment strategy? Or do they continue to take investment risk in order to retain upside potential and to hedge inflation risk so as to protect the prospect that they will be able to index their nominal obligations to (wage) inflation?

The current pension contract is rather ambiguous about which investment policy pension funds should implement at low nominal funding rates. The supervisory rules do not force pension funds to match their nominal obligations if capital buffers become very low. These rules thus leave substantial discretion to the pension funds on how to respond to low funding rates in terms of their investment policies. In fact, substantial risk-taking is observed even if nominal funding rates are close to 100 percent.[6] In this way, funds take the risk that they eventually will have to cut nominal pensions. After the nominal funding rate of a pension fund falls below 100 percent, a pension fund has three years to recover to a funding rate above 100 percent. If the fund cannot show recovery on the expected path these three years, it may have to cut nominal pension rights.

The possibility that nominal benefits could be cut came as an unpleasant surprise to many pensioners and eroded the confidence of members in pension funds. Indeed, there is a clear mismatch between what funds communicate (nominal guarantees) and how they invest. In the face of the investment policies of the larger pension funds, one can argue that the current contract does not provide guarantees and is characterized by benefits that depend on financial returns. In other words, the pension system has lost its DB nature altogether in the sense that not only indexation but also nominal pensions are no longer guaranteed. By reducing nominal funding rates, the financial crisis revealed a major weakness of the Dutch pension system, namely the ambiguity of the current pension contract in general and the status of the nominal 'obligations' in particular.

Tension between nominal and real thinking: what is a hedging portfolio?

This ambiguity of nominal guarantees can be explained as follows. On the one hand, nominal guarantees can be matched much easier by financial assets than real guarantees because the supply of inflation-linked bonds is very limited. Moreover, participants tend to suffer from money illusion and thus value nominal guarantees. On the other hand, defending nominal guarantees in the face of low nominal funding rates can be quite costly in terms of the ambition of the funds to safeguard the purchasing power of pension rights.

Indeed, in the face of fluctuating inflation expectations, funds must choose between stabilizing nominal or real funding rates (or alternatively, selecting nominal pension income or a real pension income as the risk-free asset that needs to be hedged). In particular, investing in short-term instruments allows funds to take advantage of rising nominal interest rates if inflation expectations increase so as to stabilize real funding rates and protect the purchasing power of pensions. This investment policy, however, leaves open the risk that falling nominal interest rates worsen the nominal funding rate further. This tension between meeting nominal obligations and hedging inflation risks (i.e. thinking in nominal or real terms) has become especially stark in the aftermath of the financial crisis. On the one hand, low funding rates and the desire not to cut nominal pensions encourage funds to protect their nominal funding rate. On the other hand, uncertainty about inflation is substantial after a financial crisis so that funds want to hedge inflation risks by investing in short-term bonds.

Ownership of risk and buffers ambiguous

The pension contract is ambiguous in terms of not only investment policy (and the associated guarantees and mismatch risk) but also the distribution of mismatch risk. Although pension funds have strived to make risk-sharing contracts more complete through policy ladders (see Figure 12.1), the current policy ladders tend to be silent on what happens if the funding rate (i.e. assets as a percentage of the nominal liabilities) falls below 105 percent. Whereas most pension funds thus continue to take nominal risks at the low funding rates produced by the financial crisis, it is thus unclear who the owner of this risk is.

More generally, the ownership of the collective buffers is not transparent. It is also unclear, for example, what happens if the buffers rise above the level that is necessary to finance fully indexed pensions. Moreover, the policy ladders are at present not more than guidelines for the governing board. They have no legal status and thus do not offer the same protection as legal property rights do. Indeed, the government boards of the pension funds still dispose of substantial discretion in redistributing resources across stakeholders.[7] The ambiguous ownership of risks and buffers is problematic. First of all, if risk ownership is unclear, the fund cannot target its investment policy at the risk preferences of the owners of the risk. Second, incomplete and nontransparent pension contracts may give rise to unpleasant surprises and serious conflicts if shocks hit. To illustrate, when funds became underfunded after the financial crisis, it was unclear who owned these deficits and which stakeholders would have to reduce their claims on the fund or increase resources. Third, the parties who end up with the risk ex post may not be rewarded properly ex ante. Indeed, these incomplete contracts may give rise to substantial, nontransparent value transfers between stakeholders.[8] To illustrate, the benefits in the Dutch occupational pension plans are currently heavily backloaded: the pension fund charges the same price for a deferred annuity for all age groups even though the annuities for the young are cheaper. This lack of market pricing implicit in the uniform pricing of deferred annuities implies that the young are taxed on their working effort while the old are subsidized.

Inadequate communication of risks surrounding real pension income

The ways funds communicate with their participants are still based on the DB system and have not yet adjusted to the new realities in which participants are the main risk-bearers. Nontransparent communication is also related to the nontransparent pension contract (see above). Pension funds typically communicate in terms of nominal pension rights, but are rather silent on indexation prospects and the uncertainty about these expectations. After the transition from final-pay to career-average systems with conditional indexation, information about nominal pension rights of workers is inadequate for estimating the expected replacement rate at retirement.

The financial crisis, which has reduced the indexation potential, has made better communication of the uncertainty[9] surrounding the purchasing power of pensions all the more urgent. Indeed, estimates suggest that workers can expect a decline of as much as 15 percent in their replacement rates as a consequence of inadequate indexation (van Ewijk and Teulings, 2011). As residual risk bearers in pension plans, members should be informed about the risks they face so that they can take this into account in their own financial planning. Timely communication about risks is also essential to maintain the legitimacy of and trust in the system.

Supervision focuses on nominal rights

The solvency rules in the Dutch risk-based supervisory framework in fact focus on the unconditional nominal rights rather than on the unconditional pension rights, which typically involve the ambition of the pension funds to index pension rights to prices or even wages. Hence, capital funding does not necessarily extend also to soft pension rights. This implies that the indexation potential of funds remains outside much of public regulation, even though this is a major part of the expected pension, especially of workers with a long duration. In fact, funds are discouraged from being explicit about their indexation ambitions for fear that this leads to higher funding requirements. Hence, only nominal obligations are on the balance sheets of pension funds.

'One size fits all' under discussion

The current Dutch occupational pension plans impose uniform investment and indexation rules on all participants. This limits the scope to attune risk exposure to the needs of various cohorts. Efficient risk-sharing implies that an adverse shock causes consumption of all agents to decline by the same percentage.[10] For younger workers, human wealth is the most important wealth component. For older members, in contrast, pension rights account for most of individual wealth. Hence, in order to achieve the same relative change in overall wealth for all cohorts (as required by optimal risk-sharing), the pension wealth of young cohorts should fluctuate more than that of older generations if a shock hits the pension funds. These arguments for life cycle investing have led to proposals to differentiate indexation rules across cohorts (see e.g. Molenaar and Ponds, 2011). Younger generations can then take more risks on their pension savings and benefit from the associated risk premiums, whereas the contract for the elderly is geared primarily toward protection of the purchasing power of the pension entitlements. This would alleviate the tensions between younger and older generations about the preferred investment policy. In particular, in aging pension funds, investment policies may become rather conservative under the influence of more numerous retirees, thereby raising pension costs for workers.

With risks increasingly being shifted unto participants, there is also increased interest in giving individuals a say in how much risk they want to bear. The social partners also mentioned this as an option in their pension agreement, which will be referred to in the next section. At the same time, one is very aware of the extensive literature documenting that individuals have difficulties in taking adequate financial decisions and that specification of defaults and nudges is an important task of the trustees of the fund.

Advisory committees and pension agreement

The process to redesign the Dutch pension contract was kicked off in the spring of 2010 with the reports of two advisory committees installed by the Dutch government: the Frijns committee on investments and risk management and the Goudswaard committee on sustainability of the supplementary pension system. Goudswaard et al. (2010) emphasized that the Dutch pension contract exhibits important design features that are to be valued and protected: focus on annual income until death (i.e. annuitization) rather than pension wealth at retirement, mandatory participation, low cost levels, and risk-sharing of untraded risk factors such as longevity and wage risks within a collective pension fund. At the same time, this report argued that the existing supplementary pension system is not sustainable due to a gradual erosion of the risk-bearing capacity and the lack of possibilities to tailor the contract to individual characteristics of the participants (such as their age or wealth level). Goudswaard et al. (2010) stressed the trade-off between the cost of a pension contract, the ambition level (the expected annual income), and the level of certainty. Noting that the contribution rates for supplementary pensions (which can be as high as 20 percent in the Netherlands) have reached a maximum, the committee urged the social partners to reduce either the expected annual pension income or the level of guarantees. The pension agreement by the social partners in June 2010 has made clear that they prefer to reduce the level of guarantees and introduce the so-called 'soft rights' in which pension income depends on changes in life expectancy and on returns on financial markets. These soft rights in effect provide risk-bearing capital to the pension funds so that they can continue to take investment risk on behalf of the participants.

Both Frijns et al. (2010)[11] and Goudswaard et al. (2010) stressed potential conflicts of interest between different groups of participants within a collective pension fund. To illustrate, as many papers advocating life cycle investing show (cf. Bodie et al., 1992; Viceira, 2001; Cocco et al., 2005; Teulings and de Vries, 2006), taking substantial investment risk is more attractive for young participants than for retirees. Similarly, protecting nominal guarantees by reducing equity exposure and hedging interest-rate risks is primarily in the interest of the elderly. This tension is increased because many pension funds are 'aging giants': more than 60 percent of total pension assets is earmarked for pensions that have already commenced or will commence within ten years. This means that the pension funds' investment horizon is becoming shorter, thereby reducing their ability to recover from negative investment results. Major disruptions in financial markets can thus turn ageing giants into 'sinking giants': institutions that are no longer able to meet their commitments. This worsens the risk–return trade-off so that pension funds have to invest more conservatively, but this may make the investment policy unattractive for young workers.

The reports also note that the property rights of the collective buffer in the current contract are ill-defined. Among other things, this can create incentives for excessive risk-taking because risks may be shifted to future generations. Both committees also emphasize that the purchasing power of the pension income is the relevant information and that communication to participants should emphasize expected real pension income and risks, rather than provide information only on nominal income.

In June 2010, the social partners concluded an agreement on pensions. As regarding the public pension, they agreed that the eligibility age and the statutory retirement age for mandatory retirement will be linked to life expectancy in such a way that the average number of pension years for each generation would be equal to the average expected pension years for the generations who started to collect the state pension between 2000 and 2009. On the occupation pensions, social partners agreed that contributions should not rise further. Hence, cost increases on account of increased longevity and financial shocks should be avoided. On longevity increases, the number of pension years for a fixed contribution period should be stabilized. At the same time, financial shocks should be absorbed in pension rights to make the system more shock proof. Social partners agreed that they would explore whether participants could be offered individual choices on their risk exposure.

In any case, new pension contracts should be transparent and complete. Pension funds should clearly communicate the risks implied by the pension contract and investment policies to participants. Social partners also agreed that the increases in effective retirement ages should be accompanied by measures to improve the employability of workers and improve the functioning of the labor market for older workers.

Three types of pension rights

The existing Dutch pension contract can be characterized as having individual guaranteed pension rights as well as collective buffers.[12] The reform proposals advocate the introduction of individual soft rights that explicitly depend on the uncertain development of trends in life expectancy and returns on financial markets. The remainder of the section briefly considers the strength and weaknesses of the three types of pension rights: individual guarantees, collective buffers, and individual soft rights.

Individual guarantees

Individual guarantees (hard rights) are important first and foremost because many individuals prefer guarantees and indicate they are willing to pay for them in terms of additional contributions to compensate for reduced investment returns (van Rooij et al., 2007). Guarantees are easy to communicate. Moreover, they are attractive from a regulatory perspective because solvency supervision is well established (e.g. Solvency II). Last but not least, the Dutch system is rooted in what is perceived as guaranteed nominal income contracts. Hence, it seems attractive to offer these guarantees as an option when the existing pension contract is converted into a new pension contract.

Guarantees also feature considerable disadvantages. Guarantees make a given pension ambition (in terms of an expected pension outcome) more expensive because the benefits of risk premia in financial markets are foregone. Furthermore, guarantees often imply a focus on nominal pension income, rather than on the purchasing power of pensions. In many countries, indexed-linked bond markets are not as well developed as the market for nominal bonds. This is definitely the case for the Netherlands. Bonds linked to Dutch price or wage inflation are not traded apart from small trades in the OTC market. The use of bonds linked to European price inflation yields substantial basis risks and even that market is small relative to the accumulated Dutch pension assets. The use of nominal guarantees implies substantial inflation risks.

Guarantees also discipline the investment strategy. This can be seen as either an advantage or a disadvantage. Subjective judgments by trustees are less important if guarantees are provided. If pension funds had defended their nominal guarantees during the crisis, they would have reduced investment risks, at the cost of their investment exposure when markets recovered. Finally, it should be noted that the ultimate guarantee cannot be offered. Even European sovereign bonds have shown to be potentially risky, and the crisis showed that even insurers can go bankrupt. Whereas the financial crisis has stimulated the demand for guarantees, providing guarantees that cannot be honored in extreme scenarios like the crisis can be quite misleading.

Collective buffers

Collective buffers can smooth fluctuations in financial markets. This can be attractive if agents take too little investment risk because myopic risk aversion implies that they react too much to short-term volatility (Bernatzi and Thaler, 1995). A second argument in favor of collective buffers is that they allow risk-sharing with future generations. The validity of this argument is limited by the requirement that the buffer inherited by new entrants should be large enough to make participation in the fund sufficiently attractive, as otherwise the mandatory participation will be challenged. Adequate supervision is therefore required to prevent funds from shifting too many risks onto future generations. Another drawback of collective buffers is that they reduce the scope for individual decision-making that tailors investment risk to individual preferences. Moreover, they cloud information on who actually bears risks. Last but not least, collective buffers may give rise to political risks as it is unclear which stakeholders will benefit from these buffers. Indeed, the trustees have substantial discretion in allocating these buffers across participants.

Individual soft rights

As stated before, the reform proposals advocate the introduction of *individual soft rights*. Individual soft rights deliver pension income until retirement that depends in an ex ante defined way on the developments in financial markets, for example, by linking to stock market indices or interest rates. Individual soft rights can be transferred at market value, for example, when moving to another job, and cannot be affected by discretionary decisions of the trustees. These individual soft rights serve multiple goals:

- They create risk absorbers for the pension fund and enable it to take substantial investment risk on behalf of the participants.
- They identify individual ownership of components in the collective buffer. This reduces discretion of the governing board to redistribute resources, thereby reducing political risk and providing transparency ex ante on the true risk exposure of participants.[13]
- Clear individual ownership allows capital to be transferred to other pension providers (e.g. when participants move to another job).
- They allow more tailor-made risk taking on the basis of observable individual characteristics, including age. Individual soft rights and hard rights (i.e. guarantees) can be converted into each other when changes in risk exposures are called for.
- They allow individuals to choose their own risk exposure.
- During the payout phase, pension funds can supplement income from nominal guarantees by income from soft rights. In this way, retirees can provide risk-taking capital without being forced to have an upward-sloping consumption profile. This implies, however, that retirees face the risk that their overall income declines in nominal terms after an adverse shock.

The main challenge in introducing individual soft rights is communication. If hard rights are replaced by soft rights, pension income is no longer guaranteed, but rather it depends on uncertain future developments in financial markets and in life expectancy. Communicating this uncertainty to laymen is far from trivial. Another problem is that probability statements about possible future income levels depend on various subjective elements, such as the equity premium or the correlation between risk factors. Soft rights are not new in the Dutch pension contract because they are also implicit in existing collective buffers, which provide the funds for increasing the nominal guarantees through indexation. Possible ways to communicate the uncertainty about the purchasing power of the future pension income have already been widely discussed. Clearly, however, the reform process will make the soft rights more dominant so that adequate communication about uncertainty will become more important.

Another challenge for the implementation of pension contracts with individual soft rights is designing adequate risk-sharing between stakeholders and selecting a proper investment strategy for the fund, which determines the risk features of the soft rights. One of the strengths of typical Dutch pension contracts is that risk factors that cannot be traded on financial markets (e.g. longevity risks, inflation risks) can be traded within the pension fund (see 'Strengths of Dutch occupation plans' section). To illustrate, retirees can be protected against wage inflation if the soft rights of young workers are used to buffer these risks. The fair compensation for these young workers, however, is hard to determine objectively as wage risks are not traded on financial markets, so that no market prices are available. In a similar fashion, longevity risks at older ages could be insured by soft rights—albeit objective market prices are absent due to the lack of trade in systematic longevity risk.

The investment policies of collective pension funds can be viewed as follows. First, one considers the hedging portfolios for the various participants. The nature of these hedging portfolios differs between the nominal guarantees (i.e. the hard rights) and the individual soft rights. In case of the hard rights, these hedging portfolios contain nominal bonds (with low credit risks) with durations matching the (deferred) nominal annuity payments to participants. This portfolio is a buy-and-hold portfolio.

As regards individual soft rights, the hedging portfolio matches as close as possible the average real ambitions of the participants of the pension funds; that is, price-indexed or wage-indexed benefits.[14] In addition, soft rights involve a speculative portfolio that aims at maximizing the return on the mismatch risk with the hedging portfolio. This mismatch risk may involve investment risk and interest-rate risks. The weights of the hedging and speculative portfolios can be determined in a dynamic fashion; these two portfolios, thus, typically are not buy-and-hold portfolios. In a complete contract, how these weights depend on state variables is determined ex ante. Also, the way the realized mismatch risk (which may also include mismatch risks on the hard rights if these rights cannot be completely matched) is distributed over the various participants is determined ex ante in a complete contract.[15] The risk premia on these mismatch risks can be distributed to the participants who bear these risks, but a collective fund may distribute these premia also in another way.

In principle, individuals can be offered a choice between hard rights and soft rights. The prices at which these rights can be exchanged can be based on market prices, but they do not have to be.

Contract examples

In the previous section, we outlined the types of pension rights that could be included in new Dutch pension contracts (individual hard rights, individual soft rights, and collective buffers) and analyzed advantages and disadvantages of the three kinds of pension rights. Next, we discuss a number of specific contracts and how they combine these pension rights. We explore also how the contracts contribute to having more soft rights, in response to the experience of the pension crisis and the recommendations of the government committees on pension policy reform to increase the amount of risk-bearing capital of pension funds. Moreover, we compare the potential new contracts with the existing Dutch pension contract (see 'Dutch occupational pensions' section). The comparison with individual DC contracts as they are offered in many countries worldwide is taken up in the following sections.

Defined Ambition

Boeijen et al. (2010) have suggested a pension contract that contains individual soft rights as well as a collective buffer. The contract is referred to as 'Defined Ambition' to distinguish it from conventional DB or DC plans. In the Defined Ambition model, the active participants annually accrue lifelong pension income as of a particular date of retirement. The real funding rate of the pension fund, defined as the market value of the assets over the market value of risk-free fully indexed pension benefits, determines possible adjustments of accrued (soft) rights to the fluctuating value of market assets and real interest rates affecting the value of risk-free indexed liabilities of the fund. If the real funding rate exceeds a certain upper limit, existing nominal pension rights (in terms of a deferred annuity) will be gradually increased by more than the rate of inflation; if the real funding rate is less than a lower limit, nominal pension income will increase by less than the rate of inflation and may even decline in nominal terms. The asset mix does not depend on the funding rate.

This contract differs in at least three important aspects from the existing contract. First of all the contract is complete and explicitly chooses not to defend nominal guarantees; that is, not to reduce risk levels to avoid benefit cuts if the nominal funding rate falls to 100 percent. Cutting benefits is no longer a solution as a last resort but a standard risk-sharing mechanism. Accordingly, individual soft rights replace individual hard rights. Secondly, benefit cuts and bonuses depend on the investment returns and are not constrained by the level of inflation. Finally, the funding rate determines whether real pension incomes are increased or decreased, and it is defined in real terms and thus accounts for the effect of future inflation on the liabilities of the pension fund to younger generations. In this way, premature payouts to the retirees are avoided if rising nominal interest rates on account of increasing inflation expectations inflate the nominal funded rate.

The contract is similar to the current contract in that collective buffers are used to share risks with future generations. In particular, pension rights that are accumulated after financial shocks hit are affected as these shocks continue to affect the funding rate during the period afterwards, depending on how rapidly the real funding rate is brought back to its equilibrium value of 100 percent. Contracts that contain collective buffers (which may be negative) that are not directly assigned to particular individual participants are called open systems (Bovenberg and van Ewijk, 2011*a*). In closed systems, collective buffers are absent and the property rights of the assets of the fund are allocated to current participants so that the funding rate is always 100 percent.

A return-smoothing model, for now, seems to be preferred by the Dutch social partners. This avoids individual hard rights and consists only of individual soft rights and collective buffers; hence, it is closely related to Defined Ambition with two important differences. First, the liabilities in the real funding rate are computed on the basis of not the risk-free real rate but a discount rate that includes a risk premium based on the expected returns on the actual investment portfolio of the fund. A second difference is the way that real pension incomes are adjusted if the real funding rate differs from 100 percent. In that case, a tenth of the funding gap is distributed uniformly over all participants.[16]

Age differentiation in indexation

Many of the contracts that have been proposed contain elements of life cycle investing. On the one hand, taking investment risks is obviously important to keep the pension system attractive for young participants. On the other hand, retirees typically prefer to take only limited investment risks. One possible way to reconcile the conflicting wishes of younger and older participants is to use age-dependent indexation, which increases or decreases the (accrued) pension income using a larger percentage for the young than for the elderly (see Molenaar and Ponds, 2011). As in the Defined Ambition model, the real funding rate is computed with real interest rates as discount rates, and it determines whether rights are increased or decreased. Collective buffers are used to share risks with future generations. A similar mechanism could be used to limit the risks for other groups of participants than the elderly, for example, low-income workers. Groups who face more uncertain indexation benefit from a higher expected level of indexation.[17]

Growth rate approach

Another possibility to protect retirees against sizeable fluctuations in their annual income is to design the pension contract in such a way that during the decumulation phase, the payout is adjusted only gradually to wealth shocks, just as in the current indexation mechanism with collective buffers.

This approach can be implemented in both closed and open systems. In the closed collective growth rate approach, the annual adjustment in the growth rate[18] (and the volatility in that growth rate) of the (projected) pension income is the same for all participants. The required adjustment after a shock is determined in such a way that the pension wealth that is available in the fund is in expectation exactly sufficient to realize the stochastic pension income (i.e. not only the median but in principle the entire distribution) that is communicated, including annual adjustments according to the expected growth rate. This approach implies that the exposure to the mismatch risk is proportional to the duration of the pension income and is thus cohort-specific. Whereas the adjustment of the growth rate is similar across generations, the level of the growth rate can differ depending on the shocks people have experienced during the payout phase.

In the open collective growth rate approach, in contrast, future accruals also share in the return shocks through fluctuations in a collective buffer. In these open systems, not only the change but also the level of the growth rate is uniform across cohorts. This uniform growth rate between cohorts depends on the real funding rate. The growth rate approach is described in more detail in Bovenberg and van Ewijk (2011*b*).

Combi-contract

A contract with more return-dependent pension income can also be achieved starting from a contract with guarantees, but with lower nominal guarantees than communicated currently.[19] The nominal guarantees should be matched with bonds of the same duration with low credit risk. The remaining wealth can then be invested in equities or bonds with higher credit risks. With low levels of guarantees, this remaining wealth level will be sizable. In that case, it is attractive to allocate soft rights to individuals in view of the advantages mentioned in 'The impact of the crisis' section. Moreover, in the payout phase, part of the pension income can be based on a variable annuity that can be reduced in case of adverse financial shocks.

Escalating annuity contract

The Danish ATP model combines individual hard rights with collective buffers. Individual rights are nominal guarantees and pension income is paid out only of these nominal guarantees so that pension income does not decline in nominal terms. In contrast to the situation in the Netherlands, nominal guarantees are completely hedged by nominal bonds so that these nominal guarantees are defended on financial markets. In addition, ATP has a collective buffer that is invested in equity and other risk-taking capital. If this buffer exceeds 25 percent of the value of the nominal guarantees, these guarantees are increased.

This model is in fact a collective variant of an escalating annuity (see e.g. Bodie and Pesando, 1983). In an escalating annuity, pension income never declines in nominal terms and investments in risky assets are used to raise the guarantees. The amount of risky assets can be calibrated in such a way that the nominal (deferred) annuity can be expected to be increased in line with the inflation rate. For an individual, this implies that the share of risky assets in the portfolio declines with age because the duration of the pension income (and thus the capital required to raise guarantees in line with inflation) falls with age. In a collective scheme, the required share of risky assets depends on the age composition of the fund.

One can also combine a combi-contract during the accumulation phase with an escalating annuity during the payout phase. Accordingly, the overall expected deferred annuity may decline in nominal terms during the accumulation phase, but the annuity can never decline in nominal terms during the payout phase. This implies that people can benefit from the risk premium during the accumulation phase and benefit from a nominal guarantee when retired.

Conclusion

The main aim of the many alternatives to the existing Dutch contract is that the contract is adjusted in line with the directions chosen in the reform process by the social partners in June 2010. The new contracts should stabilize contribution rates by creating mechanisms such that investment risk can be taken and allocated explicitly to groups of participants. Individual soft rights and limits on the buffer fluctuations will increase transparency and will prevent the shifting of funding deficits onto future generations.

The new Dutch pension contract will be a hybrid model between the DB and DC approaches. The DC component will be increased in the sense that the pension income is no longer guaranteed, but depends on returns in financial markets and longevity. Nevertheless, like the existing contract, the new Dutch pension contract will continue to differ in a number of important aspects from the typical DC contract implemented in many countries worldwide. In particular, the set of choice-options will be rather limited in order to protect individuals from behavioral biases. This feature contributes also to rather low-cost load. This design feature is similar to the increasing emphasis on optimal choice architectures in DC schemes. In the Dutch model, however, trustees of the fund take more far-reaching investment decisions than managers of the mutual funds in which DC participants choose to invest. This is related to the emphasis in the Dutch model on providing annuities, which is in fact the most dominant difference between the new Dutch model and the DC world as known today. This emphasis on annuity income is rooted in the Dutch Defined Benefit tradition. A vast academic literature analyzes the advantages and disadvantages of pension income (annuities) over pension wealth (lump sum). Extensive references can be found in Mitchell and Piggott (2011). The specific case of the Netherlands, where annuities are also mandatory in case of most DC contracts, was recently analyzed by Brown and Nijman (2011).

The emphasis on annuity income rather than wealth accumulation per se implies challenges to investment strategies that are not transparent in most current DC contracts. In particular, both interest-rate risk and inflation risks will be managed in the contracts outlined in the 'Three types of pension rights' section to avoid undesired fluctuations in pension income or projected pension income. As argued in 'The impact of the crisis' section, if the pension wealth is to generate stable pension income eventually, the management of interest rate and inflation risks is actually equally relevant in DC contracts. It is questionable, however, whether individuals have the skills and access to financial instruments to do so. To obtain stable real pension income, when approaching retirement, individuals should not only reduce their equity exposure (as in target date funds) but also manage interest and inflation risks; that is, replicate or buy indexed and variable deferred annuities. The new Dutch contracts impose such investment strategies on their participants.

Endnotes

1. In terms of active participants, the most important other type of pension fund is a company pension fund. A company, however, does not have to set up its own company pension fund, but can contract out the pension scheme to an insurance company.
2. The nominal funding rate of a pension fund is defined as financial wealth relative to nominal pension liabilities. The latter are defined as the sum of the

nominal pension rights that the participants of the scheme have already accumulated. The real funding rate is defined in a similar way, but defines liabilities in real terms assuming full future wage or price indexation to the pension rights that participants have accumulated.

3. In calculating the real funding rate, we assumed a duration of pension liabilities of fifteen years, a nominal interest rate of 4.5 percent, price inflation of 2 percent, wage inflation of 3 percent, and weights attached to wage and price inflation of 65 and 35 percent, respectively.
4. As pension funds with lower funding ratios tend to be relatively small, they represent only about 7 percent of the participants of pension funds.
5. For a more elaborate discussion on the development of the funding rates during the financial crisis, see Bonenkamp et al. (2010).
6. Smaller pension funds typically reduced their exposure to nominal risks more than the larger funds. Among other things, this may be due to the fact that larger pension funds would have had to trade in rather illiquid markets during the financial crisis.
7. Also, the rules for transferring pension rights across pension funds show that the individual ownership of the collective buffer is not well defined. In particular, participants can take only the value of their nominal pension rights with them if they move to another pension fund on account of a change in jobs.
8. Indeed, nontransparent redistribution may be a drawback of pension systems like the Dutch one that focus on individual annuities, rather than individual wealth positions. By changing the rules for the annuities, pension funds may redistribute wealth positions across stakeholders. In traditional DC plans, in contrast, individual wealth positions are protected better. The plans, however, tend to inadequately manage the risks of providing income streams in retirement.
9. Not only communications to participants but also recovery plans pay inadequate attention to risk. In particular, recovery plans are based on the expected path and do not look at the risk that recovery does not happen on account of financial risk.
10. This assumes that all agents feature the same constant relative risk aversion and that utility is time separable and separable in consumption of commodities and leisure. More generally, optimal risk-sharing implies that everybody's marginal utility changes with the same percentage after a shock hits. See Bohn (2005).
11. The Frijns et al. (2010) report also contains important recommendations to strengthen the role of trustees of a fund versus asset managers. We do not consider these governance issues here.
12. The supervisory rules, however, do not force pension funds to match their nominal obligations if capital buffers become very low. One can therefore argue that the current contract does not provide guarantees and is characterized by return-dependent benefits already. The ambiguity of the current pension contract is one of the main weaknesses of the Dutch pension system.
13. One can thus argue that individual soft rights make the ownership of soft rights 'harder'. Indeed, an alternative definition of 'hard' and 'soft' rights is that, in contrast to 'hard' rights, 'soft' rights leave discretion in the hands of the

governing board on how to distribute resources. With this alternative definition of soft rights, the newly introduced rights should be called 'hard'.

14. Most pension funds aim at wage-indexed pensions for workers and at price-indexed pensions for retirees. Some pension funds (particularly in the public sector and the health-care sector) aim at wage indexation also for retirees.
15. In principle, one can distribute various mismatch risks in different ways over the participants. Here, we assume, however, that all mismatch risks are distributed in the same way over the participants.
16. While many argue in favor of life cycle investing, the legal requirement to avoid age discrimination for now seems to impose that relative cuts and bonuses are to be identical for all active participants. It is still unclear whether an option to choose nominal guarantees rather than a risky investment portfolio will be offered to retirees.
17. The return-smoothing model also implies different exposures to risk of retirees and workers. In particular, retirees bear less investment risk, as their purchasing power is affected only gradually by shocks. Workers, in contrast, tend to bear the full brunt of the shocks, as they tend to retire after the smoothing period has ended. A major difference with the explicit age differentiation in indexation is that those who bear more risk are not rewarded for the additional risk they bear.
18. The growth rate is measured compared to the targeted indexation variable. To illustrate, if the pension contract aims to deliver wage-indexed benefits, the growth rate is measured compared to the growth rate of wages.
19. As argued in 'The impact of the crisis' section, real guarantees cannot be hedged in financial markets because of the lack of an indexed-linked bond market in the Netherlands. Small funds can insure inflation through the OTC market.

References

Beetsma, R. M. W. J. and A. L. Bovenberg (2009). "Pensions, Intergenerational Risk Sharing and Inflation", *Economica,* 76(302): 364–86.

Bernatzi, S. and R. Thaler (1995). "Myopic Loss Aversion and the Equity Premium Puzzle", *Quarterly Journal of Economics,* 110: 73–92.

Bodie, Z. and J. Pesando (1983). "Retirement Annuity Design in an Inflationary Climate", in Z. Bodie and J. Shoven, eds., *Financial Aspects of the US Pension System.* Chicago, IL: University of Chicago Press, pp. 291–323.

——, R. C. Merton, and W. F. Samuelson (1992). "Labor Supply Flexibility and Portfolio Choice in a Life-Cycle Model", *Journal of Economic Dynamics and Control,* 16: 427–49.

Boeijen, D., N. Kortleve, and J. Tamerus (2010). "Van toezegging naar ambitie", NEA Paper 35. Tilburg, Netherlands: Netspar.

Bohn, H. (2005). "Who Bears what Risk? An Intergenerational Perspective", in D. Blitzstein, O. S. Mitchell, and S. P. Utkus, eds., *Restructuring Retirement Risks.* Oxford, UK: Oxford University Press, pp. 10–36.

Bonenkamp, J., A. L. Bovenberg, C. van Ewijk, and E. Westerhout (2010). "Report on the Effects of the Credit Crisis on the Solvency of Dutch Pension Funds and its Economic Consequences", Netspar Discussion Paper 07/2010-035. Tilburg, Netherlands: Netspar.

Bovenberg, A. L. and C. van Ewijk (2011*a*). "The Future of Multi-pillar Pension Systems", Netspar Discussion Paper. Tilburg, Netherlands: Netspar.

—— and ——(2011*b*). "Bouwstenen voor nieuwe pensioencontracten", Netspar Discussion Paper. Tilburg, Netherlands: Netspar.

Brown, J. and T. Nijman (2011). "Opportunities for Improving Pension Wealth: Decumulation in the Netherlands", Netspar Discussion Paper 2011-8. Tilburg, Netherlands: Netspar.

Cocco, J. F., F. J. Gomes, and P. J. Maenhout (2005). "Consumption and Portfolio Choice over the Life Cycle", *The Review of Financial Studies*, 18: 492–533.

De Nederlandsche Bank (2010). "Naar nieuwe pensioencontracten: Wat zijn de voorkeuren van deelnemers?", Working Paper. http://www.dnb.nl/binaries/Bijlage%20Pensioenvoorkeuren_tcm46-243710.pdf

van Ewijk, C. and C. Teulings (2011). "Nieuw Pensioencontract Onvermijdelijk", CPB Policy Brief 1. The Hague: Centraal Planbureau.

Frijns, J., J. Nijssen, and B. Scholtens (2010). "Pensioen: onzekere zekerheid", Rapport van de commissie Beleggingsbeleid en Risicobeheer (commissie Frijns).

Goudswaard, K., R. Beetsma, T. Nijman, and P. Schnabel (2010). "Een sterke tweede pijler", Rapport van de commissie Toekomstbestendigheid Aanvullende Pensioneregelingen, Working Paper.

Mitchell, O. S. and J. Piggott (2011). *Revisiting Retirement Payouts: Market Developments and Policy Issues*. Oxford, UK: Oxford University Press.

Molenaar, R. and E. H. M. Ponds (2011). "Risk Sharing and Individual Life Cycle Investing in Funded Collective Pension Funds", Netspar Discussion Paper 2011-1. Tilburg, Netherlands: Netspar.

Ponds, E. H. M. and B. van Riel (2009). "'Sharing Risk: The Netherlands' New Approach to Pensions", Journal of Pension Economics and Finance, 8(1): 91–105.

van Rooij, M. C. J., C. J. M. Kool, and H. M. Prast (2007). "Risk-Return Preferences in the Pension Domain: Are People Able to Choose?", *Journal of Public Economics*, 9: 701–22.

Teulings, C. and C. de Vries (2006). "Generational Accounting, Solidarity, and Pension Losses", *De Economist*, 146: 63–83.

Viceira, L. M. (2001). "Optimal Portfolio Choice for Long-Horizon Investors with Nontradable Labor Income", *Journal of Finance*, 56: 433–47.

Chapter 13

How Have Public Sector Pensions Responded to the Financial Crisis?

Andrew G. Biggs

Roughly four out of five employees of state and local governments in the United States are covered by a defined benefit (DB) pension plan, versus only around one in five private sector workers. Prior to the financial market disruptions of recent years, public sector pensions were well funded, at least according to their own accounting conventions.[1] As of 2007, the average public pension plan was 84.6 percent funded. In 2009, by contrast, the average public pension plan was only 77.1 percent funded.[2]

This decline in pension health was largely due to a precipitous decline in pension assets. These plans had increasingly invested in equities, rising from roughly one-third of pension portfolios prior to the mid-1980s to around two-thirds of assets prior to the financial crisis.[3] While higher than expected returns on equities allowed states to reduce pension funding from around 6 percent of state budgets through the mid-1980s to around 3 percent prior to the crisis,[4] the downside was higher sensitivity to annual market returns. According to the Federal Reserve, state and local pension assets declined by nearly $1 trillion from 2007 to 2008 and have yet to regain their former value.

Since public pension plans generally assume an 8 percent return on assets, this implies that, even today, plan assets are more than 25 percent below levels projected as of 2007. Indeed, even if public plans returned 11.5 percent annually going forward, it would take them until 2020 to catch up to asset levels projected prior to the financial crisis. This raises the question of how public sector pensions have reacted to such changes. As a matter of law and general plan stewardship, many plans have increased contributions for employers and/or participants, helping assets catch up more quickly with projected liabilities. Such changes have been the subject of political debate in many states and localities. A number of states have attempted to reduce the generosity of benefits, principally for newly hired employees but also, in some cases, for current employees and retirees through reductions in postretirement Cost of Living Adjustments (Pew, 2011). Public plan changes for current employees are often legally problematic, and it is likely that many will be settled in court.

Here, however, we focus on investment practices to ask whether public pensions have altered their investment plans since the financial crisis, and if so, how? One hypothesis is that public pensions, with their focus on longer time horizons, would make few changes to their investment practices in response to the large market shifts. Alternately, either increased or decreased risk-taking are also plausible. Following the financial crisis and the increased attention to the differences in risk between public pension assets and liabilities, some plans might reduce the risk profile of their pension investments. Yet, other underfunded pensions might seek to recoup their losses by taking even more investment risk. This could be portrayed as an irrational reaction, similar to a gambler 'doubling down' on risk, to make up for prior losses. Different plans in different circumstances could react in different ways.

To assess the direction of such possible changes, we first analyze how public pension actual asset allocations changed between 2007, prior to the financial crisis, and 2009. These changes will be due both to choices made by plan managers and, more importantly, to relative increases and decreases in the values of various asset classes. Second, we analyze changes to plan *target* asset allocations from 2007 to 2010. While these allocations may not yet be fully realized, the targets reflect the mix of risk and return that plan managers seek to achieve and thus may be a better measure of managerial intentions. Third, we estimate the risk of target portfolios in 2007 and 2010 to analyze how plans' desired mix of investment risk and return may have changed in response to the financial crisis and other factors.

Data employed

We use several sources of data to examine public plan financing and investments. For information on the funding status of plans and changes in plans' actual portfolio allocations, we use the Center for Retirement Research's (CRR) Public Plans Database, which covers 126 plans over the period 2001–9. However, the CRR dataset does not include information on plan target portfolios. To obtain this information, we surveyed the annual reports of twenty-nine large public pension plans, obtaining target asset allocations for 2007 and 2010. In a small number of cases, data were obtained through direct contact with plans. In cases in which 2010 data were not available, we relied on plan 2009 target allocations. While not a comprehensive sample, the combined assets held by these twenty-nine plans comprise roughly 50 percent of total public pension holding as of 2010.

Investment portfolios

The financial turmoil of recent years would play havoc with any investor's portfolio, requiring active rebalancing in order to maintain a given asset allocation. Most public plans rebalance only gradually, allowing accumulation differences in relative returns across classes to alter portfolio allocations. In particular, poor returns on stocks have shifted the equity share of portfolios downward over time.

Figures 13.1 and 13.2 show the percentage of public pension portfolios allocated to different asset types for the years 2007 and 2009, based on CRR data for approximately 125 plans in each year. The data points represent median values, while the bottom and top of the bars represent the 10th and 90th percentiles of the distribution.

Due to data limitations, asset classes are aggregated. For instance, domestic and international equities are treated as a single class. From 2007 to 2009, the percentage of public pension assets held in equities declined significantly, from a 2007 median of 60 percent in equities to 52 percent in 2009. Similarly, the share of pension portfolios held in bonds grew from 2007 to 2009, from a median of 24 percent of portfolios to 26 percent. Real estate remained constant at a median value of 6 percent of assets, as did cash at 1 percent. Alternate investments increased from a median value of

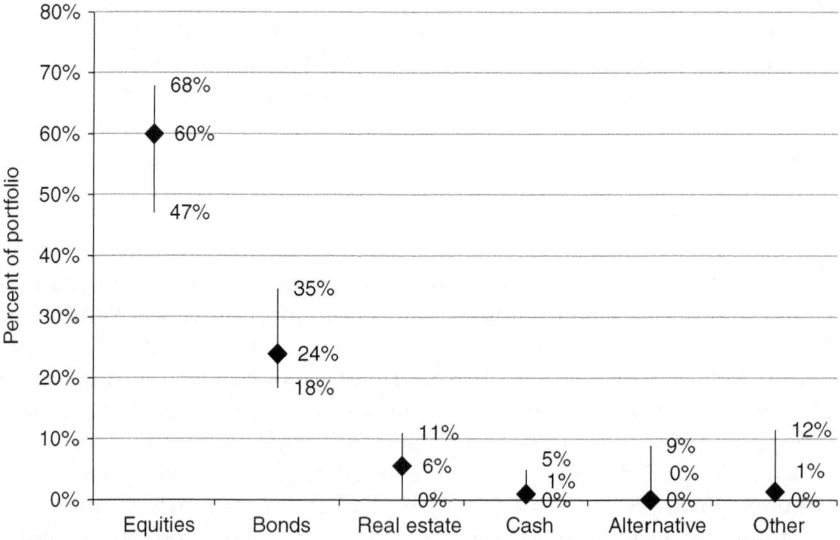

Figure 13.1 Median public pension asset allocations, with 10th and 90th percentiles: 2007

Source: Author's calculations from Center for Retirement Research data (CRR, 2011).

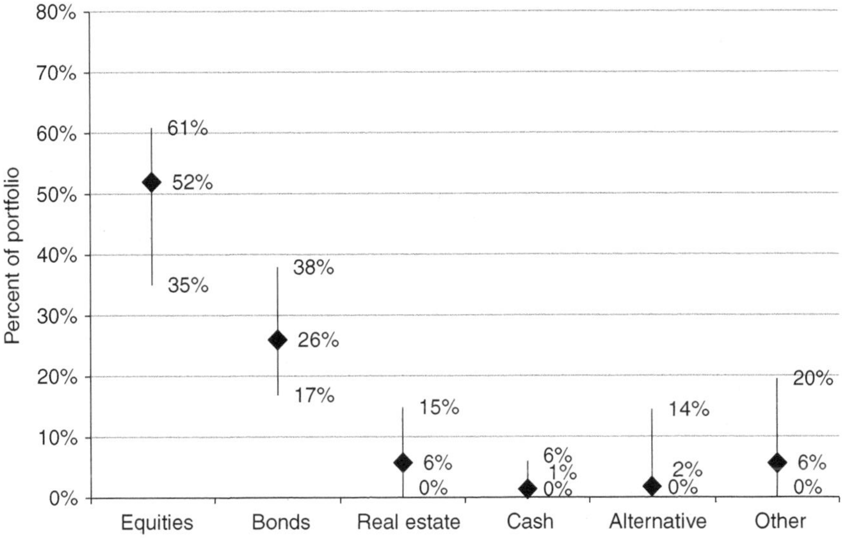

Figure 13.2 Median public pension asset allocations, with 10th and 90th percentiles: 2009

Source: Author's calculations from Center for Retirement Research data (CRR, 2011).

zero in 2007 to 2 percent in 2009. The 'other' asset class grew from a median value of 1 to 6 percent. From an examination of a number of plan reports, it appears that the 'other' investments often include assets that could be termed as alternate investments, meaning that this data may understate the uptick in alternative investment shares from 2007 to 2009.

Perhaps most striking is the increased range of portfolio allocations, meaning greater heterogeneity in asset allocations from plan to plan. In every asset class, the range from the 10th to 90th percentiles increased from 2007 to 2009. For instance, for equities, it grew from 21 percentage points in 2007 to 26 percentage points in 2009; for bonds, it grew from 16 to 21 percentage points; and for real estate, from 11 to 15 percentage points. For alternate investments, the range grew from 9 to 14 percentage points, while for 'other' the range grew from 12 to 20 percentage points.

Target portfolios

It should be borne in mind that the changes in asset allocations shown above were not primarily the result of manager choice. Rather, changing market values caused an involuntary change in most public plan portfolio allocations. To learn more about how intentions regarding asset management have changed since the beginning of the financial crisis, next we turn to public pension *target* asset allocations. The boards of most public sector plans set and disclose a target asset allocation that they will seek to reach and maintain over a period of time. How these targets change over time reveals changing management attitudes to different asset classes and to the overall risk profile that the plan seeks to maintain.

To gather information on target portfolio allocations, we focused on the 2007 and 2010 Comprehensive Annual Financial Reports (CAFRs) of twenty-nine large public pension funds, with assets representing around half of total public funds under management. For each plan, we found the target allocation as printed in the CAFR, and then tabulated those targets into five broad categories: equities, bonds, alternative investments, real estate, and cash. The results are displayed in Figure 13.3.

In 2007, almost 6 of 10 dollars in the median public pension portfolio was invested in equities, with differing allocations to domestic and international shares.[5] Bonds made up about 1 dollar in 4 dollars, and alternative investments—private equity, hedge funds, and the like—made up around 1 dollar in 10 dollars. Real estate made up around 6 percent of the average portfolio, and cash constituted the remaining small amount. Yet portfolio allocations were not uniform across plans. The difference between the 90th and 10th percentile asset shares for equities was 19 percentage points; for bonds, 16 percentage points; for alternative investments, 14 percentage points; for real estate, 11 percentage points; and for cash, 1 percentage point.

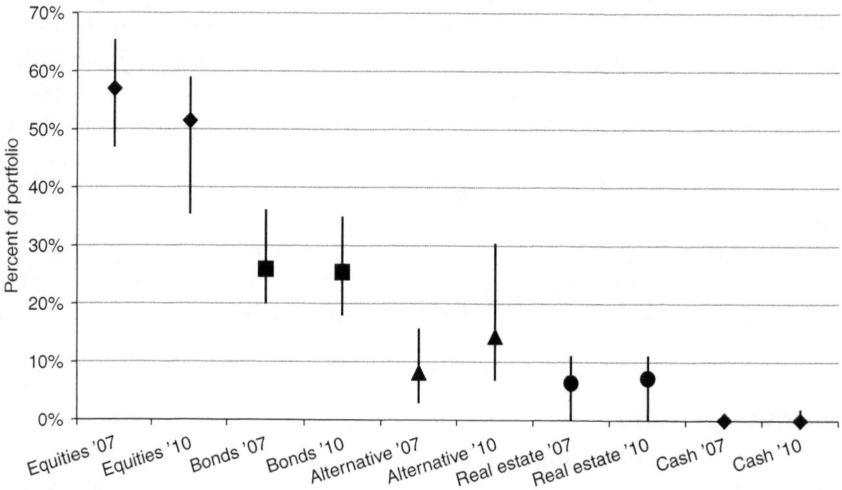

Figure 13.3 Median target asset allocations, with 10th and 90th percentiles: 2007 vs 2010

Source: Author's calculations from plan data.

By 2010, target asset allocations had shifted significantly. Equities fell from a median target share of 58 to 52 percent, while bonds and real estate remained essentially even. The largest increase was for alternative investments, which rose from 9 percent of the median target allocation in 2007 to 13 percent in 2010. In effect, the fall in equities was largely replaced by increased allocations to alternative investments. Moreover, heterogeneity in target portfolios between plans also increased. The gap between the 10th and 90th percentile portfolio shares increased for equities (from 19 to 24 percentage points), while remaining more or less steady for bonds (from 16 to 17 percentage points). The largest increase again came for alternative investments, where the difference in asset shares between the 10th and 90th percentiles grew to 24 percent, a very high level given that the median plan holds only 13 percent of its assets in alternative investments (and the mean plan only 17 percent).

Evidently, target asset allocations have changed rather markedly since the financial crisis, with pension fund managers indicating a rising interest in alternative investments. Given the poor returns on equities in recent years and pressures to maintain expected returns going forward, the shift into alternate investments may be understandable. What is unclear from the above data, however, is how this shift altered the level of risk that plans take on. To help answer that question, next we estimate the risk of plan portfolios for 2007 and 2010.

Risk of target asset allocations

Pension manager attitudes toward risk may have changed due to adverse market performance in various ways. For instance, chastened by overexposure to equities, some might shift assets toward fixed-income investments, thinking more along the lines of asset/liability management or liability-driven investment. Others might seek to win back losses by retaining or even increasing their risk exposure. Further, some might opt to 'double down'.

To our knowledge, no public plans publish their target portfolio risk in their annual reports or actuarial valuations. This constitutes a significant omission that makes it difficult for policymakers and the public to understand the contingent liabilities that they face. But with certain simplifying assumptions, we can estimate the risk of pension portfolios using projections from Wilshire Consulting (2011) regarding the mean returns, variances, and covariances of a number of asset classes.

Table 13.1 shows Wilshire's projected risk and return for the asset classes included in our tabulations. Wilshire's projections are available in more detail than shown here, but due to limitations on target portfolio data

TABLE 13.1 Expected risk and return of pension asset classes (%)

Class	Annual volatility	Expected return
Equities	16.5	7.25
Bond	4.5	3.58
Alternatives	26	9.7
Real estate	15	5.5
Cash	0	0

Source: Author's calculations using data from Wilshire Consulting (2011).

provided by plans, it is necessary to treat assets at a more aggregated level.[6] It is noteworthy that Wilshire's projected returns are lower than those used by most public plans. The typical public plan projects annual returns of around 8 percent, while Wilshire projects a median return of only around 6.5 percent.

Table 13.2 reports a correlation matrix for pension asset classes. Using these figures and Wilshire's projections of annual asset risk, we calculate the expected standard deviation of future portfolio returns for each plan. For consistency, we use the same risk and correlation assumptions for both 2007 and 2010 target portfolios.

Table 13.3 reports summary statistics on these calculations. In 2007, the mean public pension target portfolio had a projected standard deviation of annual returns of 12.2 percent; for 2010, the mean standard deviation had risen to 12.8 percent. (Medians for 2007 and 2010 were 12.2 and 12.5 percent, respectively.) In 2007, the 10th to 90th percentile range was 10.8–13.5 percent, a spread of 2.7 percentage points, while for 2010, the range was 11.5–14.2 percent, a spread that also equaled 2.7 percentage points. Yet, the standard deviation of portfolio standard deviations increased from 1 to 1.2 percentage points. Thus, while there was some widening of the differences in risk taken by plans, the more important trend seemed to be a simple shift upward.

TABLE 13.2 Correlation matrix for pension asset classes

	Equities	Bonds	Alternatives	Real estate	Cash
Equities	1	0.29	0.75	0.35	0
Bonds	0.29	1	0.32	0.15	0
Alternatives	0.75	0.32	1	0.35	0
Real estate	0.35	0.15	0.35	1	0
Cash	0	0	0	0	1

Source: Author's calculations using data from Wilshire Consulting (2011).

TABLE 13.3 Summary statistics on public pension portfolio standard deviations (%): 2007 and 2010

	2007	2010
Mean	12.2	12.8
Median	12.2	12.5
10th	10.8	11.5
90th	13.5	13.5

Source: Author's calculations (see text).

This increase in average plan risk-taking would be anticipated to boost expected returns by approximately 0.15 percentage points, assuming that portfolios were on the efficient frontier. From 2007 to 2009 (the most recent year for the CRR's Public Plans Database), the average projected nominal return increased by 0.03 percentage points, from 7.91 percent in 2007 to 7.94 percent in 2009. This change was the net of a −0.03 percentage point reduction in assumed inflation and a 0.06 percentage point increase in assumed real returns. One potential explanation is that plans were taking more risk, not just to increase expected returns but merely to maintain the returns they had already projected. This increase in plan risk is likely to be significant given the investment losses that plans suffered, and the increased policy focus on asset–liability management and on the market valuation of pension liabilities. Indeed, the typical 2010 target allocation involved more risk than did almost two-thirds of plans in 2007.

The largest increases in portfolio risk were for the South Carolina Retirement System (increase in standard deviation of 2.61 percentage points), Illinois Teachers (2.59 percentage points), and Pennsylvania Employees (2.14 percentage points). The largest *reductions* in target portfolio risk were for California State Teachers (−0.78 percentage points), Missouri Public Schools (−0.68 percentage points), and the Florida State Retirement Board (−0.47 percentage points).

Figure 13.4 details changes by plan. Eleven of the twenty-nine plans in the sample had essentially unchanged risk, meaning a change of less than 0.3 percentage points. Fourteen plans increased risk by more than 0.3 percentage points, while four plans reduced risk by more than 0.3 percentage points.

It is difficult to tell why certain plans took the paths they did. For instance, there is no simple correlation between the decline in a plan's funding ratio from 2007 to 2010 and its changed target portfolio risk. Of course, if some plans reacted to funding declines differently than others—some taking a more conservative route while others doubled down—such a pattern would be difficult to discern from the data available.

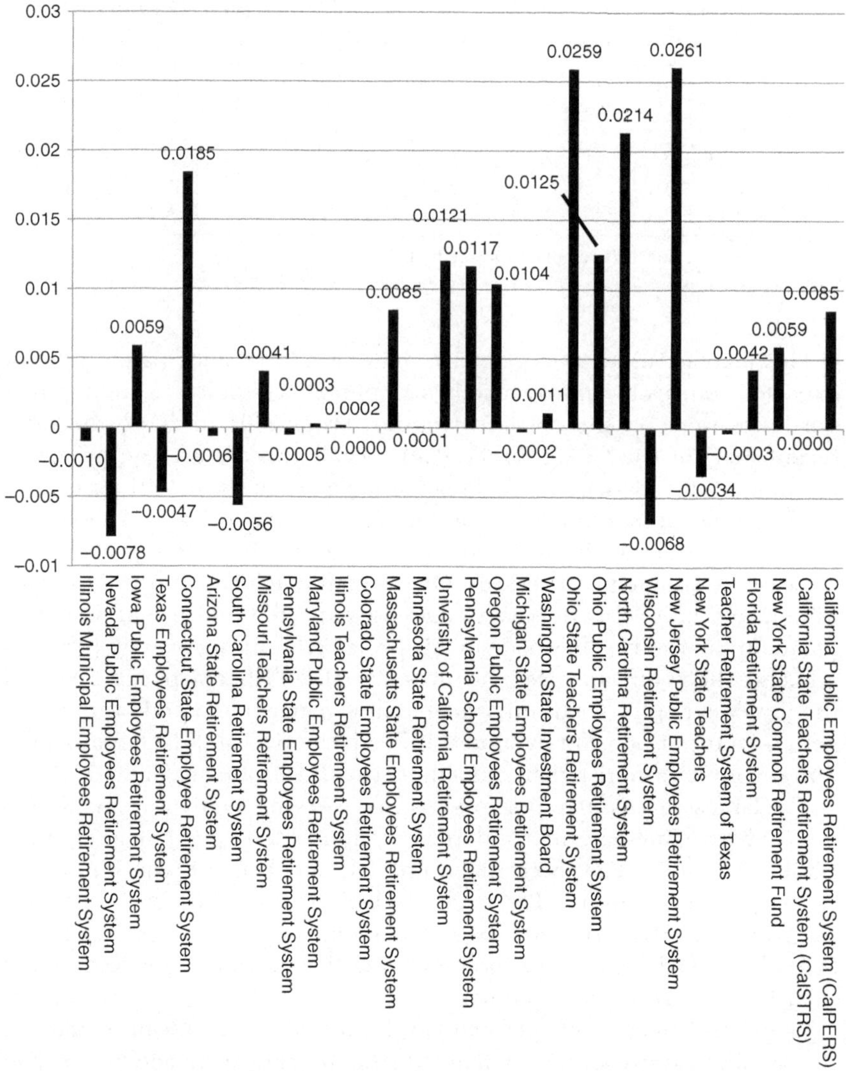

Figure 13.4 Change in standard deviation of target portfolio returns: 2007–10

Source: Author's computations.

Conclusion

The financial crisis and the subsequent recession generated significant losses to pension assets, along with declines in plan funding rates. To date, no comprehensive analysis has been conducted of how public DB plans reacted to the volatility of markets since the financial crisis. We have analyzed three aspects of pension funding: shifts in asset allocations due to changes in market values, shifts in target asset allocations due to decisions undertaken by plan managers, and estimates of the risk of plan target portfolios in 2007 and 2010. We have also sought to analyze how risk-taking by public pensions has changed over time.

Although equity price declines reduced the share of plan investments held in stocks, plan target asset allocations have tended to increase risk, often via a broader acceptance of alternative investments in public plan portfolios. The typical pension plan in 2010 targeted a level of risk that exceeded the rate of two-thirds of pensions in 2007. While the increased risk taken by the median public sector pension was modest, a small number of plans did significantly increase their target portfolio allocations, making more plausible the view that some plans may boost risk as a means to recover from market declines over the past several years. Nevertheless, risk is a double-edged sword. Pension managers should carefully consider the investment risk they are taking and make it explicit in pension reports. Otherwise policymakers and the public will not be aware of the contingent liabilities they face.

Acknowledgments

The author wishes to thank Rohan Poojara for his valuable research assistance on this project.

Endnotes

1. The so-called 'market valuation' critique of public pension accounting argues that discounting plan liabilities at the expected return on assets is misleading, as liabilities are intended to be and in most cases are guaranteed, while assets are risky. Discounting at a risk-adjusted interest rate would reduce plan funding ratios by roughly one-half and increase unfunded liabilities by a factor of around 6. See Novy-Marx and Rauh (2009) and Biggs (2010).
2. Derived by the author from the Center for Retirement Research Public Plans Database (CRR, 2011).
3. Derived by the author from FRB (2011: table L 119 (A)).
4. As reported by Munnell et al. (2010).

5. As above, due to data limitations, we aggregate domestic and international equities into a single class. Breaking out international investments would have reduced the sample size.
6. For instance, we combine domestic and international equities into a single class, with a standard deviation of annual returns equal to the unweighted average of Wilshire's projections for the two classes.

References

Biggs, A. G. (2010). "An Options Pricing Method for Calculating the Market Price of Public Sector Pension Liabilities", American Enterprise Institute Working Paper No. 164. Washington, DC: American Enterprise Institute.

Board of Governors of the Federal Reserve System (FRB) (2011). *Flow of Funds of the United States*. Washington, DC: FRB.

Center for Retirement Research (CRR) (2011). *Public Plans Database*. Chestnut Hill, MA: CRR.

Munnell, A. H., J. Aubry, and L. Quinby (2010). "The Impact of Public Pensions on State and Local Budgets", Center for Retirement Research Working Paper SLP#13. Chestnut Hill, MA: CRR (October).

Novy-Marx, R. and J. Rauh (2009). "The Liabilities and Risks of State-Sponsored Pension Plans", *Journal of Economic Perspectives*, 23(4): 191–210.

Pew Center on the States (Pew) (2011). *The Widening Gap: The Great Recession's Impact on State Pension and Retiree Health Care Costs*. Washington, DC: Pew Center on the States (April).

Wilshire Consulting (2011). *2011 Wilshire Report on State Retirement Systems: Funding Levels and Asset Allocation*. Santa Monica, CA: Wilshire Associates (February).

End Pages

The Pension Research Council

The Pension Research Council at the Wharton School of the University of Pennsylvania is committed to generating debate on key policy issues affecting pensions and other employee benefits. The Council sponsors interdisciplinary research on private and social retirement security and related benefit plans in the United States and around the world. It seeks to broaden understanding of these complex arrangements through basic research into their economic, social, legal, actuarial, and financial foundations. Members of the Advisory Board of the Council, appointed by the Dean of the Wharton School, are leaders in the employee benefits field, and they recognize the essential role of social security and other public sector income maintenance programs while sharing a desire to strengthen private sector approaches to economic security. For more information, see http://www.pensionresearchcouncil.org

The Boettner Center for Pensions and Retirement Security

Founded at the Wharton School to support scholarly research, teaching, and outreach on global aging, retirement, and public and private pensions, the Center is named after Joseph E. Boettner. Funding to the University of Pennsylvania was provided through the generosity of the Boettner family, whose intent was to spur financial well-being at older ages through work on how aging influences financial security and life satisfaction. The Center disseminates research and evaluation on challenges and opportunities associated with global aging and retirement, how to strengthen retirement income systems, saving and investment behavior of the young and the old, interactions between physical and mental health, and successful retirement. For more information, see http://www.pensionresearchcouncil.org/boettner/

Executive Director

Olivia S. Mitchell, *International Foundation of Employee Benefit Plans Professor*, Department of Business Economics and Policy, The Wharton School, University of Pennsylvania.

Advisory Board

Senior Partners

Recent Pension Research Council Publications

Financial Literacy. Olivia S. Mitchell and Annamaria Lusardi, eds. 2011 (ISBN 0-19-969681-9).

Securing Lifelong Retirement Income. Olivia S. Mitchell, John Piggott, and Noriyuki Takayama, eds. 2011 (ISBN 0-19-959484-9).

Reorienting Retirement Risk Management. Robert L. Clark and Olivia S. Mitchell, eds. 2010 (ISBN 0-19-959260-9).

Fundamentals of Private Pensions. Dan M. McGill, Kyle N. Brown, John J. Haley, Sylvester Schieber, and Mark J. Warshawsky, 9th Ed. 2010 (ISBN 0-19-954451-6).

The Future of Public Employee Retirement Systems. Olivia S. Mitchell and Gary Anderson, eds. 2009 (ISBN 0-19-957334-9).

Recalibrating Retirement Spending and Saving. John Ameriks and Olivia S. Mitchell, eds. 2008 (ISBN 0-19-954910-8).

Lessons from Pension Reform in the Americas. Stephen J. Kay and Tapen Sinha, eds. 2008 (ISBN 0-19-922680-6).

Redefining Retirement: How Will Boomers Fare? Brigitte Madrian, Olivia S. Mitchell, and Beth J. Soldo, eds. 2007 (ISBN 0-19-923077-3).

Restructuring Retirement Risks. David Blitzstein, Olivia S. Mitchell, and Steven P. Utkus, eds. 2006 (ISBN 0-19-920465-9).

Reinventing the Retirement Paradigm. Robert L. Clark and Olivia S. Mitchell, eds. 2005 (ISBN 0-19-928460-1).
Pension Design and Structure: New Lessons from Behavioral Finance. Olivia S. Mitchell and Steven P. Utkus, eds. 2004 (ISBN 0-19-927339-1).
The Pension Challenge: Risk Transfers and Retirement Income Security. Olivia S. Mitchell and Kent Smetters, eds. 2003 (ISBN 0-19-926691-3).
A History of Public Sector Pensions in the United States. Robert L. Clark, Lee A. Craig, and Jack W. Wilson, eds. 2003 (ISBN 0-8122-3714-5).
Benefits for the Workplace of the Future. Olivia S. Mitchell, David Blitzstein, Michael Gordon, and Judith Mazo, eds. 2003 (ISBN 0-8122-3708-0).
Innovations in Retirement Financing. Olivia S. Mitchell, Zvi Bodie, P. Brett Hammond, and Stephen Zeldes, eds. 2002 (ISBN 0-8122-3641-6).
To Retire or Not: Retirement Policy and Practice in Higher Education. Robert L. Clark and P. Brett Hammond, eds. 2001 (ISBN 0-8122-3572-X).
Pensions in the Public Sector. Olivia S. Mitchell and Edwin Hustead, eds. 2001 (ISBN 0-8122-3578-9).
The Role of Annuity Markets in Financing Retirement. Jeffrey Brown, Olivia S. Mitchell, James Poterba, and Mark J. Warshawsky, eds. 2001 (ISBN 0-262-02509-4).
Forecasting Retirement Needs and Retirement Wealth. Olivia S. Mitchell, P. Brett Hammond, and Anna Rappaport, eds. 2000 (ISBN 0-8122-3529-0).
Prospects for Social Security Reform. Olivia S. Mitchell, Robert J. Myers, and Howard Young, eds. 1999 (ISBN 0-8122-3479-0).
Living with Defined Contribution Pensions: Remaking Responsibility for Retirement. Olivia S. Mitchell and Sylvester J. Schieber, eds. 1998 (ISBN 0-8122-3439-1).
Positioning Pensions for the Twenty-First Century. Michael S. Gordon, Olivia S. Mitchell, and Marc M. Twinney, eds. 1997 (ISBN 0-8122-3391-3).
Securing Employer-Based Pensions: An International Perspective. Zvi Bodie, Olivia S. Mitchell, and John A. Turner, eds. 1996 (ISBN 0-8122-3334-4).

Available from the Pension Research Council web site: http://www.pensionresearchcouncil.org/

Index

Bold entries refer to **figures** and **tables**.